D1594385

Benjamin Franklin and the Politics of Improvement

THE LEWIS WALPOLE SERIES

IN EIGHTEENTH-CENTURY CULTURE AND HISTORY

The Lewis Walpole Series, published by Yale University Press with the aid of the Annie Burr Lewis Fund, is dedicated to the culture and history of the long eighteenth century (from the Glorious Revolution to the accession of Queen Victoria). It welcomes work in a variety of fields, including literature and history, the visual arts, political philosophy, music, legal history and the history of science. In addition to original scholarly work, the series publishes new editions and translations of writing from the period, as well as reprints of major books that are currently unavailable. Though the majority of books in the series will probably concentrate on Great Britain and the Continent, the range of our geographical interests is as wide as Horace Walpole's.

Benjamin Franklin

and the

Politics of Improvement

Alan Houston

YALE UNIVERSITY PRESS   NEW HAVEN AND LONDON

For Barbara, Kelsey, and Ben,
and in memory of Barkley

Published with assistance from the Annie Burr Lewis Fund.

Designed by Gregg Chase.
Set in Fournier type by Binghamton Valley Composition, Binghamton, New York.
Printed in the United States of America by Thomson-Shore, Inc., Dexter, Michigan.
Library of Congress Cataloging-in-Publication Data
Houston, Alan Craig, 1957–
Benjamin Franklin and the politics of improvement / Alan Houston.
p. cm. — (The Lewis Walpole series in eighteenth-century culture and history)
Includes bibliographical references and index.
ISBN 978-0-300-12447-7 (alk. paper)
1. Franklin, Benjamin, 1706–1790—Political and social views. 2. Political science. 3. Statesmen—United States—
Biography. I. Title.
E302.6F8H77 2008
973.3092—dc22   2008010960

A catalogue record for this book is available from the British Library.

This paper meets the requirements of ANSI/NISO Z39.48-1992 (Permanence of Paper).
It contains 30 percent postconsumer waste (PCW) and is certified by
the Forest Stewardship Council (FSC).
10 9 8 7 6 5 4 3 2 1

Contents

Acknowledgments

"Time is Money." The opportunity to research and write, free from the demands of teaching and the routine pressures of academic life, is precious. I am extremely grateful for sabbatical fellowships from the American Philosophical Society, the Center for Comparative Immigration Studies, the National Endowment for the Humanities, and the Office of the President of the University of California.

In scattered paragraphs I draw on material that appeared in the introduction to *Franklin: The Autobiography and Other Writings on Politics, Economics, and Virtue*, used here by permission of Cambridge University Press. I owe a special debt of gratitude to Quentin Skinner, who first suggested that project and thus started me down a road that led, ultimately, to this book.

"The Good particular men may do separately . . . is small, compared with what they may do collectively, or by a joint Endeavour and Interest." The record of Franklin's life is housed in vibrant public and private institutions, some of which he helped found. Like that of all modern Franklin scholars, my work is grounded in the scrupulously edited *Papers of Benjamin Franklin*, currently in its thirty-ninth volume. I have also conducted original archival research at the American Philosophical Society, the Beinecke Library of Yale University, the British Library, the Historical Society of Pennsylvania, the Houghton Library of Harvard University, the Huntington Library, the Library Company of Philadelphia, the Library of Congress, and the Public Record Office of the National Archives of the United Kingdom. Librarians and archivists at each of these institutions were unfailingly helpful; their contributions are visible on every page of this book.

"He that drinks his Cider alone, let him catch his Horse alone." Books are written by individuals, but scholarship is a collegial activity. Parts of this book have been presented at the annual conventions of the American Political Science Association and the North American Conference of British Studies and to research seminars at the American Philosophical Society; the Center for Comparative Immigration Studies of the University of California, San Diego; the Center for Research in the Arts, Social Sciences and Humanities of Cambridge University; Franklin and Marshall College; and the University of California, Berkeley. I am grateful to talented organizers and engaged audiences in each of these settings.

I have discussed my ideas with Tim Breen, Wayne Cornelius, Adam Fox, Roy Goodman, Kyle Hoffman, Istvan Hont, Sung Ho Kim, J. A. Leo Lemay, Nancy Luxon, Alan Macinnes, Phil Roeder, David Selby, Quentin Skinner, Shannon Stimson, James Strick, and Roger Thomas. The full manuscript was read by Doug Anderson, Barbara Edwards, Harvey Goldman, Don Herzog, Steve Pincus, Chris Rogers, and three anonymous readers for Yale University Press. Chris is my editor at Yale, Laura Davulis my assistant editor. Countless improvements to my original manuscript are due to the incisive comments, criticisms, and suggestions of these individuals. I am no less grateful for the support and encouragement they have given me throughout the writing of this book. To these wonderful friends and colleagues, I offer my heartfelt thanks.

Author's Note

This book is intended for general readers as well as specialized scholars. One of Franklin's greatest gifts was his ability to convey sophisticated ideas in clear and simple language. Literary style expressed moral, political, and intellectual ideals: lucid prose, he argued, is a bond of union as well as a tool for understanding. Author and audience are engaged in a conversation; good writing should not offend "the Ear, the Understanding, or the Patience." In this book I have attempted, to the best of my abilities, to meet this standard.

When quoting eighteenth-century materials, I have corrected, modernized, and Americanized spelling, lowered superscripts, and expanded symbols and abbreviations. All fourteen ways of spelling "Pensilvania" have been reduced to one, "Pennsylvania"; "labour" is rendered as "labor," "work'd" as "worked," "&c." as "etc." Unless otherwise noted, however, I have not altered punctuation, capitalization, or the use of italics. On more than one occasion Franklin lamented the growing "fondness" of printers "for an even and uniform Appearance of Characters in the Line." The practice "stripped" the text of all the capitals and italics "that intimate the allusions and mark the emphasis" in written discourse, thus bringing it "as near as possible" to the spoken word. To Franklin, this "pretend Improvement" was like repeating one of the dramatic and moving sermons of the evangelist George Whitefield "in the monotony of a school-boy." Not every eighteenth-century writer or printer was as self-conscious or consistent as Franklin. And not every twenty-first-century reader will admire his technique. But it seems fitting, in a study of Franklin's social and political thought, to defer to his judgment.

In one crucial respect, however, I have attempted to improve on Franklin's language. Like virtually all eighteenth-century writers, Franklin used the same word—man—to refer both to all humans and to the male half of the species. This creates the potential for misunderstanding: Franklin had no difficulty imagining women as members of the republic of letters, but at no point did he suggest that women might serve alongside men in the Pennsylvania militia. When referring to groups and identities that were open to men and women alike, I have used gender-neutral words like "persons" and "people"; when referring to gender-specific roles and identities, I have used words like "man" and "men," "woman" and "women."

Virtually all of Franklin's writings before 1783 are cited from *The Papers of Benjamin Franklin*. In a handful of cases—most notably the *Autobiography*—I have relied on my own text collection, *Franklin: The Autobiography and Other Writings on Politics, Economics and Virtue* (2004). All other Franklin materials · are cited from original manuscripts and printed texts. Many unprinted texts are available in the online edition of the *Papers*, at http://www.franklinpapers.org; note, however, that these texts have not been editorially corrected and may contain errors or omissions.

Franklin's face currently graces the $100 bill, the largest note in general circulation in the United States. But for most of Franklin's life, the dominant units of currency were pounds, shillings, and pence, not dollars and cents. Important equivalencies were 12 pence (12d) = 1 shilling (1s); 20 shillings (20s) = 1 pound (£1). Thus £1.3.6½ reads 1 pound, 3 shillings, 6½ pence. A guinea was 21 shillings, or £1.1. Colonists also used a Spanish silver coin known as a piece of eight, which was worth about 22½ percent of a pound sterling. Colonial currency was not standardized, and each colony set the value of its local currency at a different rate. A Pennsylvania shilling was valued at about 60 percent of a British shilling, so that £1 Pennsylvania currency = 12s sterling.

What was the value of colonial money? In 1729—the year Franklin began publishing the *Gazette*—£100 in Pennsylvania currency was roughly equivalent to $7,668 in the year 2000. In 1747—the year he organized the Pennsylvania militia—£100 in Pennsylvania currency was roughly equivalent to $6,946. Using the same modern comparison point of the year 2000, here are some illustrative figures from Franklin's accounts. On 4 July 1730 Franklin sold two hundred bail bonds to Nicholas Scull for 16s.8d, or about $63. Five years later, on 20 August 1735, he bought a pair of shoes for his son William for 2s.6d, or approximately $10. Franklin obtained a musket on 26 May 1742 for £1.18, or roughly $133. And in June 1757 his wife, Deborah, purchased "a Negro boy" for £47.10, or approximately $3,200. Calculating and comparing the value of money at different time periods is a fine art;

interested readers may wish to consult John McCusker's *How Much Is That in Real Money?* 2nd. ed. (2001) and the Economic History Services Web site, "How Much Is That?" http://eh.net/hmit/.

At the conclusion to this book are a chronology of Franklin's life and a glossary of names. For those who want to learn more, Edmund S. Morgan's *Benjamin Franklin* (2002) is an excellent short biography, while full-scale treatments begin with Carl Van Doren's vibrant *Benjamin Franklin* (1938). For additional suggestions, see the notes to the introduction.

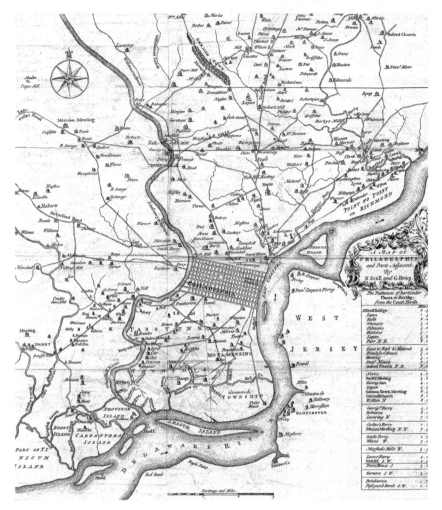

A Map of Philadelphia and Parts Adjacent, by Nicholas Scull and George Heap, 1752. (Courtesy American Philosophical Society.)

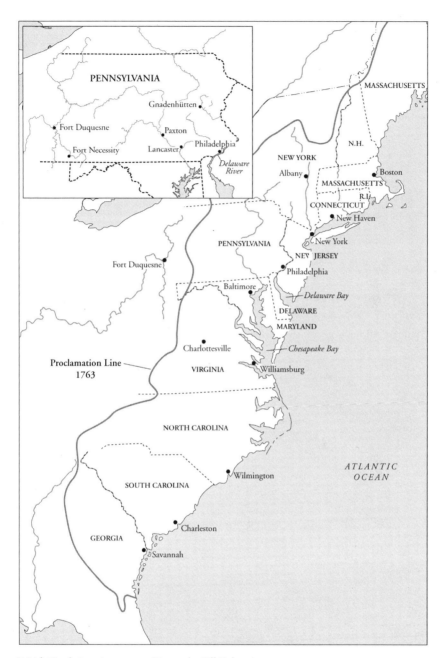

British North America, c. 1750. (Drawn by Bill Nelson.)

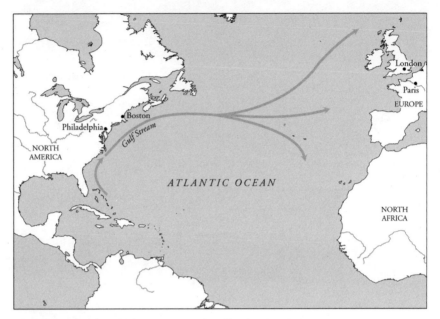

The British Atlantic World, c. 1763. (Drawn by Bill Nelson.)

Introduction

Franklin and America

Who was Benjamin Franklin? There were so many facets to his life that even his contemporaries could not agree. To Europeans he was a dazzling scientist and brilliant statesman, the man who "snatched lightning from the sky and the scepter from tyrants." To political opponents in Pennsylvania he was a "demagogue" with an "almost insatiable ambition." To fellow revolutionary John Adams, by contrast, he was a man who "loves his ease" and "hates to offend." Was Franklin a modern Prometheus? A Machiavellian schemer? Or a cagy operator whose life was "a scene of continual dissipation"?[1]

The bare facts are well known. The youngest son and fifteenth child of a Boston tallow chandler and soap boiler, Franklin received only two years of formal education before being apprenticed to his brother, a local printer. But by the time of his death he was world famous for his accomplishments. A writer of wit, grace, and intelligence, he crafted a series of complex and distinct literary voices. An experimental scientist, he conducted original research on electricity, was elected to the Royal Society, and founded the first scientific society in North America. A practical engineer, he invented the lightning rod, bifocal glasses, and the first efficient wood-burning stove. A born improver, he fathered the first subscription library, the first volunteer fire department, and the first charity hospital in North America. A political leader in colonial Pennsylvania and revolutionary America, he helped draft the Declaration of Independence, represented the United States in negotiations with France and Great Britain during the stormy period from 1776 to 1785, and participated in the Constitutional Convention.

The character of the man behind these accomplishments is less clear. What motivated him to act? What were his greatest hopes and fears? What did he value, and why? How did he conceive of his life? And how did he want to be thought of by his contemporaries and remembered in history?

Franklin's vast literary outpouring only adds to the mystery. In *Poor Richard's Almanac* of 1737 he opined, "He that can compose himself, is wiser than he that composes books." Twelve years later he added, "*Words* may show a man's Wit, but *Actions* his Meaning." What, then, are we to make of the fact that Franklin was one of the finest writers of the eighteenth century? To be sure, he was not an abstract or a systematic thinker. He disparaged "metaphysical reasoning" and made no attempt to articulate a theory of justice or defend a conception of human nature. He wrote nothing comparable to Plato's *Republic* or Hobbes's *Leviathan*. As one historian mordantly observed, "The sum total of his strictly philosophical musings about government would fill, quite literally, about two printed pages."[2] And yet *The Papers of Benjamin Franklin*—now in its thirty-ninth volume, with seven eventful years of his life still to be covered—reveal a mind of extraordinary critical intelligence. Franklin's writings reflect his engagement with the world. By trade a printer, he actively participated in the public sphere of news and communication. He wrote to influence opinions and shape events, to entertain friends and demolish enemies, to share ideas and attain commercial success. He addressed topics ranging from monetary policy to sexual mores, and from the conduct of business to the sins of slavery. He employed a wide array of literary forms, including journalistic essays, popular broadsides, public letters, political pamphlets, scientific treatises, and bagatelles. Well schooled in the use of irony, satire, and invective, he understood the value of a good hoax and delighted in the construction of dramatic personae. Some of his most famous productions were "written" by fictional characters like Silence Dogood, Father Abraham, and Richard Saunders.

Faced with these riches, scholars have found it difficult to agree on Franklin's identity. In scores of monographs he has been variously cast as Puritan, Deist, and atheist; as Newtonian empiricist and Enlightenment rationalist; as democratic populist and liberal individualist; as petit bourgeois and protocapitalist; as principled pragmatist and opportunistic scoundrel.[3]

American popular culture has had an easier time of it. Franklin's homespun wit, practical intelligence, and commitment to thrift and industry have made him a cultural icon. To many men and women, he symbolizes

Richard Feke, *Benjamin Franklin*, c. 1746. (Courtesy of Harvard University Art Museums, Bequest of Dr. John Collins Warren, 1856, H47. Photo: Katya Kallsen © President and Fellows of Harvard College.)

the American Dream. According to the dream, if you work hard and play by the rules, then you will succeed. Power and privilege are—and ought to be—the fruit of individual effort, not immutable identities like race or sex. Who you are is a function of what you do, not where, or to whom, you were born. The American Dream is closely associated with some of Franklin's most famous phrases: "A penny saved is a penny got"; "Time is Money"; "No gains without pains"; and "Early to bed and early to rise/Make a man healthy wealthy and wise."[4] Proof of these maxims is provided by Franklin's own life, which affirms the power of an individual to shape his or her own destiny.

Franklin's appeal to Americans has not been limited to adults. Children's literature—with titles like *Ben and Me: A New and Astonishing Life of Benjamin Franklin, as Written by His Good Mouse Amos* (in which Amos assumes responsibility for Franklin's discoveries and inventions), *The Hatmaker's Sign* (based on a parable Franklin told Jefferson when the latter balked at congressional attempts to edit the Declaration of Independence), and *Fart Proudly: The Writings of Benjamin Franklin You Never Read in School* (whose title derives from Franklin's satiric proposal for the scientific study of flatulence, "Letter to the Royal Academy")—testifies to the charm of Franklin's life and writings.[5] With the possible exception of George Washington, none of Franklin's contemporaries has played as important a role in the moral and political imaginations of Americans; and Washington, distant as Cato, lacks Franklin's immediacy and intimacy.

Recent studies have done little to disturb Franklin's "American" identity. Titles tell all: *The First American: The Life and Times of Benjamin Franklin* (H. W. Brands); *Benjamin Franklin: An American Life* (Walter Isaacson); *Runaway America: Benjamin Franklin, Slavery, and the American Revolution* (David Waldstreicher); *The Americanization of Benjamin Franklin* (Gordon S. Wood); *Stealing God's Thunder: Benjamin Franklin's Lightning Rod and the Invention of America* (Philip Dray); *The First Scientific American: Benjamin Franklin and the Pursuit of Genius* (Joyce Chaplin).[6]

Ironically, Franklin's importance to American culture has made it more difficult to understand his intellectual significance. Consider D. H. Lawrence's well-known attack on Franklin's ideals. In the *Autobiography* Franklin described his "bold and arduous Project of arriving at moral Perfection," complete with a table of virtues and a method for rendering them habitual. Lawrence railed against this "barbed wire moral enclosure": "The soul of man is a vast forest, and all Benjamin intended was a neat back garden." Why did Franklin do this? "Out of sheer cussedness." Franklin "hated England, he hated Europe." He "wanted to be an American," and his whole life was dedicated to "destroying the European past."[7] Lawrence was a brilliant writer and a perceptive critic, but his blistering attack was based on flawed assumptions. Like many before and after, he reduced Franklin's writings to the *Autobiogra-*

phy and *Poor Richard's Almanac*, ignoring the vast outpouring of Franklin's pen. And like many before and after, he naïvely (or perhaps mischievously) suggested that the man born in Boston was identical to the characters he created. Lawrence threw Franklin's literary artifice out the window; with it went many of the most important things Franklin actually wrote.

Lawrence identified Franklin with the desire to be an "American," and this, too, is a stumbling block. During most of Franklin's life the term *American* referred to an inhabitant of a geographic region, whether native Indian or British colonist. Only in the wake of the imperial crises of the 1760s and the revolutionary struggles of the 1770s did it begin to assume unique social, political, and cultural meanings. Franklin certainly influenced European perceptions of America and Americans. When minister to France, for example, he played to expectations of natural genius by refusing a wig and brocade jacket, wearing instead a beaver cap and simple wool coat. However, the identification of Franklin with America conflates four things that are potentially distinct: the biographical origins of an author, the social and political problems that dominated his thoughts, the audience he addressed, and the intellectual resources he drew on. Franklin spent the first two decades of his life in Boston and the following three in Philadelphia. Throughout his life his attention was riveted on the dilemmas of civic life in North America. But during long missions to England (1757–62, 1764–75) and France (1776–85) he wrote at length and with great sophistication for European audiences. And there was nothing parochial about his reading habits. As a child he eagerly consumed Bunyan's *Pilgrim's Progress* and Plutarch's *Lives;* as a lad of twenty, in a journal kept at sea, he debated Machiavellian dicta; as a budding political economist, he exploited the ideas of Marchamont Nedham and William Petty. Other early writings indicate familiarity with the poetry of Thomson, Cowley, and Pope, the philosophical reflections of Montaigne, Pascal, and Locke, the bawdy satire of Rabelais, and the savage wit of Swift. Throughout his long life he bought, borrowed, and was given books wherever he went. At his death he left a library of 4,276 volumes in English, French, Italian, Latin, Spanish, and German.[8]

One final aspect of Franklin's "American" identity should be noted, this time having to do with scholarly conventions and commitments. In the late 1950s and early 1960s a generation of academics turned from the philosophical analysis of "great texts" to the historical analysis of the intellectual contexts within which political thinking occurs. The significance of a claim or utterance could be grasped only in relationship to the range of ideas and arguments available at a given point in time. Shopworn distinctions between philosophy and history, or between reason and rhetoric, were called into question. Complex works of literature were placed alongside analytic non-fiction. In England these intellectual innovations led to vital new interpretations of familiar figures like Machiavelli, Hobbes, and Locke and to the recovery of less well-known writers like James Harrington. In the United States the new histories of political thought coincided with—and largely were absorbed by—the "republican" interpretation of the American Revolution. As late as 1955 Louis Hartz had argued that the key to American political thought could be found in the writings of John Locke. But by the early 1960s scholars had discovered, in the pamphlet literature of the mid-eighteenth century, a language of virtue and corruption that appeared to be distinct from and in tension with the liberal logic of rights and interests. Within a few short years, the concept of "classical" or "civic" republicanism dominated the landscape. Taking cues from the pioneering work of Bernard Bailyn, Gordon S. Wood, and J. G. A. Pocock, historians and political theorists recast the Revolution as a struggle to preserve republican liberty against the threat of moral and political corruption.[9]

Franklin is a strikingly marginal figure in the pages of republican revisionists, and plays no greater role in the work of critics seeking to reassert a liberal paradigm. There is a simple reason for this: he was neither a "classical republican" nor a "Lockean liberal." Though concerned with virtue and corruption, Franklin did not assume—as republican theory seemed to require—that a stable and successful polity rested on moral purity and selfless devotion to the commonwealth. Though dedicated to self-reliance and economic growth, he did not assume—as Lockean theory seemed to require—that property rights were natural, or that the language of natural rights fully captured the meaning of modern citizenship.

This lack of fit has impoverished our understanding of Franklin and of the contexts within which he lived. The loss is civic as well as scholarly. In 1782 a French immigrant to the New World, J. Hector St. John de Crève-coeur, asked, "What is an American?" What habits, thoughts, and feelings animate Americans? What distinguishes an American from any other inhabitant of the globe? Is there anything unique or distinctive about America? Not just in its material resources, but in its political ideals and cultural practices? Indeed, what *is* America? Liberalism and republicanism are two prominent answers to these questions. They are not the only answers that have been given, but in recent decades they have been the most influential.[10] They identify families of beliefs and values, practices and institutions, that have given shape to American history. From these accounts of what America is, or has been, scholars and citizens have drawn lessons about what America might become. To some, the central task facing contemporary Americans is preserving the nation's liberal heritage; to others, only the revival of long-dormant republican ideals can return the polity to good health. These arguments do not correspond to a simple left/right schema: liberalism is invoked to defend the right to private property as well as the right to vote; republicanism is summoned to justify moral reform as well as active citizenship. But in almost every case, current dilemmas are explained in terms of historical identities. Once we understand the past, we will know better how to shape the future.[11]

Franklin's contributions to American politics are remarkable. If we have not understood them, then we have not fully comprehended America.[12] Important aspects of American history and identity—including the participation of North American colonists in learned controversies that spanned the Atlantic—will remain murky and poorly understood. But Franklin's distinctiveness cannot be captured in abstract theories any more than it can be conveyed in the iconic language of popular culture. Seen through the lens of liberalism and republicanism, or of the American Dream, Franklin appears little more than a charmingly disordered mélange of ideas, abilities, and characteristics. According to an old proverb, God is in the details. Or is it the devil? Quite possibly it is both. Seemingly small matters can be of major importance; as Richard Saunders once warned, "There is no little enemy."[13] Existing interpretations do not reveal the fine-grained details that give Franklin's political thought its distinctive cast. A fresh approach is needed, one that uses the tools of historical research and conceptual analysis to bring Franklin's contributions to the theory and practice of modern politics into sharper focus.

The Politics of Improvement

If we wish to understand Benjamin Franklin's contributions to American politics, then we must begin at the beginning. Literally. Franklin learned to read at a very early age—so early that he could not recall a time when he was unable to read. His formal education was limited to two brief years between the ages of eight and ten. But that did not matter; he was "fond of Reading," and as a child spent "all the little Money that came into" his hands on books. (Well, not *quite* all. Franklin was a "bookish Lad," but books were not his only pleasure. "The Whistle" is a delightful bagatelle, written late in life but based on a lesson he had learned as an impulsive seven-year-old boy. Flush with coins, young Ben spent all his money on a toy whistle simply because its sound "charmed" him. When he returned home, his siblings pointed out that he had "given four times as much as it was worth" and laughed at his folly. Mortified, he lost all pleasure the whistle had brought him. Since that day, when tempted "to buy some unnecessary thing," he had reminded himself, "Do not give too much for the Whistle.")[14]

We often think of Franklin doing things: printing newspapers, founding libraries, fighting fires, experimenting with electricity, negotiating treaties. But Franklin's *doing* was always accompanied by *reading* and *thinking*. In his life, action and reflection were two sides of the same coin.

In his *Autobiography* Franklin identified two books as having had special influence on his later life: Daniel Defoe's *An Essay upon Projects* (1697) and Cotton Mather's *An Essay upon the Good* (1710). Defoe outlined a number of schemes for improving England, ranging from paving the roads to providing insurance for widows; Mather emphasized the importance of "doing good" in everyday life. Each book used the word *essay* in its title. To modern understanding, an essay is a formal composition of moderate length. To Defoe and Mather, an essay was also an attempt, a trial, and an experiment. In this sense, Franklin essayed as he read: he put books to the proof. Three quick examples. Exposed to the humane vegetarianism of Thomas Tryon—for whom a purified diet was a means to spiritual enlightenment—Franklin determined to forgo eating meat. The decision caused consternation: Franklin's "singularity"—his independence—was frowned on, especially as it was inconvenient for others. Nonetheless he persisted, learning to cook for himself in the process. Or, having read the Earl of Shaftesbury's *Characteristics* and Anthony Collin's *Discourse of Free Thinking*, Franklin became "a real Doubter in many Points of our Religious Doctrine." He was "indiscreet" in arguing these newfound ideas, so much so that he was "pointed at with Horror by good People, as an Infidel or Atheist." And finally, delighted by the prose style of Addison and Steele's *Spectator*, Franklin taught himself to write by systematically reconstructing it. He rewrote individual essays from memory; he turned them into verse, then back again into prose; he jumbled the order of sentences, then reassembled the original.[15]

The first page of Franklin's *Autobiography*. In printer's fashion, Franklin drafted his text in a column on the right side of the page, then made insertions and corrections on the left. (This item, HM 9999, is reproduced by permission of the Huntington Library, San Marino, California.)

Sometimes, in his enthusiasm for new ideas and vigorous arguments, Franklin sounds like a teenage intellectual: brash, aggressive, and self-satisfied. From reading his father's collection of books in "polemic Divinity," he developed "disputatious" habits. When a friend argued that the education of women was improper, Franklin "took the contrary Side, perhaps a little for Dispute sake." As luck would have it, while reading Charles Gildon's *Grammar of the English Tongue* he encountered an essay on the Socratic method. Charmed by what he read, he dropped his habit of "abrupt Contradiction, and positive Argumentation, and put on the humble Enquirer and Doubter." Especially in debating religious topics, he grew expert at "drawing People even of superior Knowledge into Concessions the Consequences of which they did not foresee, entangling them in Difficulties out of which they could not extricate themselves."[16]

Franklin found that his victims—much like Socrates'—were angered by his stratagems, and ended as enemies rather than friends. As a consequence, he gradually set aside his "positive dogmatical Manner" and retained only the habit of expressing himself "in terms of modest Diffidence, never using when I advance anything that may possibly be disputed, the Words, *Certainly, undoubtedly,* or any others that give the Air of Positiveness to an Opinion; but rather say, *I conceive,* or *I apprehend a Thing to be so or so, It appears to me,* or *I should think it so and so for such and such Reasons,* or *I imagine it to be so,* or *it is so if I am not mistaken.*" The appearance of humility was a political virtue and proved advantageous whenever Franklin "proposed new Institutions, or Alterations in the old."[17]

Franklin demonstrated a "projecting public Spirit" at an early age. Venturesome and clever, he was "generally a Leader among the Boys" and sometimes got them into "Scrapes." In the Boston of his youth

there was a Salt Marsh that bounded part of the Mill Pond, on the Edge of which at High water, we used to stand to fish for Minnows. By much Trampling, we had made it a mere Quagmire. My Proposal was to build a Wharf there fit for us to stand upon, and I showed my Comrades a large Heap of Stones which were intended for a new House near the Marsh, and which would very well suit our Purpose. Accordingly in the Evening when the Workmen were gone, I assembled a Number of my Playfellows, and working with them diligently like so many Emmets [ants], sometimes two or three

to a Stone, we brought them all away and built our little Wharf.—
The next Morning the Workmen were surprised at Missing the
Stones; which were found in our Wharf; Enquiry was made after the
Removers; we were discovered and complained of; several of us
were corrected by our Fathers; and though I pleaded the Usefulness
of the Work, mine convinced me that nothing was useful which was
not honest.—

Franklin does not reveal how his father "corrected" him or how he "convinced" young Ben that honesty was the best policy. If Mark Twain had been
telling the story, it would have ended just before the final clause ("mine convinced me . . ."). Aunt Sally would have had a switch in her hand and strong
words on her lips ("Well-a-well, man that is born of woman is of few days
and full of trouble, as the Scripture says, and I reckon it's so"); Tom would
have been scrambling to escape.[18]

Twain thought Franklin's maxims "full of animosity toward boys.
Nowadays a boy cannot follow out a single natural instinct without tumbling
over some of those everlasting aphorisms and hearing from Franklin on the
spot. If he buys two cents' worth of peanuts, his father says, 'Remember
what Franklin has said, my son,—"A groat a day's a penny a year" '; and the
comfort is all gone out of those peanuts." Twain was onto something:
Franklin showed little interest in the natural instincts of boys. None of his
characters, whether fictional or real, struggled against the adult world of
work and labor with the energy and creativity of Tom Sawyer. Yet even
Twain failed to see the irony and ambiguity in Franklin's declaration that he
had a "projecting public Spirit." In the early eighteenth century the word
projector had two distinct meanings. On the one hand, it referred to a person
who formed a project or who planned and designed an undertaking. The
connotation of this usage was neutral. Thus in 1714 the government of
Massachusetts ordered, without prejudice, that the "Projectors" of a new
bank lay their "scheme" before the Assembly. On the other hand, the word
projector could also be used to denote a person who lived by his wits, a cheat
or swindler who duped others with phony ideas. "Let not the Projector
pretend the public good," intoned one moralist, "when he intends but to rob
the rich and to cheat the poor."[19]

Franklin had a "projecting public Spirit." But did that make him an inventive planner or a conniving schemer? How could we know? Should we

focus on the means he used or the ends he achieved? On the intentions he expressed or on the actions he performed? Indeed, where are his intentions best
revealed: in the words he printed for all the world to read or in the thoughts
he saved for private conversation and correspondence?[20]

Franklin's contemporaries found these questions no less difficult than
do we. Everyone, it seemed, had a scheme or plan to offer. There were
bridges to build, morals to reform, schools to endow, balloons to float. Was
the project feasible? Desirable? Were there any alternatives? Was the projector trustworthy? Why—and for how long? Judging fact from fiction was no
easy task. At times, it appeared that every source of information was infected
with "puffery," a wonderful eighteenth-century word for the inflated prose
typical of commercial advertisements.

Like many others, Franklin justified his projects using the concept of
improvement. *Improvement* was originally an agricultural term referring to
the profitable cultivation of land. During the seventeenth century its meta-
phoric range was extended to include a host of social and political reforms
aimed at growth, development, or perfection.[21] Though rooted in political
economy, improvement was not simply, or even primarily, an economic category. The production of wealth was only part of its ethos. So, too, were the
pursuit of knowledge, the cultivation of friendship, the preservation of freedom, and the satisfaction of need. Improvement was nothing less than short-
hand for the civilizing process.[22]

The concept of improvement played an important role in eighteenth-
century European debates over the foundations of social order. Almost
everyone agreed that humans are capable of improvement and that the weaknesses of individuals are overcome through combination with others. But
what enables humans to cooperate? What ties hold them together in collective endeavors? It was here that the argument was joined. Christian moralists
invoked love and the bonds of an inclusive church. Shared values were the
cement of social order; improvement was predicated on moral and religious
reform. Machiavellians, to the contrary, appealed to the power of necessity,
imposed by a well-ordered state. Strict limits on property and mandatory
military service were needed to overcome the corrosive power of private
interests. A third group found these options—moral virtue and mortal
fear—to be politically implausible and morally unpalatable. Intrigued by the
effects of trade and commerce, they sought to explain the emergence of cooperative social relations through the power of needs and interests. At base,

they argued, humans joined together because they were useful to each other. Through the reciprocal exchange of goods and services, men and women acquired the skills and habits needed to sustain social order.[23]

Franklin was introduced to these arguments in the books and essays he read as a boy: Cotton Mather's *Bonifacius*, Daniel Defoe's *Essay on Projects*, Joseph Addison's *Spectator*, Richard Steele's *Tatler*, the third Earl of Shaftesbury's *Characteristics of Men, Manners, Opinions, Times*, John Trenchard and Thomas Gordon's *Cato's Letters: Or, Essays on Liberty, Civil and Religious*. His understanding of what was at stake in these books was deepened during his first trip to London. For eighteen months, from late 1724 until the middle of 1726, he took part in the socially and intellectually vibrant life of London's coffeehouses and taverns. Among the men of letters who frequented these locales, moral philosophy and political economy were favored topics of conversation. Just prior to Franklin's landing in the metropolitan capital, the fires of public controversy had been stoked by the publication of a third edition of Bernard Mandeville's *Fable of the Bees: Or, Private Vices, Publick Benefits*. Mandeville notoriously argued that society was an aggregation of self-interested individuals, bound together not by religious devotion or fear of punishment, but by the tenuous bonds of envy, pride, and competition. Mandeville himself was quite charming: Franklin met him in 1725 and found him "a most facetious entertaining Companion." But Mandeville's ideas were brilliantly, maddeningly paradoxical, and his readers were alternately intoxicated and infuriated by them. Francis Hutcheson's *An Inquiry into the Original of Our Ideas of Beauty and Virtue*, published in 1725, was but the latest salvo in an ongoing war of words.[24]

Franklin embraced the claim that the bonds of cooperation were forged on the anvil of utility. But his practical context was North America, not Great Britain, and the colonies of his youth lacked the institutional density of the mother country. In 1726 there were few clubs and coffeehouses for enlightened conversation, no societies to foster natural philosophy. Commercial relations were unstable and unevenly distributed; regional differences hindered common undertakings. Faced with these deficits, Franklin was forced to improvise. The debates he had been steeped in for nearly twenty years provided tools for thinking about growth and change. The backward condition of colonial life presented opportunities for enlightened action. Underdevelopment was not a permanent condition; North America could be improved. As so often would be the case, Franklin's interventions in complex debates took the form of incidental tracts and practical proposals.

Two of Franklin's best-known projects illustrate the connection he saw between development and improvement. In 1731, in an effort to increase the number and enhance the quality of books available to Philadelphia's small reading public, Franklin founded the Library Company. In a letter to Pennsylvania's Proprietor, Thomas Penn, Franklin and the Library Company's directors explained their mission:

> Your Province of Pennsylvania, Sir, happy in its Climate and Situation, and in the Constitution of its Government, is thought capable of every kind of Improvement.—
>
> But when Colonies are in their Infancy, the Refinements of Life it seems cannot be much attended to.—To encourage Agriculture promote Trade and establish good Laws must be the principal Care of the first Founders; while other Arts and Sciences, less immediately necessary, how excellent and useful so ever, are left to the Care and Cultivation of Posterity. Hence it is that neither in this nor in the neighboring Provinces, has there yet been made any Provision for a public generous Education.
>
> With a View of supplying in some Measure this Deficiency for the Present among ourselves, we have attempted to erect a common Library in Philadelphia.

Twelve years later Franklin helped found the American Philosophical Society, the first learned society in North America. The full title of the society is revealing: American Philosophical Society Held at Philadelphia for Promoting Useful Knowledge. According to Franklin's prospectus,

> The first Drudgery of Settling new Colonies, which confines the Attention of People to mere Necessaries, is now pretty well over; and there are many in every Province in Circumstances that set them at Ease, and afford Leisure to cultivate the finer Arts, and improve the common Stock of Knowledge.
>
> But as from the Extent of the Country such Persons are widely separated, and seldom can see and converse or be acquainted with each other, so that many useful Particulars remain uncommunicated, die with the Discoverers, and are lost to Mankind; it is, to remedy this Inconvenience for the future, proposed,

> That One Society be formed of Virtuosi or ingenious Men re-
> siding in the several Colonies, to be called *The American Philosophi-
> cal Society.*

An unimproved society—one that had not yet developed—was rough, rude, and rustic. With improvement a society became settled, cultivated, orderly, and polite. Individuals thrived, learning flourished, social relations were harmonized. Both the Library Company and the American Philosophical Society were intended to bring the benefits of development to the colonies.[25]

Franklin's delight at improvement leaps from almost every page he wrote. Large or small, moral or material, he relished every step forward. On more than one occasion he regretted having been "born so soon." If only he had lived "two or three Centuries hence. For Inventions of Improvement are prolific, and beget more of their Kind. The present Progress is rapid. Many of great Importance, now unthought of, will before that Period be procured; and then I might not only enjoy their Advantages, but have my Curiosity satisfied in knowing what they are to be."[26]

Franklin's longing for the future seems sincere, and in many respects it must have been. But he gave it an ironic twist. Immediately following the passage quoted above, from a letter to the Congregational minister John Lathrop, Franklin wrote: "I see a little Absurdity in what I have just written, but it is to a Friend who will wink and let it pass." A *little* absurdity. The use of an ironic afterthought was one of Franklin's favorite rhetorical strategies, undercutting any literal interpretation of his words. "*Wink*," he said with a smile, "for you know I don't *really* think this way." Improvement was not automatic, and there was no guarantee that it would continue in the future. But its possibility provided a vantage point from which to evaluate the present. In the midst of the Revolution, Franklin asked his English friend and supporter Joseph Priestley to imagine the height to which human knowledge might be carried in a thousand years: gravity might be tamed, agriculture made endlessly abundant, disease finally cured. "Oh that moral Science were in as fair a Way of Improvement, that Men would cease to be Wolves to one another."[27]

Focusing on the ideas and practices of improvement allows us to conceive of change for the better without invoking the distorting effects of its near neighbor, "progress." The latter, frequently associated with "the Enlightenment," evokes ideas like the universal power of reason, the malleability of human nature, and the disciplined application of knowledge.

Reaching its intellectual apogee in the moral philosophy of Kant, the historical vision of Condorcet, and the social reforms of Bentham, the concept of progress has been identified with many dramatic and disturbing features of the modern world. For example, belief that there was a single road to the future, and that some nations had traveled further down it than others, was sometimes used to justify the imperial ventures of Britain and France during the first half of the nineteenth century. Whole schools of thought have been dedicated to exorcising the ghost of progress from Western culture.[28] But improvement—change for the better—need not imply a taste for uniformity or a naïve faith in reason and method. It was less a philosophical doctrine or a political program than a set of priorities applied in comparative and contextual judgments. At any given point in time, what options are available? Which has the greatest advantages, or the fewest disadvantages? Can men and women be brought to support it? Using what means? And with what consequences? The lived experience of asking and answering these questions is essential to an understanding of the politics of improvement.[29]

Improvements often came in small packages, but Franklin insisted that this did not diminish their significance. In the *Autobiography* he described his efforts to have the streets of Philadelphia paved and swept. In wet weather, dirt roads turned into quagmires; in dry, they were a dusty nuisance. At first, the streets adjacent to the city market were paved in stone. When they, too, became covered in mud, Franklin persuaded his neighbors to band together and hire "a poor industrious Man" to clean the streets on a regular basis. "The inhabitants of the city were delighted" with the results and clamored to have every street similarly improved. Anticipating a skeptical "So what?" Franklin stepped back from his narrative to explain why these projects were important. "Some may think these trifling Matters not worth minding or relating: But when they consider, that though Dust blown into the Eyes of a single Person or into a single Shop on a windy Day, is but of small Importance, yet the great Number of the Instances in a populous City, and its frequent Repetitions give it Weight and Consequence; perhaps they will not censure very severely those who bestow some of Attention to Affairs of this seemingly low Nature. Human Felicity is produced not so much by great Pieces of good Fortune that seldom happen, as by little Advantages that occur every Day."[30]

Franklin's devotion to "little Advantages" did not prevent him from advocating bold measures when he thought them appropriate. Improvers need not be tinkerers. Nothing in the logic of improvement precluded radical change. When Franklin became convinced that conciliation with Great Britain was no longer possible, he embraced independence. And when he came to believe that slavery was wrong and had no place in the new nation, he called for its abolition.

Franklin brilliantly captured the spirit of improvement in his speech at the conclusion of the Constitutional Convention of 1787. Conscious that many members of the convention still harbored reservations about the document they had drafted, Franklin used his own vote as a model for accommodation:

> I confess that I do not entirely approve of this Constitution at present, but Sir, I am not sure I shall never approve it: For, having lived long, I have experienced many Instances of being obliged by better Information or fuller Consideration, to change Opinions, even on important Subjects, which I once thought right, but found to be otherwise. . . .
>
> I doubt . . . whether any other Convention we can obtain, may be able to make a better Constitution: For when you assemble a Number of Men, to have the Advantage of their joint Wisdom, you inevitably assemble with those Men all their Prejudices, their Passions, their Errors of Opinion, their local Interests, and their selfish Views. From such an Assembly can a perfect Production be expected? . . . Thus I consent, Sir, to this Constitution because I expect no better, and because I am not sure that it is not the best.[31]

The Constitution was not perfect—how could it be? It was the work of a committee—but it was preferable to the alternatives. It might even *be* the best, though, given the limits of human reason, no one could know that with certainty. To an unsympathetic critic, that might sound like damning with faint praise. But Franklin was keenly aware of the precariousness of political improvements. Innovation required cooperation; cooperation rested on organization and mobilization; organization and mobilization relied on the contingent actions of individuals who were themselves a patchwork of passions and interests. Accommodation was not (simply) a strategic compromise; it was a moral and political imperative.

Improvement was not without its complications, however. What makes a plan or project useful? Do improvements in science and politics, or in the conveniences of everyday life, truly advance human happiness? Is anything of value threatened or lost when life is organized around the need to be useful? How should we characterize a man who does so? These were the sort of puzzles that troubled D. H. Lawrence. His answers were shrill and crude, but his questions should not be dismissed out of hand. Instead, we should ask them while paying careful attention to the specific contexts within which they arise. Consider a small and private example, drawn from Franklin's life as ambassador to France. Franklin's tale of an impulsive childhood purchase, "The Whistle," was told to his French neighbor Madame Brillon to console her after she learned that her husband had, once again, been unfaithful. Franklin aspired to an affair with Brillon himself. But despite his best efforts to woo her, their relationship remained chaste.[32] "The Whistle" suggested that she falsely estimated the value of marital fidelity. Why sacrifice so much for so little, Franklin wondered? More pleasing options—an affair with him, perhaps—were available. What are we to make of this? Does Franklin's innocent tale lose some of its charm? Is there anything unattractive or unprincipled about his use of this story? Does it matter how Madame Brillon responded? (She refused the bait, insisting that she had not paid too much.) Was this Franklin's only reason for writing? If not, how do we weigh and balance various and potentially conflicting motives? Similar puzzles can be found throughout Franklin's life. For example, he sometimes profited from his public projects. Do these private gains temper our understanding of his motives for acting? Do they diminish the value of his accomplishments? Does it matter how Franklin himself would have responded? (He made no attempt to hide his returns.) Bringing these questions to the surface will add richness and depth to our understanding of Franklin.

Interpretive Strategies

The Pulitzer Prize–winning biographer Carl Van Doren once wrote that Franklin, "with his marvelous range," seems to be "more than any single man." He was a "harmonious human multitude."[33] This is probably right, especially if we do not put too much pressure on the concept of harmony. Franklin had enemies, both personal and political, and he experienced conflict, both public and private. These tensions are often revealing, and Franklin's adversaries will play important parts in our story.

This study is historical and biographical, but it is not a historical biography. Instead, I have approached Franklin as a geologist, drilling into his political thought from five different locations. Each chapter begins with a specific text or problem, then traces the seams of ideas and practices that are connected to it. These veins overlap and intersect, often in unexpected places. As a result, each chapter enhances the ones that preceded it. The composite is not complete—it does not identify every detail—but it does capture the most important features of the terrain.

These explorations have been made possible by modifying and extending current tools of research. For several decades, the most influential work in the history of political thought has been associated with the so-called Cambridge school of Quentin Skinner, J. G. A. Pocock, and John Dunn. The methodological and substantive differences between these authors are significant. But in classic essays of the 1960s and 1970s, each insisted that the full meaning of a text could not be captured unless it was located in a meticulously constructed historical context. The most important features of any historical context, in turn, are the major and minor texts circulating at that time. The history of political thought is the history of political discourse. Only by paying attention to how contemporaries used language is it possible to grasp "the point of the original intellectual enterprise."[34]

The tools of Cambridge history are necessary but not sufficient to map Franklin's political thought. Franklin read widely and deeply and was a self-conscious participant in the Atlantic republic of letters. But when he set pen to paper, he was not simply reacting to the words and concepts of others; he was also responding to actual social and political problems. To understand his thought, we need to bring into focus not just language but also reigning social practices and contingent political developments. The meaning of the terms he used and the justification for the claims he advanced were in part determined by these background conditions. Alongside texts and arguments, therefore, readers of this book will find social history, demographic data, economic analysis, and the like. These are not ancillary to Franklin's thought, but essential to its intelligibility.[35]

What does this mean in practice? In writing this book, I have employed four interpretive strategies. First, I locate Franklin within a broad Atlantic context, extending from North America to Great Britain, Europe, and Africa. Franklin is sometimes called the first American, but it is more accurate to say that he was the first person to fully inhabit the Atlantic world. He lived for extended periods in Boston, Philadelphia, London, and Paris, and moved with relative ease between these locations. He read six languages and corresponded with men and women in England, Scotland, Germany, Russia, Italy, Spain, Portugal, France, and every colony in North America. He both studied and contributed to the circulation of people and goods. He bought and sold European books and actively participated in international scientific debates. He studied the Gulf Stream and sent seeds from North America to European collectors and scientists. The wide horizon of Franklin's world is captured by the maps at the front of this book. Though Philadelphia was his home, and North America his enduring concern, his thoughts and experiences ranged across the Atlantic.[36]

Second, I treat Franklin as a public intellectual, consciously contributing to both learned controversies and civic policies. Today, political and intellectual life are dominated by specialists. The ability of an individual to contribute to more than one domain of life is limited by the need for technical expertise. Boundary crossing was more common in Franklin's day, as any visitor to Monticello can testify. Thomas Jefferson innovated in architecture, engineering, agricultural production, and small manufactures. But for all his versatility, Jefferson looked on his home in Virginia as a sanctuary, removed from the rough-and-tumble of politics; geographic isolation embodied important divisions in his life. Franklin sought no retreat. An engaged and enthusiastic city-dweller, he slipped easily between work and home, public and private, political and intellectual. Consider printing: was it his vocation or his avocation? A source of income, a form of recreation, a forum for ideas, or a tool for influencing public opinion? The correct answer—all of the above, often at the same time— reflects the richness and complexity of his engagement with the world.

Third, I attend to Franklin's sophistication as a writer. Eighteenth-century prose was inflected with irony, satire, bombast, sarcasm, raillery, and a dozen other literary modes or styles. Franklin mastered them all. His writings often occupy more than one level, and the ideas that appear first, on the surface, are not always the most important. More than one reader, from his day to ours, has mistakenly believed a hoax to be true or an ironic aside to be literally meant. Franklin was capable of extraordinary, breathtaking clarity. Why did he sometimes choose to run the risk of misunderstanding? What does his use of language tell us about his political objectives?

Finally, I pay careful attention to what Franklin *did* as well as *said*. In Franklin's life, reflection and action, thinking and doing, were intertwined.

Important aspects of his political thought are revealed in concrete actions, not abstract arguments. Franklin's deepest insights into the nature of citizenship in a polity divided by religion and class were embedded in his plans for the Association, a militia mustered to defend Pennsylvania in 1747. His most profound reflections on the logic of political institutions in an extended polity were contained in his 1754 proposal for intercolonial union.

Lived experiences are constituent features of Franklin's political thought. It is essential to note, however, that "lived experiences" are not strictly "local experiences," especially if the latter is narrowly conceived. Social practices and political institutions, not to mention memory and imagination, extend the horizons of life beyond its immediate locale. As a boy in Boston, Franklin's experience of the world was shaped in part by the magical-mystical doctrines of a seventeenth-century English healer, Thomas Tryon. As an adult, struggling to understand the effects of population growth on human well-being, Franklin's experiences were shaped in part by decades of political and economic decisions taken by imperial authorities in London. The variety of contexts for Franklin's political thought is matched only by the richness of his ideas. To them we now turn.

1. Commerce

The Use of Money is all the Advantage there is in having Money.
— Benjamin Franklin, *Poor Richard's Almanac* (1737)

" 'Tis hard for an empty Bag to stand upright"

Benjamin Franklin had a money problem. In the spring of 1726, after eighteen eventful months, he had "grown tired of London." Having reached the age of twenty, he longed to return to Pennsylvania. He had a career waiting for him, as clerk to the Philadelphia merchant Thomas Denham. The starting salary was modest, just £50 a year, but colonial trade was on the upswing, and his prospects for improvement were excellent. There was just one problem: he did not have enough money to pay for his passage home.[1]

"A penny saved is a penny got," but Franklin was having difficulty saving his pennies. He had traveled to London at the behest of Pennsylvania's governor, Sir William Keith. Keith considered Franklin "a young Man of promising Parts" and had offered to set him up in the printing business. Franklin sailed in expectation of letters of recommendation and instruments of credit that would enable him to obtain the supplies needed to set up a colonial print shop. To his horror and dismay, on reaching England he discovered that Keith had provided neither. Just three years earlier Franklin had run away from the Boston print shop of his brother and master, James. When he arrived in Philadelphia in the fall of 1723, he was penniless and friendless, possessing little more than the clothes on his back. Now, once again, he was on his own. A fellow passenger advised that he make the best of it; "among the Printers here . . . you will improve yourself; and when you return to America, you will set up to greater Advantage."[2]

Franklin immediately found employment at Samuel Palmer's print shop and set about exploring the city. He was not alone; he had been accompanied on the voyage by James Ralph, a Philadelphia friend who aspired to become an actor. Or a writer. Or a copyist. (Eventually he settled on teaching.) Ralph had no money, so he borrowed from Franklin. Together they went to the theater, listened to speeches and sermons, and visited clubs, coffeehouses, and taverns. Both were charmed by the women of London. Ralph took up with a "sensible and lively" young milliner. When Ralph left London to seek employment, she turned to Franklin for comfort and financial support. He "grew fond of her Company," but the only thing his "attempted Familiarities" brought was a firm rebuff from the milliner and a "Breach" in his friendship with Ralph.[3]

In the *Autobiography* Franklin tells us that he left Palmer's for Watts's, near Lincoln's Inn Fields, so that he could begin saving money. He "spent but little" upon himself; his poverty was due to Ralph, who refused to repay the £27 he had borrowed. A story passed down by the descendents of Zabdiel Boylston, a Boston physician who visited London in 1725, suggests otherwise. Boylston would have been well known to Franklin—he had been James Franklin's doctor—and Franklin is reported to have appeared before him in "extreme distress," "without money, friends or counsel," asking for help. Boylston is said to have given him 20 guineas. The Franklin scholar J. A. Leo Lemay dismisses this as "apocryphal." After all, Franklin was gainfully employed almost from the moment he set foot in London. But Thomas Denham's account book gives credence to Boylston family memories. In April 1726 Denham lent Franklin £10 for passage to Philadelphia. But over the previous six months—before his offer of employment—Denham appears to have lent Franklin over £6 for "cash" and "sundries." Later, Poor Richard would warn, "Rather go to bed supperless, than run in debt for a Breakfast." These were lessons learned in the breach. Even without Ralph's help, Franklin lived beyond his means.[4]

From start to finish, Franklin's sojourn in London was defined by relationships of credit and debt, trust and betrayal. The lending and collecting of money was only one facet of these bonds. Keith offered Franklin financial assistance but also the power of personal recommendation. He reneged on both. Ralph sponged Franklin's money, shared his louche life, and then, when seeking employment outside London as a tutor, borrowed Franklin's name as well. Denham offered Franklin small loans to help tide him over. More important, he offered to bring Franklin into his Philadelphia home, where he would teach him business skills and treat him as a future partner.

The Franklin visible in London contrasts sharply with the man of lore and legend. Joseph Dennie, a Federalist appalled by the rise of Jeffersonian democracy, denigrated Franklin as a small-minded man, the kind of person "who has the *pence table* by heart and knows all the squares of multiplication." Nathaniel Hawthorne thought that *Poor Richard*'s proverbs were "all about getting money, or saving it." The most inspired of these attacks—and the only one that matches Franklin's wit—came from Mark Twain: "His simplest acts" were "contrived with a view to their being held up for the emulation of boys forever—boys who might otherwise have been happy. . . . . Franklin once said in one of his inspired flights of malignity, 'Early to bed and early to rise/Make a man healthy and wealthy and wise.' As if it were any object to a boy to be healthy and wealthy and wise on such terms. The sorrow that that maxim has cost me through my parents' experimenting on me with it, tongue cannot tell." Finally, there is the influential argument of Max Weber, the German sociologist who suggested that Franklin exhibited the "spirit of capitalism" with "almost classical purity." Weber's analysis was free of moralizing cant, but he agreed with Hawthorne: Franklin's whole life was subordinated to the task of making more and more money. (Weber's depiction of Franklin is explored in detail in the appendix.)[5]

Finding passages in Franklin's writings to support these views is not difficult. For example, Franklin famously advised young tradesmen to "remember that Time is Money. He that can earn Ten Shillings a Day by his Labor, and goes abroad, or sits idle one half of that Day, though he spends but Sixpence during his Diversion or Idleness, ought not to reckon That the only Expense; he has really spent or rather thrown away Five Shillings besides." That certainly sounds like the way to wealth. But is it? And is it expressive of Franklin's deepest insights into work and labor? Franklin retired from business at the age of forty-two, with the expectation that the "moderate Fortune" he had acquired as printer and bookseller would secure him "Leisure to read, study, make Experiments, and converse" with friends. In comparison, the character described by Dennie, Hawthorne, Twain, and Weber seems wooden and one-dimensional, like a prop on a stage or a mannequin in a store window. But what of Franklin's pithy phrases? Don't they reveal something distinctive about his economic ethos? Perhaps. But recall that Franklin was a voracious reader. The vast majority of Poor Richard's proverbs were the "Gleanings" of his studies. "A penny saved is a penny got"? "No gains without pains"? "Haste makes waste"? "Rather go to bed supperless, than run in debt for a Breakfast"? " 'Tis hard for an empty Bag to stand upright"? These were already well known in seventeenth-century Britain. And what of Twain's nemesis, that deepest and most distinctive expression of Franklin's priorities, "Early to Bed, and early to rise, makes a Man healthy, wealthy and wise"? With only slight variation—"Early to go to bed and early to rise, makes a man healthy, wealthy and wise"—it, too, was familiar decades before Franklin was born. Franklin was a brilliant writer and a creative thinker, but he was not autochthonous. He lived and wrote in relationship to others, in an intellectual context as vast as the Atlantic.[6]

If we are to grasp the sophistication and originality of Franklin's thoughts on work and labor, then we cannot restrict our attention to the words of Poor Richard or the facts of Franklin's life. We must also explore Franklin's participation in eighteenth-century Atlantic debates over the theory and practice of commercial society. In Franklin's day, the word *commerce* carried the familiar meaning of truck and barter, "the Exchange of one Commodity or Manufacture for another." This was its core. But circulating around it were other meanings, many of which have been lost or forgotten in the intervening centuries. Commerce referred to association with others, as in "the free and easy commerce of social life." Some of these associations were illicit ("the illegal commerce of the sexes"), others were exemplary (Jesus's "commerce with his disciples"). Commerce also referred to the exchange of thoughts and ideas, as in "a constant commerce of letters." Franklin invoked several senses of the word in 1753, when he offered, as postmaster, to use his franking privileges to facilitate the trade of ideas between two philosophically minded friends. "Let me be the Medium of your literary Commerce," he suggested. "It behooves us all to join Hands for the Honor" of "American Philosophy."[7]

Commerce concerned the circulation of raw materials and finished goods, rough ideas and refined sentiments. It involved much more than simply buying and selling. (Or, perhaps better, commerce is much more complicated than we often allow.) Traders associate for exchange. They haggle and bargain, threaten and seduce. Sometimes they gain from their interactions; sometimes they go home empty-handed, or worse. All but the simplest exchanges involve credit and debt, hence uncertainty and risk.

Even correspondence can be measured in these terms. Who has not begun a letter, as Franklin once did, with the confession that although "it is a long time since I have had the Pleasure of a Line from you . . . I have not deserved it; for I am Debtor on Account of several of your Favors that remain unanswered"?[8]

Commerce provided a model for cooperative social relations based on the power of needs and interests: humans join together because they are useful to each other. The theory of commercial society provided a vibrant alternative to accounts of cooperation based on moral virtue (we cooperate because we hold specific other-regarding beliefs and values) or mortal fear (we cooperate because we dread the coercive sanctions imposed by governments). During the eighteenth century theories of commercial society played an increasingly important role in public debates. Throughout the Atlantic world philosophers and politicians, playwrights and pamphleteers, pursued a number of questions with vigor and sophistication. Why do individuals engage in commerce? How are relationships of credit and debt sustained? Why should those engaged in trade, often separated by vast distances, trust each other? How strong are the bonds of cooperation forged by commerce? Does trade give rise to enduring or hazardous forms of conflict? These questions had moral and psychological, as well as political and economic, dimensions. As Franklin learned from Keith's false promises and Denham's generous support, trustworthiness resided in an individual's character as well as in the policies governing his or her actions. Tracing Franklin's contributions to the manifold debates concerning commercial society will provide important first clues to the nature and purpose of the politics of improvement.

Sociability

Franklin's interest in trade and commerce dated to his youth. One of the books that captured his attention as a boy, for example, was Daniel Defoe's *An Essay upon Projects.* Defoe proposed a number of measures for the "Improvement of Trade," from creating a network of local banks to publicly maintaining England's roads and highways. One of his projects concerned the fate of widows, who often fell into poverty when their husbands died. Why not make provision for this predictable event? A system of "friendly societies" would allow couples to make small regular contributions to a collective fund, against which widows could draw after their partners' deaths. Franklin thought highly of this idea and reprinted it in his tenth "Silence Dogood" essay. ("Silence" was the pseudonym Franklin chose for his contributions to James Franklin's *The New-England Courant*. Silence had a sharp wit and a satiric tongue as well as a "natural Inclination to observe and reprove the Faults of others." She was also a widow. Was her decision to call attention to Defoe's proposal self-interested? Should it matter? What of the fact that, unknown to the *Courant*'s readers, she was a he, and a sixteen-year-old boy at that? Determining the trustworthiness of an informant can be treacherous.)[9]

Eighteenth-century reflections on trade and commerce do not look like the writings of contemporary economists. "Economy" was originally the art or science of managing a household; an "economist" was a person who practiced that art. Closely related was the use of the word *economy* to refer to thrift or the careful management of resources. It was not until 1767 that an English-language book appeared with the phrase "political economy" in its title; another forty years passed before writers referred to individuals concerned with managing the material resources of a nation as "economists."[10] To be sure, systematic concern for national wealth predated these usages by at least two centuries. And many of the questions asked in the eighteenth century—Do gains in the wealth of one country augment or diminish the wealth of other countries? Is agricultural production or market exchange the key to growth and development? Do high wages make an economy grow or contract?—continue to be asked. But early investigations of economic phenomena were not conducted within a distinct intellectual or professional discipline. Adam Smith was undoubtedly the greatest political economist of the eighteenth century, but his arguments are spread across books with titles like *The Theory of Moral Sentiments* and *Lectures on Jurisprudence* as well as *An Inquiry into the Nature and Causes of the Wealth of Nations*. Economic thinking encompassed ideas and arguments that are now treated separately by economists, historians, sociologists, anthropologists, psychologists, political scientists, lawyers, and philosophers.

One set of questions that preoccupied early political economists was essentially moral and psychological. Improvement—constructing roads, building hospitals, funding "friendly societies"—was impossible without economic growth and development. As Poor Richard quipped, "*Necessity has no Law; Why? Because 'tis not to be had without Money.*"[11] Even the simplest of governmental tasks had a price tag. But what of the men and women who made growth possible? What did they think about work and labor? Inherited moral traditions held that the pursuit of wealth was morally suspect. Greed—an inordinate or excessive desire for gain—was a vice. It corrupted the soul and created social conflict. In medieval theology avarice was considered a deadly sin; its antonym was charity, the unselfish love of others. Could the pursuit of profit be morally rehabilitated? If so, could it also be made psychologically attractive? Everyday observation suggested that many workers preferred a little more leisure to a little extra income. Laborers often responded to increased wages by cutting back on the number of hours or days they worked. How might they be motivated to become more industrious? And finally, how would the spread of trade—an increase in the number and diversity of things bought and sold—affect social order? Would it provide new bases for cooperation? Or would the experience of economic competition lead to fragmentation and conflict? Indeed, what *were* the traits and habits, beliefs and practices, that enabled humans to cooperate?

Franklin meditated on this last question—the bases of cooperation—during his long voyage back to Philadelphia. He left London on 21 July 1726. After six days hard winds forced his ship, the *Berkshire,* to take shelter near Portsmouth. Allowed to go on shore with the captain, he heard stories about the "severity" of a recent governor. Seeing "Johnny Gibson's Hole," a wretched dungeon where soldiers were confined "for trifling misdemeanors," Franklin was led to reflect on the "common maxim, that without severe discipline it is impossible to govern the licentious rabble of soldiery." In *The Prince,* Machiavelli famously—and notoriously—argued that it was better to be feared than loved. The bonds of love were weak and easily broken. But the fear of punishment never left a person; it was a permanent brake on misbehavior. Hannibal's great military successes, Machiavelli suggested, were owed to his reputation as a "harsh and cruel" leader. Franklin thought this mistaken, countering that "Alexander and Caesar, those renowned generals, received more faithful service, and performed greater actions by means of the love their soldiers bore them, than they could possibly have done if . . . they had been hated and feared by those they commanded."[12] Fear paralyzed individuals, sapping their vigor and motivation; love mobilized their energy through admiration, respect, and loyalty.

Two weeks later the winds changed and Franklin's ship took leave of land. On the open ocean, he delighted in the natural world. He marveled at flying fish, studied crab embryos in seaweed, and caught dolphins. (The latter, he recorded in his journal, tasted "tolerably well.") He stayed up to observe an eclipse of the moon and was astonished by a near-total eclipse of the sun. But much of the time he did what sea travelers have done for centuries: he fought tedium and ennui with idle distractions. "I rise in the morning and read for an hour or two perhaps, and then reading grows tiresome. Want of exercise occasions want of appetite, so that eating and drinking affords but little pleasure. I tire myself with playing at draughts [checkers], then I go to cards; nay there is no play so trifling or childish, but we fly to it for entertainment. A contrary wind, I know not how, puts us all out of good humor; we grow sullen, silent and reserved, and fret at each other upon every little occasion."[13]

During one of an endless series of card games, a fellow passenger was accused of cheating. A court of justice was constituted. Witnesses were heard, evidence was examined, and the jury returned a verdict of guilty. The knave refused to accept his punishment, the payment of a fine, and in frustration a rope was tied about his middle and he was hoisted in the air and left to hang, "cursing and swearing, for near a quarter of an hour." Finally, when his face turned black and he seemed near death, the passengers and crew relented. Instead of further physical punishment, they "excommunicated" him: everyone on board refused "to play, eat, drink, or converse with him" until he paid his fine.[14]

Ostracism was a powerful corrective. After five days the convicted cardsharp found exclusion from society too painful to bear. Agreeing to pay his fine, he was "received . . . into unity again." Franklin's comment on this episode is extraordinary:

> Man is a sociable being, and it is for aught I know one of the worst
> of punishments to be excluded from society. I have read abundance
> of fine things on the subject of solitude, and I know 'tis a common
> boast in the mouths of those that affect to be thought wise, *that they
> are never less alone than when alone.* I acknowledge solitude an agreeable refreshment to a busy mind; but were these thinking people
> obliged to be always alone, I am apt to think they would quickly find
> their very being insupportable to them. I have heard of a gentleman
> who underwent seven years close confinement, in the Bastille at
> Paris. He was a man of sense, he was a thinking man; but being deprived of all conversation, to what purpose should he think? There

is no burden so grievous to man as time that he knows not how to dispose of. He was forced at last to have recourse to this invention: he daily scattered pieces of paper about the floor of his little room, and then employed himself in picking them up and sticking them in rows and figures on the arm of his elbow-chair; and he used to tell his friends, after his release, that he verily believed if he had not taken this method he should have lost his senses. One of the philosophers, I think it was Plato, used to say, that he had rather be the veriest stupid block in nature, than the possessor of all knowledge without some intelligent being to communicate it to.

This passage is brimming with ideas. Franklin dismissed out of hand the ascetic ideal of solitude. (He surely had in mind the French mathematician and philosopher Blaise Pascal, who once wrote that "the sole cause of man's unhappiness is that he does not know how to stay quietly in his room.")[15] "Man is a sociable being," and thrives in the company of others. But what, precisely, does this mean? Franklin had a gregarious soul and made friends wherever he went. He relished the company of others. Yet here he linked sociability to the movement of pieces of paper on the floor of a prison cell. How can these be related?

The concept of sociability played an important role in seventeenth- and eighteenth-century moral, political, and economic debates. At the time of Franklin's voyage, major discussions on the subject could be found in the writings of Hugo Grotius, Thomas Hobbes, Samuel Pufendorf, John Locke, and the third Earl of Shaftesbury. In later years, important contributions were made by Francis Hutcheson, David Hume, Jean-Jacques Rousseau, and Adam Smith. Franklin read the work of all these men and was friends with several of them. But he was not a "footnoter"; in his own writings, he rarely cited the books and arguments of others. Moreover, he inhabited a world in which a great many arguments were conducted orally, in coffeehouses, taverns, and salons. (Recall that Franklin met Bernard Mandeville, a critic of the doctrine of natural sociability, at the Horns, an alehouse in Cheapside.) To understand what Franklin meant when he said that "man is a sociable being," we must reconstruct key pieces of his mental furniture.

The seventeenth-century English political philosopher Thomas Hobbes argued that civilized life is not possible without the absolute authority of a sovereign. In a state of nature—a condition in which resources are scarce, and there is no "common power" to keep people in "awe"—each person threatens (or is a potential threat to) the well-being and survival of the others. Cooperation is fragile, because people have no good or enduring reasons to trust each other. Each is responsible for his own security. In such a world, Hobbes wrote, life is "solitary, poor, nasty, brutish, and short."[16]

Hobbes's *Leviathan* was written in the middle of the English civil war (1642–60) and drew rhetorical power from that bloody conflict. Sociability is not natural. Just look around you, Hobbes suggested, if you want to see what life is like without a stable, coercive government.[17] Not every observer came to that conclusion, however. From the start there were critics who insisted that Hobbes's observations and arguments were mistaken. The breakdown of social order during the civil war did not prove that humans were naturally vicious. The eighteenth-century moral philosopher Francis Hutcheson, for example, claimed that sociability was a "primary" human attribute. Love or benevolence (Hutcheson thought them equivalent) lead us to help others even when our own pleasures or interests are not involved. They do not always do so; violent passions, like the thirst for revenge, may drown them out. But friendship, gratitude, and affection provide a natural moral and psychological foundation for cooperation.[18]

The arguments of Hobbes and Hutcheson, and variations on them, enjoyed wide circulation on both sides of the Atlantic. In 1737 the esteemed Philadelphia scholar James Logan asked Franklin to comment on a draft essay, "Moral Good or Virtue." Logan's original has been lost, but Franklin's reactions survive. Logan apparently veered too close to Hutcheson for Franklin's tastes: the essay was "a little too severe upon Hobbes, whose Notion, I imagine, is somewhat nearer the Truth than that which makes the State of Nature a State of Love: But the Truth perhaps lies between both Extremes."[19] Where was that middle ground? One influential answer lay in the writings of the German jurist Samuel Pufendorf. According to Pufendorf, utility (and not fear or love) was the glue of society. Humans lack the capacity to survive on their own. Natural instincts and physical abilities are insufficient to ensure self-preservation. Individuals are driven together by practical needs, not moral ideals. As Adam Smith suggested in the *Wealth of Nations,* "it is not from the benevolence of the butcher, the brewer, or the baker that we expect our dinner, but from their regard to their own interest. We address ourselves, not to their humanity but to their self-love, and never talk to them of our own necessities but of their advantages."[20]

Franklin had this cluster of ideas in mind when he wrote that "man is a sociable being." He did not worry about the details—he rarely did—but he accepted the claim that sociability was grounded in the satisfaction of needs, not in fear or love. That was one of the lessons of life on board ship. The convicted cardsharp finally paid his debt not because he felt remorse for his actions, or because he was concerned for the well-being of his fellow passengers, or even because he feared being hung from the mast once again, but because he wanted to be allowed back into the game. The passengers were sullen and fretful, and they had no particular concern for each other, but they preferred the petty pleasures of cooperation to the deadening silence of the sea.

Franklin's story of the French gentleman who endured seven years' solitary confinement adds psychological complexity to these observations. Lacking companions to engage his thoughts and feelings, he was reduced to playing a simple game, over and over, to stave off insanity. "There is no burden so grievous to man as time that he knows not how to dispose of." The foundation for this insight was laid in John Locke's *An Essay concerning Human Understanding*, a book Franklin read with care as a boy in Boston. According to Locke, the will is determined by a sense of "uneasiness," or the "want of some absent good." Bodily pains call to mind the comforts and pleasures we lack and lead us to seek relief. So, too, do discomforts of the mind. Release is not always possible, however, and that only magnifies our sense of unease. Who has not felt, at one time or another, the truth of the proverb that "hope deferred maketh the heart sick"?[21] Perhaps so intensely that the only alternative to misery and despair seems death? To survive, the French prisoner had to turn his thoughts from unbearable isolation to a narrow and mechanical task.

Sociability is grounded in utility. But as Franklin's examples suggest, he did not think of utility in narrowly economic terms, nor did he think usefulness could be straightforwardly measured in terms of profits and losses. Utility and usefulness were blanket terms used to capture the ability of people and things to be advantageous or beneficial. Some objects of utility were tangible, like food and shelter. Others were more abstract: the Library Company was a "useful" institution, and the American Philosophical Society dedicated itself to the pursuit of "useful" knowledge. The company of others was useful in a thousand different ways, from bringing pleasure to keeping us sane. Older women, Franklin once remarked, were "the most tender and useful of all Friends when you are sick."[22] We need not agree to see his point: cooperation is grounded not in Christian charity or Hobbesian fear, but in our ability to assist each other.

The Habits of Virtue

We join in cooperative ventures in order to satisfy our needs and interests. But that does not mean that we naturally, spontaneously, or automatically act in ways that are useful to ourselves or others. Life on board the *Berkshire* proved that. So, too, had Franklin's life in London. Though he had worked hard and had many interesting experiences, he had also fallen under the influence of dissolute friends and freethinking ideas and had committed a number of painful indiscretions. The story of the solitary prisoner in the Bastille pointed to an important fact: our customs, habits, and beliefs are malleable. We can modify and adapt ourselves as well as change our surroundings. This was crucial to how Franklin thought about his own life, and it had profound implications for how he thought about the dynamics of commercial society.

While at sea in the summer of 1726 Franklin drafted a "plan" for "regulating my future Conduct in Life." He had never settled on a "regular design" for his life, and as a consequence the things he did were incongruous. But now, as he returned to Philadelphia to work for Thomas Denham, he had the opportunity to begin anew. "Let me, therefore, make some resolutions, and form some scheme of action, that, henceforth, I may live in all respects like a rational creature." Franklin settled on four goals: frugality, sincerity, industry, and charity. He was in debt and needed to repay his creditors. He was a young man, with little more to trade on than his reputation for honesty. He was susceptible to temptation and could not afford to sacrifice long-term interests to short-term passions. And he had a sharp and critical tongue that often caused him trouble.[23] Were he to make himself a useful man, he needed to reform.

Three or four years later Franklin ratcheted up the stakes and conceived a "bold and arduous Project of arriving at moral Perfection." He recounted his experiences in his *Autobiography;* the character of that extraordinary document is relevant to our understanding of his narrative purposes. Franklin began writing his memoirs in the summer of 1771, while visiting Jonathan Shipley, bishop of St. Asaph, at his country estate near Twyford. He completed the first draft of part 1 within six weeks but did not write part 2 until 1784, during his residence in France. Parts 3 and 4 were written in Philadelphia between 1788 and 1790. Franklin intended to review his entire life, but ill health prevented him from completing the manuscript, and the narrative breaks off abruptly in 1757. At the outset he admitted to mixed motives: he wanted to write a family history, vindicate his reputation, and indulge his vanity. These objectives are visible on almost every page. So, too, is Franklin's desire to craft a work of moral and political education. Franklin thought his life "fit to be imitated." As he explained to a friend, he hoped "to benefit the young reader, by showing him from my example, and my successes in emerging from poverty, and acquiring some degree of wealth, power, and reputation, the advantages of certain modes of conduct which I observed, and of avoiding the errors which were prejudicial to me."[24] These reasons for writing overlap and intersect; a single story often served multiple purposes. And given Franklin's brilliance as a writer, they are often delivered with delightfully ironic wit.

Franklin tells us that he "wished to live without committing any Fault at any time," conquering "all that either Natural Inclination, Custom, or Company might lead me into." He knew—or thought he knew—right from wrong, and did not see why he "might not *always* do the one and avoid the other." But to his chagrin he found the task exceedingly difficult. While he was guarding against one fault, another would surprise him. Habit took "Advantage of Inattention. Inclination was sometimes too strong for Reason." He knew what he wanted to do, but he could not bring himself to do it. Legislating reform—even self-legislating reform—was generally ineffective.[25] Anyone who has ever dieted or taken up an exercise program will easily understand Franklin's difficulties.

The intellectual foundation for this "discovery" lay, once again, in Locke's *Essay*. According to Locke, moral freedom rests on the capacity to "*suspend* the prosecution of this or that desire, as everyone daily may Experiment in himself." Each man has the capacity to "be determined in *willing* by his own Thought and Judgment." But it was "not easy for the Mind to put off those confused Notions and Prejudices it has imbibed from Custom, Inadvertency, and common Conversation." Overcoming these impediments to a moral life was emotionally and intellectually demanding, pitting an individual against his or her own desires as well as against the expectations of others. What might motivate a person to embrace such a strenuous vocation? Locke argued that the answer to this question lay in a keen awareness of humanity's utter dependence on God. Only knowledge of the "Rewards and Punishments of another Life"—"exquisite and endless Happiness" or "infinite Misery"—gave people strength to resist the temptations of the temporal world.[26]

Franklin did not deny that the threat of eternal punishment made some persons moral. But he did not think that true of all. Other motives, less absolute and more closely tied to everyday life, could be equally effective. Moral character was a matter of habit, and what Franklin needed was an art or method for securing the virtues he had and acquiring the ones he lacked. He began by distilling the many and varied lists of virtues he had encountered in his reading. There were thirteen in all:

1. Temperance. Eat not to Dullness. Drink not to Elevation.
2. Silence. Speak not but what may benefit others or yourself. Avoid trifling Conversation.
3. Order. Let all your Things have their Places. Let each Part of your Business have its Time.
4. Resolution. Resolve to perform what you ought. Perform without fail what you resolve.
5. Frugality. Make no Expense but to do good to others or yourself: i.e. Waste nothing.
6. Industry. Lose no Time.——— Be always employed in something useful.———Cut off all unnecessary Actions.———
7. Sincerity. Use no hurtful Deceit. Think innocently and justly; and, if you speak, speak accordingly.
8. Justice. Wrong none, by doing Injuries or omitting the Benefits that are your Duty.
9. Moderation. Avoid Extremes. Forbear resenting Injuries so much as you think they deserve.
10. Cleanliness. Tolerate no Uncleanness in Body, Clothes or Habitation.———
11. Tranquility. Be not disturbed at Trifles, or at Accidents common or unavoidable.
12. Chastity. Rarely use Venery but for Health or Offspring; Never to Dullness, Weakness, or the Injury of your own or another's Peace or Reputation.———
13. Humility. Imitate Jesus and Socrates.———

Franklin's original list included only twelve virtues. But a Quaker friend informed him, in no uncertain terms, that he was "generally thought proud," and provided several examples of his "overbearing" and "insolent" behavior. Franklin did not dispute the charge—if anything, his account of the incident twinkles with delight—but he did add "humility" to his list of virtues.[27]

To help make these virtues habitual, Franklin devised a novel system of moral bookkeeping. In a small book he drew a table with a row for every virtue and a column for each day of the week. Every time he committed a fault, he made a black mark in the appropriate square. Each week he focused his attention on one of the virtues; after thirteen weeks, he began the cycle again. Franklin imagined himself a kind of moral gardener, picking weeds one at a time. Over time, he hoped to experience the pleasure of "viewing a clean book."

Perfection proved impossible. As Franklin sardonically reported, "I was surprised to find myself so much fuller of Faults than I had imagined." The tone of this observation is essential to its meaning. At times Franklin found the pursuit of perfection utterly exhausting and totally futile. Order was an impossible goal; he would never learn to keep his shop tidy. On such occasions he was reminded of the man who wanted the whole surface of his ax to shine as brightly as the edge. The blacksmith agreed, so long as the customer turned the grinding wheel. "The Smith pressed the broad Face of the Ax hard and heavily on the Stone, which made the Turning of it very fatiguing." At length the man became exhausted and resolved to take the ax as it was. "No, says the Smith, Turn on, turn on; we shall have it bright by and by; as yet 'tis only speckled." Yes, said the worn-out man, "but—*I think I like a speckled Ax best.*" Franklin sometimes felt like the man with the ax and was tempted to stop before he had polished all of his character. At other times he worried that his scheme was "a kind of Foppery in Morals." A fop was a fool, overly precise in his appearance and manners, foppery the vain and silly acts of such a person. How ridiculous to be an ethical dandy, excessively concerned with the small stains and broken creases that mark any comfortable and well-worn suit of moral clothes. Such scrupulous attention to the smallest details was offensive. And yet, Franklin realized that he was "a better and a happier Man" than he would have been had he not attempted to perfect himself. Changing habits was like learning to write: by tracing perfectly printed letters, a person's penmanship is improved. It was never as good as

Project and my Studies; Resolution once become habitual, would keep me firm in my Endeavours to obtain all the subsequent Virtues; Frugality & Industry, by freeing me from Debt, & producing Affluence & Independance would make more easy the Practice of Sincerity and Justice, &c. &c... Conceiving then that agreable to the Advice of Pythagoras in his Golden Verses, daily Examination would be necessary, I contriv'd the following Method for conducting that Examination.

I made a little Book in which I allotted a Page for each of the Virtues. I rul'd each Page with red Ink so as to have seven Columns, one for each Day of the Week, marking each Column with a Letter for the Day. I cross'd these Columns with thirteen red Lines, marking the Beginning of each Line with the first Letter of one of the Virtues, on which Line I might mark by a little black Spot every Fault I committed respecting that Virtue upon the Day.

my remaining

Insert these Lines that divide it in a Note

Form of the Pages

| Temperance. |
| Eat not to Dulness. |
| Drink not to Elevation. |

	S	M	T	W	T	F	S
T							
S	•	•		•		•	
O	•	•		•		•	•
R			•				
F		•	•				
I							
S							
J							
M							
C							
T							
C							
H							

Folio 99 of the *Autobiography*, with Franklin's sketch of a page from the "little Book" in which he tracked his moral habits. Each mark represented a failure, in this instance, of the virtue of temperance. (This item, HM 9999, is reproduced by permission of the Huntington Library, San Marino, California.)

the original, but it was "tolerable." These insights combined to create a rich and multifaceted lesson for Franklin's young readers. Strive to do the right thing: your life will be improved by the effort. But don't be priggish about it. And above all, don't confuse a shiny surface for a sharp edge.[28]

The rhetorical framework of the *Autobiography* would have been familiar to Franklin's audience from seventeenth- and eighteenth-century Christianity. A man of promise and ability leads a life of dissipation; awakening to this fact, he is disgusted with himself and resolves to change; through reflection and self-observation, he struggles to purge himself of vice; over time, with the helping hand of God, he moves ever closer to a life of purity and perfection. This narrative, concerned with the fate of a single soul, was deeply personal. But it was told for public purposes, and not simply that we might learn from the struggles and mistakes of others. The self created through self-discipline was an exemplary self. It represented the qualities and characteristics of a life infused with God's grace, and it expressed God's grace through benevolent action in the world. Good works were an outward manifestation of inner piety. As Cotton Mather put it in *An Essay upon the Good*—another work that Franklin read with care—"a workless faith is a worthless faith."[29]

Franklin often expressed his moral ideals in these terms: "What is Serving God? 'Tis doing Good to Man." This phrase looks similar to Mather's, but Franklin has inverted its meaning. In Franklin's moral scheme there were thirteen virtues, ranging from temperance to humility. He constructed no comparable table of vices, but we can infer them from his characterizations of men and events. The list would have been short: argumentativeness, idleness, and indecision. These traits were vicious because they made people useless to themselves and to each other. "Vicious Actions are not hurtful because they are forbidden, but forbidden because they are hurtful, the Nature of Man alone considered." Mather could not have disagreed more: "Study no other *Ethics*, but what is in the *Bible*."[30]

The distance between these two perspectives was displayed in an exchange between Franklin and his parents in the spring of 1738. Josiah had just turned eighty; Abiah was a decade younger. They had been married in Boston's Old South Church in 1689 and still lived in the Union Street home to which they had moved when Benjamin was six. In separate letters, Josiah and Abiah expressed concern for Franklin's opinions. As good New England

Congregationalists, they had reason to worry. He had ceased attending services (he found the sermons "very dry, uninteresting and unedifying, since not a single moral Principle was inculcated or enforced"). He had written four long and impassioned pamphlets defending Samuel Hemphill, a visiting Irish preacher whose nondogmatic emphasis on the practice of virtue had incurred the wrath of the local synod. And he had joined the Freemasons, a fraternal organization whose secret practices and esoteric ideas aroused suspicion.[31]

Franklin's response to his parents, filled with corrections, additions, and alternative formulations, is preserved in his commonplace book. It is an extraordinary manuscript, recording a son's struggle to find words that would comfort his parents yet still be truthful. In the first draft, Franklin was truculent and defensive: "you both seem concerned for my Orthodoxy. God only knows whether all the Doctrines I hold for true, be so or not." In the next version, he softened his tone: "you both seem concerned lest I have imbibed some dangerous Errors." The final draft is conciliatory: "you both seem concerned lest I have imbibed erroneous Opinions. Doubtless I have my Share." Franklin then pleaded his case: "I think Opinions should be judged of by their Influences and Effects; and if a Man holds none that tend to make him less Virtuous or more vicious, it may be concluded that he holds none that are dangerous; which I hope is the Case with me." The Freemasons were "a very harmless sort of People." Doctrinal differences were not important. "Vital Religion" suffers when "Orthodoxy is more regarded than Virtue. And the Scripture assures me, that at the last Day, we shall not be examined what we *thought*, but what we *did*."[32]

Franklin's carefully crafted letter to his parents accomplished its objective. One month later he wrote again, expressing his "great Pleasure" that his mother "approved of my Letter and was now satisfied with me." But behind this resolution to a painful family conflict deep differences remained. According to Franklin, morality was a matter of actions and effects, not motives and intentions. In 1749 Poor Richard opined: "*Words* may show a man's Wit, but *Actions* his Meaning." We sometimes say that actions speak louder than words, especially when we hope to expose the hypocrisy of others. "Don't listen to what he says—watch what he does, and you will see his true intentions." Franklin had something different in mind: moral identity is established by, and known through, action. Properly speaking, it is not a matter of will, at least not as the will was understood by Puritan moralists. The self was a constellation of passions and interests, integrated into a productive whole through good habits. It could not be changed quickly. Franklin rejected the rhetoric of conversion and rebirth: "men don't become very good or very bad in an Instant, both vicious and virtuous Habits being acquired by Length of Time and repeated Acts." The self was, however, malleable. The most effective strategies were indirect. The key was to begin with actions. "It was a wise counsel given to a young man, *Pitch upon that course of life which is most excellent, and* CUSTOM *will make it the most delightful*." *Do* the right thing, and in time you will learn to *want* to do the right thing.[33]

Franklin's contemporary Jonathan Edwards, the fiery Congregational minister, vehemently rejected this idea. According to Edwards, virtuous actions were the fruit of virtuous motives. Without a pure heart, it was not possible to act virtuously. A theory based on habit could not explain an original commitment to virtue. "How came he," wondered Edwards, "by that virtue from which he acted when he first began to reform?" Nor could such a theory protect men and women against the sins of hypocrisy and self-deception. Edwards doubted the sufficiency of works as an expression of goodness. Seemingly virtuous actions can mask base motives. (Most shopkeepers are honest; is that because they think it is the right thing to do or because they fear being caught and punished for cheating?) Edwards thus insisted that purity of heart was morally, psychologically, and ontologically prior to action in the world.[34] But Franklin did not participate in the Puritan inner drama of guilt, self-doubt, and self-accusation. Nor did he linger, with fear and trembling, over moral backsliding and the inevitable reappearance of sin. He tallied his mistakes—his "errata"—and sought to change himself by changing his habits. In this effort he did not insist that his motives be pure. As he quipped in the *Autobiography*, vanity and pride made him a better man.

Franklin came from Puritan stock, but he did not share the faith of his forebears. The habits of virtue were not designed to calm an anxious spirit, nor were they grounded in a sense of unworthiness. To the contrary, they were expressions of existential confidence. Franklin did not doubt that improvement was possible, nor did he hesitate to suggest that the measure of improvement was utility or usefulness. These beliefs proved crucial as Franklin turned from the moral and psychological bases of cooperation to the practices and policies that governed economic exchange.

The Politics of Money

By the late 1720s, as a result of reading, conversation, and personal experience, Franklin had come to embrace the following ideas: society is grounded in mutual needs and interests, not mortal fear or Christian love; virtue is measured by actions, not intentions; character is shaped by habits, which can themselves be changed; and improvement, personal and collective, is possible. All of these ideas came together in his first pamphlet to address a major public controversy, *A Modest Enquiry into the Nature and Necessity of a Paper-Currency* (1729).

A Modest Enquiry concerned Pennsylvania monetary policy. Seventeenth-century colonial economies were plagued by a shortage of circulating media of exchange. Gold and silver were extremely scarce: mercantilist policies led Parliament to prohibit the export of coin to the colonies in 1695, and English creditors generally required balance-of-trade payments to be made in the few coins that could be found. At times the colonies came close to operating on a barter basis. This was massively inefficient and posed substantial obstacles to economic development. Beginning in 1690, colonial governments sought to resolve this liquidity crisis by issuing paper money in the form of bills of credit. Massachusetts was among the first to experiment with public and publicly regulated measures to extend credit and expand the money supply. Pennsylvania followed suit by issuing £15,000 of paper money in 1723, and the success of that venture led to a renewal in 1726. These schemes were relatively simple. Pennsylvanians mortgaged their real property to a loan office, and received newly minted paper money in return. As the loans were repaid, the trustees of the loan office destroyed bills taken in. At the end of the loan cycle, the money supply would have returned to its original level; but while the bills remained in circulation, they provided vital instruments of exchange. These measures pleased many, especially merchants and debtors; but because the expansion of the money supply was accompanied by inflation, it dismayed landowners and creditors. Heated debates ensued; *A Modest Enquiry* was Franklin's attempt to influence their outcome.[35]

According to Franklin, "*Commerce*, or the Exchange of one Commodity or Manufacture for another, is highly convenient and beneficial to Mankind" because it eliminates the inefficiencies and instabilities of barter exchange. Money is simply a socially agreed-upon medium of exchange; the true standard for value is provided by labor. "Thus the riches of a Country

A MODEST

E N Q U I R Y

INTO THE

Nature and *Necessity*

OF A

PAPER-CURRENCY.

—————— *Quid asper*
Utile Nummus habet ; patriæ, charisq; propinquis
Quantum elargiri deceat. ————
                                        Pers.

PHILADELPHIA:
Printed and Sold at the New PRINTING-
OFFICE, near the Market. 1729.

Title page of Franklin's first major contribution to Pennsylvania politics. The Latin epigram is from Persius, *Satires*, 3:69–71: "What good there is in fresh-minted coin; how much should be spent on country and on your dear kin." (Courtesy the Library Company of Philadelphia.)

KNOW ALL MEN by these Presents,
That I *Eleazer Doane of Middletown
in the County of Bucks Yeoman*
am held and firmly bound unto
Samuel Carpenter, Jeremiah Langhorne, William Fishbourn, and
Philip Taylor, Trustees of the GENERAL LOAN-
OFFICE of the Province of Pensylvania, in the Sum of
Forty Pounds
Lawful Money of the said Province, to be paid unto the said
Trustees or their Successors; To which Payment well and
truly to be made, I do bind my Self, my Heirs, Executors,
and Administrators firmly by these Presents. Sealed with my
Seal, Dated the *fourth* Day of *November* in
the Year of our Lord One Thousand Seven Hundred and
twenty nine

THE CONDITION of this Obligation
is such, That if the Above-bounden *Eleazer Doane*
or his Heirs, Executors, or Administrators, do well and truly
pay unto the said Trustees or their Successors, at the Place where their
Office shall be kept for the Time being, the Value of *Twenty Pounds*
in Bills of Credit cur-
rent by the Law of the said Province, or in Current Money of America,
with Interest for the same at *Five per Cent. per Annum*, And every
Part thereof, in such Proportions, at such Days and Times, and in such
Manner and Form as is particularly directed by a certain Indenture bearing
even Date with the above-written Obligation, and made between the
Above-bounden *Eleazer Doane* of the one Part,
and the said Trustees of the other Part, for securing the same Money as is
herein mentioned, according to the Tenor, Form and Effect of the same
Indenture; Then the above Obligation to be Void and of no Effect, or
else to be and remain in full Force and Virtue.

Sealed and Delivered in
the Presence of us

Eleazer Doane

Mortgage bond of the Pennsylvania General Loan Office. In this instance, Eleazer Doane of Middletown, Bucks County, borrowed £40 on 4 November 1729. (Courtesy American Philosophical Society.)

are to be valued by the Quantity of Labor its Inhabitants are able to purchase, and not by the Quantity of Silver or Gold they possess." A plentiful money supply does, however, enable efficient market institutions to develop. In so doing it spurs immigration and serves as a stimulus to growth. Scarce money, by contrast, frustrates commercial exchange and encourages recourse to barter. When that happens, prices increase, the value of commodities varies, labor is discouraged, and population growth is depressed.[36]

Some of these ideas, like the labor theory of value, were drawn from William Petty's seventeenth-century discussion of the issue in Ireland, *A Treatise of Taxes and Contributions*. Others reflect the work of John Wise, a Boston contemporary of Franklin's.[37] Franklin's unique contribution lay in his explicit attention to the political determinants of economic development. In Massachusetts, for example, Wise had argued for a private bank of credit, under the direction of "Landed Men, and Great Merchants," to manage the money supply. The natural play of interests would ensure that these gentlemen acted "to promote the Public Good." After all, Wise reasoned, "if they hurt others, they hurt themselves."[38] To Franklin this was an absurdly naïve view of commercial societies. Social order is grounded in relationships established to provide for the satisfaction of needs and interests. But needs and interests are not self-interpreting or self-limiting, and they do not automatically mesh with each other. Common wisdom held that "interest will not lie": if you know an individual's interests, then you know how that person will behave. But what if one did not know one's interests, or if one ignored or rejected them? Beliefs and passions, embedded in bad habits, often got in the way. That had been one of the lessons Franklin had learned from his experiments with moral reform. He had not always known what was in his interest; and even when he did, he was often unable to act on it.

Moreover, Franklin argued, interests are not objective facts, like height or weight, that can be known apart from a person's social and political context. Our interests are shaped by the laws we live under, the customs and habits we share, the social roles we inhabit. Even property rights are conventional.[39] Calculations of interest were insufficient to establish order and facilitate growth, for the simple reason that the existing regime of property rights expressed deep conflicts of interest. In colonial Pennsylvania there were classes of men who did not favor commercial development. "Men will always be powerfully influenced in their Opinions and Actions by what appears to be their particular Interest," and it was the interest of those who profited from inefficiency—the very wealthy, moneylenders, and lawyers who built their business on failed contracts—to keep money scarce.[40] These men were represented in the Assembly, where they tenaciously pursued their interests. Each new election seemed to bring a different coalition into the majority. The dynamics of electoral politics led to fluctuating monetary policies; this, in turn, exacerbated Pennsylvania's economic woes. Politics and economics were inseparable. The key to commercial growth was political integration.

Did Franklin have a stake in Pennsylvania monetary policy? What were *his* interests? These are important questions, but they need refinement. We have seen that Franklin had a long-standing *intellectual* interest in the arguments of political economists. And we have no reason to doubt that he had a genuine *civic* interest in the health and well-being of Pennsylvania. But that is not what most people have in mind when they ask about Franklin's interests; they want to know about his *material* interests in order to determine whether the position he took simply reflected his own profit or advantage. (That we ask this narrow version of the question says a great deal about our own priorities but very little about the concept of interest itself.)[41]

What of Franklin's interests in this narrow, economic sense? He made little if any profit from *A Modest Enquiry*. Franklin's pamphlet appears to have sold well enough, but he printed more copies than the market would bear and was still trying to unload remainders two years later. And he gained nothing from printing the money itself; that lucrative contract—worth £80—went to his competitor, Andrew Bradford. But Franklin's friends in the Assembly, who appreciated his efforts on behalf of the money bill, did reward him with "a very profitable Job": printing the registers of the General Loan Office. Did the prospect of a reward cast Franklin's integrity into doubt? He did not think so; he proudly broadcast the Assembly's "help" in his *Autobiography*.[42] Was he mistaken?

Finally, what of money itself? One of Franklin's best-known essays, "Advice to a Young Tradesman, Written by an Old One," suggested a provocative metaphor. "Remember," the young tradesman was counseled, "that Money is of a prolific generating Nature. Money can beget Money, and its Offspring can beget more, and so on. . . . He that kills a breeding Sow, destroys all her Offspring to the thousandth Generation. He that murders a Crown, destroys all it might have produced, even Scores of Pounds."

Franklin's metaphor is extraordinary, and has led some to conclude that he thought of money as a living thing, possessed of soul and spirit, to be cherished and nurtured as life itself. If that were true, then those who destroyed money—whether recklessly, through simple inattention, or as a conscious choice—committed a grievous sin. But this was clearly not Franklin's view. His language is earthy, amusing, and slightly menacing. The man who "murders a Crown" flirts with a politically volatile image (regicide) at the same time that he practices bad economics. By contrast, an ambitious young tradesman who views money through the eyes of a hog farmer is unlikely to fall victim to avarice. Money, like pigs in a poke, could be increased (through debt finance) or destroyed (by retiring debt). Neither entailed ethical failure. As Richard Saunders put it in 1737, "the Use of Money is all the Advantage there is in having Money."[43]

Credit and Debt

Expanding the money supply was a necessary but not sufficient condition for the economic development of British North America. Imperatives of credit and debt called for personal improvement as well. The population of eighteenth-century North America was swiftly growing but still highly dispersed. Trade followed a similar pattern: rapidly increasing—especially imports from England—but widely distributed. Commercial exchange occurred primarily in local settings where the stability of transactions rested more on personal character than impersonal market mechanisms. In the absence of sufficient circulating media, a substantial proportion of commercial exchange was conducted on credit. "Philadelphia records indicate that dry-goods merchants sold as much as 90 percent of their goods on credit. In the Chesapeake colonies the figure was about 80 percent. New England storekeepers apparently followed the same practice." Overseas exchanges were no different. As Adam Smith noted, credit, not cash, ruled colonial transactions.[44]

Franklin's own business ledgers meticulously record credits extended, debts owed, and payments made to and received from virtually every producer and consumer he dealt with. Individual figures were typically quite small, but collectively they represented substantial sums of money. Others might lack Franklin's means, but they conducted business on the same terms. In the cash-starved colonies, book credit—accounts of transactions that

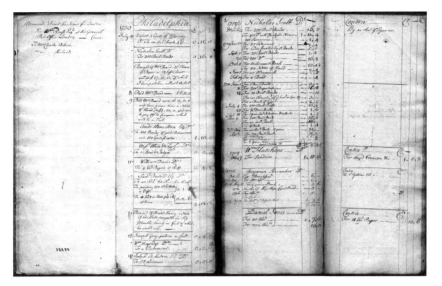

Folios 1 and 172–73 of Ledger A&B, Franklin's earliest surviving account book. At the front is a running tally of sales; in the back, a cumulative list of credits and debts. Nicholas Scull's purchase of two hundred bail bonds on 4 July 1730 is listed on each of the pages printed here. (Courtesy American Philosophical Society.)

were typically small, local, and personal, kept in a book or ledger by tradesmen and merchants and backed by nothing more than personal assurance—was the foundation of exchange. Book credit often served as a medium of exchange, substituting for money.[45] In these exchanges, interest was not charged, and records were simple lists of debtors organized by name. Periodically creditors and debtors would reconcile their books with each other, eliminating overlapping commitments. But like many merchants, Franklin was unable to collect all that was owed him. All those "small sums" for books and supplies, advertisements and postage, added up to "something considerable." In his will, he bequeathed these unpaid debts to the Pennsylvania Hospital in hopes that its administrators could recover what he had not.[46]

In the *Autobiography* Franklin noted that in order to secure his "Credit and Character as a Tradesman," he "took care not only to be in *Reality* Industrious and frugal, but to avoid all *Appearances* to the Contrary. I dressed plainly; I was seen at no Places of idle Diversion; I never went out a-fishing or shooting . . . and to show that I was not above my Business, I sometimes brought home the Paper I purchased at the Stores, through the Streets on a Wheelbarrow." This was not a confession—Franklin was unembarrassed by his success at performing a role—but a testament to the importance of a reputation for industriousness. Commercial success rested on networks of credit; credit on trust; trust on personal reputation. And reputation, in turn, was a matter of appearance, of living up to the expectations of an audience. In this instance, Franklin's audience—the merchants and traders of Philadelphia—was attuned to his capacity for work. It mattered that Franklin worked late into the night and began again early in the morning. His industry was visible to his neighbors and gave him "Credit and Character." As his reputation spread, his business grew. As Franklin boasted, "Being esteemed an industrious young Man . . . I went on swimmingly."[47]

According to one English contemporary, "to support and maintain a man's private credit, 'tis absolutely necessary that the world have a fixed opinion" of his "honesty and integrity." Merchants and traders scrutinized the creditworthiness of potential customers by grasping at every scrap of information. As colonial historian Bruce Mann explains, "before Dun and Bradstreet pioneered centralized credit reporting in the nineteenth century, the decision to extend or withhold credit rested on personal ties or experience, or, absent those, on second- or third-hand information reported by someone whom the creditor knew—in short, on reputation, rumor, opinion, even fact." Eighteenth-century economic literature is filled with aphorisms and apothegms that played on the double meaning of credit as reputation and financial resource. In the words of one shopkeepers' guide, "Of the Trade of this Nation you may reckon at least two Thirds is carried on upon Credit: But pray what does this *Credit*, or *Trust* arise from? Why from that *Credit*, or *Reputation*, that the Tradesman has acquired by his Industry, Integrity, and . . . other Virtues and good Qualities."[48]

Maintaining one's credit did not come easily. It was hard work and required focused energy and extraordinary self-control. One merchant advised his son to handle a difficult Dutch merchant in the following manner: "I would have you go to him in as genteel a manner as possible and inform him of his mistake, and whatever he says to you be as determined to keep your temper and behave like a Stoic philosopher." When Franklin's English friend and editor Benjamin Vaughan sent his younger brother to the United States on business, he urged him to "be calm, and *seem* calm. . . . You must conduct business on an European, and not on an American plan."[49] To these young men, the commercial ethos of an economy of credit was an ascetic discipline, embraced out of the desire to succeed.

Failure to maintain a good reputation spelled disaster. In a South Carolina newspaper, "Honestus" complained that small merchants were especially vulnerable to attacks on their reputation. "Credit is undone in Whispers. . . . An ill Word may change Plenty into Want." A Rhode Island debtor who went by the name "An Impartial Hand" bluntly warned that when a tradesman's creditors learn that they have no good reason to trust him, "he is soon discovered, hunted down, and perhaps cast into prison." Impartial Hand's worries were justified. Daniel Defoe—who knew indebtedness firsthand—lamented that bankruptcy was treated as "a Crime so Capital" that debtors were "cast out of Human Society, and exposed to Extremities worse than Death." Richard Steele—like Defoe, one of Franklin's favorite authors—concurred. Bankruptcy was "the most dreadful of all Humane Conditions." In every colony, and later every state, imprisonment for debt was permitted. The conditions were often Dickensian: dirty, cruel, and corrupt.[50]

In this context, Franklin's "Advice to a Young Tradesman" acquires yet another layer of meaning. Franklin's old tradesman warns his young colleague that "Time is Money" and reminds him that "money is of a prolific generating Nature." Each of these observations is important. But the weight of the old trader's advice falls on the behavior appropriate to a man living on credit. Success went to those who earned a reputation for industry and frugality. "The most trifling Actions that affect a Man's Credit, are to be regarded. The Sound of your Hammer at Five in the Morning or Nine at Night, heard by a Creditor, makes him easy Six Months longer. But if he sees you at a Billiard Table, or hears your Voice in a Tavern, when you should be at Work, he sends for his Money the next Day. Finer Clothes than he or his Wife wears, or greater Expense in any particular than he affords himself, shocks his Pride, and he duns you to humble you. Creditors are a kind of People, that have the sharpest Eyes and Ears, as well as the best Memories of any in the World."[51] The simple movements of work—the swinging of a hammer, the pushing of a wheelbarrow—conveyed a man's character better than any oath or proclamation. Through repetition they became habitual and, as habits, industry and frugality were essential virtues. Here, then, was another manifestation of Poor Richard's belief that we are what we do. "*Words* may show a man's Wit, but *Actions* his Meaning."

Because the basic unit of life was the household, the reputations of wives, children, and servants had economic repercussions. Fine food, expensive clothes, idle habits: all these reflected on the tradesman and had the potential to undermine his credit.[52] Franklin has sometimes been faulted for his treatment of his wife, Deborah, and his daughter, Sally, during his long sojourns in England and France. During the Revolutionary War, for example, Sally asked him to send a few creature comforts from Paris: long black pins, lace, and feathers. Franklin responded that this "disgusted me as much as if you had put salt into my strawberries. . . . You are to be dressed for the ball! you seem not to know, my dear daughter, that of all the dear things in this world, idleness is the dearest, except mischief." This may seem hard-hearted and hypocritical, especially given the comparative ease of Franklin's life in Paris. Reading Sally's response, which chafed at her father's "severe reprimand," it is difficult not to feel supportive of her. But perhaps we should view this admonishment not in terms of a modern, emotionally intimate family but in terms of a (patriarchal) eighteenth-century economic unit.[53]

When thinking about his wife, Deborah, Franklin recalled the English proverb "He that would thrive/Must ask his Wife." It was "lucky for me that I had one as much disposed to Industry and Frugality as myself. She assisted me cheerfully in my Business, folding and stitching Pamphlets, tending Shop, purchasing old Linen Rags for the Paper-makers, etc. etc. We kept no idle Servants, our Table was plain and simple, our Furniture of the cheapest." In morality tales of this sort, of course, there must always be temptation. In this instance, it came in the form of conspicuous consumption: "My Breakfast was for a long time Bread and Milk, (no Tea,) and I ate it out of a two penny earthen Porringer with a Pewter Spoon. But mark how Luxury will enter Families, and make a Progress, in Spite of Principle. Being Called one Morning to Breakfast, I found it in a China Bowl with a Spoon of Silver. They had been bought for me without my Knowledge by my Wife, and had cost her the enormous Sum of three and twenty Shillings, for which she had no other Excuse or Apology to make, but that she thought *her* Husband deserved a Silver Spoon and China Bowl as well as any of his Neighbors."[54]

Sally's request for pins and lace was simply the latest in a series of downfalls; Deborah's vanity and pride had already introduced luxury into the Franklin household. The problem with luxuries was not simply that they were expensive but that they symbolized a loss of emotional and familial control by male heads of households. Women were the primary purchasers of consumer goods in colonial America, and anxieties about luxury often

took the form of a battle of the sexes. As historian Tim Breen has sardonically observed, "the downfall of eighteenth-century American women was
a tale told in terms of cloth. Everywhere colonial males looked, they were
confronted by females decked out in gaily colored 'Silks and Lawn' tailored
to the latest fashion. Their bodies had become a highly visible index to the
advance of luxury." The situation was all the harder for men to accept because "these female slaves to fashion seemed to have minds of their own."[55]
Unruly women threatened the order and discipline that gave a man credit in
the world of commerce. A trader whose household was consumed by luxury
was a trader who ought not to be trusted.

Securing one's credit was a matter of economic survival and called on
collective as well as individual resources. One of Franklin's earliest "projects" in Philadelphia was the Junto, a "Club for mutual Improvement"
formed in 1727. Meeting on Friday evenings, members of the Junto—
printers, scriveners, shoemakers, and joiners—provided mutual support, exchanged information, and discussed moral, political, economic, and scientific
topics. Franklin considered it "the best School of Philosophy, Morals, and
Politics that then existed in the Province." It was also a hardheaded practical
institution, combining moral uplift and self-help in roughly equal proportions. At each meeting members asked themselves questions like "Has any
citizen in your knowledge failed in his business lately, and what have you
heard of the cause?"; "Have you lately heard of any citizen's thriving well,
and by what means?"; "Has anybody attacked your reputation lately? and
what can the Junto do towards securing it?"; and "Have you lately heard any
member's character attacked, and how have you defended it?"[56]

John Locke's plans for a society for "improvement in useful Knowledge," as well as Cotton Mather's call for neighborhood "Religious Societies," may have provided models for the Junto. Closer to home, in purpose
if not location, were the artisanal clubs and associations Franklin would have
encountered during his eighteen months in London. In Britain, as in the
colonies, an acute shortage of specie forced merchants, traders, and craftsmen to rely on informal credit networks in their daily business. And in
Britain, as in the colonies, a reputation for probity and creditworthiness was
essential to success. As Defoe put it in *The Complete Tradesman*, "The loss of
money or goods is easily made up, and may be sometimes repaired with advantage; but the loss of credit is never repaired; the one is breaking open his
house, but the other is burning it down." Englishmen met this threat by

banding together. According to one contemporary, "Tradesmen's clubs . . . meet at taverns, inns, coffee and ale houses, wherein they have their respective orders for their better government, whereby during the times of their several meetings virtue is not only promoted, and vice punished, but likewise a good correspondence cultivated, for the mutual improvement of their respective businesses, by dealing with one another."[57] So, too, the Junto sought to enhance the credit—the reputations and resources—of small traders and craftsmen in Philadelphia.

Consumption

Poor Richard's ethos of industry and frugality was a strategic response to the challenges of an economically backward society. It was also a weapon in the growing imperial conflict. By the middle of the eighteenth century, one out of every three consumers of British products lived in North America. "Around half of all English exports of copperware, ironware, glassware, earthenware, silk goods, printed cotton and linen goods, and flannels were shipped to colonial consumers. Between two-thirds and three-quarters of all exported English cordage, iron nails, beaver hats, linen, and Spanish woolen goods went to British America." The consumer market penetrated the innermost recesses of the colonies. It went far beyond basic or absolute needs, and was increasingly driven by taste and fashion.[58]

Colonists' preference for British goods drove them deeper and deeper into debt. As Archibald Kennedy put it in 1750, "in Debt we are, and in Debt we must be, for those vast Importations from *Europe*." Father Abraham, one of Franklin's mouthpieces in *Poor Richard's Almanac*, was livid at colonial spending habits. "What Madness must it be to *run in Debt* for these Superfluities! . . . Think what you do when you run in Debt; *You give another Power over your Liberty*." But what was superfluous, and what was necessary to life? Almost any consumer good could be considered a luxury. Was it possible to draw a sharp line between what was merely desirable and what was truly indispensable? These were painfully difficult questions for Europeans and Britons as well as North Americans. Luxury was not simply an economic condition; it was also a complex moral and political category.[59] Mere subsistence needs seemed an impossibly low threshold. As one Maryland writer argued, without luxury "life would be tasteless, and a heavy burden." But what kinds of pleasures, and at what levels of intensity, were acceptable? Cotton

Pennsylvania 20 shilling note, 1739. Franklin perfected the technique of "nature printing," using impressions of actual leaves to help prevent counterfeiting. (Courtesy Stacks Rare Coins, New York City.)

cloth instead of woolen? In what textures and colors? And if cotton, then why not silk and lace? To be sure, past generations survived without fine clothes. But perhaps increasing levels of consumption were the natural consequence of improvement. A Connecticut author proclaimed that "man in his nature is a progressive being." Though he begins with "rude materials," he "natural rises, from the necessaries of life, to the conveniences, the delicacies, and the luxuries."[60] Luxury goods made life easier and more enjoyable; they were part of the civilizing process.

The growing market for consumer goods linked consumer behavior and commercial growth. Franklin explained the logic to his young English friend Benjamin Vaughan in the summer of 1784. "Is not the Hope of one day being able to purchase and enjoy Luxuries a great Spur to Labor and Industry? May not Luxury therefore produce more than it consumes, if without such a Spur People would be as they are naturally enough inclined to be, lazy and indolent?" Franklin illustrated this argument with an example. Years before, the skipper of a small ship that worked the Delaware River performed a "small Service" for Franklin but refused any pay. On learning that he had a daughter, Deborah sent her a "new-fashioned Cap." Three years later the skipper visited Franklin, with a local farmer in tow.

He mentioned the Cap and how much his Daughter had been pleased with it; but says he it proved a dear Cap to our Congregation—How so? When my Daughter appeared in it at Meeting, it was so much admired, that all the Girls resolved to get such Caps from Philadelphia; and my Wife and I computed that the whole could not have cost less than a hundred Pound. True says the Farmer, but you do not tell all the Story; I think the Cap was nevertheless an Advantage to us; for it was the first thing that put our Girls upon Knitting worsted Mittens for Sale at Philadelphia, that they might have wherewithal to buy Caps and Ribbons there; and you know that that Industry has continued and is likely to continue and increase to a much greater Value, and answers better Purposes. Upon the whole I was more reconciled to this little Piece of Luxury; since not only the Girls were made happier by having fine Caps, but the Philadelphians by the Supply of warm Mittens.

Emulation was a powerful force, inducing men and women, boys and girls, to invest time and energy in productive activity. Anchored in jealousy, driven by ambition, it fostered competition, growth, and development.[61]

Luxury was unavoidable in a "great State." Franklin's words consciously echoed a train of ideas that ran from Bernard Mandeville to Adam Smith. In the first decades of the eighteenth century, Mandeville had taunted British moralists by declaring that they were caught on the horns of a dilemma. They wanted both material prosperity and moral purity, and they set about reforming English society to bring it into accordance with their ideals. But, argued Mandeville, they could not have both. It was impossible to enjoy "all the most elegant Comforts of Life that are to be met with in an industrious, wealthy and powerful Nation, and at the same time be blessed with all the Virtue and Innocence that can be wished for in a Golden Age." Mandeville illustrated this paradox with a fable of the bees:

> A spacious Hive well stocked with Bees,
> That lived in Luxury and Ease;
> And yet as famed for Laws and Arms,
> As yielding large and early Swarms.

The hive thronged with activity, as millions worked to satisfy each other's needs and desires. What motivated the bees? What was the source of their energy and vitality? Envy, vanity, and pride. *Especially* pride. Without it, a bee was like "a huge Wind-mill without a breath of Air."[62] These base passions did not make the bees virtuous, but they did make them industrious. Each sought to better its own position by emulating others. Even leisure had its place; the pursuit of ease, not a disciplined sense of duty, was one of the most powerful motivating forces in a vibrant economy.

In Franklin's day, civic and religious reformers often acted as if intentions and outcomes were correlated. Moral intentions yield moral outcomes; immoral intentions yield immoral outcomes. Honesty breeds trust; dishonesty is corrosive of social order. Luxury was problematic because it seemed to rest on corrupt motives (envy, pride, covetousness, indolence). One of the key ideas developed by eighteenth-century theorists of commercial society was that intentions and outcomes were not necessarily correlated. Under the right conditions, private vices could yield public benefits. Franklin drove this point home with a simple example. "A vain silly Fellow builds a fine House, furnishes it richly, lives in it expensively, and in a few Years ruins himself, but the Masons, Carpenters, Smiths and other honest Tradesmen have been by his Employ assisted in maintaining and raising their Families, the Farmer has been paid for his Labor and encouraged, and the Estate is now in better Hands." The pursuit of luxury, even when it is self-destructive, is "not always an Evil to the Public."[63] (Assuming, of course, that the "vain silly fellows" paid their bills. If they did not, then "honest tradesmen" suffered miserably. The enforcement of contracts was essential to the plausibility of Franklin's tale.)

The rise of commercial society shattered the claim that good intentions and desirable consequences were always and everywhere connected. The web of beliefs and practices that held together the social world was simply too complex for that idea to remain plausible. Pure motives did not guarantee sought-after results; useful actions were sometimes based on morally suspect intentions. Closely linked to this emphasis on the unintended consequences of our actions was a move away from thinking about human character in terms of a single, unified structure. Mirroring the complexity of the social world was the belief that the self was "an adulterated compound, a heap of contradictions." As Franklin had discovered through experience and reflection, purity and consistency were not possible. Nor were they necessary; sometimes a speckled ax *was* best. This had profound consequences for older standards of behavior. The satisfaction of needs could not be ensured by the cultivation of love or fear alone. The conditions of modern commerce made the ideals of the Christian saint and the classical citizen anachronistic.[64]

The Political Economy of Empire

Debt is an inescapable feature of commercial societies. "Unless commerce consists of simultaneous exchanges of goods or services and the payment for them . . . people must conduct business on promises."[65] But trading in promises can be risky. Every debtor runs the risk of insolvency. In the eighteenth century the consequences could be disastrous. Assets could be seized, and individuals might be imprisoned. During the second half of the eighteenth century, in an attempt to insulate creditors and debtors from unpredictable fluctuations in the market, colonies and states in North America began experimenting with bankruptcy laws. Safety nets were erected to halt an economic free fall and enable debtors to return to the world of exchange. Typically, however, bankruptcy proceedings were available only to commercial debtors and did not provide relief for insolvent consumers.

The law did not protect individual consumers from the temptation of luxury goods. But the boundaries of consumption could be politically negotiated. The interdependence of British producers and colonial consumers made the restraint of trade a powerful bargaining tool in imperial struggles. As Franklin explained to Parliament in 1766, "The goods [the colonists] take from Britain are either necessaries, mere conveniences, or superfluities. The first, as cloth, etc. with a little industry they can make at home; the second they can do without, till they are able to provide them among themselves; and the last, which are much the greatest part, they will strike off immediately. They are mere articles of fashion, purchased and consumed, because the fashion in a respected country, but will now be detested and rejected." The nonimportation agreements of the 1760s were designed to influence British commercial policy by creating a crisis in the merchant community. In so doing, they made the consumption patterns of ordinary Americans a matter of strategic concern. Industry and frugality were the public virtues of a colonial society struggling to influence the conduct of its imperial master. This suggests another context for Franklin's brusque response to Sally Franklin's request for lace and feathers. The salt in his strawberries was political as well as personal. The boundaries between necessities, conveniences, and superfluities were defined not by moral theories or religious precepts but by the dictates of war. Sally was not showing the self-restraint of a virtuous consumer.[66]

Nonimportation was a second-best strategy; Franklin's first preference was for freedom of trade. Both concerned the political economy of the British Empire in the wake of the Seven Years' War. In October 1759 news of the fall of Quebec reached London, and peace seemed near. Public debate turned to the contours of the postwar world. Great Britain had made two major conquests in the Americas, Canada and Guadeloupe, but it could keep only one of them. Which? Canada promised vast and unsettled land; Guadeloupe, the riches of the sugar trade. Within a short span of time over sixty-five pamphlets and countless newspaper articles were printed on the topic. Franklin mapped his position in a letter to Henry Homes, Lord Kames: "I have long been of Opinion, that the Foundations of the future Grandeur and Stability of the British Empire, lie in America; and though, like other Foundations, they are low and little seen, they are nevertheless, broad and Strong enough to support the greatest Political Structure Human Wisdom ever yet erected." The North American colonies ought to be "considered as the frontier of the British empire" on the western side of the Atlantic. The fate of the colonies "directly and fundamentally concerned" the interest "of the *whole* nation."[67]

One of the greatest obstacles to thinking about the empire as a single integrated unit was the widespread anxiety that the colonies in North America were a long-term threat to the economy of Great Britain. As an anonymous pamphleteer put it in 1761, "As America increases in people, so she must increase in arts and sciences, in manufactures and trade . . . [and] the more she increases in these, the less she must want from Britain; the more she rises above a certain pitch, her utility and advantage to Britain must proportionally decrease."[68] Vast and unsettled, the colonies of North America could become an economic leviathan. A growing population would provide the demographic foundation for American manufactures, undercutting one of the cornerstones of the British imperial economy. And as the colonies became conscious of their strength, they could be expected to unite and declare their independence. (Historians focused on constitutional conflicts and the claims of political philosophy trace thoughts of independence to the late 1760s and early 1770s. Concerns of political economy, however, clearly put this possibility on the table much sooner.)[69]

In 1760, in an attempt to ease metropolitan anxieties, Franklin scoffed at this idea. The colonies had "different forms of government, different laws, different interests, and some of them different religions and different manners. Their jealousy of each other is so great that . . . a union of the whole is impossible."[70] As we shall see, Franklin's analyses of the politics of population growth, and of the prospects for colonial union, were richer and more provocative than this suggests. At this point it is necessary to anticipate a few of his ideas.

Metropolitan authorities generally agreed that the colonies were, and ought to be, economically subordinate to Great Britain. As one writer put it in 1763, "The British Colonies are to be regarded in no other light, but as subservient to the commerce of their mother country; the colonists are merely factors for the purposes of trade, and in all considerations concerning the Colonies, this must be always the leading idea."[71] Franklin considered this politically misguided and economically shortsighted. In 1729 he had attempted to address the relationship between political integration and economic development by appealing to a legislative consensus within the Pennsylvania Assembly. After 1760 he was forced to consider a much larger and more complex set of issues. He took his bearings from David Hume's 1758 essay, "Of the Jealousy of Trade." According to Hume, the harshly competitive world of international commerce encouraged nations to think of each other as rivals. Each imagined that it was impossible for a neighbor to flourish "but at their expense." Against this "narrow and malignant opinion," Hume argued that the "diversity of geniuses, climates, and soils" made national economies interdependent. "States are in the same condition as individuals. A single man can scarcely be industrious, where all his fellow-citizens are idle. The riches of the several members of a community contribute to increase my riches, whatever profession I follow." The alternative, in Hume's estimation, was not a zero-sum competition but a universal decline in wealth. When "jealousy of trade" gave rise to tariffs and other protective measures, growth and development ground to a halt.[72]

Franklin warmly embraced this argument. As he wrote Hume in September 1760, "It cannot but have a good Effect in promoting a certain Interest too little thought of by selfish Man, and scarce ever mentioned, so that we hardly have a Name for it; I mean the *Interest of Humanity*, or common Good of Mankind: But I hope particularly that from that Essay, an Abatement of the Jealousy that reigns here of the Commerce of the Colonies, at least so far as such Abatement may be reasonable."[73] This was not (simply) special pleading. As the success of Pennsylvania's monetary policy was built on the integration of conflicting groups, classes, and interests, so, Franklin argued in the 1760s, the success of the British Empire rested on the consolidation of distinct regions and economies into an integrated whole.

Cooperation in a commercial society is based on utility. But usefulness is not a natural property of individuals or groups; it has to be cultivated personally, through the formation of habits of virtue, and collectively, through the political and economic integration of groups and interests. The resilience of relationships based on credit and debt, trust and confidence, is dependent on the degree to which these conditions are met. Reinforcing and extending their effects was another vital force: voluntary association.

2. Association

The Good particular men may do separately . . . is small, compared with
what they may do collectively, or by a joint Endeavor and Interest.
—Benjamin Franklin, *Pennsylvania Gazette* (8 August 1751)

Citizens and Soldiers

In the summer of 1747 privateers entered Delaware Bay. No one was certain
whether they were Spanish or French. But their "boldness" was indisputable,
and it was only a matter of time before they reached Philadelphia.[1] Anxious
colonists appealed to the Assembly for protection. But the Assembly was
dominated by Quakers, and as a matter of principle Quakers refused to mobilize for war. The colony was without defense. By fall the situation seemed
desperate. After consulting key friends, Franklin took the initiative. "Protection is as truly due from the Government to the People, as Obedience from
the People to the Government," he thundered. If the Assembly would not
defend Pennsylvania, then Pennsylvanians would have to defend themselves.
In a carefully orchestrated campaign, colonists were called to join the Association, a voluntary self-defense society. On the first day twelve hundred
men took the oath of engagement; over the coming weeks, thousands more
joined them. Companies were formed, officers were elected, flags were
sewn, forts were built. Spring came and went without sign of privateers, and
calm gradually returned to the province. The men of the Association were
hailed for their "zeal and activity" in time of crisis.[2]

The Association is a striking illustration of the capacity of voluntary
organizations to address unmet needs. In *Democracy in America*, the
nineteenth-century French writer Alexis de Tocqueville argued that no nation made better or more extensive use of societies, groups, and private

associations than the United States. "Americans of all ages, all stations in life, and all types of dispositions are forever forming associations. There are not only commercial and industrial associations . . . but others of a thousand different types—religious, moral, serious, futile, very general and very limited, immensely large and very minute."[3] Franklin's own life is illustrative. Among the associations he *joined* were the Freemasons, a secret international fraternal organization; the Royal Society, the oldest scientific society in the world; the Club of Honest Whigs, an informal circle of friends who gathered for supper in London coffeehouses; and the Pennsylvania Society for the Abolition of Slavery, the first antislavery society in America. Among the associations Franklin *founded* were the Junto, a club for the "mutual improvement" of artisans and traders; the Library Company, a subscription library supported by its shareholders; the Union Fire Company, Philadelphia's earliest volunteer fire brigade; and the American Philosophical Society, the first learned society in North America. Among the associations Franklin *dreamed of* was the Society of the Free and Easy, a latitudinarian sect of unmarried young men dedicated to moral and political reform. And finally, among those associations Franklin *drifted away from* or *quit* was the New England Congregational Church of his youth.

This abbreviated list—and it *is* abbreviated—confirms Tocqueville's observation: the breadth and depth of associational life in America is extraordinary. But it also suggests that Tocqueville was mistaken to think that the phenomenon he observed was uniquely or essentially American. Voluntary associations are an integral part of commercial societies, a crucial mechanism for negotiating relationships of interest, taste, and value. They meet needs and provide important settings within which habits are formed, characters are shaped, and identities are confirmed. During the eighteenth century they "penetrated every nook and cranny of British social and cultural life."[4]

In this world, the Association was an association of a very specific sort: it was a militia, a body of civilians raised locally for military service. During the seventeenth century every colony in North America, with the exception of Pennsylvania, organized a militia system. (Pennsylvania's Quaker government rejected militias on moral and religious grounds.) By the turn of the eighteenth century, colonial militias performed a variety of tasks. They helped secure property and maintain social order, they quelled riots and patrolled slaves, and they fought Indians and repelled brigands. They also helped shape the local community. Training days "bound high and low to-gether politically," as "officers put the men through their paces, and then they all got drunk together, at the officers' expense."[5]

The close connection between militias and local communities proved especially important in the growing conflict with Great Britain. Colonial militias provided manpower and organization for Stamp Act riots and helped enforce nonimportation agreements. They suffered valiantly at Bunker Hill and responded with alacrity at Lexington and Concord. And they provided a ready contrast to the British army, whose soldiers were in the pay—and hence under the thrall—of a distant administrative apparatus. As Josiah Quincy Jr. proclaimed in 1774, the army that occupied Boston was a "stand-ing army," an instrument of tyranny and a destroyer of right and law. "Booty and blind submission" are "the science of the camp"; "what will they not fight for—whom will they not fight against? . . . No free government was ever founded or ever preserved its liberty without uniting the characters of citizen and soldier in those destined for defense of the state." George Ma-son concurred: "A well regulated Militia . . . is the natural Strength and only safe and stable security of a free Government."[6]

As fighting began in earnest, professional soldiers in America com-plained that militias were ill trained and undisciplined. Militiamen retained "the tender feelings of domestic life." Having never been "steeled by habit or fortified by military pride," they were unprepared for "the shocking scenes of war." Faced with these problems, Congress was forced to "regu-larize" the Continental Army. But even George Washington, a fierce advo-cate for professionalism, could not resist the allure of the citizen-soldier. At the end of the war he argued that "every Citizen who enjoys the pro-tection of a free Government, owes . . . his personal services to the de-fense of it." Every man from eighteen to fifty should be enrolled in the militia, so that "the Total strength of the Country" might be mobilized on "Short Notice." Washington did not believe that every soldier should be a citizen. But, like other proponents of militias, he held that every citizen should be a soldier.[7]

What enabled a man to bear arms in defense of his country? One com-mon answer, derived from the republican writings of Niccolò Machiavelli and James Harrington, was virtue. A virtuous citizen had a manly spirit and remained vigorous, strong, and stout in the face of adversity. A virtuous cit-izen controlled his passions so that anger, greed, or lust did not interfere with his duties. Above all, a virtuous citizen assigned higher priority to the public good than to his own private interests. This was particularly clear in time of war, when a citizen-soldier risked his life to protect his country. But the potential for tension between the public good and private interests pervaded life. A virtuous citizen, like Cato of old, refused to sacrifice even the smallest part of the commonwealth for private gain. A man who inverted these civic priorities was considered vicious and corrupt.[8]

Republican virtue was austere and demanding. How could it be sustained and reinforced? What threatened or undermined it? These questions plagued eighteenth-century supporters of the militia idea. One source of special concern was the growth of trade and commerce. Many worried that an economy of exchange was inherently corrupting. Wealth—especially mobile wealth—distracted people with luxury. Paper money and sophisticated instruments of credit subjected people to the play of volatile markets. Even wage labor was problematic, for wage earners were dependent on the goodwill of their employers, and their conduct could be controlled by pulling their purse strings. At its core, republicanism was an agrarian ideology. The ideal citizen was an "independent country gentleman," economically insulated from the market and free to serve his country with his reason, his will, and his arms.[9]

Against this backdrop, the Association is a striking anomaly, and not simply because Franklin—unlike Washington—was not an independent country gentleman. Franklin's first public appeal for the Association was the anonymous work of "A Tradesman of Philadelphia," and it explicitly appealed to trade as a bond of union and motive for valor. The Association itself was funded through a lottery, making the virtuous activity of citizen-soldiers dependent on a frivolous game of chance. These extraordinary characteristics of the Association reflect Franklin's insight into the challenges and opportunities of associated activity in a commercial society divided by religion, nationality, and economic interest. Voluntary association provided a potent challenge to the shibboleths of classical republicanism.

Mobilization

At first glance the quandary confronting Pennsylvanians in the fall of 1747 looks familiar. Everyone agreed that the colony was in danger, but no one was willing to provide for its defense. It was easier—and perhaps even more

Forms used by the Library Company of Philadelphia: *above*, a subscription receipt; *below*, a borrowing slip. (Courtesy the Library Company of Philadelphia.)

rational—to let others bear the costs. Of course, since everyone thought and acted this way, no one was secure.[10]

Franklin cut his teeth on problems like this. From an early age he had a "projecting public Spirit," and the *Autobiography* is overflowing with schemes for collective improvement. The Library Company of Philadelphia is exemplary. The members of the Junto were avid readers, but as modest young tradesmen they could not afford many books. Franklin suggested that they pool their treasures in a "common library." They did so, only to discover that their combined collection was much smaller than expected. Worse yet, over time their books were mistreated and mislaid. After one year the experiment was ended; each participant retrieved his books and retreated to his private study. In response to this crisis of the commons—familiar to anyone who has worked in an office in which cleaning and refilling the coffeepot is a collective responsibility—Franklin "set on foot" his proposal for the Library Company. Fifty subscribers agreed to make annual contributions for fifty years; opinions were solicited, lists were drawn, and books were ordered; officers were appointed and hours were set; rules of use were issued and enforced. Franklin proudly reported that "the institution soon manifested its utility" and was imitated in other towns and provinces.[11]

Defending Pennsylvania was little different than securing books; all that was needed was "Order, Discipline, and a few Cannon." Or so it might seem. But the challenge of mobilizing a colony was far greater than that of organizing a club of bibliophiles. The Library Company was founded by men who shared a goal—the creation of a "common Library"—but lacked means to accomplish it. Company rules and policies, many of which were hammered out during the library's first years of existence, provided an institutional substitute for personal virtue. Returning books on time proved especially difficult; late fees accomplished what individual goodwill could not.[12] In the fall of 1747, however, Pennsylvanians were divided over ends as well as means. Security meant different things to different people. Coming to grips with this fact was Franklin's first task.

Quaker Pacifism

Quaker pacifism dated to the Restoration of Charles II. The Society of Friends emerged in mid-seventeenth-century England as a Christian sect dedicated to the "Inward Light" of God, lived without formal creed or clergy. Early generations were anything but quietist; their style was provocative, their methods confrontational. They disrupted church services, refused to swear oaths or pay taxes, and insisted on referring to all, even their social betters, in terms normally reserved for inferiors. Quaker beliefs and practices seemed to threaten the social order, and Friends were ruthlessly persecuted as enemies of the state. In an attempt to remove some of the "Jealousy and Suspicion" directed at them, George Fox announced in 1660 that Quakers rejected "all bloody Principles and Practices . . . all outward Wars, and Strife, and Fighting with outward Weapons, for any end, or under any pretence whatsoever."[13]

Fox's "peace testimony" announced Quaker pacifism to the world. But it left unanswered many difficult questions, including whether Quakers should pay taxes to support a government at war, or whether in the eyes of Quakers the state could legitimately fight a war if it did not require their participation.[14] These questions haunted William Penn's "Holy Experiment" in North America. Pennsylvania was founded as a refuge for Quakers seeking relief from persecution in England. It was also intended to demonstrate the strength and vitality that flowed from religious freedom. Penn's Charter of Privileges guaranteed the civil and political liberties of all denominations, and the promise of religious toleration and economic opportunity proved a potent lure for European immigrants. Amish, Mennonites, Dunkers, Schwenkfelders, and Moravians poured into the colony. So, too, did Lutherans and Scots-Irish Presbyterians and a dozen other religions and nationalities. All reveled in Pennsylvania's relative peace and harmony. As one colonial politician put it, Quaker influence ensured a quiet "medley of all kinds of People and denominations."[15] But no matter what the policy of the Quakers, Pennsylvania was a part of the British Empire, and Britain was at war during significant portions of the first half of the eighteenth century. In a predictable pattern, London called on the Assembly to muster a militia for local defense and provide men and matériel for long-range campaigns, while pirates and privateers threatened havoc up and down the Delaware. Quakers worked out compromises wherever possible. They voted money for "the King's Use," for example, tacitly acknowledging but not formally approving its use for military measures.[16] But they would not create a militia, nor would they directly fund war efforts. And while some non-Quakers were grateful for the practical consequences of Quaker pacifism, others found it extremely noxious. Many Pennsylvanians saw no necessary conflict between religious belief and self-defense. To them, imperatives of faith as well as considerations of safety dictated unambiguous military measures.[17]

The political limits of Quaker pacifism were reached in the mid-1750s, during the first phase of the Seven Years' War. Confronted with strident British demands, and increasingly fearful of Indian attack—the French were mobilizing allies along the frontier—the Assembly found it impossible to resist taking action. On 19 November 1755 Franklin introduced a militia bill; six days later, over Quaker opposition, it was approved. The newly formed Association, like its 1747 namesake, was strictly voluntary. It explicitly acknowledged the rights of those who "are conscientiously scrupulous of bearing Arms." And it insulated militiamen from the strict rules and harsh punishments of British military law. But experience quickly convinced Franklin that even "a voluntary Militia of Freemen" needed discipline. In March 1756 he persuaded the Assembly to make mutiny and desertion crimes punishable by death.[18] Three months later six Quakers in the Assembly resigned their seats. As they explained, many of their constituents believed military measures necessary. But "a Conviction of Judgment" prevented them from acting on these instructions. "We conclude it most conducive to the Peace of our Minds, and the Reputation of our religious Profession, to . . . [resign] our Seats." Significantly, the Quakers emphasized personal integrity, not public policy. They did not attempt to block preparations for war within the Assembly, nor did they attempt to sway public opinion by staging a dramatic protest. Instead, they insisted that for their own sake, and for the sake of their religion, they would not dirty their hands. Franklin was relieved: "all the Stiffrumps except One, that could be suspected of opposing the Service from religious Motives, have voluntarily quitted the Assembly."[19]

These events occurred nearly a decade after Franklin founded the Association, but they shed light on the challenges he faced in 1747. How was it possible to mobilize the colony amid such men? To be sure, not all Quakers were opposed to self-defense. Certainly not the venerable scholar and statesman James Logan, who "heartily" wished Franklin "all possible success": "I have clearly seen that government without arms is an inconsistency."[20] Logan, who had come to America in 1699 as William Penn's private secretary and subsequently served lengthy terms on both the Provincial Council and the Supreme Court, was not alone in thinking that defensive wars were legitimate. But Logan was unique in his ability to take a public stand that directly challenged Quaker pacifism. Other Friends were not so fortunate, and they were disowned by the Philadelphia Meeting.[21]

The quandary facing Quakers who favored defensive measures was rooted in an increasingly important feature of colonial life: the differentiation of social roles.[22] Toleration was meant to separate politics and religion. To the extent that it succeeded, the rights and obligations of citizenship did not directly correspond to the beliefs and practices of faith. Citizens could be Presbyterian or Quaker or even religiously indifferent without endangering their standing in the polity. Devout Lutherans could fulfill the obligations of citizenship without risking their place among the faithful. These were aspirations, of course; in everyday life, tensions between political and religious roles were frequent and sometimes difficult to manage. Franklin believed that there were many Quakers who supported the Association, but understood that they were reluctant to do so publicly. Navigating the boundary between politics and religion required indirection and a willingness to tolerate inconsistency. Franklin captured this insight in an anecdote concerning the Union Fire Company:

> It had been proposed that we should encourage the Scheme for building a Battery by laying out the present Stock, then about Sixty Pounds, in Tickets of the Lottery. By our Rules no Money could be disposed of but at the next Meeting after the Proposal. The Company consisted of Thirty Members, of which Twenty-two were Quakers, and Eight only of other Persuasions. We eight punctually attended the Meeting; but though we thought that some of the Quakers would join us, we were by no means sure of a Majority. Only one Quaker, Mr. James Morris, appeared to oppose the Measure: He expressed much Sorrow that it had ever been proposed, as he said *Friends* were all against it, and it would create such Discord as might break up the Company. We told him, that we saw no Reason for that; we were the Minority, and if *Friends* were against the Measure and outvoted us, we must and should, agreeable to the Usage of all Societies, submit. When the Hour for Business arrived, it was moved to put the Vote. He allowed we might then do it by the Rules, but as he could assure us that a Number of Members intended to be present for the purpose of opposing it, it would be but candid to allow a little time for their appearing. While we were disputing this, a Waiter came to tell me two Gentlemen below desired to speak with me. I went down, and found they were two of our Quaker Members. They told me there were eight of them assembled at a Tavern just by; that they were determined to come and vote with us if there should be occasion, which they hoped would not be the Case; and desired we would not call for their Assistance if we could do without it, as their Voting for such a Measure might embroil them with their Elders and Friends; Being thus secure of a Majority, I went up, and after a little seeming Hesitation, agreed to a Delay of another Hour. This Mr. Morris allowed to be extremely fair. Not one of his opposing Friends appeared, at which he expressed great

Surprise; and at the Expiration of the Hour, we carried the Resolution Eight to one.

Political theorists and public observers sometimes suggest that democracy
rests on free and frank speech. Complexity and indirection are marks of corruption; virtue, like truth, rests on "simple facts, plain arguments, and common sense." Franklin's experience with the Fire Company suggested a
different set of ideals: flexibility, compromise, negotiation, and a measured
dose of hypocrisy. Intriguingly, these goals did not necessarily sacrifice personal integrity. The six Quakers who resigned their seats in the Assembly in
1756 kept their hands clean and preserved the sanctity of their faith. At the
same time, and as they intended, the demands of their constituents were met.
The "politics of persuasion" was filled with puzzles of this sort.[23]

Flexibility was particularly difficult for Quakers, thought Franklin, because they had "published it as one of their Principles, that no kind of War
was lawful," and "once published, they could not afterwards, however they
might change their minds, easily get rid of it." Printed doctrines were obstacles to the truth. This was an extraordinary conclusion for Franklin, a
printer's printer, to come to, and needs elaboration. Printing transformed intellectual life in early modern Europe by making communicative acts durable
and easily duplicable.[24] The same text—precisely the same words and
numbers—could be read by men and women living in different places and at
different times. This kind of stability was unavailable in oral or scribal cul-
tures, where each recitation or copy was inescapably unique. It was vital to the
emerging practices of modern science, permitting the systematic repetition
of experiments and accurate comparison of observations and data. But the
permanence of written expression was a liability in morals and politics,
thought Franklin, because it encouraged dogmatism. Far better the practice
of the Dunkers, who refused to publish their doctrines for fear it would
freeze them in place. "When we were first drawn together as a Society," the
Dunker Michael Welfare once told Franklin, "it had pleased God to en-
lighten our Minds so far, as to see that some Doctrines which we once esteemed Truths were Errors, and that others which we had esteemed Errors
were real Truths. From time to time he has been pleased to afford us farther
Light, and our Principles have been improving, and our Errors diminishing.
Now we are not sure that we are arrived at the End of this Progression, and
at the Perfection of Spiritual or Theological Knowledge; and we fear that if

we should once print our Confession of Faith, we should feel ourselves as if bound and confined by it, and perhaps be unwilling to receive farther Improvement; and our Successors still more so, as conceiving what we their Elders and Founders had done, to be something sacred, never to be departed from." Improvement required flexibility, the ability to learn and grow and change. Every life, every doctrine, every confession was marred by "errata"—a printer's term for errors—that needed to be noted and corrected. As Franklin mischievously put it in an epitaph he drafted as a young man,

The Body of
B. Franklin,
Printer;
Like the Cover of an old Book,
Its Contents torn out,
And stripped of its Lettering and Gilding,
Lies here, Food for Worms.
But the Work shall not be wholly lost:
For it will, as he believed, appear once more,
In a new and more perfect Edition,
Corrected and amended
By the Author.

The good life was constantly being revised and rewritten.[25] This was—or ought to be—true of groups as well as individuals. It was the Quakers' misfortune to have publicly committed themselves to an inflexible doctrine. Through skillful stratagems, Franklin sought to make it possible for as many as possible to amend their own beliefs and support the Association.

Needless to say, many Quakers did not see things this way and were unwilling to compromise the "peace testimony." As a result, Franklin pursued a much riskier strategy: he argued that they misunderstood their own faith. For years Franklin had sold copies of Robert Barclay's *An Apology for the True Christian Divinity*. Barclay was born Scottish and raised Calvinist, but in 1667 he had converted to Quakerism. Like his mentor William Penn, he sought to combat the persecution of Quakers by writing books; the *Apology*, first published in 1676, is often held up as a classic statement of Quaker principles. In late 1747 Franklin, using his considerable skill as a ventriloquist, and hiding behind the neutral mask of editor, used Barclay and a series of fabricated documents and letters to challenge Philadelphia Quakers in the pages of the *Pennsylvania Gazette*. First he printed a poem written by a "Gentleman on his first reading Barclay's Apology." Like a bright ray of light, Barclay had pierced the clouds that darkened the gentleman's mind. He no longer cursed and mocked the Quakers; instead, he loved them. Two weeks later Franklin printed a letter to the editor, from a "reader" who had been moved by the gentleman's poem to read Barclay himself. To the reader's great surprise (!), he had discovered that Barclay's pacifism was "very moderate" and allowed wars in self-defense.[26] Franklin printed another letter in mid-November, this time from a "reader" who had been prompted by the discussion of Barclay to recall another well-known Quaker, William Edmonson. Edmonson did not merely defend the principle of self-defense; during the Glorious Revolution he had "very justly" called on the government in Ireland to provide "military Defense" against roving bands of "Men who make Plunder and Destruction their Business." Wise men, men concerned for "the public Good," took "all prudent and reasonable Provisions against Danger." This was as the Bible taught. Lest the lesson be missed, Franklin followed this front-page letter with a translation of the Latin quotation that graced the cover of *Plain Truth:* "Be not deceived—Divine Assistance and Protection are not to be obtained by timorous Prayers, and womanish Supplications. To succeed, you must join salutary Counsels, Vigilance, and courageous Actions."[27]

These pieces in the *Gazette* were followed by a full-scale pamphlet war. Franklin did not relish doctrinal disputes and turned over the assignment to Gilbert Tennent, a well-known Presbyterian evangelist. Tennent was guaranteed to incite. George Whitefield once observed that "hypocrites must either soon be converted or enraged at his Preaching. He is a *Son of Thunder.*" Tennent's first salvo was a sermon preached on 24 December. Taking Exodus 15:3 ("The Lord is a Man of War") as his text, Tennent sought "to remove the Scruples of such, who by their *Religious Principles*, are hindered from joining in the Association." Come into "the *Camp* of CHRIST," he exhorted, "and enlist under his *Colors.*"[28] Quakers were incensed by the "deceit and Quirks" of Tennent's sermon. John Smith quickly drafted an official response; others followed in the coming weeks and months.[29]

Tennent's arguments ranged from the relationship between Jewish and Christian law to the status of natural law. Alongside Scripture he quoted classical and contemporary authorities, from Cicero to Grotius. His critics contested each and every point. The precise details of these exchanges are less important than the basic contrast they reveal. Tennent's argument rested on a simple means-ends calculation. God intended humans to live in peace, and "when any End is enjoined by divine Authority, apt Means directing to it are enjoined likewise." And as he mockingly put it in a sermon delivered in early January, "if any imagine that their *Faith* and *Piety* are sufficient to *protect* them from a *temporal Enemy*, without the Use of *temporal Means*, let them try for a while, if they please . . . and see what they can do; possibly this may convince them of their unhappy Mistake!" But this was precisely what Quaker pacifists were willing to do. According to Smith, Friends believed that all men were called "to forsake a Dependence upon human Means, and trust in God alone." Self-defense was not the "only Barrier against Injustice and Violence." Many "depend and confide solely in another Barrier, viz. The Eternal and Beneficent Providence." "Piety and prayers" were "the only acceptable Means necessary to obtain Protection from Heaven."[30]

From a distance this exchange looks like a garden-variety (albeit high-stakes) policy dispute, the kind that happens every day in boardrooms, households, and legislative assemblies. Tennent identified an end (peace) and a means of achieving it (defensive war); Smith accepted the end, but proposed an alternative means (piety and prayer). Of course, if this were a policy dispute, then the next step would be toward the bargaining table, where each side would hope to negotiate a favorable solution. That did not happen, because this was not a simple policy dispute. Tennent's sermons focused on "the public Interest and Safety" of the colony. "All will doubtless acknowledge, that human or civil *Happiness* consisting in the Security and Protection of our *Lives*, *Liberties*, and *Properties*, is a *Good* or *End* worthy to be aimed at." Smith did not appeal to the value of safety or security, nor did he use the language of interest. Peace was a spiritual condition, marked by the overcoming of sin. Defensive wars were still wars, and the violence and bloodshed they brought were corrupt and corrupting.[31] Tennent played on Pennsylvanians' fears, warning that "the fatal Consequences of the Enemy's finding us unprepared for defense, I need not mention, every body of common Understanding may easily imagine!" (He could afford to be discreet: previously Franklin had pointed to the "Miseries" that would accompany an attack, and William Currie had painted the scene in graphic detail.)[32] Smith argued that adhering to the "peace testimony" diminished the risks; even privateers were inhibited by a calm refusal to return violence for violence.

Tennent invoked the well-known Roman motto *Si vis pacem para bellum* (If you seek peace, prepare for war).[33] Smith countered with "our Savior's Word": "For whosoever will save his Life, shall lose it, and whosoever will lose his Life for my sake, shall find it. For what is a Man profited if he shall gain the whole World, and lose his own Soul? Or what shall a Man give in Exchange for his Soul?"[34]

We are at an important political and intellectual boundary. Political philosophers sometimes argue that the desire for self-preservation is the foundation for legitimate political authority. Imagine, as Thomas Hobbes once did, what life would be like in the absence of government: "In such condition, there is no place for Industry; because the fruit thereof is uncertain: and consequently no Culture of the Earth; no Navigation, nor use of the commodities that may be imported by Sea; no commodious Building; no Instruments of moving, and removing such things as require much force; no Knowledge of the face of the Earth; no account of Time; no Arts; no Letters; no Society; and which is worst of all, continual fear, and danger of violent death; And the life of man, solitary, poor, nasty, brutish, and short." This "state of nature" is unremittingly bleak, and people will do anything to escape it. Hobbes thought the only hope was a sovereign powerful enough to secure social order. Accordingly, there is a "mutual Relation between Protection and Obedience." Subjects are obligated to obey "as long, and no longer," than the sovereign is "able to protect them." Franklin clearly had this argument in mind when he composed *Plain Truth*. "*Protection*," he urged, "is as truly due from the Government to the People, as *Obedience* from the People to the Government."[35] Tennent concurred. If Quakers were to remain in the Assembly, then they must accept their responsibility, as governors, to protect the colony from attack. Doing so required that they separate their identity as Quakers from their role as legislators.[36] Franklin and Tennent suggested that the failure of Quakers to do so represented a basic misunderstanding of politics.[37] But it is more accurate to say that the Quakers simply did not share the same conception of legitimacy as their critics. Fear was not a universally available motivator, nor was it a shared justification for authority.

This distinction helps explain why the Quakers were not necessarily "free riding" on the defensive efforts of others. The concept of free riding is used by economists and social scientists to help explain the failure of a market or a political system to provide public goods. A key characteristic of public goods is that they are nonexcludable: once they are made available, specific individuals or groups cannot be prevented from consuming them. Free riders take advantage of this characteristic of public goods by consuming more than their fair share of a good, or by shouldering less than their fair share of its cost, without fear of being excluded from enjoying its benefits. Defense is a classic example of a public good. Once a territory is protected, everyone living within it is protected; it is not possible to defend one person without defending all persons. A free rider in defense will seek to avoid paying for being defended, knowing that he or she will still be protected just as well as those who actually do contribute. It is crucial for the logic of the argument that free riders and their patsies consume the same thing. But many Quakers did not want the same thing as Franklin and his supporters. Indeed, the very means used by the Association to secure the peace were destructive of the ends sought by Quaker pacifists. In mid-eighteenth-century Pennsylvania, defense was not a public good.

The Proprietary Party

Fear of violent death was not universal. It might have captured the basal worries of many Pennsylvanians. But to Quakers strictly committed to the peace testimony, it was neither morally relevant nor psychologically motivating. It did not justify the use of force, and it did not inspire them to act. So much for Hobbes.[38]

Hobbes's eighteenth-century critics pursued this thought with vigor and sophistication. In the preface to *De Cive* (1642), Hobbes had approved the well-known Roman maxim *Homo homini lupus* (Man is a wolf to man). Humans are predators. If unconstrained, they will hunt and destroy each other in a ruthless struggle for survival. Even the best of people cannot escape recourse to "the virtues of war." Only a strong and centralized state—a Leviathan—is capable of containing the disintegrative forces of life in the state of nature. Anthony Ashley Cooper, the third Earl of Shaftesbury, thought this "absurd, when one considers that wolves are to wolves very kind and loving creatures." History and experience teach that humans are naturally sociable, born with a desire for "fellowship," constantly "combining" and "confederating" in groups and associations of all sorts and sizes. These sentiments provide a foundation for moral judgments and a motive for virtuous actions. We know what we ought to do, and then actually do it, because we feel these moral sentiments. Francis Hutcheson concurred.

Humans have more than five senses, he argued. In addition to sight, smell, taste, touch, and hearing, we have a sense of beauty, a moral sense, and a few others. Like sight or smell, these senses enable us to perceive essential features of the world. When we observe a compassionate action, we approve; when confronted with a malicious action, we disapprove. We do so because such acts exhibit (or fail to exhibit) benevolence or love. "There is in human Nature a disinterested ultimate Desire of the Happiness of others."[39]

Franklin had intimate knowledge of Shaftesbury and Hutcheson.[40] And he had extensive experience with the social world they sought to capture with concepts like "sociability" and "benevolence": the world of clubs and societies in Hanoverian Britain. In these settings, conversation served as stimulant and corrective. It brought individuals together, where the desire to please and be pleased sharpened their wits and softened their manners. "We polish one another and rub off our rough corners by a sort of amicable collision." A new social virtue—politeness—emerged. [41] Some of these associations, like Franklin's Junto, were designed to facilitate "mutual Improvement." In Westminster, a club of men gathered in an alehouse to learn mathematics so that "by their mutual assistance and indefatigable industry they are now become master . . . of logorithmetical arithmetic." Others, like Franklin's Union Fire Company, sought to coordinate the efforts of individuals to address pressing collective problems. Mutual aid societies provided pensions for widows and orphans, while subscription societies raised bridges, provided street lighting, and opened regional hospitals. A few made the pursuit of benevolence their guiding principle. The three basic tenets of the Freemasons were "Brotherly Love, Relief and Truth," and Masonic sermons emphasized the importance of serving the public good.[42] In the midst of these activities, participants also sought relaxation and happiness. At the meetings of clubs and societies "they would take part in the formal business and then sit around with friends, usually with a drink, to hear the latest news or scandal, to join in a song, to escape from the tedium of work and the family." Small wonder that a 1744 visitor to Philadelphia proclaimed that he could "Learn More of the Constitution of the Place, their Trade, and manner of living, in one hour" in a tavern "than a Week's Observation Sauntering up and down the City could produce."[43]

Unfortunately, the spirit of brotherly love did not extend to Pennsylvania politics. In Franklin's day Quakers constituted a minority of the colony's population but dominated Philadelphia civic life and controlled the Assembly. The Proprietor, Thomas Penn, did not live in Pennsylvania, and had abandoned many Quaker beliefs and practices. But he was the colony's single largest landholder and possessed important political powers, including the right to name the governor. Around him a party had arisen, dominated by Anglicans and Presbyterians but defined by its opposition to the Quakers. Conflicts between the Proprietary Party and the Quaker Party were bitter and destructive. As Franklin explained in *Plain Truth:*

> Is our Prospect better, if we turn our Eyes to the Strength of the *opposite Party,* those Great and rich Men, Merchants and others, who are ever railing at *Quakers* for doing what their Principles seem to require . . . but take no one Step themselves for the Public Safety? They have so much Wealth and Influence, if they would use it, that they might easily, by their Endeavors and Example, raise a military Spirit among us, make us fond, studious of, and expert in Martial Discipline, and effect every Thing that is necessary, under God, for our Protection. But ENVY seems to have taken Possession of their Hearts, and to have eaten out and destroyed every generous, noble, Public-spirited Sentiment. *Rage* at the Disappointment of their little Schemes for Power, gnaws at their Souls, and fills them with such cordial Hatred to their Opponents, that every Proposal, by the Execution of which *those* may receive Benefit as well as themselves, is rejected with Indignation. *What,* say they, *shall we lay out our Money to protect the Trade of Quakers? Shall we fight to defend Quakers? No; Let the Trade perish, and the City burn; let what will happen, we shall never lift a Finger to prevent it.* . . . . 'Til of late I could scarce believe the Story, of him who refused to pump in a sinking Ship, because one on board, whom he hated, would be saved by it as well as himself. But such, it seems, is the Unhappiness of human Nature, that our Passions, when violent, often are too hard for the united Force of *Reason, Duty* and *Religion.*[44]

Franklin's frustration with the Proprietary Party is palpable. He prided himself on his complaisance and consciously avoided confrontations. This is one of the few occasions in all his writings on which he gave such feelings public expression.

Franklin's caustic description of "the opposite Party" reflects the influence of Shaftesbury and Hutcheson. Moral sentiments are but one kind of passion or feeling coursing through the human soul. There are others: joy and pity, courage and gratitude, but also insolence and pride, fretfulness and discontent. Some, like compassion, are generous and other-regarding; others, like malice, are brutal and selfish. Some, like love of parents, calm the soul and bring pleasure; others, like desire for revenge, tear it apart. The self is a composite, "an adulterated compound, a heap of contradictions." Any attempt to reduce the motives for action to a single factor—whether self-interest or pride or even benevolence—was doomed to failure. According to Shaftesbury, "there are more wheels and counterpoises in this engine than are easily imagined. It is of too complex a kind to fall under one simple view or to be explained thus briefly in a word or two."[45] As a consequence, benevolence was natural but not automatic. It was "strengthened by Esteem, Gratitude, Compassion, or other kind Affections" and "weakened by Displicence [displeasure], Anger, or Envy." Living a moral life required a kind of emotional horticulture, in which the passions were pruned and shaped to preserve a "Balance of Affections." Reason was a poor tool for this task. It might help point the way, but it was incapable of directly changing a person's sentiments.[46] Knowing what you ought to do did not lead you to do it. Passion must balance passion.

Here, then, was the problem with "the opposite Party": its members had succumbed to "*Pride, Envy* and *implacable Resentment*" and were unwilling to act generously or patriotically. Here, too, was the reason for Franklin's harsh criticism: he could not hope to rationally persuade them that they were mistaken. Against envy and rage his only weapon was to evoke an equally powerful passion: shame. He appears to have succeeded. Immediately after the publication of *Plain Truth*, a letter to the *Pennsylvania Gazette* complained that "the Party opposite to the Quakers" had been unfairly maligned. In the heat of partisan conflicts a few members had let loose one or two "inconsiderate Expressions." But they were now, as they "always have been . . . sincerely and heartily determined to exert themselves, according to their several Abilities, for our common Security."[47] We have no way of knowing how many members of "the opposite Party" joined the Association, but their leader, William Allen, a prosperous Philadelphia merchant, did serve as treasurer of the Philadelphia lottery.

The Middling People

Quakers seemed immune to fear. Their enemies were consumed by envy. Who was left? "The middling People, the Farmers, Shopkeepers and Tradesmen of this City and Country." This was a large and diverse group, ranging from Scots-Irish on the western frontier to Germans in the vicinity of Philadelphia and from hardscrabble farmers to thriving craftsmen. Franklin estimated that there were at least sixty thousand "Fighting Men" in the colony.[48] Could they be moved to action?

One obstacle was fragmentation and indifference to the plight of others. City-dwellers said to themselves, "*An* Indian *War on the Frontiers will not affect us. . . . Let those concerned take Care of themselves,*" while those living in the countryside imagined, "*The Enemy will be satisfied with the Plunder of the Town. . . . Let the Town take care of itself.*" Franklin thought these sentiments shortsighted and mistaken. To refresh the imaginations of his compatriots, he dipped his cup into a very old barrel: "Is not the whole Province one Body, united by living under the same Laws, and enjoying the same Privileges? Are not the People of City and Country connected as Relations both by Blood and Marriage, and in Friendships equally dear? Are they not likewise united in Interest, and mutually useful and necessary to each other? When the Feet are wounded, shall the Head say, *It is not me; I will not trouble myself to contrive Relief?* Or if the Head is in Danger, shall the Hands say, *We are not affected, and therefore will lend no Assistance?* No. For so would the Body be easily destroyed. But when all Parts join their Endeavors for its security, it is often preserved."[49] The body politic was an ancient metaphor, a cherished analogy for the organic and interdependent relationships of a well-ordered society. A political community, like a human body, is a composite of different parts. The health of the whole depends on the union of the parts.

The body politic was a staple of early modern political thought. Examples abound; Franklin's words easily could be replaced by those of Richard Morison, a humanist scholar in the court of Henry VIII: "A commonwealth is . . . nothing else but a certain number of cities, towns, shires . . . united and knit together by the observation of the laws: these kept, they must needs flourish, these broken, they must needs perish. . . . A commonwealth is like a body, and so like, that it can be resembled to nothing so convenient, as unto that." Morison's language is archaic, but his meaning is clear, and Franklin would have had no difficulty accepting it. But in sixteenth- and seventeenth-century Britain the metaphor of the body politic also signified hierarchy and subordination. Though the parts of the body were united, they were not equal. Royal heads were made for commanding; royal subjects—the hands and feet of the polity—were made to obey. Thus in 1566 it made perfect sense for Queen Elizabeth to put bumptious parliamentarians in their place by reminding them that it was "a strange thing that the foot should direct the head in so weighty a cause."[50]

Franklin gutted the concept of the body politic of these traditional meanings and stuffed it with new ideas. Unity was a function of interdependence, not hierarchy. It did not require that the hand command the foot, or the hand defer to the heart. Instead, it called for each part to acknowledge its dependence on the others. His touchstone was the tightly woven world of commerce. "Whatever different Opinions we have of our Security in other Respects, our TRADE, all seem to agree, is in Danger of being ruined in another Year." Without adequate defense against privateers, the hazards of importing and exporting will grow. Ship owners and overseas merchants will be forced to take out additional insurance. As a result, the cost of imports will rise, and the value of exports will fall. Shopkeepers will be forced to raise their prices, while the decline in trade will lead to a loss of employment. Credit will be stretched to the limit, and debts will remain unpaid. The value of land and houses will drop. All will suffer the consequences of economic devastation.[51]

Franklin's appeal to "the middling People" rested on their needs. The body politic was a commercial society, its bonding force the mutual satisfaction of needs and interests. Society emerges from "the practice of exchanging either goods or services," and the relationships of "one man to another" were those of "buyer to seller, service provider to customer, or partner in a common enterprise of labor."[52] Utility, alongside satisfaction and pleasure, was a core principle of association.

Many of the associations Franklin either founded or joined were explicitly based on needs and interests. The Junto is exemplary of the tight relationship between individual need, social context, and associational activity. The members of the Junto were artisans in the early stages of their careers. In the world of their ancestors, the bonds between masters and apprentices had been pillars in a patriarchal and paternalistic social order. Apprenticeship was a form of bonded servitude, in which the master's responsibilities were like those of a father, and the apprentice's obligations were like those of a son. Masters ensured the apprentice's health and moral well-being at the same time that they provided education and technical training. In exchange for their labor, apprentices received professional skills and entry into a craft guild. It was expected that once a young man had been apprenticed he would practice his trade for life. As a mode of social organization, apprenticeship was well suited to a world in which economic resources were limited, avenues of investment were restricted, bonds between generations were stable, and knowledge was tradition bound. But in North America the wilderness—the sheer presence of undeveloped land, with its opportunity for growth and development and its ability to induce chronic labor shortages—helped undermine the bonds of apprenticeship. Masters began to demonstrate less interest in and commitment to the noncommercial aspects of their role. Apprentices began to view masters as impediments to their improvement.

By the end of the eighteenth century paternal labor relations were largely replaced by impersonal market transactions. Masters and apprentices turned to private institutions and voluntary organizations to provide training and education. The Junto was an early response to these changes. As we have seen, the Junto was a hardheaded, no-nonsense institution, fine-tuned to the needs and interests of tradesmen confronting a complex and changing commercial world. Lacking patrons and disparaging masters, Franklin and his associates turned to each other to secure their credit. At each meeting they probed recent successes and failures in business, and worked to secure each member's reputation. But the Junto was not simply practical, nor were the concerns of its members purely commercial. The Junto was also a debating society in which members pursued moral, political, and scientific questions with vigor and sophistication. Among the topics discussed were: "Whence comes the Dew that stands on the Outside of a Tankard that has cold Water in it in the Summer Time?"; "Does the Importation of Servants decrease or advance the Wealth of our Country?"; and "Is it justifiable to put private Men to Death for the Sake of public Safety or Tranquility, who have committed no Crime?" [53]

According to Bernard Bailyn, projects like the Junto were informed by the sense that the universe was open-ended: "What lay behind the interest in mutual instruction, in informal education of all sorts, and in extemporized institutions like evening schools was the recognition that one's role in life had not been fully cast, that the immediate inheritance did not set the final limits, that opportunities beyond the expectation of birth lay all about and could be reached by effort." In Franklin's memorable phrase, he lived in "the Age of Experiments."[54] Improvement was a collective undertaking, association a crucial means of achieving it.

In 1747 the various members of "the middling People" had to be persuaded that their needs and interests were linked, and that they were all vulnerable to the effects of war. They also had to be convinced that they could do something to improve their situation. Passivity, resignation, and fatalism were tremendous obstacles to action. Rational proof was insufficient; passions had to be engaged. Franklin attempted to do so in the opening pages of *Plain Truth* with a story thrice told. That he did so may testify to his sense of urgency. It may also reflect his insight into contemporary reading practices. Literacy is difficult to measure, and figures for the eighteenth century are necessarily imprecise. But in 1747, approximately 60 percent of adult white males living in rural Lancaster County, and approximately 80 percent of urban white males living in Philadelphia, were able to sign their name. (Signature literacy is thought to correspond to a middle range of literacy skills, or roughly to the ability to read fluently.) We do not have reliable figures for women and servants, though they were surely lower.[55] But even if we did, it would be a mistake to rely on numerical rates alone to understand reading practices. Colonial books, pamphlets, and newspapers were not read silently by solitary readers; nor were they read once and then either shelved or discarded. Often they were read and discussed out loud: in the home, on the street corner, in the tavern; and always they were shared, so that a single newspaper might be read by many people over a long period of time. As a consequence, the audience for a printed text was not restricted to those who were literate; many heard a text even though they could not read it. Franklin was keenly aware of this fact. In his own printing he made extensive use of italics and capitalization to bring written texts "as near as possible to those spoken." Doing so made it easier for readers to convey the sense of the words to their listeners. (Ever on the lookout for improvements, Franklin also thought that English-language printers should adopt the Spanish practice of putting a question mark at the beginning as well as the end of a sentence, so that the voice is not "wrongly modulated" in reading it.)[56]

The cover page of *Plain Truth* includes a passage from Sallust's *Conspiracy of Catiline*. This was an inspired choice. Greek and Roman authors were well known and widely read in the eighteenth century. They were a virtually limitless trove of ideas and arguments, examples and events, providing a common stock of mental furniture with which writers could fill their pages. Scarcely a pamphlet was written, or a sermon delivered, without the grace of at least one Latin quotation. Two popular touchstones were Roman politicians of the first century BCE, Catiline and Cato. Catiline epitomized moral degradation and political corruption; Alexander Pope considered him the human equivalent of the plague. In 63 BCE Catiline had attempted to overthrow the republic. He collected an army, enlisted supporters, and cultivated the poor and discontented. Despite the threat he posed, the Senate refused to believe that Rome was imperiled and responded slowly. Only when confronted with incontrovertible evidence did the Senate agree to crush Catiline's forces. While Catiline was still in the field, his coconspirators in Rome were convicted of treason and sentenced to death. In the debate that followed, Caesar argued for clemency, while Cato urged resolution. The quotation Franklin printed—in Latin—was from Cato's speech:

> *Should the City be taken, all will be lost to the Conquered. Therefore if you desire to preserve your Buildings, Houses and Country Seats, your Statues, Paintings, and all your other Possessions, which you so highly esteem; if you wish to continue in the Enjoyment of them, or have Leisure for any future Pleasures; I beseech you . . . Be not deceived—* DIVINE ASSISTANCE AND PROTECTION ARE NOT TO BE OBTAINED BY TIMOROUS PRAYERS, AND WOMANISH SUPPLICATIONS. *To succeed, you must join* SALUTARY COUNSELS, VIGILANCE, *and* COURAGEOUS ACTIONS. *If you sink into Effeminacy and Cowardice; if you desert the Tender and Helpless, by Providence committed to your Charge; never presume to implore the Gods:—It will provoke them, and raise their Indignation against you.*[57]

Cato's integrity was unimpeachable. So, too, was his association of courageous action with men and cowardly prayer with women. Cato's words reflect the masculine ethos of Roman republicanism. Citizens—good citizens—ought to be firm and unyielding, not soft and pliant. In order to defend women, it was necessary not to become like a woman. Gender, sex, and social role blended together, creating a powerful incentive to bear arms in defense of the city.

Franklin's second exhortation to action was equally inspired, though less esoteric: a woodcut illustration of the lesson "He that won't help

"Of the Waggoner and Hercules," *Plain Truth* (Philadelphia, 1747).

himself, shall have help from nobody." In 1747 Franklin printed the first American edition of Thomas Dilworth's *A New Guide to the English Tongue*. The *New Guide* was a "spelling book" designed to be used in grammar schools. It consisted of word lists, a treatise on grammar, and reading selections that included fables, moral lessons, and prayers. First published in England in 1740, it was extraordinarily popular: there were 12 North American editions before the Revolution and nearly 150 editions in Britain and America through the nineteenth century. Franklin carried advertisements for imported copies in early 1746, and in 1747 announced his own edition "just published, and sold by B. Franklin."[58]

Part 4 of Dilworth's *New Guide* included a dozen fables with "proper Sculptures [illustrations], for the better Improvement of the Young Beginner." The first was from Aesop, "Of the Waggoner and Hercules."

As a Waggoner was driving his Team, his Wagon sunk into a Hole, and stuck fast.

The poor Man immediately fell upon his Knees, and prayed to *Hercules*, that he would get his Wagon out of the Hole again.

Thou Fool, says *Hercules*, whip thy Horses, and set thy shoulder to the Wheels; and then if thou wilt call upon *Hercules*, he will help thee.

The Interpretation.

Lazy Wishes never do a Man any Service; but if he would have Help from God in the Time of Need, let him not only implore his Assistance, but make Use of his own best Endeavors.

Many in Franklin's audience would have read or heard this fable. Even the illustration would have been familiar, not just from Dilworth but from similar woodcuts in any one of a number of popular translations of Aesop. When Franklin used this image in *Plain Truth*, however, the only caption was the words "Non Votis, etc.," a reference to Cato's exhortation "Divine Assistance and Protection are not to be obtained by timorous Prayers, and womanish Supplications."[59]

Franklin self-consciously used images to engage an audience. Pictures, even more than words, are open-ended. They have the ability to stimulate a manifold of ideas and passions, without requiring that these reactions be resolved into a single, consistent whole. For those who did not know the fable, who was the figure in the clouds? God? If so, then why was he carrying a club? Against whom could it be used? And what was the man by the wagon praying for? His life? His wagon? His town? What *should* he be praying for? These and similar questions are stimulated by the print, engaging the hearts and minds of those who viewed it. This was an essential first step in Franklin's larger campaign: to bring "the middling People" to action.

Finally, after Sallust's Latin and Dilworth's woodcut came Franklin's clear and forceful prose:

It is said the wise *Italians* make this proverbial Remark on our Nation, *viz*. *The English* FEEL *but they do not* SEE. That is, they are sensible of Inconveniences when they are present, but do not take sufficient Care to prevent them: Their natural Courage makes them too little apprehensive of Danger, so that they are often surprised by it, unprovided of the proper Means of Security. When it is too late they are sensible of their Imprudence: After great Fires, they provide Buckets and Engines: After a Pestilence, they think of keeping clean their Streets and common Shores: and when a Town has been sacked by their Enemies, they provide for its Defense, etc. This Kind of AFTER-WISDOM is indeed so common with us, as to occasion the vulgar, though' very significant Saying, *When the Steed is stolen, you shut the Stable Door.*

Franklin had used the same Italian proverb twelve years earlier, in a call for the creation of a Philadelphia fire company. Franklin was brilliant at adopting and adapting mottoes, phrases, and proverbs; *Poor Richard's Almanac* was, by his own admission, an exercise in creative recycling. In this instance, he drew on the seventeenth-century English republican James Harrington, who was in turn improvising on an idea he found in the writings of the sixteenth-century Italian Niccolò Machiavelli.[60] Common to all three was the thought that our understanding of the world is shaped by our experiences. Our ability to anticipate the future is limited by what has happened to us in the past. As a consequence we have difficulty imagining things outside our daily lives. To Machiavelli this gave a prince room for maneuver, since most of the prince's subjects knew him only through the image he chose to project. To Franklin, writing to the valley (the people) and not the mountain (the prince), the imperfections of everyday prudence had a different implication: the imaginations of "the middling People" had to be roused if disaster were to be avoided. As one who had seen further and more deeply than others, it was his "duty" to speak "freely, openly, and earnestly" so that "those who seem to sleep, may be awakened."[61]

The "Form of Association"

Plain Truth appeared on 17 November 1747. Franklin printed two thousand copies at his own expense.[62] A campaign to build support was put into effect. On 21 November Franklin caucused with "150 Persons, mostly Tradesmen, in Chancellor's Sail Loft." He addressed the men as "the first Movers in every useful undertaking that had been projected for the good of the City—the Library Company, Fire Companies, etc." He then read a draft copy of the "Form of Association," which all approved and offered to sign. But Franklin demurred, suggesting that they first present it to the provincial elite. Their support would prove helpful, and they would surely want to think that they were essential to the scheme, and not an afterthought. And so a second gathering was held on the 23rd at Robert's

Coffee-House, where "the principal Gentlemen, Merchants and others" unanimously approved the Association. Finally, an open meeting was called for the 24th. As Franklin recalled, the New Building "was pretty full. I had prepared a Number of printed Copies" of the "Form of Association" and placed pens and ink "all over the Room. I harangued them a little on the Subject, read the Paper and explained it, and then distributed the Copies, which were eagerly signed, not the least Objection being made." Approximately five hundred men subscribed on the spot. To ensure wide circulation, Franklin printed five hundred copies of the "Form of Association" and then reprinted the entire document, with explanatory notes, in the *Pennsylvania Gazette*. Ultimately, some ten thousand men joined the Association. *Plain Truth* had done its intended work: it had "wonderfully spirited us up to defend ourselves and [our] Country."[63]

What had these men agreed to? What *was* the Association? The first thing to note is that, unlike every other colonial militia, it was voluntary. In New York, every man between sixteen and sixty was required to enlist; in Virginia, every man between twenty-one and sixty. There were, of course, exceptions. Massachusetts exempted "magistrates, legislators, Harvard educators, school teachers, church leaders, physicians, ship captains, fishermen, and certain kinds of artisans"; Virginia excluded political and legal officers, ministers, teachers, students at William and Mary, and the overseers of slaves. All colonies either restricted or prevented the enlistment of transients, indentured servants, Indians, and African Americans. And in no instance did the militia include women.[64] But despite these exceptions, the obligation to serve extended to the vast majority of freeholders. Within the horizon of eighteenth-century assumptions and expectations, the ideal— every citizen a soldier, and every soldier a citizen—appeared tantalizingly possible. But not in Pennsylvania, where Quaker pacifism posed a seemingly insuperable obstacle to the creation of a compulsory state militia. Franklin's language is revealing. Men did not "enlist" in the Association. They were "subscribers," just as the members of the Library Company and the Fire Company were "subscribers."[65] This was the language of a joint stock company, in which the members agreed to contribute to a common fund for specific and limited purposes.

What held subscribers to their agreement, especially after the first flush of enthusiasm wore off? Even voluntary associations use sanctions to enforce good behavior. Debates in the Junto were to be "conducted in the

sincere Spirit of Enquiry after Truth, without Fondness for Dispute, or Desire for Victory." But in the heat of battle men became argumentative, aggressive, and inflexible. To break the power of these passions, members
found it necessary to impose small fines for uncivil conduct. The Library
Company, we have seen, used fines to ensure that subscribers returned books
on time and in good condition. And the Union Fire Company fined men who
failed to keep their buckets and bags ready to hand and in good condition.
These fines were rigorously enforced, as one member learned to his dismay.
When he moved to Lancaster, he took his equipment with him. Though he
now lived some seventy miles from Philadelphia, he was still obligated to
present his buckets and bags at the monthly meetings![66]

Against this background, it is striking that Franklin specifically rejected
the use of sanctions to enforce the rules of the Association. Individual companies might choose to impose small fines for misconduct on their own members. But the highest authority in the Association, the General Military
Council, was barred from imposing "any Pecuniary Mulcts, Fines, or Corporal Penalties, on any Account whatever." As Franklin explained, "A Militia of FREEMEN, ought not to be subject to any corporal Penalties. In worthy
Minds, the Principles of *Reason, Duty* and *Honor,* work more strongly than
the Fears of Punishment. The Military Council therefore is not empowered
to appoint any such, nor yet even pecuniary Mulcts or Fines; that it may
clearly appear we act only on the most honorable Motives." Whips and
"wooden horses" were basic tools of the British army, part of a "ferocious
disciplinary system" that maintained order through exemplary punishments.
Floggings were routine, with offenders receiving hundreds of lashes.[67] For
some offenses soldiers were forced to ride the wooden horse, sitting astride a
plank or rail, weights tied to the feet, for a specified period of time. These
punishments were agonizing and potentially fatal. They were also deeply
humiliating: cruelty and horror were intended to make a man humble.[68]

Corporal punishment helped establish hierarchy and subordination
within the British army. Colonial militias did not abjure it.[69] But militia officers, at least in some colonies, preferred to admonish soldiers rather than co-
erce them. Discipline depended on "consistency, solidarity, entreaty and
instruction." As one horrified Massachusetts soldier discovered during the
Seven Years' War, "We now see what it is to be under martial law and to be
with the regulars, who are but little better than slaves to their officers." This
private's lament relied upon a familiar metaphor. Early modern Britons

frequently used the concept of slavery to define the boundaries of acceptable behavior. The distinctions they drew were inherently hierarchical. Seventeenth-century gentlemen argued that they "ought not to be shamed by 'slavish' punishments like whipping or the stocks"; these were reserved for lesser men. The presence of human chattel in the colonies sharpened the underlying metaphor and altered its social referents. But it did not change its fundamental meaning. To be a free man was to be free from the punishments inflicted on slaves.[70]

As a young man, sailing home from London, Franklin had been repulsed by "Johnny Gibson's Hole"—a wretched military dungeon in Portsmouth—and wrote in his journal that the greatest generals of antiquity had motivated their soldiers with example and affection, not fear and terror. The Association embodied his belief that reason and duty were sufficient to ensure good behavior. To all appearances, his expectations were justified. In early December six hundred men assembled for their first meeting. Franklin proposed dividing the city into districts and companies, and the men dispersed. On New Year's Day they appeared "under Arms," elected officers, and marched in review. "The whole was performed with the greatest Order and Regularity, and without occasioning the least Disturbance." In early 1748 the men of the Association learned to drill, helped erect a fort on the Delaware, and kept watch over the city. To aid these endeavors, Franklin reprinted a standard drill manual to coincide with the first formal meeting of the Association.[71] Franklin sang the praises of the men in the Association in the *Gazette*. Their "Zeal and Industry" were exceptional, their "Sobriety and good Order" commendable. To have made such progress "in so short a time" was "truly extraordinary." He was not, of course, a neutral observer. But even those with the greatest reason to be suspicious of the Association— the Proprietors and their colonial supporters—commended its conduct.[72]

As Franklin made clear in *Plain Truth*, however, it was not virtue alone that motivated the men of the Association. "The middling People, the Farmers, Shopkeepers and Tradesmen of this City and Country," were united by trade. Commercial interests reinforced the voices of reason, duty, and honor. This deserves emphasis. In the republican tradition, mercenaries— professional soldiers—could not be trusted. As Machiavelli noted, "They have no cause to stand firm when attacked, apart from the small pay which you give them." To remain free, a republic had to depend on the virtue of citizen-soldiers. And according to republican theorists, commerce was inherently corrupting. The instruments of trade—stocks and bonds, bills of credit, and paper money—were "imaginary," embodying "the power of opinion, passion and fantasy." Men who lived from trade were fatally dependent on forces outside their control. A man who farmed his own land, by contrast, was free to act as virtue commanded. A successful republic—a virtuous republic—was "a republic of armed proprietors."[73] These arguments were widespread in the eighteenth century, leading some to conclude that "the right of the people to keep and bear arms," guaranteed by the Second Amendment, is a direct descendent of Machiavelli's praise for citizen-soldiers.[74]

The Association—arguably the most important militia prior to the Revolution—flies in the face of these ideas. Civic virtue and commercial interest were not antithetical; instead, they reinforced each other. But noting this fact barely scratches the surface. In classical republicanism, the militia was an educational as well as a military institution. It hardened men's minds and disciplined their souls, imbuing them with manly energy and enabling them to defend their country in time of war.[75] It also reinforced social hierarchy. There was a direct connection between military office and social position. The highest offices were to be held by men of "quality," men with land, fortune, and education. Members of the gentry were distinguished from freeholders by honor and position. Both groups were distinguished from servants and day laborers, who were ineligible for militia duty. (In James Harrington's influential model, these distinctions were marked first by excluding servants—their dependence made them ineligible for citizenship—then by dividing the militia into "horse" and "foot." To be a member of the horse, a man had to have an estate with a substantial annual income.)[76]

Using the militia to teach social hierarchy was not unique to classical republicanism; it was an essential ingredient of actual militias in Britain and North America as well. As Edmund S. Morgan has observed, "Service in the militia was a school of subordination, where the structure of society was most visibly displayed, especially on the annual or semiannual or even monthly training days." But in forming the Association, Franklin explicitly rejected this practice. Officers were to be directly elected by the men in each company. As he explained, "Where those to be commanded choose those that are to command, it is to be presumed the Choice will naturally fall on Men of the best Character for their military Skill; on such too, from whose Prudence and Good-nature there may be no Fear of Injustice or military

Oppression."[77] In itself, this did not guarantee the differentiation of military organization and social structure. The only other colony to permit the election of officers was Massachusetts, and historians have suggested that elections in the Bay Colony did little to disrupt traditional hierarchies. In selecting leaders, militiamen naturally deferred to their betters. What of the Association? No muster lists have survived, and thus we have no record of rank-and-file membership. The names of officers were published in the *Gazette*, however, and they are revealing. Each of the eleven original companies in Philadelphia elected three officers: a captain, lieutenant, and ensign. Of these thirty-three men, twenty-nine can be identified. Eight were prosperous merchants, two were physicians, one was a lawyer. Eight were artisans. Six others either were or became members of the Assembly or Council. The artisans were skilled craftsmen—saddlers, upholsterers, carpenters, engravers—but they were by no means members of the provincial elite.[78]

The Association's relative independence from existing social hierarchies was reinforced by its regional structure. The original subscription lists were chaotic, "signed promiscuously by Persons dwelling in all Parts of the Town." The first order of business was to divide the "associators" into companies of between fifty and one hundred men. The only requirement was that they live near each other. This was partly a matter of convenience; mustering men to drill was far easier when they came from the same part of the city. But it was also a matter of principle. As Franklin explained, division by locale "is intended to prevent People's sorting themselves into Companies, according to their Ranks in Life, their Quality or Station. 'Tis designed to mix the Great and Small together, for the sake of Union and Encouragement. Where Danger and Duty are equal to All, there should be no Distinction from Circumstances, but All be on the Level." In daily life men were merchants and farmers, gentlemen and artisans, creditors and debtors. They were unequal in wealth, power, and status. But the organization of the Association reflected the fact that in one basic respect they were equal. Regardless of the clothes they wore, or whether they worked with their hands or their head, they were all vulnerable to assault by an "enterprising" and "cruel" enemy.[79]

Vulnerability, not martial virtue, defined "the middling People." " 'Tis true, with very little Notice, the Rich may shift for themselves. The Means of speedy Flight are ready in their Hands; and with some previous Care to lodge Money and Effects in distant and secure Places, though they should lose much, yet enough may be left them, and to spare. But most unhappily circum-stanced indeed are we, the middling People, the Tradesmen, Shopkeepers, and Farmers of this Province and City! We cannot all fly with our Families; and if we could, how shall we subsist?" The rich could flee danger with little or no loss; their wealth was mobile. Not so the middling People. Lacking an exit, their only option was to mobilize for self-protection. Shared vulnerabil-ity justified the Association: "*Protection* is as truly due from the Government to the People, as *Obedience* from the People to the Government."[80]

Intriguing confirmation of the link between vulnerability and civic identity can be found in a proposal Franklin drafted in 1775. At that time Pennsylvania's militia was involuntary, and Quakers were confronted with a legal obligation that violated the peace testimony. Franklin proposed an oath of allegiance for conscientious objectors. The second half of the oath ex-pressed willingness to perform alternate service. Though pacifists would not bear arms, they could fight fires, provide medical assistance, and care for the infirm. The first half of the oath committed them to "share the Fate of our Fellow Citizens": "We will not in any time of danger, attempt separately to secure ourselves our Families and private Property, by withdrawing them from Situations of Danger, while others are engaged in the common De-fense; nor take any Measures for such purpose but in Concert with the Pub-lic."[81] The risks of war varied enormously. Some faced greater hazards than others, and the opportunity to flee dramatically changed the odds. Shared vulnerability was a condition of equal citizenship.

The Association was an association of equals, its regional structure af-firming a basic moral and political principle. It was also a practical organi-zation intended to meet the colony's need for protection. What looks like a principle of equality from a philosophical point of view can also be seen as a characteristic of associational life from a sociological point of view. Recall that toleration was meant to separate religion and politics, so that the beliefs and practices of faith did not directly map onto the rights and obligations of citizenship. Religious association and civic life were (or ought to be) distinct. Each was strengthened by its separation from the other. The same idea could be applied within an association. Vibrant debate in Franklin's Junto was made possible by the willingness of each member to tolerate the religious be-liefs and practices of every other member. Each member was required to "sincerely declare" that no person "ought to be harmed in his body, name or goods, for merely speculative opinions, or his external way of worship."

Similarly, fellowship among Freemasons, who came from all classes and countries, was facilitated by a willingness to set aside religious and political quarrels.[82] Learned conversation among persons of different backgrounds and levels of education in the American Philosophical Society was eased by rules forbidding ridicule of a member's manner of speaking or writing. Equality among subscribers to the Library Company, who varied substantially in wealth, was preserved by ensuring that no one held more than one share.[83] In each of these instances, equality within an association was preserved by carefully separating membership in it from other roles and identities. "Corruption" occurred when a member attempted to dissolve the boundaries that defined the association: by refusing to chat amiably with a person because of his religious beliefs, or by using money to influence the decisions of a philosophical society. The success of the Association rested on its remaining distinct from the roles and identities of everyday life.

The Lottery Scheme

The "Form of Association" provided for order and discipline. But what about cannon? Associators were responsible for their own weapons, but cannon were expensive and exceeded the grasp of all but the wealthiest.[84] To be effective, moreover, cannon needed fortification. How could a voluntary association afford such mighty weapons?

The associators petitioned the Proprietors for a "generous Supply of Cannon and small Arms."[85] As expected, the Penns turned them down. Though sensitive to the colonists' apprehensions, the Proprietors considered the Association "Criminal." Franklin was flirting with anarchy. Or worse. Less than two years earlier the British government had been panicked by the second Jacobite uprising. Under the standard of Charles Edward Stuart, "Bonnie Prince Charlie," hundreds of armed men descended from Scotland to within 125 miles of London. The Jacobites were crushed, and the Scottish clans were ruthlessly suppressed. But to the Penns the lesson seemed clear. Arming and organizing men was not a legitimate private activity—it was a dangerous threat to government. (Social order was not the only worry of the Penns. Buried in their response to the Association was a sly political gambit. If the Assembly would pass a militia law, then the Proprietors would be quite willing to lend their support. Passing a militia law would, of course, regularize the Association. It would also destroy the Quaker Party.)[86]

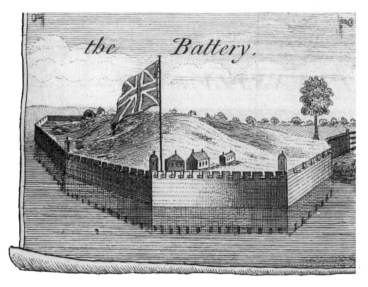

The Association battery on the Delaware River. Detail from "The East Prospect of the City of Philadelphia," engraving after George Heap, *London Magazine*, 1761. (Courtesy the Library Company of Philadelphia.)

Requests to borrow cannon from Massachusetts and New York brought slightly better results. Governor Shirley of Massachusetts turned the associators down; he had none to spare. Governor Clinton of New York was inclined to help, but his military engineers advised against it. A small delegation was sent to persuade him. As Franklin recalled, wine and conversation succeeded where reason failed: "He at first refused us peremptorily: but at a Dinner with his Council where there was great Drinking of Madeira Wine, as the Custom at that Place then was, he softened by degrees, and said he would lend us Six. After a few more Bumpers he advanced to Ten. And at length he very good naturedly conceded Eighteen."[87] (A bumper was a glass of wine, filled to the brim and drunk as a toast.) The New York cannon were excellent weapons, but they were borrowed, and borrowed cannon were at best a stopgap solution to the colony's defensive needs. From the beginning Franklin planned for the Association to purchase cannon from England and build a battery on the Delaware. Funds would be raised through a lottery.

When we think of community institutions in colonial North America, we often think of town meetings, public markets, civic parades, and religious festivals. With time we may add schools and taverns as well as various social conventions governing status or standing. We may even recall the militia.

But we rarely think of lotteries, even though they, too, were essential features of colonial life. Individuals used lotteries to dispose of large pieces of property. They were often driven to this expedient by debt. As Thomas Jefferson explained, "An article of property, insusceptible of division at all, or not without great diminution of its worth, is sometimes of so large value as that no purchaser can be found while the owner owes debts, has no other means of payment, and his creditors no other chance of obtaining it but by its sale at a full and fair price. The lottery is here a salutary instrument for disposing of it, where many run small risks for the chance of obtaining a high prize." Thus in 1768 George Washington sought to expand his landholdings by purchasing twenty tickets in the lottery of Colonel William Byrd III, a desperately indebted Virginia planter who was raffling "the entire towns of Rocky Ridge and Shockoe."[88]

Individuals were not the only beneficiaries of lotteries. Prior to the development of a stable bond market, lotteries were an indispensable source of capital for community projects. Schools, roads, churches, bridges, and a dozen other kinds of improvement were funded through lotteries. In the early seventeenth century the Virginia Company sought to fund the settlement of Jamestown with a series of small lotteries. In the eighteenth century Harvard College, King's College, the College of New Jersey, and Yale College held lotteries to fund their educational missions. The governments of Massachusetts, New York, and Virginia used lotteries to help pay for the Seven Years' War. In 1776 Congress followed their example, authorizing the first of several U.S. lotteries. Even John Adams could not resist temptation—he urged Abigail to buy a ticket in the name of their children. "Let us try their Luck," he implored.[89]

The association of lotteries with luck and chance gave them an ambiguous moral tinge. If a man is known by the company he keeps, then the title of an early eighteenth-century English pamphlet says it all: *Jack Puddings Disappointment, Or: A General Lamentation Amongst Cooks, Players, Rope-dancers and Fiddlers, Whores, Lottery-men, Pickpockets and Jugglers for the Lord Mayors Order for a discontinuing of Bartholomew Fair.* Lotteries were akin to gambling, and many considered them vicious. They made sport of God's providence and exposed weak-willed men to the machinations of "projectors" and "adventurers." The target of lotteries, to use a lovely seventeenth-century word, were *cullies*, dupes and gulls who could easily be deceived. There was never a shortage of such people, for they were animated by failure:

Lotteries are a Spot, that managed right,
Raises vast Crops, like Mushrooms, in a Night.
By often paring, and reducing low,
Like Vines, by pruning, they more fruitful grow.[90]

Lotteries thrive on mistaken beliefs regarding random events. We are poor calculators of odds, overestimating our chances of success and underestimating our chances of failure. As Joseph Addison observed in the *Spectator*, every lottery ticket is "as likely to succeed as any of its fellows." But the "Pastimes and Extravagances of Human Reason" are such that people will favor one number above another. "Some are pleased to find their own Age in their Number; some that they have got a Number which makes a pretty Appearance in the Ciphers, and others because it is the same Number that succeeded in the last Lottery." To critics of lotteries, the consequences of miscalculation were disastrous: "the distress of individuals, the ruin of families, the extravagance and luxury of the successful, and the rage and fraud of those that miscarry."[91]

Opponents of lotteries attempted to banish them from the colonies, but they were singularly unsuccessful. A particularly vigorous campaign was waged in Pennsylvania by the Quakers. In the first meeting of the Assembly, Quakers passed a code punishing all who were "Convicted of playing Cards, Dice, Lotteries, or such like enticing, vain and evil Sports and Games." This and similar acts were annulled by the English government as an unjust restriction of "innocent Diversions." (Competition may have played a role in the decision. The English were major players in the lottery business.) In 1729 the Assembly passed a law proscribing public and private lotteries. Those convicted were fined £100, half of which went to the governor, the other half to the party who brought charges. This act was allowed to become law. "But the citizens were not to be denied," and over the next three decades "at least fifty-two quasi-legal lotteries were held" with the governor's "connivance."[92] The arrangement was clever and simple: suit was brought by a member of the organization holding the lottery, and both complainant and governor forfeited his portion of the penalty. In this way, although the act was technically enforced, it was practically voided. When it came time to instruct young colonists in mathematics, it made perfect sense to use lottery tickets as an example of large numbers. None would have missed the reference or its relevance.[93]

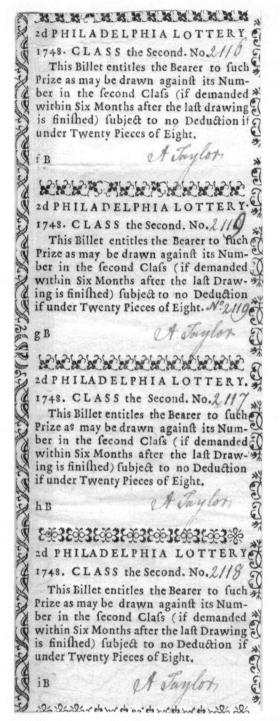

2d PHILADELPHIA LOTTERY.
1748. CLASS the Second. No. 2116
  This Billet entitles the Bearer to such Prize as may be drawn againſt its Number in the ſecond Claſs (if demanded within Six Months after the laſt drawing is finiſhed) ſubject to no Deduction if under Twenty Pieces of Eight.

f B   *A. Taylor*

2d PHILADELPHIA LOTTERY.
1748. CLASS the Second. No. 2119
  This Billet entitles the Bearer to ſuch Prize as may be drawn againſt its Number in the ſecond Claſs (if demanded within Six Months after the laſt Drawing is finiſhed) ſubject to no Deduction if under Twenty Pieces of Eight. *N°2119*

g B   *A. Taylor*

2d PHILADELPHIA LOTTERY.
1748. CLASS the Second. No. 2117
  This Billet entitles the Bearer to ſuch Prize as may be drawn againſt its Number in the ſecond Claſs (if demanded within Six Months after the laſt Drawing is finiſhed) ſubject to no Deduction if under Twenty Pieces of Eight.

h B   *A. Taylor*

2d PHILADELPHIA LOTTERY.
1748. CLASS the Second. No. 2118
  This Billet entitles the Bearer to ſuch Prize as may be drawn againſt its Number in the ſecond Claſs (if demanded within Six Months after the laſt Drawing is finiſhed) ſubject to no Deduction if under Twenty Pieces of Eight.

i B   *A. Taylor*

Lottery tickets, second class. Four of thirty thousand tickets printed for the second lottery, held to raise 9,375 pieces of eight for the defense of Pennsylvania. (Courtesy Beinecke Rare Book and Manuscript Library, Yale University.)

The first Association lottery was announced in early December 1747. To give confidence in the enterprise, Franklin printed a detailed "Account of the Manner of Drawing a Public Lottery" in the *Gazette*. Every step was "done in Public" and designed to prevent fraud. By early February, ten thousand tickets at 40 shillings each had been sold, and winners were drawn and paid. Prizes ranged from £3 to £500; there were over two thousand of the former, but just two of the latter. Fifteen percent of the gross, or £3,000, was left for "the Public Use."[94]

Franklin was a shrewd organizer. He noted with pride the success of the first lottery and immediately followed with a second and slightly different form of lottery. The first had had a single class: all prizes were distributed in a single drawing. This restricted the size of the lottery. Perhaps more important, it also limited the incentive to play. Accordingly, the second lottery was divided into four classes. The price of a ticket was divided into "four gradual Payments, to be made, if the Buyer pleases, at four different and distant Times." The first class was the least expensive, encouraging wide participation. Each succeeding class was more expensive; correspondingly, the value of the prizes grew.[95] The entire scheme was designed to maximize revenue by keeping ticket holders engaged through all four classes.

Franklin was not normally a gambler. He believed that happiness "is produced not so much by great Pieces of good Fortune that seldom happen, as by little Advantages that occur every Day." But he understood the lure of lotteries. In 1790 the New York merchant Nathaniel Hazard wrote Alexander Hamilton proposing a lottery to sink the national debt. Anticipating Hamilton's concern that the highest prize was too great, Hazard recalled "an opinion of the late Dr. Franklin," which was that if there were a lottery with ten thousand tickets and only one prize of £1,000, all the tickets would sell and "he himself would become an Adventurer." Only one ticket could win; "why not his as well as any other?" Hamilton concurred with Franklin's judgment. When he came to draft his own lottery plan three years later, he favored a small number of large prizes rather than a large number of small prizes, "for adventurers would as leave lose altogether as acquire trifling prizes and would prefer a small chance of winning *a great deal* to a great chance of winning little. Hope is apt to supply the place of probability and the Imagination to be struck with glittering though precarious prospects."[96]

Hamilton is sometimes cast as the American Caesar, a proponent of empire and interest. At other times he is held up as the architect of a radically new conception of America's economy. In both cases he is contrasted with republicans, like Thomas Jefferson, who favored virtue over interest, agriculture over commerce, and militias over standing armies. It is true that Hamilton was skeptical of militias. He thought them unattractive to modern citizens and inappropriate to modern combat. To the extent that a militia was needed under the Constitution, it ought to be under the control of the national government.[97] Thus it is all the more striking that Hamilton and Franklin understood lotteries in the same way. This was no minor matter—it went to the core of their assumptions about the structure of the psyche and the motives for action in a modern society. Purity of heart and singleness of purpose were not necessary to civic life. The Association demonstrates that militias could be consistent with, not antithetical to, the play of passions and interests in a commercial economy.

Action

After scouting locations, the lottery managers decided to build the Association battery at Wicaco, on the banks of the Delaware just outside Philadelphia. Materials were ordered and men were hired. Construction was nearly complete in late April 1748, just in time to receive cannons on loan from New York. As shown in George Heap's "An East Prospect of the City of Philadelphia" (1761), it was an impressive structure, four hundred feet long and built to house more than two dozen cannons. Lottery records list the names of over 120 men and women who were paid for its construction and maintenance; countless more are listed simply as "workers" or "laborers." Some of the disbursements—for cannons, or for land to build on—were quite large. But there were scores of smaller payments. Isacchia Price was paid £2 to cut trees for gun carriages; John Moore hauled them for £1. Captain Sibbald hired a gang of men to mount the guns for £5.3.15; Samuel McCall sold gunpowder to the Association for £9. Joseph Kent was paid £10 for his work as a lottery clerk. Whatever else it was, the Association battery was a massive public-works project, providing employment for Philadelphians of every class and skill.[98]

All this time the associators continued to muster and drill. A group of women, using devices and mottoes provided by Franklin, presented "Silk Colors" to regiments in and near Philadelphia. Arrangements were made for cooperation between city and country troops, and a second and smaller battery was erected near Society Hill. Periodic reports of privateers kept everyone on edge. In June river traffic was placed under a curfew and guard was mounted every night. On one occasion, near New Castle, shots were fired. But otherwise the guns of the associators remained quiet, and were used only on ceremonial occasions. Ironically, the cannons purchased by the Association did not arrive until after the king announced an end to hostilities in the War of the Austrian Succession.[99]

Franklin may not have minded the fact that the associators never saw combat. By no means a pacifist, he thought peace vastly preferable to war. As he delighted in saying during the Revolution, "There never was a good War, or a bad Peace."[100] There were, however, untold benefits to the hustle and bustle of militia life. Nearly a decade after forming the Association, Franklin led a troop of soldiers, now under the authority of the Assembly, to build a string of forts on the western frontier of Pennsylvania. The weather was miserable—wet and cold—and often the men were unable to work. This led Franklin "to observe, that when Men are employed they are best contented. For on the Days they worked they were good-natured and cheerful; and with the consciousness of having done a good Days work they spent the Evenings jollily; but on the idle Days they were mutinous and quarrelsome, finding fault with their Pork, the Bread, etc. and in continual ill-humor: which put me in mind of a Sea-Captain, whose Rule it was to keep his Men constantly at Work; and when his Mate once told him that they had done everything, and there was nothing farther to employ them about; O, says he, *make them scour the Anchor.*" Franklin's sea captain spoke with the folk wisdom of a thousand voyages. His words have a slightly unsavory ring to them. We all know make-work when we see it. But Franklin's observation can be dressed in finer garb. As previously noted, John Locke argued that the will is determined by "uneasiness" or the "want of some absent good." Bodily pain disquiets the mind and causes us to want to ease it—so, too, do discomforts of the mind. Locke insisted that our sense of unease reflected present conditions, not necessarily long-term needs, interests, or values. Intense pain, violent love, and thirst for revenge take root in our sense of unease, even though their satisfaction need not be to our advantage.[101]

In Franklin's adaptation of Locke's arguments, actions and events were more important than motives and intentions. What was needed was an art or technique for securing the virtues we already possess and acquiring the ones we lack. This was the foundation for Franklin's "bold and arduous Project" of moral reform. We ought to view the Association in the same light. It was an attempt to channel desire and ease disquiet through habit and action. Organizing, drilling, and building calmed and reassured as they protected. Even lotteries—which take advantage of our cupidity—had a part to play. Virtue was not an expression of human excellence. It was not even a necessary precondition to life as a citizen-soldier. Instead, it was the consequence of active participation in complex, habit-forming institutions. All that was needed was "Order, Discipline, and a few Cannon."

Aftershocks

Not all were satisfied with the Association. As previously noted, Thomas Penn considered the Association illegal and unconstitutional. He also believed that it threatened his interests: "This association is founded on a Contempt to Government, and cannot end in anything but Anarchy and Confusion. The People in general are so fond of what they call Liberty as to fall into Licentiousness, and when they know they may Act . . . by Orders of their own Substitutes, in a Body, and a Military manner, and independent of this Government, why should they not Act against it?" The Association sought to establish "a Military Common Wealth," and its supporters were guilty of "little less than Treason." Franklin, whose leadership of the Association was widely acknowledged, was of special concern. "He is a dangerous Man and I should be very Glad he Inhabited any other Country, as I believe him of a very uneasy Spirit, however he is a Sort of Tribune of the People, he must be treated with regard."[102] The historian Robert Middlekauff has suggested that Penn's reaction to the Association was "skewed" by "peculiar, almost morbid, suspicion." It does seem more than a little hysterical to accuse Franklin of stirring up "the Wild unthinking Multitude." [103] Penn's instinctive reaction to provincial initiatives was sullen and distrustful. But in this instance his anxiety was not entirely misplaced. Within ten years Franklin would travel to London in an attempt to end the Penn family's power over the government of the colony.

Thomas Penn's apprehensions were founded on the philosophical premise of *Plain Truth:* "*Protection* is as truly due from the Government to the People, as *Obedience* from the People to the Government." Though Penn did not dispute the principle, he was concerned about its application. Who had the authority to decide whether the people of Pennsylvania were being protected? Using what criteria? Should they conclude that the government was failing to protect the people, what were they entitled to do? Regardless of the merits of the Association, the principle by which it was justified was potentially explosive.[104] Once again, Penn's worries were not without foundation. Within twenty years a violent frontier movement, the Paxton Boys, would demonstrate the dangers inherent in popular self-defense movements.

Until the 1750s Euro-Americans and Indians enjoyed "unparalleled peace" in Pennsylvania. Following William Penn's lead, Quaker governments sought to treat Indians with "Humanity and Justice." Conflicts, when they arose, were for the most part resolved fairly and impartially.[105] But steady westward expansion, the growth of settler communities that did not share Penn's vision, and conflicts within and between Indian tribes all contributed to increasing tension. Finally, under the intense pressure of the Seven Years' War, frontier harmony was shattered, never to return. Within a few short years thousands of men, women, and children, both settler and Indian, were killed, wounded, captured, or displaced. Encounters were fierce and brutal, the carnage broken only by brief periods of dread and suspicion. The accidental discharge of a weapon, or the unexpected setting of a fire, could send entire communities into a deep and dangerous panic.[106]

Western settlers unsuccessfully petitioned the governor and Assembly for assistance. Desperate and feeling abandoned, they formed themselves into militia companies and elected officers.[107] But the depredations continued. Finally, in late 1763, Scots-Irish frontiersmen from the vicinity of Paxton (near present-day Harrisburg) reached a breaking point. Settlers had long suspected that small enclaves of "friendly" Indians were in fact fifth columnists, providing support and information to hostile or "wild" Indians. Believing that they had found proof implicating the Indians living at Conestoga, a band of about fifty men descended on the settlement on 14 December and killed the two men, three women, and one child they found. Local authorities rounded up fourteen surviving members of the Conestoga band and placed them in the Lancaster workhouse for their protection. But the men of Paxton considered these Indians equally guilty, and on 27 December they broke into the workhouse and slaughtered them as well. A contemporary witness reported that he saw

> a number of people running down street towards the jail, which enticed me and other lads to follow them. At about six or eight yards

from the jail, we met from twenty-five to thirty men, well mounted on horses, and with rifles, tomahawks, and scalping knives, equipped for murder. I ran into the prison yard, and there, oh what a horrid sight presented itself to my view! Near the back door of the prison lay an old Indian and his squaw, particularly well known and esteemed by the people of the town on account of his placid and friendly conduct. His name was Will Soc; across him and squaw lay two children, of about the age of three years, whose heads were split with the tomahawk, and their scalps taken off. Towards the middle of the jail yard, along the west side of the wall, lay a stout Indian, whom I particularly noticed to have been shot in his breast; his legs were chopped with the tomahawk, his hands cut off, and finally a rifle ball discharged in his mouth, so that his head was blown to atoms, and the brains were splashed against and yet hanging to the wall, for three or four feet around. This man's hands and feet had also been chopped off with a tomahawk. In this manner lay the whole of them, men, women and children spread about the prison yard; shot, scalped, hacked and cut to pieces.[108]

When news of these massacres reached Philadelphia, the governor denounced the killers and offered a reward for their apprehension. He also recommended that about 140 Indians who had lived under the guidance and protection of Moravian religious communities be removed to Philadelphia to prevent further violence.

In late December 1763 men from Paxton and neighboring towns began planning a march on Philadelphia. They sought government recognition for their sufferings. They also planned to interrogate—and if necessary punish—the Indians who had taken refuge in the city. "Companies of volunteers were formed and stores of arms and powder were collected for the expedition. Contributions were soon received to defray expenses of the poorer volunteers." The Assembly responded with "An Act for preventing Tumults and Riotous Assemblies," but that did not deter the frontiersmen. In early February 1764 a body of armed men, rumored to be anywhere from 700 to 1,500 strong, crossed the Schuylkill and camped at Germantown. (In fact, they numbered closer to 250.) The governor invoked the Riot Act and called on the citizens of Philadelphia to defend the city. With Franklin's house serving as headquarters, nearly 1,000 men "entered into an Association, and took Arms for the Support of Government, and Maintenance of good

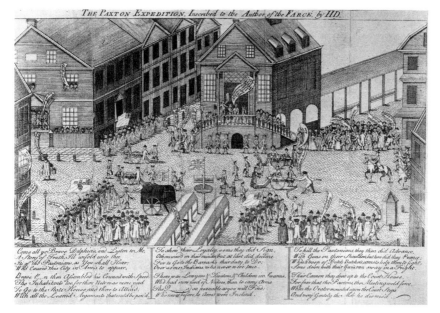

Henry Dawkins, *The Paxton Expedition, Inscribed to the Author of the Farce by H.D.,* 1764.
(Courtesy the Library Company of Philadelphia.) Based on David Dove's *The Paxton Boys, a*
Farce, the engraving shows panicked associators preparing to fire their cannon at a troop of
"Dutch" (German) butchers who had come to help. In the upper left is the Quaker meeting-
house, used as shelter in the cold February rain.

Order." Six companies of foot, one of artillery, and one troop of horse were
formed. A delegation of prominent citizens, including Franklin, was sent to
negotiate with the men from Paxton. After several hours' parley, the men
agreed to disband and return home on condition that two be allowed to remain behind and present their grievances to the governor and Assembly.
Armed conflict was averted, and the immediate crisis was ended.[109]

The first half of the Paxton Boys' *Declaration and Remonstrance* woefully recited the background to the massacres, contrasting the government's
concern for Indians with its indifference to settlers. The second half of the
Declaration began with an institutional explanation for why this had happened: underrepresentation of the frontier counties in the Assembly. As
"Free-Men and *English* Subjects" they were entitled to "the same Privileges
and Immunities" as those living in Philadelphia and the eastern counties. But
seats were allocated in such a way that those living in the east had over twice
as many representatives as those living in the west. Philadelphia and the

eastern counties had twenty-six seats, while the five western counties had only ten seats. According to one historian, had apportionment been fair according to the standards of the day, the east would have had only twenty-one seats, while the west would have had twenty-two. The Paxton Boys thought this "oppressive, unequal and unjust, the Cause of many of our Grievances and an infringement of our natural Privileges of Freedom and Equality."[110] Those living "in and around Philadelphia" lived a "pleasant, protected life." They simply had "no feeling" for the trials and tribulations of those living on the frontier. In an unpublished "Apology" the "Paxton Volunteers" proclaimed their certainty that "if we had had a proper Number of Representatives in Assembly . . . so many of our Brethren had not been murdered and captivated [by Indians]. Something would have been done sooner for our Relief and Assistance."[111]

No one was ever prosecuted for the massacre of the Conestoga Indians or for the march on Philadelphia. Incipient racism festered and grew. Old distinctions between "peaceable" and "wild" Indians withered, replaced by homogenizing racial identities.[112] As one contemporary put it, "the White People most in General, hates any Thing that Savors of the Name of an Indian." Franklin thought these appeals to fixed identities nonsense and in his powerful and passionate *Narrative of the Late Massacres, in Lancaster County* mocked frontier logic: "If an Indian injures me, does it follow that I may revenge that Injury on all Indians? It is well known that Indians are of different Tribes, Nations and Languages, as well as the White People. In Europe, if the French, who are White-People, should injure the Dutch, are they to revenge it on the English, because they too are White People? The only Crime of these poor Wretches seems to have been, that they had a reddish brown Skin, and black Hair; and some People of that Sort, it seems, had murdered some of our Relations. If it be right to kill Men for such a Reason, then, should any Man, with a freckled Face and red Hair, kill a Wife or Child of mine, it would be right for me to revenge it, by killing all the freckled red-haired Men, Women and Children, I could afterwards any where meet with." Franklin's argument may have helped ease tensions in late January and early February 1764. But in the long run it had little effect. In Alden Vaughan's blunt words, "The Paxton Boys's principal legacy was 'open season' on the Indians, friend or foe."[113]

For all their differences, Franklin and the Paxton Boys shared a basic premise: protection and obedience were reciprocal. Both defended their actions by pointing to the Assembly's unwillingness to protect their lives and property. Backcountry rebels in other regions—the Regulators in North and South Carolina, Daniel Shays's followers in Massachusetts—pitched their arguments along similar lines.[114] Critics feared the "Contempt showed the Government" by these movements. Such "Violent Encroachment upon the Laws of the land" could only have "bad consequences."[115] But in Pennsylvania these fears were fraught with irony. The Paxton Boys were an eerie reflection of Franklin's original Association. Both were popular self-defense movements. And it was a vestige of the Association, in turn, that protected government and preserved lives in the face of the Paxton Boys threat. "*Protection* is as truly due from the Government to the People, as *Obedience* from the People to the Government." But who are the people? What can they do when governments fail to protect them? Who speaks for them? These questions demanded answers; Franklin's first formulations came in the form of a treatise on population growth.

3. Population

People are indeed the essential of commerce, and the more people the
more trade; the more trade, the more money; the more money, the more
strength; and the more strength, the greater the nation.
—Daniel Defoe, *Review of the State of the British Nation* (1709)

There is no Science, the Study of which is more useful and commendable
than the Knowledge of the true Interest of one's Country.
—Benjamin Franklin, *A Modest Enquiry* (1729)

Population Politics

Miss Polly Baker was slightly flustered, and more than a little indignant. For
the fifth time she had been "dragged" before a Connecticut court "for having
a Bastard Child." Twice, in accordance with the law, she had been fined;
twice more, she had been punished. But the law itself was unreasonable.
How could having children be a crime? "Abstracted from the Law, I cannot
conceive (may it please your Honors) what the Nature of my Offence is. I
have brought Five fine Children into the World, at the Risk of my Life; I
have maintained them well by my own Industry, without burdening the
Township, and would have done it better, if it had not been for the heavy
Charges and Fines I have paid. Can it be a Crime (in the Nature of Things I
mean) to add to the Number of the King's Subjects, in a new Country that
really wants People? I own it, I should think it a Praise-worthy, rather than a
punishable Action." Fertility was a civic virtue, wasn't it? If anyone deserved punishment, it was "the great and growing Number of Bachelors in
the Country" who "leave unproduced (which I think is little better than

Murder) Hundreds of their Posterity to the Thousandth Generation. Is not this a greater Offence against the Public Good, than mine?"[1]

"The Speech of Miss Polly Baker" is one of Franklin's best-known and most-loved compositions. First printed in London in early 1747, it was quickly reprinted in newspapers and journals throughout England and North America. Because the speech appeared without attribution, many assumed that Polly was a real person, brought to the bar of a real court. This was not a matter of ignorance or literary naïveté. One of the more delightful anecdotes from Franklin's Paris ministry involved the *philosophe* Abbé Raynal, who had included Polly's speech in his *Histoire philosophique et politique* (1770) as an example of the severity of New England laws. Raynal insisted with vehemence that the speech was authentic; only Franklin's confession—which came *after* he had allowed the matter to be debated for some time—persuaded him otherwise.[2]

Franklin was a brilliant literary artist, and "Polly Baker" is one of his finest productions. But for all its japes and puns, innuendo and sly satire, Polly's speech addressed a serious topic: the relationship between population growth and the public good. (It treated other topics, like the separation of church and state, but these are not of immediate concern to us.) Governments exist not in isolation but as part of complex international systems. Competition within these systems is fierce, as regimes experiment with fresh policies and novel institutions. At key moments, the international system changes; this, in turn, affects the prospects for particular forms of government. For example, the Peace of Westphalia (1648) marked the inauguration of a new international system based on sovereign states. Alternative forms of organization—the Holy Roman Empire of central Europe, the city-states of Italy, or the Hanseatic League in northern Europe—were unable to compete and died off. And as sovereign states consolidated their power, they encountered new risks and incurred new obligations. On the one hand, changes in the scale and technology of international warfare imposed vast new fiscal demands on states. Large armies and powerful navies were frightfully expensive. Territorial ambitions and confessional claims had to be subordinated to economic needs. Trade, in David Hume's estimation, became "an affair of state." On the other hand, growing numbers of philosophers and politicians embraced the claim that states are responsible for the welfare of their inhabitants. If the people suffered from malnutrition, unemployment, or other forms of deprivation, then states were obligated to respond. Taken together, these two sets of considerations—the state's ability to prosper in competitive international markets and its obligation to provide for the welfare of its inhabitants—called for extraordinary political and intellectual innovations.[3]

One of the most important tools fashioned in response to these challenges was "political arithmetic," or "the art of reasoning by figures, upon things relating to the government."[4] Political arithmetic applied the science of numbers to a state's economy and society. The measurement and analysis of wages and prices, credits and debts, played an essential role. So, too, did the study of birth and death, fertility and morbidity. No less critical were migration, emigration, and immigration, the free and forced movement of people within and between states.

"The Speech of Miss Polly Baker" was a witty and ironic contribution to eighteenth-century political arithmetic. Human increase—a growing population—was vital to improvement. More people brought more trade; more trade brought greater wealth; greater wealth brought improvements in human well-being. Yet time-honored moral principles, underwritten by Christianity, were obstacles to population growth. Prostitution? Birth out of wedlock? Franklin hinted that these ought not to be considered problems, if the goal is increasing the number of inhabitants. Even worse was the double standard that permitted men to evade their responsibility to procreate or to procreate without taking responsibility. These antique customs and values had outlived their usefulness. (Throughout his life Franklin was impatient with what he regarded as flinty old customs. As a boy he chafed at the time taken by family prayers. One year, when the winter's provision of meat had been salted, he urged his father to say grace over the whole cask once for all. Daily repetition was a waste of time.)[5]

Franklin was intrigued by political arithmetic. As a boy of sixteen, wearing the guise of "Silence Dogood," he approvingly reprinted Daniel Defoe's scheme for insuring widows. His first pamphlet as a Philadelphia printer, *A Modest Enquiry*, concerned colonial monetary policy. Many of the civic schemes he proposed during the 1730s and 1740s rested on calculations of life expectancies. Sometime during the 1740s he turned his attention to population growth. Polly's "Speech" appeared in 1747. Three years later Richard Saunders included population statistics and bills of mortality in his almanac. He also wondered what "the natural Increase of Mankind" might be. In 1751 Franklin drafted his answer, in the form of a small scientific treatise: *Observations concerning the Increase of Mankind, Peopling of Countries, etc.* In this work he made two predictions that proved remarkably accurate: that the population of North America would double every twenty-five years and that the population of North America would outstrip that of Great Britain within one hundred years.[6]

Population has bearing on many crucial features of modern life: laws and customs governing reproduction; the size of budgets for schools and hospitals, roads and police; wage rates and the location of different types of jobs; the movement of people from the countryside to cities and from one nation to another. The politics of improvement was based on the belief that humans can shape their world through judgment and choice. Political arithmetic sought to identify limits to agency, the boundaries that separated what was contingent (and thus could be changed) from what was necessary (and thus beyond human control). To ignore these limits—to act as if all things are possible—was irresponsible; to misunderstand these limits—to imagine limits that do not actually exist—was self-defeating and potentially unjust.[7]

Improvement required a keen appreciation of the limits and possibilities of population growth. Hence, it is not surprising that Franklin reflected on immigration as well as natural increase in his *Observations.* What is surprising, especially to modern readers, is the tone and substance of some of his comments. Lamenting the "swarm" of German immigrants who threatened to make Pennsylvania "a Colony of *Aliens,*" Franklin called for policies designed to protect and increase the number of English settlers.[8]

What are we to make of the *Observations?* Was it a landmark in the history of demography? The major premise of Franklin's predictions—that population grows up to, but cannot exceed, the limits of subsistence—was an important precursor to modern population doctrines. Or was the *Observations* the work of a nativist, a man who believed that German immigrants must either assimilate or be excluded from British North America?[9]

Each of these interpretations contains a kernel of truth: Franklin was an extraordinary scientist, *and* he sometimes expressed himself in ethnically charged terms. But the dichotomy underlying these alternatives—between, roughly, "science" and "prejudice"—obscures more than it reveals. Eighteenth-century investigations of population occurred at the intersection of natural philosophy, natural history, and natural theology. In modern terms, these fields of investigation roughly correspond to the natural sciences (biology), the social sciences (economics and anthropology), and the humanities (philosophy and religious studies). If we are to understand Franklin's arguments, and their contribution to the politics of improvement, then we must begin with this apparently tangled disciplinary web.

The Practice of Science

Benjamin Franklin was an electrician, perhaps the first; he coined the word in 1751. He also gave currency to such now-common terms as *plus* or *positive, minus* or *negative, electrify, non-conducting,* and *battery.* Franklin's most famous experiment was flying a kite in a thunderstorm; his best-known invention was the lightning rod.[10]

Franklin's science was the science of electricity. Or so it might seem. But in the eighteenth century science was not divided neatly into subjects and disciplines, nor was it restricted to the study of the material universe. "The word *Science,*" Isaac Watts explained in a popular book of logic, "is usually applied to a whole Body of regular or methodical Observations or Propositions which learned Men have formed concerning any Subject of *Speculation.*" Science was as vast as the universe. Its domain was on display in Franklin's 1743 prospectus for the American Philosophical Society. Among topics of interest were "all new-discovered Plants, Herbs, Trees, Roots . . . All new-discovered Fossils in different Countries . . . New and useful Improvements in any Branch of Mathematics . . . New Inventions for saving Labor . . . Surveys, Maps and Charts of particular Parts of the Seacoasts, or Inland Countries . . . New Methods of Improving the Breed of useful Animals . . . [and] new Improvements in Planting, Gardening, Clearing Land, etc." The men who met to discuss this promiscuous list of topics were amateurs and generalists, not specialists and experts. Franklin was a printer; Thomas Bond, a physician; John Bartram, a farmer; Thomas Hopkinson, a merchant, lawyer, and judge. None considered himself a "scientist" (the word was not used until the nineteenth century). They were "Virtuosi or ingenious Men." Or—to use another word Franklin coined—they were "academicians," men who belonged to an academy or society that promoted the arts and sciences.[11]

Franklin understood and shared the intense intellectual curiosity and excitement of the virtuosi. As a young man in London he befriended Henry Pemberton, a physician and mathematician who was editing Sir Isaac Newton's *Principia mathematica.* Pemberton promised a meeting with Newton,

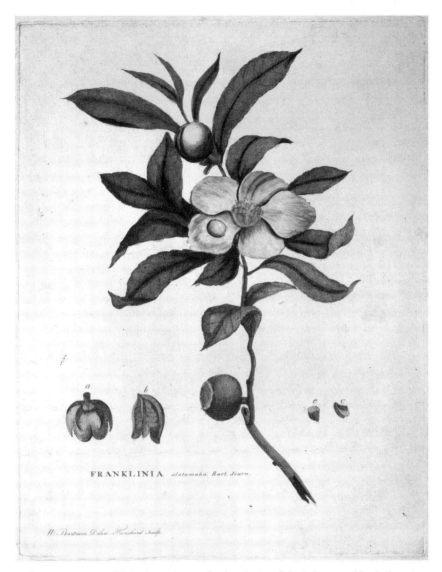

FRANKLINIA *alatamaha. Bart. Journ.*

William Bartram, *Franklinia alatamaha*. Hand-colored print of shrub discovered by the botanist John Bartram and his son William in the vicinity of the Alatamaha River and named after Franklin. (Courtesy American Philosophical Society.)

but to Franklin's great disappointment "this never happened." Instead, he caught the attention of the physician and collector Sir Hans Sloane, using an American curiosity—a purse made of asbestos—as bait. Back in Philadelphia, Franklin helped cement a circle of correspondents that included the English naturalist Peter Collinson, the Pennsylvania botanist John Bartram, and the New York physician Cadwallader Colden.[12] Though amateurs, these men were not dabblers. Collinson, like Pemberton, was a fellow of the Royal Society; Newton and Sloane were presidents of that esteemed association. Colden and Bartram were internationally known for their botanical investigations.

Unlike most modern scientists, eighteenth-century virtuosi did not sharply distinguish between knowledge and human interests. Many topics of investigation were chosen for their potential to contribute to the quality of life. In Franklin's case, his first scientific experiments concerned the design of fireplaces; his final, the temperature of water in the Gulf Stream. Franklin's work on fireplaces reflected his "interest in the human body—its constitution, its health, its productivity." To his dying day, friends sought his advice on how to minimize and control the noxious smoke produced by wood- and coal-burning fires. Franklin's study of the Gulf Stream was grounded in a common sailors' observation that the length of time needed to cross the Atlantic depended not just on distance but on the route taken. But from the beginning Franklin emphasized the political and economic importance of the Gulf Stream. This was in keeping with the purview of the American Philosophical Society: "all philosophical Experiments that let Light into the Nature of Things, tend to increase the Power of Man over Matter, and multiply the Conveniences or Pleasures of Life." Science and improvement were bound at the hip.[13]

As these examples suggest, Franklin's scientific interests were wide-ranging. One of the most charming anecdotes involving Franklin and John Adams—in truth, the *only* charming episode from the frosty relationship between these two men—comes from a diplomatic mission to meet with the commander of the British forces in North America, Lord Howe, in early September 1776. The taverns in New Brunswick were so full that Franklin and Adams were forced to share a small room with a single bed. Adams, who was "afraid of the Evening Air," shut the window. "Oh!" exclaimed Franklin, "don't shut the Window. We shall be suffocated. . . . Open the Window and come to bed, and I will convince you" that the night air is not dangerous. "Opening the Window and leaping into Bed," Adams recorded in his autobiography, "I said I had read his Letters to Dr. Cooper in which he had advanced, that Nobody ever got cold by going into a cold Church . . . but the Theory was so little consistent with my experience, that I thought it a Paradox. However I had so much curiosity to hear his reasons, that I would run the risk of a cold. The doctor then began an harangue, upon Air and cold and Respiration and Perspiration, with which I was so much amused that I soon fell asleep, and left him with his Philosophy together."[14]

Human interests did not simply influence the subjects of science, they also affected the logic of scientific argument. The Dutch lawyer and mathematician Willem Jakob 's-Gravesande, elected to the Royal Society in 1715, suggested that since "we cannot immediately judge of all Physical Matters by our Senses," we must have "recourse to another just way of reasoning": "We must look upon as true, whatever being denied would destroy civil Society, and deprive us of the Means of Living." This blunt identification of truth and utility, natural philosophy and social theory, reflected a widespread belief that the earth—intricate, varied yet orderly—had been devised for human habitation. The moral and physical worlds revealed each other, for each was the work of the same designer. Nowhere was there tragedy or waste. As William Derham put it in his wildly popular collection of sermons, *Physico-Theology* (1713), "we see nothing wanting, nothing redundant, or frivolous, nothing botching, or ill-made."[15]

To natural theologians like Derham, the book of nature was legible to men of science. The investigation of nature gave testimony to the glories of the Creation. The English naturalist and theologian John Ray—like Derham, a fellow of the Royal Society—compactly summarized the argument from design in the title of his best-selling book, *The Wisdom of God Manifested in the Works of the Creation: in two parts: viz. The Heavenly Bodies, Elements, Meteors, Fossils, Vegetables, Animals, (Beasts, Birds, Fishes, and Insects) more particularly in the Body of the Earth, its Figure, Motion, and Consistency, and in the admirable Structure of the Bodies of Man, and other Animals, as also in their Generation, etc.* (1692). As Douglas Anderson has emphasized, the imperatives of natural theology were "as much civic and political" as they were "religious and scientific." At one point in *The Wisdom of God*, Ray gave voice to the Deity's intentions in designing the world: "I have provided thee with Materials whereon to exercise and employ thy Art and Strength . . . I have distinguished the Earth into Hills, and Valleys, and Plains, and Meadows, and Woods; all these parts capable of Culture and Improvement by thy Industry . . . I have furnished thee with all Materials for Building, as Stone, and Timber, and Slate, and Lime, and Clay, and Earth whereof to make Bricks and Tiles." And, perhaps most important, "I have planted in thy Nature a desire . . . for the improvement and advance of thy

Knowledge."[16] This was enough to make a (prospective) member of the Royal Society proud.

Franklin thought highly enough of Derham and Ray to commend *Physico-Theology* and *The Wisdom of God* in his curriculum for the Philadelphia Academy. Intriguingly, he put them under the heading "natural history." Their purpose was exhortation: Franklin hoped they would spark curiosity about the book of nature, leading young scholars to acquire knowledge that would be "of great Use to them" in their adult lives. Though Franklin had included Ray in the private liturgy he composed in 1728, "Articles of Belief and Acts of Religion," he had little use for theological speculation or doctrinal disputes. Work was the most important form of worship, and Ray's "natural piety" expressed itself through the improvement of the world.[17]

At times, Franklin's insistence that knowledge be useful went so far that he questioned the need for causal explanations. In the concluding section of *Experiments and Observations on Electricity* (1751), he boldly asserted that it was unnecessary to know "the Manner in which Nature executes her Laws; 'tis enough if we know the Laws themselves. 'Tis of real Use to know, that China left in the Air unsupported will fall and break; but how it comes to fall, and why it breaks, are Matters of Speculation. 'Tis a Pleasure indeed to know them, but we can preserve our China without it." The value of an opinion or conjecture was determined by its utility. If it was merely speculative, then it was not important. (Recall, however, that Franklin held an expansive view of utility. In 1783, while living in Paris, he witnessed one of the first successful balloon flights. A skeptic in the crowd wondered, What good is a balloon? It is a mere toy, serving no useful purpose. To this Franklin famously replied, What good is a newborn baby? As no one could predict all that a child might grow into, so no one could foresee the uses to which balloons might be put. Immediate use was an inappropriate standard for scientific research. After all, Franklin's own "first Experiments" with electricity had been "mere Matters of Amusement.")[18]

Scientific explanations were inseparable from human purposes. Franklin cut his logical teeth on a treatise widely known as *The Port-Royal Logic*, Antoine Arnauld and Pierre Nicole's *Logic; or, The Art of Thinking*. (Port Royal was the location of the French Catholic monastery to which Arnauld and Nicole belonged.) Franklin was not alone; the *Logic* enjoyed "almost unparalleled success" in England and on the Continent until the end of the nineteenth century. According to the Port Royalists, there are two kinds of truth, necessary and contingent. Necessary truths concern the "immutable essence" of things, independent of their existence. Classical geometry is concerned with this kind of truth. Contingent truths, by contrast, "concern existing things, especially human and contingent events, which may or may not come to exist when it is a question of the future, or which may not have occurred when it is a question of the past." Contingent truths do not admit of certainty; they are inferences under conditions of uncertainty, calculations of probability.[19]

According to Arnauld and Nicole, our assessment of contingent truths ought to combine a measure of their probability with an assessment of their importance. All too often, however, we fail to do so. For example, thunder makes some individuals apprehensive that they will be struck by lightning. "It is easy to show that this is unreasonable. For out of two million people, at most there is one who dies this way. We could even say that there is hardly a violent death that is less common. So then, our fear of some harm ought to be proportional not only to the magnitude of the harm, but also to the probability of the event." By the same token, we sometimes underestimate the significance of an event, even when we accurately forecast its probability. Franklin's "Advice to a Young Tradesman" called attention to the importance of the smallest events to a man's reputation. As Richard Saunders once warned, "Creditors have better memories than debtors." All too often, young tradesmen underestimated the cost of conduct that cast poor light on their character. Personal improvement was impossible for such men. True wisdom combined an appreciation for the likelihood of an event and an awareness of its human significance.[20]

Franklin's lack of interest in "matters of speculation" did not signal a complete abandonment of natural theology, however. From it he retained the idea that the world was complex and interdependent. Historians of science have frequently noted that Franklin's experiments and observations relied on a cluster of related concepts: circulation, flow, balance, equilibrium, and conservation. As an electrician, for example, Franklin's "primary claim to fame" lies in his formulation of what we now know as the principle of the conservation of charge: electric charge flows, but its quantity never changes; it can neither be created nor destroyed.[21] In natural history, this idea took the form of an appreciation for the delicate balance between an organism and its environment: "Whenever we attempt to mend the scheme of Providence and to interfere in the Government of the World, we had need be very circumspect lest we do more harm than Good. In New England they once thought Black-birds useless and mischievous to their corn, they made [Laws] to destroy them, the consequence was, the Black-birds were diminished but a kind of Worms which devoured their Grass, and which the Black-birds had been used to feed on increased prodigiously; Then finding their Loss in Grass much greater than their saving in corn they wished again for their Black-birds." Phenomena in the natural world are interdependent; changes in one area can have dramatic and unexpected consequences in another. The vital residue of natural theology in Franklin's thought was the belief that an organism is functionally integrated into its environments.[22]

How did population fit into this matrix of ideas? Franklin's friend and fellow scientist Ezra Stiles once wrote that population was "as properly a subject of systematical Science, as the theory of agriculture or raising and improving stock." Properly understood, the "general laws" of population would have "very useful and interesting applications." Stiles was thrilled at the prospect and more than a little impatient to make progress in this science. "The World is under a most amazing Improvement."[23] Stiles was not the first to imagine a systematic study of population. To understand Franklin's innovations in population theory, we need to learn more about the ideas and practices that preceded him.

Political Arithmetic

Populousness—an abundance of people—was a desideratum of European statecraft from the final third of the seventeenth century until the end of the eighteenth century.[24] It was a concern that crossed every cultural, linguistic, and national boundary. The seventeenth-century English political economist Sir William Petty argued that "fewness of people, is real poverty, and a Nation wherein are Eight Millions of people, is more than twice as rich as the same scope of Land wherein are but four." The leading German demographer Johann Peter Süssmilch agreed: "A state which has only half as many inhabitants as its circumstances and food permit, will be only half as fortunate, powerful and wealthy as it could and should be." Similar ideas were articulated from France to the Netherlands, Scotland to Italy. The first step to preserving a state was to increase its population.[25]

Europeans had, of course, long been concerned with population growth. All lived under the biblical injunction to "be fruitful, and multiply"

(Genesis 1:28), as all knew that "in the multitude of people is the king's honor" (Proverbs 14:28). Fertility was the work of Providence, and a large and thriving population was a sign of God's grace and favor. These traditional perspectives on population survived into the eighteenth century, when the French and English fought for bragging rights over the relative size of London and Paris. The larger of the two, everyone assumed, was greater and more glorious, giving testimony to the national preferences of Providence.

During the seventeenth century perspectives on population began to change. Prior to about 1650 populousness, as a political objective, was subordinated to dominion. The continental wars and colonial ventures of early modern kings and empires were organized around the pursuit of territory. Land was the key to strength and stability. Spain pursued the ideal of a "universal monarchy," combining spiritual dominion and unlimited territorial sovereignty. France and England sought to check Spain by adding to their own dominions.[26]

By the middle of the seventeenth century it was increasingly clear that the strength, stability, and grandeur of a state rested not simply on its acquisition of lands but also on its mastery of trade. This was closely connected to changes in warfare. Technical and tactical innovations, including both massive increases in the size of land forces and increased reliance on sea power, imposed overwhelming fiscal and political demands on states.[27] The costs of war exceeded the capacities of existing institutions and compelled reliance on a new and challenging source of wealth: the international market. And "for the nation, the state . . . to ground its military strength, national glory, and political stability upon commercial success . . . created a wholly new situation. It required a redefinition, or at the least a significant modification, of the very notion of strength."[28]

New perspectives on populousness were a direct outgrowth of this transformation in European statecraft. State survival rested on commercial success, achieved in the face of menacing international rivalries. As Charles Davenant argued in 1699, in the wake of England's war with France, "It is not extent of territory that makes a country powerful, but numbers of men well employed, convenient ports, a good navy, and a soil producing all sort of commodities."[29] A large population contributed to a nation's strength in several distinct yet related ways. It increased the number of productive hands, extending a nation's tax base and enabling greater quantities of labor to be invested in commodities. (Hence the concern with unproductive or idle hands. Mere numbers were not enough; as Gregory King famously argued, it was necessary to distinguish between those who "added to" and those who "subtracted from" the wealth of the kingdom.)[30] A large population also increased the breadth and depth of a nation's internal market, enabling a more extensive division of labor and greater circulation of commodities within the realm. (Hence the growing interest in the moral psychology of emulation. Dense urban populations encouraged interpersonal comparison; vanity and pride increased consumption.)[31] Most important of all, a large population helped keep wages low. According to widely accepted economic doctrines, the key to a nation's wealth lay in maintaining a favorable balance of trade. A nation had to sell—and sell cheap—to maintain its advantage in a competitive international market. One of the most important factors in the price of a commodity was the cost of labor. The cost of labor, in turn, was inversely related to population. When workers were scarce, wages increased; when workers were plentiful, wages declined. A large population was a critical mechanism for keeping wages low and commodities cheap. (Hence, too, the importance of the concept of a subsistence wage. Many writers assumed that laborers preferred leisure to labor, and that the amount of work they were prepared to undertake was directly related to the amount of money required to satisfy a set of basic needs. High wages simply decreased the number of hours an individual was willing to work.)[32]

The importance of population helped spur the emerging discipline of "political arithmetic," or "the art of reasoning by figures, upon things relating to government." According to one of its earliest practitioners, "The foundation of this art is to be laid in some competent knowledge of the numbers of the people." Political arithmetic sought to quantify life expectancy and population growth on the basis of a distinction between natural and artificial, or restrained and unrestrained, growth. For example, John Graunt's *Natural and Political Observations made upon the Bills of Mortality*— predicated on the belief that "the Art of Governing, and the true *Politics*, is how to preserve the Subject in *Peace* and *Plenty*"—sought to "understand the Land, and the hands of the Territory to be governed, according to all their intrinsic, and accidental differences."[33] The life expectancy of an individual represented a potential, from which he or she might deviate owing to the accidents of disease and misfortune or the good fortune of peace and a strong constitution. The rate of reproduction for groups was typically expressed in terms of its "doubling rate," or the period of time required to double its current population. And it was almost universally agreed that observed doubling rates were substantially below what nature made possible.[34]

The bound of nature was an imaginary ideal, given practical content by contemporary observation. For British writers, the distance between actual and potential was graphically demonstrated by the demographic paradox of London. As Graunt observed in 1662, London's bills of mortality recorded far more burials than christenings, while its building rates soared. The former indicated population loss—more deaths than births—while the latter suggested population growth. The solution to this puzzle, Graunt argued, was in-migration. London was "supplied" with people from the countryside. And supplied it was: according to modern demographers, London grew from approximately 200,000 inhabitants in 1600 to approximately 575,000 in 1700. This extraordinary growth occurred against a backdrop of relative stagnation in England's population as a whole. Having reached a peak of 5.5 million in the 1650s, England did not begin to grow again until the middle third of the eighteenth century. Given London's high mortality rates, the city's growth during the seventeenth century was purchased through the in-migration of nearly 900,000 individuals. As Graunt concluded, population growth in the countryside was sufficient to provide "the People, both of *London*, and itself."[35]

What accounted for the unnatural and low birth rate of London? Explanations varied. To some it was a problem of public health. London's air and water were notoriously bad, exposing its inhabitants to all manner of illness and diseases. Others viewed it as a problem of residency. English men lived in the city for months on end to conduct business, leaving their wives in the countryside. Some thought that hard labor made men more fertile and that the relatively sedentary life of the city lowered the birth rate. To these (and many other) factors were added the moral and physical hazards of prostitution and fornication. Sex that was too frequent, or with too many partners, was thought to render men and women barren.[36]

Regardless of the impact of environment or sexual mores, however, it was generally agreed that the greatest impediment to population was the difficulty of marriage. Between the sixteenth and eighteenth centuries, a distinctive form of household emerged in northwest Europe, in which "social and cultural norms dictated that couples wishing to marry and procreate should possess sufficient resources to establish an independent household." The norm of the "simple nuclear family" meant that individuals married on the expectation of economic independence and well-being. If economic opportunities were perceived to contract, then fewer men and women married, and they did so at a later age. This, in turn, lowered the birth rate. As Edmund Halley remarked in 1693, "The Growth and Increase of Mankind is not so much stinted by anything in the Nature of the *Species,* as it is from the cautious difficulty most People make to adventure on the state of *Marriage,* from the prospect of the Trouble and Charge of providing for a Family."[37]

Given this consensus on the causes of population decline, a wide range of policies designed to enable more people to marry at an earlier age were put forward. Marriage taxes, passed in time of war, should be revoked. New duties should be imposed on bachelors or anyone else who chose to remain celibate. (Miss Polly Baker would have approved.) Bounties should be offered to those with large families. Ready employment should be offered the poor. Sir William Petty thought that Ireland's population could be dramatically increased by encouraging "short marriages," dissolved after six months should the couple fail to conceive. He even suggested the possibility of "Californian Marriages," in which six men and six women were "conjugated" in a complex pattern "in order to beget many and well conditioned children." Petty's proposals might seem outlandish, but they reflected a growing willingness to view marriage in terms of its contribution to the public weal. The family was more than a metaphor for politics; it was a human institution, subject to regulation and manipulation, through which children were produced and cared for.[38]

To many European observers, efforts to directly manipulate population through policies governing family, taxation, sexuality, and immigration were inadequate. It appeared, particularly during the first half of the eighteenth century, that Europe's population was declining, giving rise to one of the great intellectual "set pieces" of the period: the debate over the populousness of the ancients and the moderns. In the *Persian Letters* Montesquieu had wondered "why it is that the world is so thinly populated in comparison with former times?" Nature itself seemed exhausted and decayed: the ancient world held many times more people than the present, and if the current rate of decline continued, the world would soon become "a desert." But the burden of responsibility for the earth's depopulation fell not on nature but on humans and the customs, habits, and forms of government they imposed on themselves. "Gentle methods of government have a wonderful effect on the propagation of the species," while "arbitrary power" led to poverty and depopulation. In the *Spirit of the Laws* Montesquieu extended the psychological and political range of this argument. The fertility of animals, he argued, is relatively constant. "But in the human species, the way of thinking, character, passions, fantasies, caprices, the idea of preserving one's beauty, the encumbrance of pregnancy, that of a too numerous family, disturb propagation in a thousand ways." Political centralization and territorial expansion, pursued by the kings of France, rendered life precarious. Fear and anxiety, no less than war and destruction, undermined population. New "laws are needed to favor the propagation of the human species." Montesquieu was doubtful of success; "an almost incurable ill is seen when depopulation is of long standing because of an internal vice and a bad government." He imagined but one possibility, modeled on the practice of the Romans: distribute land "to all of the families who have nothing" so that "not a moment for work is lost."[39]

Montesquieu gave intellectual weight to the depopulationist argument; others extended its range and compass. Population was an index of social health; depopulation indicated decay and corruption. Though Montesquieu did not indict commercial society in the decline of population, his proposed solution to depopulation was distinctly agrarian and noncommercial. Others made the connection explicit. According to the Scottish clergyman Robert Wallace, "The question concerning the number of mankind in ancient and modern times . . . is not to be considered as a matter of mere curiosity, but of the greatest importance; since it must be a strong presumption in favor of the customs or policy of any government, if, *caeteris paribus*, it is able to raise up and maintain a greater number of people." Wallace's *Dissertation on the Numbers of Mankind* was written to demonstrate that "ancient policy, ancient manners, and ancient customs, were better calculated to make nations great and populous, than modern policy, modern manners and modern customs."[40] By "modern" Wallace meant the whole cluster of customs, habits, and policies associated with commercial society.

David Hume recognized the importance of this challenge. "Of the Populousness of Ancient Nations"—written in response to a manuscript presented by Wallace to the Philosophical Society of Edinburgh in the summer of 1751—is the longest and most historically detailed of Hume's *Essays.* Hume thought it improbable that ancient civilizations were more populous than modern ones. "Their wars were more bloody and destructive, their governments more factious and unsettled, commerce and manufactures more feeble and languishing, and the general police more loose and irregular." By contrast, the "improvements and refinements" of modern society "seem all extremely useful to the encouragement of art, industry, and populousness."[41]

Wallace and Hume used population as a proxy for social and political health. Standing just to the side of their debate, however, were dramatic and violent events that complicate the picture. In 1745 the Scottish Highlands had served as a staging ground for the last Jacobite rebellion. (Jacobitism arose in response to the Glorious Revolution, in which the Catholic James II was deposed and the Protestants William of Orange and Mary Stuart brought to the throne. Jacobites, with the support of European powers, sought to restore the House of Stuart to the throne.) As in the failed rising of 1715, the rebellion was crushed, and scores of rebels were either publicly executed or hunted down and killed. Alongside a ruthless campaign to pacify the Highlands, Whigs sought to underwrite a policy of "state-sponsored improvement." According to Wallace, the Highlands were "almost a desert . . . whose present inhabitants are overwhelmed with ignorance and barbarity." The "late unprovoked rebellion" had prompted laws by which "the inhabitants of the Highlands may be brought from a state of barbarity and of slavery, to a state of civility and of independence." But commercial improvement was predicated on the presence of large numbers of laborers, and the effects of those reforms were limited to the most populous regions. It was necessary to "make opulence and industry penetrate into their innermost and most distant parts." Highlanders "can only be civilized, by being made industrious."[42] Economic development and population growth went hand in hand. Together, they would teach the virtues of industry and frugality and soften the warlike manners that had been sustained by clan culture. Debating Hume, Wallace had worried that the spread of commerce led to demographic disaster; confronted with rebellion in the Highlands, however, he embraced the power of commerce to channel passions, transform identities, and pacify societies.

The Peopling of British North America

If a growing population was the key to prosperity, then by the middle of the eighteenth century the Anglo-American world suffered from an embarrassment of riches. The combined population of the British Isles and mainland

North America grew from roughly 8.4 million in 1700 to 13.3 million in 1770. This growth was unevenly distributed in space and time. It was most visible in North America, which grew from one-twentieth of the population of the British Isles in 1700 to nearly one-fifth in 1770. The impact of population growth and movement was profound. In Scotland and Ireland, shortages of land drove thousands into poverty, spurring waves of emigration to North America in the decades prior to the Revolution. From Germany came thousands more, pushed by war, poverty, and religious persecution and pulled by independent immigration brokers who exchanged ocean passages for a term of indentured servitude. In the backcountry of North America, restive settlers seeking land pressed up against Native Americans, prompting increasingly hostile and frequently violent conflicts. These phenomena were unexpected and only dimly understood. They challenged the capacities of basic social and political institutions on both sides of the Atlantic.[43]

The British government feared that the flow of emigrants would lead to depopulation and economic devastation. If the population of Great Britain declined, then the labor pool would shrink. This would force up the price of wages. In turn, the cost of British manufactures would increase, and international competition would drive the British out of the market.

One long-standing bone of contention was the production of iron. The colonies contained astonishing mineral deposits. Most merchants and policy makers in London believed that as a source of raw materials (pig iron) the colonies were invaluable, but that as manufacturers of finished products like nails they were an economic threat. Even the production of bar iron— iron wrought into malleable bars—was dangerous. Colonial manufacturers would compete with the British on international markets and eliminate them from the fast-growing North American consumer market. Population doctrines were crucial to these arguments. As the merchant Joshua Gee explained to Parliament in 1738, "If their Forges and Manufactures are suffered to increase in the manner they now do, they will constantly drain this Kingdom of great Numbers of our People. . . . Want of Work at home, and a Prospect of higher Wages under new Masters abroad" will lead them to be "continually going from us to them, to the great Depopulation of their Mother Country."[44] Gee's fears were not unfounded. By the third quarter of the eighteenth century, British workers had discovered that the threat of emigration could be used as a bargaining chip in labor negotiations.[45] The Iron Act of 1750 reflected these conflicting imperatives and fears. To strengthen the imperial economy by decreasing reliance on foreign goods, it eliminated all duties on the importation of American pig and bar iron into Britain itself. But to prevent damage to the British iron industry—the bill was passed in the wake of a petitioning campaign by ironmasters, mine owners, and forest growers—it forbade the construction in the colonies of mills for rolling and slitting iron, forges for hammering iron, and furnaces for making steel.

Franklin had skewered moral and religious objections to uninhibited procreation in "The Speech of Miss Polly Baker." Countering the Iron Act—a piece of legislation backed by powerful economic interest groups— called for a different strategy. In *Observations concerning the Increase of Mankind, Peopling of Countries, etc.*, Franklin turned from social satire to the straitlaced methods of political arithmetic. (This distinction is provisional; as we shall see, *Observations* is a rhetorically complicated document.) Franklin's argument, presented in twenty-four crisply written sections, was breathtakingly simple: "There is . . . no Bound to the prolific Nature of Plants or Animals, but what is made by their crowding and interfering with each other's Means of Subsistence. Was the Face of the Earth vacant of other Plants, it might be gradually sowed and overspread with one Kind only; as, for Instance, with Fennel; and were it empty of other Inhabitants, it might in a few Ages be replenished from one Nation only; as, for Instance, with Englishmen." No one, prior to Franklin, had argued that population levels are strictly determined by the available means of subsistence.[46] Changing the customs and laws of marriage might alter the rate of reproduction, but it could not "increase a People beyond the Means provided for their Subsistence." Neither could restricting emigration or creating opportunities for immigration. In all but the shortest of time frames, "natural Generation" ensured that there were no "vacancies" in a country's population.[47] (Fifty years later this claim seized the attention of Thomas Robert Malthus, with surprising consequences. We will return to this topic in the final section of this chapter.)

Population was determined by the means of subsistence, but the latter, Franklin argued, varied with a territory's stage of development. When first discovered, North America was fully settled—but with hunters, not husbandmen. "The Hunter, of all Men, requires the greatest Quantity of Land from whence to draw his Subsistence," while "the Husbandman" subsisted on "much less," and "the Manufacturer" required "least of all." The introduction of agriculture by Europeans created ecological space for a population explosion. "Hence Marriages in America are more general, and more generally early, than in Europe."[48]

Franklin's argument was an early contribution to the "four stages" theory of history. According to four stages theory, societies "naturally" or "normally" progress over time through "four more or less distinct and consecutive stages, each corresponding to a different mode of subsistence": hunting, pasturage, agriculture, and commerce. "To each of these modes corresponded different sets of ideas and institutions relating to law, property, and government, and also different sets of customs, manners, and morals." Four stages theory provided a model for the unintended but lawlike development of societies. It bears an obvious affinity with the concept of improvement and played a crucial role in eighteenth-century social and political theory. In the 1750s there were pioneering formulations of four stages theory in Scotland (Lord Kames, Adam Smith) and France (Turgot, Helvétius). Franklin became friends with each of these men, but only *after* he had written the *Observations;* indeed, the *Observations* precedes the published work of any of Franklin's European peers. Perhaps we should not look for direct influences; we may be dealing with a moment in which similarly minded men, independently working on common problems, came to comparable conclusions. We know, for example, that Franklin was familiar with the classical and contemporary authors who provided the intellectual foundations for the four stages theory. In 1749 alone he borrowed James Logan's copy of Lucretius and recommended Grotius, Pufendorf, and Locke in his curriculum for the Philadelphia Academy. Unfortunately, Franklin rarely noted the sources with which he was working when he developed his ideas, and we cannot be sure whether, or how, these works fit into the *Observations.*[49]

If there were a proximate cause of Franklin's embrace of four stages theory, it was undoubtedly his exchanges with the Scottish-born and Boston-based physician and historian William Douglass. Franklin and Douglass had a long history together: in 1722 Douglass had been one of the "ingenious Men" who contributed to James Franklin's *New-England Courant,* and in that capacity he was among the first to read, and commend, sixteen-year-old Benjamin's "Silence Dogood" essays. No direct correspondence has survived, but it is clear that Franklin and Douglass remained in contact; around the time Franklin composed the *Observations,* they exchanged notes on colonial population and disease. Moreover, Franklin knew, and recommended to others, Douglass's *A Summary, Historical and Political, of the First Planting,*

Progressive Improvements, and Present State of the British Settlements in North America. In the first volume, published in 1747, Douglass suggested that society appeared in its rudest and most imperfect form among some of the natives of North America. They may be considered "the youngest Brother and meanest of Mankind." They have "no Civil Government, no Religion, no Letters; . . . they do not cultivate the Earth by planting or grazing . . . they do not provide for To-Morrow . . . [and] when they have good Luck in Hunting, they eat and sleep until all is consumed and then they go a Hunting again."[50]

Contemporaries sometimes expressed this idea by saying that Indians lived in a "natural state." Franklin did so himself in marginal notes to Allan Ramsay's *Thoughts on the Origin and Nature of Government* (1769).[51] It is crucial to distinguish this "natural state" from the "state of nature" familiar from social contract theories like that of John Locke. In the latter, individuals are said to be naturally free and independent, subject only to the law of nature. This condition is "inconvenient"—there is no settled law to establish right and wrong, no fair or independent judge to resolve disputes, and no power to enforce justice—and so individuals consent to join with others to create a civil society and authorize a government to act on their behalf. In social contract theories, the state of nature is not a moment in time but a juridical condition, a conceptualization of the moral identities individuals possess even when they lack a government. The point of this abstraction is to call attention to the conditional character of political authority. As Thomas Jefferson put it in the Declaration of Independence, when government violates its end and purpose, "it is the Right of the People to alter or to abolish it."

Franklin, Douglass, and others committed to the four stages theory of history did not look to the "natural state" of humans to provide a moral foundation or conceptual bedrock on which to build legitimate governments. Quite the opposite: it was antifoundational, a historical (and conceptual) reference point from which to measure the accomplishments of civilization. In a well-known letter to Peter Collinson, written in 1753, Franklin claimed that

> the proneness of human Nature to a life of ease, of freedom from care and labor appears strongly in the little success that has hitherto attended every attempt to civilize our American Indians, in their present way of living, almost all their Wants are supplied by the spontaneous Productions of Nature, with the addition of very little

labor, if hunting and fishing may indeed be called labor when Game is so plenty, they visit us frequently, and see the advantages that Arts, Sciences and compact Society procure us, they are not deficient in natural understanding and yet they have never shown any Inclination to change their manner of life for ours, or to learn any of our Arts; When an Indian Child has been brought up among us, taught our language and habituated to our Customs, yet if he goes to see his relations and make one Indian Ramble with them, there is no persuading him ever to return.

As Franklin makes clear in the next sentence, he was not making an ethnographic generalization about indolent Native Americans in contrast to energetic Europeans. Instead, he was addressing a general feature of human nature: "That this is not natural [to them] merely as Indians, but as men, is plain from this, that when white persons of either sex have been taken prisoners young by the Indians, and lived a while among them, though ransomed by their Friends, and treated with all imaginable tenderness to prevail with them to stay among the English, yet in a Short time they become disgusted with our manner of life, and the care and pains that are necessary to support it, and take the first good Opportunity of escaping into the Woods, from whence there is no reclaiming them." Franklin was not imagining things; the unwillingness of English and French settlers, once having been taken captive by Indians, to return to European colonial lives was well known to his contemporaries. This phenomenon cast glaring light on the paradoxical nature of improvement. The institutions of civilization—cities and states, private property and public markets, but also clubs and taverns, newspapers and journals, as well as norms of behavior like politeness and sociability—emerged in time, as societies moved through the stages of historical development. The justification for these institutions did not lie in their coherence with the law of nature, or in an original act of consent, but in their capacity to improve the quality of human life. And as the behavior of "the white Indians of colonial America" indicated, that was not a foregone conclusion. Adam Smith, working independently in Scotland, came to a similar insight. "Power and riches . . . keep off the summer shower, not the winter storm." They leave an individual "as much, and sometimes more exposed than before, to anxiety, to fear, and to sorrow; to diseases, to danger, and to death." And yet—Smith relished the paradox—"it is well that nature" deceives us into pursuing "baubles and trinkets," for it is this deception that "keeps in continual motion the industry of mankind." Neither Franklin nor Smith doubted the virtues of civilization; neither glorified the life of the "noble savage." But both were keenly aware of the complex, contingent, and sometimes ironic character of improvement. Four stages theory provided a model for the historical development of modern societies, but it did not compel its adherents to view that process as a simple, linear progression.[52]

"A Nation well regulated is like a Polypus"

The sheer size of the North American landmass ensured that it would remain agricultural for many generations. Until it was "fully settled, Labor will never be cheap," and high wages were inconsistent with manufacturing.[53] The abundance of uncultivated land made manufacturing unprofitable. As Adam Smith observed twenty-five years later in the pivotal third book of *Wealth of Nations*, the prosperity of North America "is founded altogether in agriculture." England's riches, by contrast, were founded in commerce and manufactures. This distinction enabled a vibrant division of labor between the mother country and her colonies. Franklin sought to be reassuring: "The Danger therefore of these Colonies interfering with their Mother Country in Trades that depend on Labor, Manufactures, etc. is too remote to require the Attention of Great-Britain."[54]

While land in North America provided refuge for many a poor Scotch or Irish farmer, it was not a drain on the population of the British Isles. To capture this thought, Franklin used an extraordinary metaphor. "A Nation well regulated is like a Polypus; take away a Limb, its place is soon supplied; cut it in two, and each deficient Part shall speedily grow out of the Part remaining. Thus if you have Room and Subsistence enough, as you may by dividing, make ten Polyps out of one, you may of one make ten Nations, equally populous and powerful; or rather, increase a Nation tenfold in Numbers and Strength."[55]

Franklin described the "singular Properties of that most unaccountable of all Creatures the Polyp" in *Poor Richard Improved* of 1751. "Found at the Bottom of Ditches, and standing Waters " and often visible only under a microscope, polyps "do not seem to be of different Sexes" but instead reproduce by "Buds and Branches." Even more "wonderful, and almost beyond

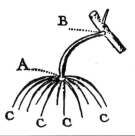

The Figure of the Fresh-water Polypus, *sticking to a Twig.*

"Observations and Experiments upon the Fresh-water Polypus, by Monsieur Trembley, at the Hague," *Philosophical Transactions* 42 (1742). "The *Polypus* multiplies more or less, as he is more or less fed, and as the Weather is more or less warm. If plenty of Food, and a sufficient Degree of Warmth concur, they multiply prodigiously. . . . If the Body of a *Polypus* is cut into two Parts transversly, each of those Parts becomes a complete *Polypus*. . . . It creeps, it eats, it grows, and it multiplies; and all that, as much as a *Polypus* which never had been cut."

Belief . . . when cut into a great many Pieces, each several Piece becomes a complete Polyp."[56]

Franklin was not alone in his fascination with polyps. First brought to the attention of European scientific communities in 1741, polyps were scrutinized for their astonishing and apparently unlimited reproductive power.[57] Polyps were freshwater animals, but they reproduced like plants, from cuttings. Contemporaries were fascinated and horrified. "The story of the Phoenix who is reborn from its ashes, fabulous as it is, offers nothing more marvelous than the discovery" of the polyp. "Nature goes farther than our chimeras."[58] Investigators created tiny armies of polyps, multiplying one into a hundred in the well of a microscope. In a macabre eighteenth-century version of bioengineering, they experimented with the polyp's potential for mutation. By cutting a polyp at the right time in the right place, it was possible to fabricate a creature with seven heads and bodies, joined by a single tail.

The discovery of the polyp raised difficult and disturbing questions. Some concerned basic categories of classification. Was the polyp a plant or an animal? Other questions—no less a part of eighteenth-century natural philosophy—were speculative and metaphysical. As previously noted, arguments from design, like that of William Derham, held that the visible world confirmed the Creation. Only God could have created the wondrously varied yet intricately interrelated patterns and structures of nature. And if there was a plan to nature, then the processes of nature were confined to the patterns and purposes established by God. The identity of plants and animals was fixed at the Creation. The polyp, by its ability to grow and reproduce on its own, and by its capacity for novel mutation, threatened to shatter this idea. In France, especially, the discovery of the polyp helped spur the development of materialist doctrines, according to which living matter had a capacity to organize itself in ways that were not directly under God's control. Nature was not preformed; it was alive, changing, in constant flux. The evolutionary perspectives of La Mettrie, Buffon, and Diderot owe their origins to the humble polyp.[59]

Opponents of materialism fought back. In France, Rousseau mocked the "vain" objects of science, which included the study of insects that "reproduce in an extraordinary way." Voltaire—an antievolutionist as well as an antimaterialist—sought to discredit the polyp as a scientific irrelevance. In England, the physician, antiquary, and fellow of the Royal Society James Parsons called attention to the mistaken ideas "inadvertently drawn from the late curious and useful Experiments upon the Polypus." The debate played out for decades.[60] In many respects, it has never died out.

Franklin, with his brilliant ear for language, saw in the polyp a powerful metaphor for political communities.[61] The polyp grew and reproduced with ease, limited only by the available means of subsistence. As a metaphor for the body politic, the polyp did not suggest hierarchy and differentiation. That had been the function of natural analogies in the great chain of being, and the concept remained crucial to the argument from design. Even the division of species into male and female seemed to imply inequality. The polyp, by contrast, was an organism capable of division and replication, in which each part was capable of becoming a whole. As a metaphor, it pointed to horizontal ties between equal parts. As we will see in chapter 4, that is precisely how Franklin imagined the British Empire: as an association of equals. Hence, when it came to population growth, he did not see disruption and instability, as when a child outgrows its parents, but mutual benefit. The doubling rate for the population of North America was an astonishingly short twenty-five years. In one hundred years "the greatest Number of Englishmen will be on this Side the Water. What an Accession of Power to the British Empire by Sea as well as Land! What Increase of Trade and Navigation! What Numbers of Ships and Seamen!"[62]

Immigration and Identity

Franklin's analysis of the relationship between land, economic development, and population growth gave him confidence that North America could be occupied. But by whom? In a satiric essay of 1751, "Rattle-Snakes for Felons," Franklin lampooned the British practice of transporting criminals to the colonies. Colonists had complained of convict transportation since the early eighteenth century. According to one Virginian, transportation threatened to turn the colony into "hell upon earth, another Siberia." But Parliament persisted, defending it as vital to the "improvement and well peopling [of] the colonies." Franklin sharpened his quill, thanked "our *Mother Country*" for her "tender *parental* Concern," and offered, as a token of gratitude, to send a rattlesnake to England for every convict relocated to America.[63]

Some 55,000 convicts were transported to the colonies of North America prior to the Revolution, constituting just under 7 percent of the total pool of immigrants to this time. Another 200,000, or 25 percent of the total, were bound laborers. The largest group were slaves: approximately 322,000, or 41 percent of the total, during the same period. These numbers are stunning and bear repetition: "From the founding of Jamestown until the Revolution, nearly three-fourths of all immigrants to the thirteen colonies arrived in some condition of unfreedom."[64]

Franklin's relationship to slavery is complex, and it changed over the course of his life. It will be explored in depth in chapter 5. Here we need note simply that when Franklin wrote the *Observations* he was clear in his mind (though not in his practice) that slavery was economically irrational, morally corrupting, and physically destructive. "The Labor of Slaves can never be so cheap here as the Labor of working Men is in Britain. Any one may compute it." Why, then, did Americans purchase slaves? Because their movements could be controlled. "Hired Men are continually leaving their Master . . . and setting up for themselves"; slaves did not have this option. But slavery came at a cost. The children of families that owned slaves learned to be "disgusted with Labor," and were "educated in Idleness," making them "unfit to get a Living by Industry." The slaves themselves were physically destroyed. "Worked too hard, and ill fed, their Constitutions are broken, and the Deaths among them are more than the Births; so that a continual Supply is needed from *Africa*."[65]

Ideally, the flow of immigrants into North America would no longer include convicts or slaves. So much seems clear. But then, in the final two paragraphs of the *Observations*, immediately after declaring that "a Nation well regulated is like a Polypus," Franklin advanced a set of ideas that have proven jarring and problematic, from his day to ours:

> Since Detachments of English from Britain sent to America, will have their Places at Home so soon supplied and increase so largely here; why should the Palatine Boors be suffered to swarm into our Settlements, and by herding together establish their Language and Manners to the Exclusion of ours? Why should Pennsylvania, founded by the English, become a Colony of *Aliens,* who will shortly be so numerous as to Germanize us instead of our Anglifying them, and will never adopt our Language or Customs, any more than they can acquire our Complexion.
>
> Which leads me to add one Remark: That the Number of purely white People in the World is proportionally very small. All Africa is black or tawny. Asia chiefly tawny. America (exclusive of the new Comers) wholly so. And in Europe, the Spaniards, Italians, French, Russians and Swedes, are generally of what we call a swarthy Complexion; as are the Germans also, the Saxons only excepted, who with the English, make the principal Body of White People on the Face of the Earth. I could wish their Numbers were increased. And while we are, as I may call it, *Scouring* our Planet, by clearing America of Woods, and so making this Side of our Globe reflect a brighter Light to the Eyes of Inhabitants in Mars or Venus, why should we in the Sight of Superior Beings, darken its People? why increase the Sons of Africa, by planting them in America, where we have so fair an Opportunity, by excluding all Blacks and Tawneys, of increasing the lovely White and Red? But perhaps I am partial to the Complexion of my Country, for such Kind of Partiality is natural to Mankind.[66]

What are we to make of these blunt words? Contemporary scholars cannot agree. Sympathetic biographers have called Franklin's position "insular," "prejudiced," and "ethnocentric." But they have also insisted that these paragraphs are momentary failures and do not reflect Franklin's deepest values or most enduring beliefs.[67] Literary critics have countered that Franklin's prose should not always be taken at face value. Franklin was a master of raillery and ridicule; some of his most important essays seethe with bitter irony and savage satire. In this instance, Franklin's final sentence tips his hand: he has, once again, pursued a "strategy of indirection," invoking cultural and racial identities in order to call them into question.[68] Franklin's critics, from political philosophers and historians of immigration to students of race and ethnicity, have rejected these possibilities. Franklin meant what he said and said what he meant. Or perhaps he simply saw political value in the image of an all-white North America. In either case, he was an early contributor to the rhetoric of nativism. Like those who followed in his footsteps, he suggested that economic growth and political development were inseparable from the preservation of racial and national homogeneity.[69]

At stake in this dispute are Franklin's character and standing. But that is not all; how we make sense of Franklin depends on what we mean by terms like *race, ethnicity,* and *nation.* What beliefs and practices do these terms refer to? What role ought they to play in our explanation of complex events? How do they intersect with other dimensions of life, like sex and gender or politics and economics? Were Franklin's comments about complexion racially tinged or racially motivated? Did his anxieties about German ethnic identity determine his position on immigration, or did they simply reinforce and exacerbate views rooted in economic competition or political struggles? [70]

To understand Franklin's politics of population, we need to know more about the contemporary meaning of the language of color (black, white, tawny) and categories of ethnicity and nationality (German, English, American). Until the final third of the eighteenth century, categories of complexion were ambiguous and unstable. Personal attributes like social standing or possession of good manners were "more explicitly important" to British assessments of themselves and others than were "physical attributes such as skin color, shape of the nose, or texture of the hair." To be sure, the binary distinction between "black" and "white" had assumed increasingly well-defined and socially significant meanings in North America. But these circulated fluidly among a great many categories of identity and difference, inclusion and exclusion.[71] For example, a draft table of demographic data for the colony of New Jersey, compiled for *Poor Richard Improved,* included two different sets of classifications. A 1737–38 survey (bottom right) divided the population into "Whites" and "Negroes and other Slaves," noting the basic age distribution of the groups. A survey taken eight years later (top right) indicated how many of the whites were Quaker and referred simply to

Census of New Jersey, 1737, 1738, 1745, prepared for *Poor Richard Improved*, 1750 . (Courtesy American Philosophical Society.)

"slaves." (The reason for counting Quakers is not given but undoubtedly had to do with calculating the number eligible for military service.) Of course, not all Negroes were slaves. Indeed, not all Africans were black, nor were all blacks of African descent. Pennsylvania enlistment papers from the Seven Years' War often indicated a soldier's complexion alongside his height, age, trade, and place of birth. This information was especially useful in rounding up troops who deserted. In one collection, ten out of eighty-six recruits are identified as having a "black" complexion; in another, four out of seventeen. Some of these soldiers may have been freedmen; in a depressed economy, military service was often the best employment option available to Africans who were not enslaved. But over half the "black" soldiers were born in Germany, Ireland, or England.[72]

The relationship between skin color and specific racial or ethnic characteristics remained unsystematic until the latter half of the eighteenth century. The consolidation of Native American identities into a single Indian race appears to have crossed a threshold in the early 1760s. Frontier settlers like the Paxton Boys mobilized against what they considered to be a single "Indian" enemy. Native American spiritual leaders, in turn, sought to foster pan-Indian unity in opposition to Euro-Americans. "In parallel ways, Pontiac and the Paxton Boys preached the novel idea that all Native people were 'Indians,' that all Euro-Americans were 'Whites,' and that all on one side must unite to destroy the other."[73] The emergence of a consolidated and racialized black identity came later, during the Revolution, when the theory and practice of slavery came under mounting pressure from abolitionists.[74]

Where does Franklin fit into this shifting set of ideas? He often invoked national identities in order to call attention to their plasticity. In the same breath he spoke of Germans with contempt and low humor, praised their "industry and frugality," and attributed their distinctiveness to the effects of custom, habit, and law. "Nature" could not account for the differences between English and German settlers; "it must arise from Institution." And as we have seen, he mocked the Paxton Boys' racialized rhetoric of collective guilt. Was it "right" to kill men because they have "reddish brown Skin, and black Hair," and "some People of that Sort" have killed our relatives?[75] These comments and observations were consistent with four stages theory, which conceived of the differences between societies in terms of stages of historical development, and not natural or essential differences. But like most eighteenth-century natural philosophers, Franklin wondered whether there were any stable distinctions within the human species. Were "Negroes" less susceptible to the heat and more vulnerable to cold than "whites"? Franklin was unsure; he was skeptical of the former, since it was "alleged" to prove the "necessity" of using African slaves on sugar plantations, but he had observed several instances of the latter.[76]

Public reception of the *Observations* only partially solves this mystery. For several years copies of the manuscript circulated among Franklin's friends in North America and Great Britain. Reactions were generally enthusiastic. Cadwallader Colden and John Bartram took "exception" to the final paragraph of Franklin's treatise, but otherwise we have no recorded response to Franklin's invocation of an all-white America.[77] Indeed, there *was* no audience for it, either in the colonies or in Great Britain. No one in a position of authority talked openly or seriously about the elimination of slavery or the slave trade in the early 1750s. (Very few outside circles of power did so, either.) The very implausibility of the idea lends credence to the suggestion that Franklin's racially and ethnically homogenized vision was meant satirically. He simply could not have hoped to have gotten political mileage out of it.

For unknown reasons Franklin—who was not normally shy—resisted publication. Finally, in the winter of 1754, he alerted William Shirley that he "would not object" if his treatise were printed as an appendix to a pamphlet on imperial affairs by William Clarke. Clarke was dilatory—Shirley was still trying to edit his manuscript seven months later—but finally, in the summer of 1755, Franklin's *Observations* was printed in Boston.[78] Copies almost immediately appeared in London. When Franklin reprinted the *Observations* in 1760 as an appendix to his own essay *The Interest of Great Britain Considered, With Regard to Her Colonies,* he removed the two final paragraphs. He also changed the language of a key sentence, so that it no longer declared every slave "*by Nature* a Thief." Instead, it held that every slave was "from the nature of slavery a thief." These modifications in the text suggest a change of heart. But what kind of change? Had Franklin revised his views? Was he embarrassed by what he had written? Were the final two paragraphs no longer politically relevant? Or did he conclude that they were too opaque, an ironic gesture that had failed? Unfortunately, the record is silent.

Four years later things had changed. Copies of Franklin's original treatise, including the final two paragraphs, were reissued by his opponents in the run-up to the 1764 Assembly election. Franklin's reference to "Palatine Boors" was viewed as a slur—it was like calling Germans "a *Herd* of *Hogs*," wasn't it?—and news of Franklin's perfidy spread through every Dutch coffeehouse. Franklin claimed not to understand the flap and defensively argued that the word *boor* meant nothing more than "peasant." But the damage had been done, and his support among German voters evaporated. One

The German Bleeds, 1764. (Courtesy the Library Company of Philadelphia.) The man in the broad-brimmed hat is Israel Pemberton, a hated symbol of Quaker pacifism to frontier people. To the left is Franklin, with a copy of the Assembly's resolution calling for an end to proprietarial government. "The German Bleeds & bears the Furs / Of Quaker Lords & Savage Curs / Th' Hibernian frets with new Disaster / And kicks to fling his broad brim'd Master / But help at hand Resolves to hold down / Th' Hibernian's Head or tumble all down."

clever writer suggested that Germans "swarm" into Philadelphia on election day and "herd together" at the polling place. That is precisely what they did, and for the first time Franklin was defeated in an Assembly election.[79]

This heated reaction suggests that the real work of Franklin's final paragraphs in the *Observations* concerned the regulation of German immigration, not the creation of an all-white America. Between 1683 and 1783 approximately 500,000 men, women, and children left Germany for Hungary, Russia, Spain, and Great Britain. Roughly 125,000 came to British North America. Most landed at Philadelphia, and about three-fourths settled in Pennsylvania. By 1775 one out of every three Pennsylvanians was German speaking. This massive migration, which one historian has called a "prototype of later, nineteenth-century, transatlantic mass migrations," was "not the result of a *concerted* governmental effort." Instead, it was built on a private and market-driven recruiting network, in which "redemptioneers" sought out potential migrants and offered them transportation to the colonies in exchange for five years of indentured servitude.[80]

Prior to the Seven Years' War, Pennsylvania Germans resisted assimilation. They supported German printing houses, patronized German stores, and taught their children in German. Christopher Sauer—the man who drove Franklin's German-language paper, the *Philadelphische Zeitung*, out of business—"assaulted all proposals that hinted at closer English-German union in religious or political affairs in Pennsylvania." Sauer had "one simple lesson" he "hammered home": "Support the Quakers and avoid courts, lawyers, politics, and unnecessary involvement with English-speakers that might endanger our language, our families and customs, and our faith."[81]

Franklin's ire at German immigrants began to crystallize in 1747, when they refused to heed his call to join the Association. Franklin had praised "the *brave* and *steady* GERMANS." And he had translated, printed, and distributed a German-language edition of *Plain Truth*. But it was to no avail; his campaign was immediately countered by Sauer, and very few Germans took the oath of engagement. Their reasoning—that if they remained neutral, then it did not matter whether the British or the French governed the colony—disturbed Franklin. Would German immigrants make "good Subjects" and remain "faithful to the British Interest"?[82] (Franklin's reaction points to the porous boundary between "private" and "public," or "voluntary" and "compulsory," forms of organization. Though the Association was voluntary and private, failure to join was taken as a sign of civic untrustworthiness by individuals in positions of power.)

Franklin was not the only English speaker to be worried by the independence of German settlers. By law, aliens entering Pennsylvania were required to take an oath of allegiance to the crown and to the government of the colony. At midcentury this formal gesture seemed inadequate. Loyalty oaths were notoriously feeble devices for uncovering a person's intentions. Any liar or hypocrite could evade them. Complicating matters, some immigrants, like the Mennonites, refused oaths on religious grounds. Was this simply a ploy, enabling them to evade civic obligations like militia service? Even the Mennonites acknowledged that there was no easy answer to this question.[83] Colonial and metropolitan authorities struggled to find alternative ways of identifying and measuring a person's commitment to the British Empire. One increasingly popular option was to measure loyalty in terms of cultural identification with Britain.

By the early 1750s parliamentarians and members of the metropolitan elite solicited Franklin's views on German immigration. Manuscript copies of the *Observations* were eagerly read and discussed.[84] In private correspondence Franklin embraced proposals to establish free English schools in German communities, to require that all legal documents be written in English, and to require that all public officials be competent speakers of English. But he backpedaled before more draconian proposals circulating in London, including forced intermarriage and the suppression of German-language printing houses. "Methods of great tenderness should be used, and nothing that looks like a hardship be imposed. Their fondness for their own Language and Manners is natural: It is not a Crime. When People are induced to settle a new Country by a promise of Privileges, that Promise should be bona fide performed, and the Privileges never infringed: If they are, how shall we be believed another time, when we want to People another colony?" All that was needed was a plan to distribute German immigrants more evenly rather than allow them to cluster in Pennsylvania.[85]

The one practical consequence of these conversations was the creation of the Society for Promoting Religious Knowledge and English Language among the German Immigrants in Pennsylvania. At its height the society sponsored eleven schools, serving about 750 students. Opposition within the German-speaking community was fierce, however, and the schools closed after only six years.[86] To colonial observers, however, it was increasingly obvious that formal programs of assimilation were unnecessary; the incorporation of German-speaking Pennsylvanians was already under way. Ironically, the initiative often came from within the German community. Established immigrants complained loudly of the low moral standards and poor behavior of the recently arrived. German-language publishers responded with advice manuals, using dialogues between *Einwohner* (well-settled Germans) and *Neukomer* (the newly arrived) to provide cultural instruction. These did not call simply for the re-creation of Palatine life in North America. English-language manuals were printed for the first time between 1748 and 1751. German speakers began to write wills and avail themselves of English courts as they discovered the limits of customary practices in new social settings. Churches sought formal recognition by the government as a means of strengthening their internal institutions. Across Pennsylvania, German-language settlers were finding new ways in which public law could be put to use in private life.[87]

Coda: The Half-life of an Idea

The quasi-voluntary incorporation and assimilation of Pennsylvania's German-speaking community is precisely what advocates of commercial society intended. Empires are *always* about identities, about the destruction of "old" peoples and the construction of a "new" people. This was no less true of the commercial empire of the eighteenth century than of the territorial empires of ancient Rome. Indeed, it was precisely the power of commerce to change identities that made it attractive to so many. Without this capacity, Franklin and others could not have looked to the spread of commercial society as a civilizing force.[88]

To end here, however, would be to miss the dramatic second act of Franklin's *Observations*. As previously noted, Franklin deleted the final two paragraphs of his treatise when he reprinted it as an appendix to his 1760 pamphlet *The Interest of Great Britain*. In this form, the *Observations* ended with the evocative metaphor "a Nation well regulated is like a Polypus." It made no reference to German immigration, nor did it express a preference for "White People." Franklin included this version in the landmark 1769 edition of *Experiments and Observations*. In this edited form, it became the touchstone for Franklin's reputation as a student of population. The impact of Franklin's two key claims—that population levels were determined by the available means of subsistence and that the doubling rate for the population of North America was an astonishingly short twenty-five years—was immediate and profound. For example, the radical English philosopher Richard Price responded to the *Observations* in a lengthy public letter that was printed as an independent pamphlet in 1769, quickly reprinted in the *Philosophical Transactions* of the Royal Society, and then included in Price's own widely read financial and demographic treatise, *Observations on Reversionary Payments* (1771). And Samuel Johnson—no friend of the Revolution—ended the original page proofs of his rebuke of the colonies, *Taxation no Tyranny* (1775), with a rebuttal of Franklin's prediction that the population of the colonies would soon exceed that of Great Britain.[89]

Not every reference to Franklin's ideas mentioned the *Observations*. Adam Smith argued in the *Wealth of Nations* that "the most decisive mark of the prosperity of any country is the increase of the number of its inhabitants. In Great Britain, and in most other European countries, they are not expected to double in less than five hundred years. In the British colonies in

North America, it has been found that they double in twenty or five-and-twenty years." Smith's modern editors suggest that the unacknowledged source for these figures was Richard Price. Price, in turn, vouched for his data by citing the work of Franklin and Ezra Stiles. Stiles, a Congregational minister from Connecticut and the future president of Yale College, was dedicated to the study of meteorology and demography. His own calculations concerning the growth of North America rested on the work of a friend and fellow natural philosopher—Benjamin Franklin.[90] Similar stories can be repeated scores of times. Eighteenth-century rules of intellectual etiquette were lax; the recycling of texts and arguments was widespread and generally went unpunished. Franklin's observations were embraced and duplicated, even after the connection to his essay had been lost.

One route through the intellectual thicket merits special attention. In the late eighteenth century an intense row broke out over the state of Britain's population. Was it rising or declining? In particular, was it rising too fast for the public good? Growing poor rolls suggested that that might be the case. But actual numbers were hard to come by. The government's attempt to take a census in 1754 had been blocked in Parliament, and a private effort to in 1781 was halted when poll takers were threatened with everything from fists to the loss of employment.[91] The first official census was not taken until 1801. In the absence of hard facts, the debate was speculative, abstract, and philosophical.

In this context, the English novelist and radical philosopher William Godwin sought to prove that the perfection of the human species was possible through the free exercise of reason. Our actions, Godwin argued, depend upon our beliefs about the world; if we change our beliefs, then we also change our actions. Moreover, there are no inherent limits to reform. If, through the continual application of reason, we are able to free ourselves from the shackles of custom, habit, and tradition, then vice can be "extirpated from the world." The first step is to overhaul (and drastically curtail) government, since it inhibits improvement "by its very nature." Once that is done, life on earth can be humanized. Freedom and equality will replace domination and degradation, and an increased standard of living will be made available to England's growing population. Godwin combed the past for kindred spirits and claimed to have found one in Franklin: "Who shall say where this species of improvement must stop? . . . The celebrated Franklin conjectured, that 'mind would one day become omnipotent over matter.' "[92]

Godwin met his match in Thomas Robert Malthus, a young minister in the Church of England. Malthus was no rhetorical slouch. His 1798 *Essay on the Principle of Population*—arguably the most important work in the history of population studies—was written from the ironic point of view of a disappointed and disheartened idealist. Malthus ardently wished that Godwin were right. He, too, dreamed of perfection. But "he has not acquired that command over his understanding which would enable him to believe what he wishes, without evidence, or to refuse his assent to what might be unpleasing, when accompanied with evidence." Dreams were no substitute for hard thinking. It was time for a bracing slap from reality. The pursuit of perfection was a fantasy. What was the truth of science that forced Malthus's dreams down to earth? That population always and everywhere increases faster than the means of subsistence. In his famous formulation: "The power of population is indefinitely greater than the power in the earth to produce subsistence for man. Population, when unchecked, increases in a geometrical ratio. Subsistence increases only in an arithmetical ratio."[93] To prevent catastrophe, something had to hold population growth in check: natural causes like old age, human miseries like war, or moral restraints like abstinence.

When Malthus penned these words, he wrote as a moralist, with heat and passion and indignation. He was long on argument and short on facts. Even his famous ratios—geometric increases in population (2, 4, 8, 16, etc.) vs. arithmetic increases in the food supply (1, 2, 3, 4, etc.)—were illusory, pretending to an unjustified degree of precision. Immediately after the publication of the first edition of the *Essay*, he began a detailed study of population doctrines. He turned to four authors in particular: Joseph Townsend, Sir James Steuart, Johann Süssmilch, and Benjamin Franklin. The fruit of this study was a second edition of the *Essay*, published in 1803. Malthus's treatise grew dramatically, from fifty-five thousand words to over two hundred thousand. It also changed in orientation. Malthus's ambitions were no longer limited to dashing the utopian hopes of Godwin and his ilk; he wanted to integrate his ideas about population into a comprehensive and realistic economic theory. He retained, however, his belief that "necessity, that imperious all pervading law of nature," imposed strict limits on what could be accomplished through social policy.[94]

Franklin appeared on the first page of the second edition of Malthus's *Essay*. The greatest obstacle to human happiness is "the constant tendency in all animated life to increase beyond the nourishment prepared for it. It is observed by Dr. Franklin, that there is no bound to the prolific nature of plants or animals, but what is made by their crowding and interfering with each other's means of subsistence. . . . This is incontrovertibly true."[95] Perhaps we should not attribute too much to this reference; Franklin was not the only writer to influence Malthus. But Franklin's *Observations* helped define Malthus's framework for thinking about the relationship between population and subsistence and in this way entered the stream of modern population doctrines.

Malthus's critics—of which there were many—were furious. Godwin fought back, taking Malthus to task for, among other things, his misplaced trust in Franklin's *Observations*. (Having once invoked Franklin as a forerunner, Godwin now considered him a "vague" thinker whose "nerves" were stronger than his intellect.) Others challenged Malthus's skill as a political economist, his vision as a social theorist, and his ethics as a public moralist.[96] We need not follow these debates, nor need we worry about the adequacy of Malthus's models for population and subsistence.[97] We need note only that one of Malthus's readers—Charles Darwin—took him seriously, and precisely on the issues over which Franklin had exercised such influence.

Darwin's voyage on the *Beagle* lasted five years, from 1831 to 1836. According to popular legend, Darwin hit upon the idea of evolution while surveying the Galapagos Islands. But in truth, Darwin was not fully aware of the significance of what he had observed until *after* he returned to London. The theory of natural selection took several years of intense reflection to crystallize. Darwin's *Autobiography* explained the process as follows: "In October 1838 . . . I happened to read for amusement Malthus on *Population*, and being well prepared to appreciate the struggle for existence . . . from long-continued observation of the habits of animals and plants, it at once struck me that . . . favorable variations would tend to be preserved and unfavorable ones to be destroyed. The result of this would be the formation of new species. Here, then, I had at last got a theory by which to work; but I was so anxious to avoid prejudice, that I determined not for some time to write even the briefest sketch of it."[98] Darwin began reading Malthus's *Essay* on 28 September 1838 and finished it by 3 October. Scholars working with Darwin's unpublished notebooks and correspondence have dated the genesis of the theory of natural selection to these five days. "It was only when Darwin read Malthus that the harmonious conception [of nature] was shattered for him." Reading Malthus was "a crucial step in the formation of the theory of natural selection." Of this "there can be little doubt."[99]

What role did Franklin play in this discovery? Darwin had strong family ties to Franklin. His grandfather Erasmus Darwin had befriended Franklin during Franklin's long stays in England. Fellow members of the Lunar Society—a club of Birmingham luminaries that included Josiah Wedgwood, James Watt, and Joseph Priestley—Erasmus and Franklin shared interests in science and improvement. Erasmus was a freethinking physician and early evolutionist.[100] In epic poems like *The Botanic Garden* and *The Temple of Nature*, he celebrated nature and explored the origins of life. Franklin, "Immortal FRANKLIN," appeared often in these works. Erasmus's son Robert—Charles's father—studied medicine in Paris in the early 1780s, where he often saw Franklin. As a boy, Charles was treated to stories of Franklin's "wit" and "affection."[101]

Against this background, it is unsurprising to learn that Charles Darwin read Franklin's *Autobiography* and that he considered it "very good." Unfortunately, there is no evidence that Darwin read Franklin's *Observations* or any of Franklin's other scientific writings.[102] And yet, a crucial paragraph of Notebook D—the notebook Darwin's modern editors consider to provide the "first formulation of natural selection"—begins with Malthus's statement of the relationship between population and subsistence: "population in increase at geometrical ratio in FAR SHORTER TIME THAN 25 YEARS—yet not until the one sentence of Malthus no one clearly perceived the great check amongst men."[103] The conflict between geometrical and arithmetical growth was Malthus's. But the core idea—"There is . . . no Bound to the prolific Nature of Plants or Animals, but what is made by their crowding and interfering with each other's Means of Subsistence"—was Franklin's. So, too, was the claim that the natural rate of increase for humans, visible in North America, was twenty-five years.

We have no way of knowing what Franklin would have thought about the trajectory his ideas had taken. The theory of evolution held that species were constantly in flux, coming into and going out of existence. Natural selection appeared to leave no room for the plan of a Creator. It is possible that Franklin would have found this troubling.[104] But as we have seen, Franklin had his doubts about the argument from design. One of the bagatelles he composed in Paris—the kind he relished sharing with Robert Darwin and other guests at Passy—gently mocked the pieties of natural theology with a series of "Christian, moral, and philosophical reflections" on the drinking of wine. After several biblical stories and multilingual puns—the root of the

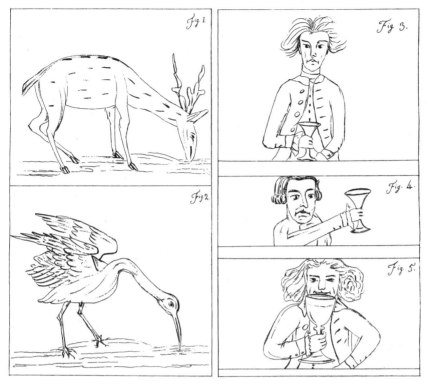

"*In vino veritas*, says the wise man,—*Truth is in wine*." Drawn by William Temple Franklin, in M. Lémontey, ed., *Mémoires de l'abbé Morellet* (Paris, 1821).

word "divine," he asserted, was the French word for wine, *vin*—Franklin ended with an argument from design:

> To confirm still more your piety and gratitude to Divine Providence, reflect upon the situation which it has given to the *elbow*. You see (Figures 1 and 2) in animals, who are intended to drink the waters that flow upon the earth, that if they have long legs, they have also a long neck, so that they can get at their drink without kneeling down. But man, who was destined to drink wine, must be able to raise the glass to his mouth. If the elbow had been placed nearer the hand (as in Figure 3), the part in advance would have been too short to bring the glass up to the mouth; and if it had been placed nearer the shoulder, (as in Figure 4) that part would have been so long that it would have carried the wine far beyond the mouth. But by the actual situation, (represented in Figure 5), we are enabled to drink at

our ease, the glass going exactly to the mouth. Let us, then, with glass in hand, adore this benevolent wisdom;—let us adore and drink!

This was a playful jest. Perhaps it reflected Franklin's belief that the argument from design was secure: so secure, indeed, that it could be made the butt of a good-humored story. But perhaps it signaled something more radical: that the argument from design was risible, and nothing of real significance depended on it. It would not be the first time Franklin used an ironic smile to undermine the shibboleths of natural theology.[105]

Whether or not Franklin would have approved of Darwin's theory of natural selection, he would have immediately understood the firestorm that erupted when Darwin published *On the Origin of Species* in 1859. Natural selection, like the peopling of countries, was a science, but a science that sat at the intersection of a wide range of human interests: biology, paleontology, and geography, to be sure, but also anthropology, religion, and political economy. Perhaps it is no accident that evolution, population growth, and immigration are still among the most publicly contentious domains in modern science. Each has an important part to play in the politics of improvement.

4. Union

Long did I endeavor with unfeigned and unwearied Zeal, to preserve from
breaking, that fine and noble China Vase the British Empire.
—Benjamin Franklin to Lord Howe (20 July 1776)

May I presume to whisper my Sentiments in a private Letter? Britain and
her Colonies should be considered as one Whole, and not as different States
with separate Interests.
—Benjamin Franklin to Peter Collinson (28 May 1754)

Internal Improvements

On 12 September 1787 the Committee of Style submitted a "revised and
arranged" draft of the U.S. Constitution to the Philadelphia convention. Three
arduous months of compromise and negotiation were coming to a close. All
that remained was to review the draft, line by line, to ensure that it accurately
reflected decisions taken over the course of the summer. Members were eager
to finish, impatient of delay. But they recognized the importance of the task before them. As draftsmen, they knew that seemingly small matters—the choice
of a word, the placement of a semicolon—could alter the meaning of the Constitution. And so they replaced "servitude" with "service" in the definition of
apportionment in Article 1, section 2, and corrected the punctuation of the
"general welfare" clause of Article 1, section 8. As politicians and patriots,
moreover, they knew that this was their last chance to influence the document
that would be presented to the people for ratification. George Mason lobbied
for a measure to curb consumption, especially of foreign goods. (It was allowed to die in committee.) James Madison sought authorization for a nonde-

nominational national university. (He was denied.) And Benjamin Franklin "moved to add after the words 'post roads' " in Article 1, section 8: "a power to provide for cutting canals when deemed necessary." James Wilson of Pennsylvania seconded, and the floor was opened for debate.[1]

Franklin had long been interested in canals. At midcentury he used the movement of water through channels and locks to explain atmospheric phenomena such as the Aurora Borealis. Like water in a canal, electricity was a "fluid" whose discharge created a wave that moved in the opposite direction. Later, Franklin turned to the direct investigation of canals. During a 1766 trip through the Netherlands, a boatman flatly declared that it was "well known" that vessels traveled slower in shallow water. At first Franklin was doubtful. But he respected the boatmen's practical wisdom and formulated a tentative explanation. After returning to England he used a wooden trough and toy boat to demonstrate and measure the effect of water depth on boat speed.[2] His curiosity was not idle: the English were digging canals at a feverish pace, and colonists were eager to follow suit.[3] Wagon haulage was difficult, slow, and costly; inland waterways provided a much more efficient means of transportation for bulk commodities like grain and coal. And while rivers were "ungovernable Things, especially in Hilly Countries," canals were "quiet and very manageable." Franklin's research suggested that while deeper canals cost more to construct, they might be cheaper to operate.[4]

Franklin's contemporaries shared his enthusiasm. In the *Wealth of Nations* Adam Smith proclaimed that "good roads, canals, and navigable rivers, by diminishing the expense of carriage, put the remote parts of the country more nearly upon a level with those in the neighborhood of the town. They are upon that account the greatest of all improvements." Alexander Hamilton thought this argument "sufficiently judicious and pertinent" to quote it at length in his landmark "Report on Manufactures."[5]

Smith and Hamilton emphasized the economic significance of inland navigation. Roads and waterways were critical to growth and development. But the impact of canals was not simply or narrowly economic. Internal improvements created channels of communication, permitting the movement of people and transmission of ideas as well as the exchange of goods. Enabling contact across longer distances in shorter times, they made it possible for previously isolated individuals and groups to interact on a regular basis.

James Madison called attention to the political importance of canals in *The Federalist*. Opponents of the Constitution had objected that the nation was too large for republican government. As Machiavelli and Montesquieu testified, self-government was only possible in polities that are small and homogeneous. As numbers grow, differences multiply, conflicts are magnified, and governments are corrupted. Republican government was appropriate to individual states; a republic on a national scale, however, was doomed to failure. In a brilliant riposte, Madison countered that small states are *less* stable because they are less diverse. "The fewer the distinct parties and interests," the more likely it is that a single group will constitute a majority, able to dominate weaker and smaller groups. "Extend the sphere," however, and "you take in a greater variety of parties and interests," making it less likely that a single group will have both the interest and the ability to "invade the rights of other citizens."[6]

What, according to Madison, was the "natural limit of a republic"? It was "that distance from its center, which will barely allow the representatives of the people to meet as often as may be necessary for the administration of public affairs." And "let it be remarked" that "intercourse throughout the union will be daily facilitated by new improvements. Roads will everywhere be shortened, and kept in better order; accommodations for travelers will be multiplied and meliorated; and . . . communication between the western and Atlantic districts, and between different parts of each, will be rendered more and more easy" by "numerous canals" that will be connected and completed. Madison returned to this theme in his seventh annual presidential message of 1815: "Among the means of advancing the public interest," one of the most important is that of "establishing throughout our country the roads and canals which can best be executed under the national authority. No objects within the circle of political economy so richly repay the expense bestowed on them. . . . These considerations are strengthened, moreover, by the political effect of these facilities for intercommunication in bringing and binding more closely together the various parts of our extended confederacy." Madison was echoing words Thomas Jefferson had uttered during one of *his* presidential addresses: through public improvements in roads and canals, "new channels of communication will be opened between the States; the lines of separation will disappear, their interests will be identified, and their union cemented by new and indissoluble ties."[7]

Canals, like roads and rivers, ports and post offices, helped integrate the nation. They were part of the material foundation of the public sphere, no less important than clubs and coffeehouses or books and newspapers. By decreasing the time and cost of travel, they made it possible to exchange news and information as well as goods and services across ever greater distances. In so doing, they helped give rise to a shared national identity.[8] In a very literal sense they were causes of union. Somewhat paradoxically, they were also union's consequence. Proponents argued that large-scale internal improvements were too costly and too risky for private or local authorities. Complex problems of coordination in the planning and execution of such projects could be solved only by the national government.[9] And so, when the convention reached Article 1, section 8 of the draft Constitution, Benjamin Franklin proposed that Congress be authorized to "provide for cutting canals where deemed necessary." Roger Sherman, a delegate from Connecticut, immediately objected: "The expense in such cases will fall on the U[nited] States, and the benefit accrue to the places where the canals may be cut." Why should the many assist the few? Why should the nation fund projects with regional benefits? Why, indeed, should Connecticut pay for canals in Pennsylvania? James Wilson countered that canals could easily be made a source of revenue, not expense. National benefits accrued from regional investments. Madison, fearing that there might be other instances in which the national interest in "easy communication" and "free intercourse" could not be advanced by the actions of individual states, proposed that Franklin's motion be enlarged to include a general power to grant "charters of incorporation." If "political obstacles" were removed, then the "natural ones" would follow. Rufus King of Massachusetts balked. The power to grant charters of incorporation was either unnecessary or dangerous, and quite possibly both. Wilson snapped back: "It is necessary to prevent a State from obstructing the general welfare." But King would not budge, and finally Virginia's George Mason called a vote on the narrow question of canals. The suspicions voiced by Sherman and King could not be overcome. Franklin's motion was rejected, 8 to 3, with only Pennsylvania, Georgia, and Virginia in the affirmative.[10]

The failure of Franklin's motion set the stage for one of the most intriguing political puzzles of the early Republic. Despite strong public support and the backing of Congress and four different presidents, the federal government failed to implement a coherent and sustained program of internal improvements during the first half century of the nation's existence. Part of the problem was constitutional. Presidents Jefferson, Madison, and Monroe encouraged the construction of roads and canals, but they were adamant that they would not sign appropriate legislation without a constitutional

amendment authorizing internal improvements.[11] Had Franklin's motion
passed, they would have had no grounds for complaint. There were overt
political problems as well. Congressional supporters "were slow to build and
effectively use the legislative tools and structures" that would have facilitated policy formation. And the growing power of sectionalism made cooperation increasingly difficult.[12]

These obstacles to improvement were not unique to the early Republic, nor even to the United States. They are endemic to human life, found
anywhere it is necessary to coordinate the actions of groups and individuals.
Human needs and interests often conflict. Even when they coincide, our
powers of reason are limited, and our judgments are inescapably partial. Interactions are rarely (if ever) transparent, and in dealing with others it is often difficult to know whether to trust or betray, cooperate or defect.[13]

In the middle of the eighteenth century the Scottish philosopher David
Hume suggested that governments originated in an attempt to solve these
problems. According to Hume, our actions originate in our passions, among
the most problematic of which are selfishness and shortsightedness. We prefer the present over the remote, immediate satisfaction over future gain.
These traits make it difficult for us to cooperate with others in large and complex projects. "Two neighbors may agree to drain a meadow, which they
possess in common: because it is easy for them to know each other's mind;
and each must perceive, that the immediate consequence of his failing in his
part, is the abandoning [of] the whole project. But it is very difficult, and indeed impossible, that a thousand persons should agree to any such action; it
being difficult for them to concert so complicated a design, and still more difficult for them to execute it; while each seeks a pretext to free himself of the
trouble and expense, and would lay the whole burden on others." Hume
thought it impossible to change our "natures"; selfishness and shortsightedness are permanent features of the human condition. But we can change our
"situation." In a different environment, under the authority of well-
designed government, we are better able to cooperate. Everywhere we look,
this is how "bridges are built, harbors opened, ramparts raised, canals
formed, fleets equipped, and armies disciplined."[14]

"The care of government" enables cooperation. But not just any government will do. For the sake of clarity Hume assumed that the institutions
of government could be arranged to ensure that justice was "the immediate
interest" of persons in power. This was a useful analytic simplification,

allowing Hume to highlight the constructive powers of government. But Hume was a historian as well as a philosopher, and he knew full well that existing governments rarely, if ever, met this standard. The actual rules of the political game, formal and informal, made the conduct of governments complex and often enigmatic. Sometimes governments helped solve problems of collective action; sometimes they made them worse. For those living in the stream of time and not speculating outside of it, Hume's analysis posed a difficult challenge: can actual governments be brought closer to the ideal?

Franklin had greater faith in voluntary association than Hume and might have suggested a different outcome to Hume's story about neighbors draining a meadow. After all, he had organized ten thousand men to defend Pennsylvania without benefit of government! But the Association, like all of Franklin's organizations, was defined by the way it regulated the conduct of its members. Franklin never doubted the power of rules and procedures to influence outcomes. This was especially evident when institutions failed. Franklin expressed this insight with startling clarity in his afterthoughts about the British Empire. As he remonstrated with the English author and colonial administrator Francis Maseres in 1785, "The ancient system of the British empire was a happy one, by which the colonies were allowed to govern and tax themselves. Had it been wisely continued, it is hard to imagine the degree of power and importance in the world that empire might have arrived at. All the means of growing greatness, extent of territory, agriculture, commerce, arts, population, were within its own limits, and therefore at its command. I used to consider that system as a large and beautiful porcelain vase, I lamented the measures that I saw likely to break it, and strove to prevent them; because once broken I saw no probability of its being ever repaired. My endeavors did not succeed: we are broken, and the parts must now do as well as they can for themselves." Franklin frequently mourned the loss of "that fine and noble China Vase the British Empire." As he wrote to Sir Joseph Banks in the summer of 1783, "What an extension of Agriculture even to the Tops of our Mountains; What Rivers rendered navigable, or joined by Canals; what Bridges, Aqueducts, new Roads and other public Works, Edifices and Improvements, rendering England a complete Paradise, might not have been obtained by spending those Millions in doing Good which in the last War have been spent in doing Mischief!"[15]

Empires, no less than individuals and colonies, can be improved. Ties can be strengthened, resources can be developed, lives can be enhanced. But how? What kinds of institutions are appropriate to imperial growth and development? How can the many and diverse parts of an empire be held together? Where, and how, should decisions be made? Over what policy domains? Were the fruits of empire to be spread among its constituent members or concentrated in just one part? What, indeed, was an empire? A tightly unified system of rule, extending over a vast territory? A federation of loosely coordinated polities? Or something altogether different?

Franklin approached the British Empire with the same "projecting public Spirit" that he brought to everyday life in Philadelphia. Independent states, like isolated individuals, are weak; improvement requires cooperation. Cooperation, in turn, rests on utility, on the ability of men and women, or colonies and states, to be useful to each other. And though many forms of cooperation emerge through voluntary association, or commercial exchange, there is no substitute for well-designed political institutions. Franklin first sketched the structure of a union for improvement in the early 1750s, when he campaigned to reform the British Empire in North America. His insights and arguments were prescient. Ideas that seemed novel in 1787, from a federal division of power to the representation of individuals and the construction of canals, had been prefigured in imperial debates over three decades before.

Visions of Empire

Franklin first broached the topic of colonial union in a 1751 letter to James Parker. Franklin was a silent partner in Parker's print shop, and Parker had solicited Franklin's thoughts on a manuscript concerning Indian affairs by a New York colonial official, Archibald Kennedy. Franklin was encouraging and used the opportunity to slip into print some of his own thoughts.[16] (Franklin's letter was published as an appendix to Kennedy's tract. Though anonymous, its provenance would have been obvious to most readers.)

Kennedy's theme was captured by his title: *The Importance of Gaining and Preserving the Friendship of the Indians to the British Interest, Considered.* When British settlers first arrived in North America, they were welcomed by the Indians. A "Covenant Chain" established an alliance between northern colonists and the tribes of the Iroquois Confederacy. At first the chain was bright and strong. But in time it began to rust. Unsavory men, especially commissioners and traders, "abused, defrauded, and deceived . . . innocent

[and] well-meaning" Indians. As a consequence, the chain was nearly broken. Adding to the stress were the actions of the French, Britain's "natural Enemies and Competitors in every Corner of the World." The French were "indefatigable in cultivating the Friendship" of Indian allies. Should they succeed in weaning the Six Nations from the British interest, the results would be fatal. The future of "the whole Continent" hinged on restoring the Covenant Chain.[17]

Metropolitan officials were receptive to this line of analysis. In 1748 the Treaty of Aix-la-Chapelle had ended King George's War, the American phase of the War of the Austrian Succession. Great Britain and France were once again at peace. But the treaty did little to resolve underlying colonial and commercial conflicts between these two empires, and each continued to jockey for advantage. Both recognized that Indians had the ability to tip the balance. At stake was an extraordinary prize: mastery of the land, trade, and peoples of North America.

Kennedy recommended a combination of military, commercial, and administrative measures. A new fort, with a permanent garrison and ample arsenal, would protect the colonies from northern invasions. (Kennedy, a Scot, favored soldiers from the Highlands, "the wilder, the better.") A string of armed townships would constitute a "Barrier" along the frontier. Official interpreters would ease communication; authorized blacksmiths would provide vital craft skills as well as instruction in the English language. An annual "grand Fair" would ensure that Indians were offered the best merchandise at fair prices. Each of these steps was to be "put under the Direction of one single Person of Capacity and Integrity, of his Majesty's Appointment . . . in the Nature of a *Superintendant of Indian Affairs*, with full Powers to do summary Justice upon all Occasions." And because the cost of these efforts exceeded the capacity of any single colony, Kennedy called for an annual meeting of colonial commissioners "to fix their respective Quotas for the general Expense."[18]

Franklin subtly but profoundly transformed this mélange of ideas. Kennedy, disdainful of colonial assemblies, called on Parliament to impose these changes.[19] Franklin thought this mistaken. Characteristically, his argument focused on practical consequences: "A voluntary Union entered into by the Colonies themselves, I think, would be preferable to one imposed by Parliament; for it would be perhaps not much more difficult to procure, and more easy to alter and improve, as Circumstances should require, and

Experience direct." Franklin then skillfully explained why previous efforts to mobilize the colonies had failed. Many governors are "on ill Terms with their Assemblies." Some attempt to play both sides of the issue, publicly favoring union while privately opposing it. Others simply fail to "see the Necessity of it." As a consequence, when assemblies consider plans of union, they do so unaided. No one in the debate has the interest, information, and influence needed to sway their decisions. Franklin suggested, as an alternative, that New York send out a team of "half a Dozen Men of good Understanding and Address" to engage the "leading Men" of the other colonies in the scheme. "For reasonable sensible Men, can always make a reasonable Scheme appear such to other reasonable Men, if they take Pains, and have Time and Opportunity for it; unless from some Circumstances their Honesty and good Intentions are suspected."[20]

Franklin's suggestions went beyond the method of adoption. His language reveals thinking on an altogether different plane. First, Franklin identified the central objective of Kennedy's proposals as the creation of a colonial union: not the introduction of a superintendent of Indian affairs, not the construction of forts, not the creation of barrier communities along the frontier, but a "Union of the Colonies." Second, Franklin imagined this union as a quasi-independent and self-organizing entity. This was implicit in his preference for "a voluntary Union": a colonial pact would be easier to amend than would a plan imposed by Parliament. It became explicit in Franklin's elaboration on its organization: "Were there a general Council formed by all the Colonies, and a general Governor appointed by the Crown to preside in that Council, or in some Manner to concur with and confirm their Acts, and take Care of the Execution; every Thing relating to Indian Affairs and the Defense of the Colonies, might be properly put under their Management." Franklin's "general Governor" was not a superintendent acting on orders from London but an agent of the council, confirming and executing its acts. Finally, Franklin addressed the political consequences of this new institution: "Perhaps if the Council were to meet successively at the Capitals of the several Colonies, they might thereby become better acquainted with the Circumstances, Interests, Strength or Weakness, etc. of all, and thence be able to judge better of Measures proposed from time to time." Regular meetings would facilitate mutual understanding, sharpen policy decisions, and help overcome notoriously fractious relations between the colonies.[21]

Franklin's letter to Parker contained a sketch, more hint than plan, of colonial union. Despite Franklin's profession of ignorance—he claimed to "have little Knowledge, and less Experience in these matters"—it suggested a mind busy at work, thinking, probing, and investigating the possibilities and limits of colonial politics. And it resonated with his contemporaneous *Observations concerning the Increase of Mankind*, which proclaimed that population growth in North America would be an extraordinary "accession" to the British Empire. If Britain's conflicts with France were resolved, and if sufficient land were secured, then colonial growth might increase the "Nation tenfold in Numbers and Strength."[22]

Franklin invoked the potential of North America in order to claim equal membership within the empire. The identity he claimed was British, not American. As he "whisper[ed]" to Peter Collinson in 1754, "Britain and her Colonies should be considered as one Whole, and not as different States with separate Interests."[23]

What was the British Empire? What did it mean to say that Great Britain was an imperial power? An empire is a system of domination. The Latin root for empire, *imperium*, means the right to rule or command. Thus an *imperator*, or emperor, is the commander in chief or sovereign. An empire is also an extended polity. In his celebrated dictionary of 1755, Dr. Johnson illustrated this sense of "empire" with the words of Sir William Temple: "A nation extended over vast tracts of land, and numbers of people, arrives in time at the ancient name of kingdom, or modern of empire." And an empire is a unique form of civilization. As historian Anthony Pagden has emphasized, an empire is a distinctive kind of society, a community "governed by the rule of law" that demands "adherence to a particular kind of life."[24]

The "dominant conception of the British Empire" in the mid-eighteenth century was that it was "Protestant, commercial, maritime and free."[25] Protestantism was the glue of British national identity during the seventeenth century, helping to bond England, Scotland, and Wales into a coherent whole. It was nurtured by memories of Protestant martyrdom and sustained by deeply held fears and hatreds. Anti-Catholicism could take virulent form. But it was not (entirely) irrational; confessional differences were essential ingredients of international conflicts throughout the early modern era. Part of what made the Glorious Revolution of 1688 "glorious" was that it saved Britain from the Catholic scheming of James II. The presence of millions of French just across the Channel, presumably massed against them, helped sustain

Britain's sense of precariousness throughout the eighteenth century. Imperial conflicts embodied this divide.[26]

The British Empire was also commercial. This should come as no surprise, given previous discussions of political economy and population growth, but it bears emphasis. Prior to the seventeenth century, the greatness of an empire was measured by the extent of its territories. Strength, stability, and grandeur rested on conquest. But the scale and duration of international wars placed ever greater financial demands on the states fighting them. The costs of war exceeded existing fiscal capacities and compelled reliance on a new and challenging source of income: the market. As Charles Davenant argued in 1699, "It is not extent of territory that makes a country powerful, but numbers of men well employed, convenient ports, a good navy, and soil producing all sorts of commodities." The colonies provided staple goods for British consumption and manufacture. As they grew and prospered, they also created vibrant new markets for British goods. According to one economic historian, exports were "the most dynamic sector of the English economy in the first three quarters of the eighteenth century," with a seven- or eightfold increase to North America alone.[27] Contemporaries were keenly aware of the commercial importance of the empire. Small wonder, then, that interest in the colonies was "disproportionately concentrated in the bigger ports and the important inland marketing centers for manufactures."[28]

As the empire was commercial, so, too, was it maritime. Britannia ruled by ruling the waves. The integrity of Britain was secured by its command of the seas. Naval superiority, not territorial conquest, was the foundation of the empire. The enormous cost of maintaining an imperial navy was borne by trade and shipping: the expansion of trade generated new sources of revenue, while the shipping industry provided vessels, craftsmen, and a ready supply of trained seamen. From a European point of view, this "blue-water policy" was isolationist; Britain had no enduring territorial commitments or ambitions on the Continent.[29] But from a global point of view, Britain's blue-water policy entailed the active pursuit of resources and markets. Great Britain ensured its safety and prosperity by keeping the seas open for its commerce.

Finally, the empire was free. Britons prided themselves that their empire was built not by military conquest—as with Spain or France—but through commerce and trade. The plantations and colonies had been settled by freeborn British subjects, men and women who respected the ancient constitution and obeyed the common law.[30]

In short, "the British empire was imagined to consist of flourishing and commercially viable colonies, populated with free British subjects, that served as bulwarks of trade, prosperity, naval strength and political virtue for the parent state." This vision enjoyed broad support. It was articulated by pamphleteers, commemorated by artists, deployed by politicians, and embraced by merchants and traders. Parades celebrated it, coins and medals memorialized it, plays and poems elaborated on it.[31] This imperial imagery encouraged midcentury Britons to think of themselves as partners in a single, integrated polity.[32] But unity was not the same as equality, and virtually no one in Great Britain doubted that the colonies were and ought to be subordinate to the needs and interests of the mother country. Among the governing elite and those who sought to advise them, this was said with clarity and candor. In a 1751 memorandum to the Earl of Halifax, Henry McCulloh emphasized "the necessity of keeping the Colonies within due Bounds and in a proper dependence on their Mother Country." An anonymous author— possibly Halifax himself—thought it "of the utmost Consequence to regulate" the colonies, "that they may be useful to, and not rival in Power and Trade their Mother Kingdom." The colonial agent and politician James Abercromby declared that "the first principle" of "Colony Government, whether amongst ancient, or Modern Nations, has ever been, to make their Colonies, Subservient to the Interest of the Principal State." Malachy Postlethwayt, an esteemed economist, held that "colonies ought never to forget what they owe to their mother country, in return for the prosperity and riches they enjoy. Their gratitude in that respect, and the duty they owe, indispensably oblige them to be immediately dependent on their original parent, and to make their interest subservient thereunto."[33] In the decade following the Stamp Act, British opinion began to divide and harden. But prior to that time the position taken by these four men was entirely unexceptional. For example, the Iron Act of 1750—the very legislation that prompted Franklin to write his *Observations concerning the Increase of Mankind*—was justified in terms of the subordinate place of the colonies in the imperial economy.

Though belief that the British Empire was "Protestant, commercial, maritime and free" dominated the middle decades of the eighteenth century, it was under severe pressure from two directions. As hoped and expected, the colonies of North America experienced extraordinary growth. Their populations exploded, their economies broadened and deepened. This made the colonies increasingly valuable to Great Britain. But, as if to demonstrate the wisdom of the old saying "Be careful what you wish for; you just might get it," this also made imperial officials progressively more anxious. Improvement was a double-edged sword. Contemporaries assumed that development brought thoughts of independence, and by 1750 "fears of colonial independence were everywhere manifest in Britain." These apprehensions touched every aspect of colonial life. Thus Pennsylvania's Proprietor, Thomas Penn, thought Franklin's plans for the Philadelphia Academy were "premature": "I find people [in London] think we go too fast with regard to the matter and it gives an opportunity to those fools who are always telling their fears that the Colonies will set up for themselves."[34]

From a British point of view, the perils of colonial development were compounded by flaws in the institutions of colonial governance. In the infancy of the empire, special rights and privileges were granted to the colonies "as an Encouragement to new Settlers." No one imagined that these accommodations would give rise to thoughts of "Independency." But they had. Colonial assemblies intruded in the day-to-day business of government and truculently defended their rights. Colonial governors, as agents of the crown, found it increasingly difficult to maintain their power and independence. Matters were not helped by disorder within the British government, where there was neither coordination nor clear lines of responsibility for colonial policy. Metropolitan authority was thought weak and fragile, and there were insistent calls to shore it up.[35]

The shape of reform was influenced by a second source of pressure on the imperial imagery: France. While the British colonies were busy defending their privileges and squabbling with their governors, the French were constructing a string of forts along the western frontier. The "great Object" of this effort was "joining the two Provinces of Canada, and Louisiana, and confining the English to their present Settlements." At the same time the French were shoring up relations with the Indians. Henry McCulloh worried that if the French and Indians joined, "although they are not near so numerous as the English Settlers," they would be "nevertheless capable of greatly distressing and even ruining the English Colonies by hemming them in, and making the back Settlers retire to places of Safety." Archibald Kennedy was apocalyptic: "*Delenda est Carthago* [Carthage must be destroyed]. There is no Alternate. . . . This Continent cannot hold us both."[36]

The French were feared and reviled for their strength on the North American continent. But they were also admired and envied for their administrative competence and their economic prowess.[37] Conventional opinion held that freedom was a precondition to economic development. Commercial prosperity followed on the heels of political liberty. But as early as 1742 David Hume noted that the growing commercial wealth of France challenged this equation. Malachy Postlethwayt concurred. The "masterly Strokes of the French Policy" were obvious. "Every impartial Man," he wrote despairingly, "must discern the wide Difference there is between the French and the British System of commercial Policy." One "is calculated, by the utmost Stretch of Wisdom and Sagacity, to raise the Commerce" of France to "its utmost Pitch of Splendor," while "the other is calculated to sink and depress the British Trade to its primitive Nothingness."[38]

France's commercial success in the first half of the eighteenth century influenced debates over colonial reform. British authorities coalesced on the idea that enhancing the metropolitan government's power was the key to preserving the empire. This was difficult in America, where there were so many "distinct and Separate States or Governments." Colonies were not like corporations or even counties in Great Britain; each was unique, with its own set of legislative and executive institutions. James Abercromby argued that the government of the colonies was sui generis and "must stand, upon its own Principles." But he was also insistent that the "Capital Object in Colonial Government" was to ensure the colonies' "Subservience." Authorities were generally agreed on the need to "revise the Constitutions of the Settlements abroad, and to regulate them." Rules and regulations dating to the seventeenth century were no longer appropriate. Greater speed and efficiency were called for, and that necessitated the centralization of information and authority. Henry McCulloh lobbied for "a regular Plan or System" on the French model. France successfully maintained central control over its colonies, preserving "one regular uniform and entire Rule of Action" throughout the empire.[39]

McCulloh's enthusiasm for French officialdom may have been extreme, but there can be no doubt that British reformers were determined to reconstitute the formal and informal structures of provincial government. Many in London thought tightened control over the colonies essential to the preservation of imperial order. Archibald Kennedy's pamphlet on Indian affairs and Franklin's letter responding to it were attempts to influence these opinions.

So, too, was Franklin's *Observations concerning the Increase of Mankind*, which had argued for a natural congruence of economic interests between the colonies and Great Britain. Franklin did not return to these topics until 1754. When he did so, it was in three vigorous and sophisticated documents: the Albany Plan of Union, a plan for settling western colonies, and a series of letters to Governor Shirley of Massachusetts. Franklin's goal was to sketch an alternative to the French model that combined unity, diversity, and decentralization.

"Join, or Die"

On 18 September 1753 the Board of Trade ordered the governor of New York to convene an intercolonial conference on Indian affairs. The previous summer Hendrick, chief of the Mohawks, had declared the Covenant Chain broken. This frightened imperial authorities in London, who were keenly aware of the strategic importance of the Six Nations of the Iroquois as well as of French attempts to "withdraw them from the British interest." It was essential that colonists and Indians "bury the Hatchet." Governor Delancey dutifully called on nine colonies—New Hampshire, Massachusetts Bay, Rhode Island, Connecticut, New York, Pennsylvania, New Jersey, Maryland, and Virginia—to meet at Albany the following June.[40]

The board's anxiety was justified. Great Britain's simmering conflict with France was about to boil over. In the spring and summer of 1754, soldiers from Virginia—including a young and very green officer, George Washington—engaged French troops in the Ohio valley. The numbers were small and the locations were remote. "Nothing could have been further from Washington's mind, or more alien to the designs of the men who had entrusted him with troops . . . than beginning a war." But that is precisely what happened. Frontier conflicts set in train the Seven Years' War. Warriors from the Six Nations of the Iroquois were pivotal in these confrontations, and to the shock of the Virginians they were neither steady nor pliant allies.[41]

Franklin reported the first of these clashes in the 9 May edition of the *Pennsylvania Gazette:* "Friday last an Express arrived here from Major Washington, with Advice, that Mr. Ward . . . was compelled to surrender his small Fort in the Forks of the Monongahela to the French, on the 17th past. . . .'Tis further said, that besides the [1,000] French that came down from Venango, another Body of near 400 is coming up the Ohio; and that

Franklin's cartoon "Join, or Die" for the *Pennsylvania Gazette*, 9 May 1754.

600 French Indians, of the Chippewa's and Ottawa's, are coming down Siota River, from the Lake, to join them; and many more French are expected from Canada; the Design being to establish themselves, settle their Indians, and build Forts just on the Back of our Settlements in all our Colonies; from which Forts, as they did from Crown-Point, they may send out their Parties to kill and scalp the Inhabitants, and ruin the Frontier Counties." Confronting these ominous developments, colonists had but one plausible course of action: they must unite. If they failed to do so they would be destroyed. There was no middle ground. Franklin drove home this urgent message with a simple image.

Franklin's snake cartoon was brilliant, equal to his best efforts as a prose stylist. It quickly and powerfully conveyed Franklin's twined themes: strength in union, vulnerability in isolation. Others agreed. Within weeks "Join, or Die" was reprinted in New York and Boston; by the end of the summer it had been referred to by newspapers in South Carolina and Virginia. In time, with minor adaptations, it became one of the most widely used political images in eighteenth-century America.[42]

When composing the maxims and proverbs of Poor Richard, Franklin scoured his library for inspiration. He appears to have followed the same procedure in this instance; the snake cartoon bears a striking resemblance to a seventeenth-century French emblem in which a picture of a snake cut in two is accompanied by the motto *Un Serpent coupe en deux. Se rejoinder ou mourir* (A serpent cut in two. Either join or die). A snake was no polyp, capable of regenerating a severed limb. As any colonial farmer could testify, a divided snake was a dead snake. To survive, it must remain intact. Nonetheless, the snake was a potentially risky iconographic choice. Virtually all of Franklin's readers would have been familiar with the story of the Garden of Eden, in which the serpent "beguiled" Eve into eating the fruit "of the tree of the knowledge of good and evil." For this the snake was "cursed above all cattle, and above every beast of the field; upon thy belly shalt thou go, and dust thou shalt eat all the days of thy life." The snake was cunning, treacherous, deceptive, and filled with malice. It denoted a lurking danger or a suspicious person, as in familiar warnings against "a snake in the grass."[43]

To these general considerations we may add a biographical flourish. One of Franklin's favorite authors was John Milton. Contemporary references indicate that *Paradise Lost* was on his mind at this time. In Milton's epic, "the spirited sly Snake" is the mouthpiece of Satan. Eve's temptation precipitated the fall; earthly tyranny was its consequence. To Franklin this was a stern warning. Base passions—arrogance, envy, insolence, and all their vile sisters and brothers—had the power to deface the soul and deform the polity.[44]

What can have prompted Franklin to represent colonial union with a snake? Twenty years later, in a letter to the *Pennsylvania Journal,* he tallied the virtues that made a rattlesnake an appropriate symbol for America: courage, generosity, vigilance, strength. The rattles at first puzzled him, until he realized that in the drawing he had seen there were thirteen, "exactly the number of the Colonies united in America; and I recollected too that this was the only part of the Snake which increased in numbers. . . . 'Tis curious and amazing to observe how distinct and independent of each other the rattles of this animal are, and yet how firmly they are united together, so as never to be separated but by breaking them to pieces.—One of those rattles singly, is incapable of producing sound, but the ringing of thirteen together, is sufficient to alarm the boldest man living." This was in December 1775, after the battles of Lexington, Concord, and Bunker Hill. In November the Continental Congress had authorized the creation of a naval force, and the image Franklin was responding to had been painted on the drum of Philadelphia Marine: a rattlesnake, coiled to strike and sporting the motto "Don't Tread on Me."[45] But in 1754, when Franklin first conceived the snake cartoon, there were no comparable uses of this image. No one else conceived of the colonies as a snake, and no one—least of all Franklin—advocated war with Great Britain.[46] The visual and political vocabulary of 1775 owed its origins to Franklin's imaginative engagement with a quite different set of circumstances.

In 1754 (rattle)snakes had two iconographic virtues. First, they were unique to the New World and an object of horror and fascination in the Old. As we have seen, Franklin took advantage of this territorial association in his 1751 hoax, "Rattle-snakes for Felons." For every felon transported from Great Britain to North America, Franklin proposed returning a rattlesnake. What better way to display colonial gratitude, Franklin sneered, than to return these indigenous reptiles for the "*Human Serpents* sent us by our *Mother Country*"?[47] Second, and crucially, snakes have neither hands nor feet. For centuries British political thought had relied on organic metaphors to convey ideas of unity and coherence. The body politic was a *body,* with head and heart, hands and feet. The head commanded, the heart provided vigor and courage, the feet supported the load. Social order, like bodily health, required that each part perform its appointed role. This "great chain of being" was still potent in Franklin's day, and its implication of inequality would have been devastating to Franklin's ambitions. Already, in *Plain Truth,* he had invoked a body politic whose unity was a function of interdependence, not hierarchy. The image of the snake permitted him to extend this idea. No state need worry which was above and which was below; all were level (though South Carolinians may have found their location—at the snake's tail—less than flattering).

The snake cartoon expressed a potent aspiration: intercolonial union. It also captured a frightening reality: intercolonial fragmentation. For members of Franklin's generation, things had never been different. From its foundation in 1696, the Board of Trade was besieged with complaints about the unwillingness of the colonies to cooperate with each other. As one mid-century traveler put it, "Fire and water are not more heterogeneous than the different colonies in North-America. Nothing can exceed the jealousy and emulation, which they possess in regard to each other." The snake cartoon reflected these differences. Like the colonies, the snake was already divided into pieces. Without bold action, it would die. Patterns in the distribution of the cartoon mirrored the hazardous condition of the colonies. Though widely reproduced, the snake cartoon was frequently modified, sometimes subtly, sometimes substantially, thus revealing "the persistence of local identities and prejudices." Franklin was dismayed by the fractious habits of his fellow colonists. "The Confidence of the French . . . seems well-grounded on the present disunited State of the British Colonies, and the extreme Difficulty of bringing so many different Governments and Assemblies to agree in any speedy and effectual Measures for our common Defense and Security."[48] Join or die: those were the options. But for the colonies to join, a plan of union had to be framed, and a method for its adoption had to be established.

Plans of Union

The Albany Congress convened on 19 June 1754 in the city courthouse. The weather was warm, windy, and wet; during the first week it rained so hard that the Hudson rose fourteen feet and flooded the countryside. James Delancey, lieutenant governor of New York, presided; twenty-four men, representing seven colonies, were in attendance. After reading their instructions, the commissioners appointed a committee to draft Delancey's speech to the Indians. This prompted controversy. During the "interviews" with the Indians, which colony should be seated first? Should this honor be given to the largest colony? To the one most exposed to risk? Or perhaps to the colony that had incurred the greatest expense? Delancey, in an effort to quell the dispute, suggested that the colonies be seated in geographic order. But did this mean south to north or north to south? North it was. And to the chagrin of New Hampshire, Massachusetts—which then included the district of Maine—took pride of place.[49] This was a minor squabble, to be sure, but it illustrates just how fraught intercolonial cooperation could be.

The commissioners turned their attention to colonial union on the 24th, when they agreed that it was "absolutely necessary for their security and defense." Franklin and five others were asked to prepare a plan "with all Imaginable Speed." The committee submitted its draft on 28 June; after a thorough vetting, the final version was approved on 10 July. Unfortunately, no detailed record of these deliberations exists. Scholars have had to reconstruct the plan's development from a handful of sketches, memos, and notes. Among these is Franklin's "Short Hints towards a scheme for uniting the Northern Colonies," drafted on the road from Philadelphia to Albany. In the *Autobiography* Franklin recalled that several plans were considered by the committee, but "mine happened to be preferred, and with a few Amendments was accordingly reported" to the congress. The commissioners debated it daily, "hand in hand with the Indian Business. Many Objections and Difficulties were started, but at length they were all overcome, and the Plan was unanimously agreed to." Franklin did not agree with every change but still considered it "my Plan."[50] Over the years this claim has been challenged by scholars seeking to drive a wedge between Franklin and the Albany Plan.[51] But the strongest arguments and the best evidence confirm his memory. The plan was based on Franklin's "Short Hints." It was developed in committee and amended in congress, but Franklin's fundamentals were not altered. Franklin composed the final draft and wrote the only detailed explanation of its logic. As James Madison is the father of the U.S. Constitution, so Benjamin Franklin is the father of the Albany Plan of Union.

Franklin's "Reasons and Motives for the Albany Plan of Union" was written soon after he returned to Philadelphia. Intended for imperial authorities, it began with a familiar refrain: under existing conditions the colonies were incapable of cooperating in "general measures for the common defense." Contemporaries often said that the colonies were "jealous" of each other. By this they did not mean that they were intolerant of rivals but that they were wary, suspicious, watchful, apprehensive. But why? What made the colonies distrust each other? Most pointed to diversity as the cause. Trust was undermined by the existence of so many different forms of government, systems of law, religious persuasions, and regional customs. Difference gave rise to apprehension; apprehension bred distrust; distrust thwarted cooperation. As modern game theory has made clear, "cooperative behavior does not emerge simply because it is mutually beneficial." Joint ventures make each party dependent on the others. Participants, even when they are predisposed to cooperate, will defect if they are sufficiently uncertain of the motives of their partners. The cost of misplaced trust (relying on a partner who proves unfaithful) often exceeds the cost of distrust (refusing to cooperate).[52]

Thomas Hobbes placed this problem at the center of his seventeenth-century masterpiece, *Leviathan*. According to Hobbes, cooperation is rational only when we can be confident that the terms of our agreement will be enforced. In every joint venture someone must go first, and "he that performs first, has no assurance the other will perform after . . . without the fear of some coercive Power." We can trust each other only when we are subject to the authority of a well-ordered state. Sovereignty precedes sociability.[53] As noted in chapter 1, this line of argument provoked furious debate over the moral and psychological foundations of human conduct. But its impact was not limited to philosophers; it also informed comparisons of French and British imperial practices in the 1750s. The "Advantages" of the French "Form of

Government" were considerable, especially "in Time of War." Every French settlement, no matter how small, was "under the absolute Command of the Governor of Canada." The British colonies, by contrast, were "independent" and "generally disunited."[54] To growing numbers on both sides of the Atlantic, France provided a model response to colonial fragmentation.

Franklin did not deny that the colonies behaved in a "jealous" fashion. Every invitation to cooperation was taken to be a sign of weakness and led to opportunistic bargaining in which each colony pushed for "favorite laws, powers, or points that . . . could not at other times be obtained." Colonies refused to cooperate when it appeared that another would "reap more immediate advantage." And on those rare occasions when joint ventures were undertaken, each held back, "afraid of doing more than its share, or desirous of doing less."[55] These traits were deep seated, but they could be altered. The colonies were unable to band together on their own. Union had to originate in an act of Parliament. (I will say more about this topic below.) But ongoing cooperation did not require permanent imperial administration. The experience of union would change colonial beliefs and practices. "By the frequent meetings-together of commissioners or representatives from all the colonies, the circumstances of the whole would be better known, and the good of the whole better provided for; and . . . the colonies would by this connection learn to consider themselves, not as so many independent states, but as members of the same body; and thence be more ready to afford assistance and support to each other." By working together, the colonies would come to see themselves as partners in a common enterprise. Ongoing relationships would shape their imaginations and constrain their behavior. Once inaugurated, colonial union was (potentially) self-sustaining.[56]

For closely related reasons, Franklin opposed the creation of "partial Unions." Some of the commissioners suggested forming "two or three distinct unions." According to the Massachusetts delegation, "smaller geographic districts would unite colonies with common frontiers, Indian neighbors, and economic interests."[57] This appeared to lower the stakes of union and made intuitive sense in the context of colonial jealousies. To Franklin, however, partial unions were partial solutions. They were less efficient and less potent than a general union. Should the strength of the whole be required—and war with France was on the horizon—the colonies would be no better off. Conflicts would emerge between the partial unions, and continental cooperation would remain an impossible aspiration.

These arguments were stock-in-trade. Then came a novelty, revealing Franklin's intellectual and political creativity, that ought to have astonished his fellow commissioners. "Where particular colonies have *selfish views,* as New York with regard to Indian trade and lands; or are *less exposed,* being covered by others, as New Jersey, Rhode Island, Connecticut, Maryland; or have *particular whims and prejudices* against warlike measures in general, as Pennsylvania, where the Quakers predominate; such colonies would have more weight in a partial union and be better able to oppose and obstruct the measures necessary for the general good, than where they are swallowed up in the general union."[58] Partial unions are more susceptible to partial passions and interests because they magnify the power of their constituent members. New York, one-thirteenth of a general union, would be one-third or one-fourth of a partial union. As a consequence, its influence would be much greater. The grand scale of a continental union, frightening to many, was its greatest asset. It decreased the relative power of each colony and thus increased the likelihood that the common good would be served.

This argument is familiar to modern audiences from James Madison's *Federalist,* 10. According to Madison, all societies are subject to the influence of factions, groups of citizens "united and actuated by some common impulse of passion, or of interest, adverse to the rights of other citizens, or to the permanent and aggregate interests of the community." The causes of faction are "sown in the nature of man" and cannot be removed. Their effects, however, can be controlled by increasing the size of the community: "The smaller the society, the fewer probably will be the distinct parties and interests composing it; the fewer the distinct parties and interests, the more frequently will a majority be found of the same party." But if you "extend the sphere," then "you take in a greater variety of parties and interests; you make it less probable that a majority of the whole will have a common motive to invade the rights of other citizens . . . [or] act in unison with each other." One of the advantages "the Union" enjoyed over "the States composing it" is that it was larger and thus less vulnerable to the distorting effects of faction. Madison considered this a "republican" remedy for a republican "disease," and in 1787 it may have been.[59] But in 1754, when it was first sketched by Benjamin Franklin (and when Madison was but three years old), it was intended to strengthen and preserve the British Empire in North America.

The political virtues of union were especially attractive to Franklin because, to use Samuel Beer's felicitous phrase, he thought "on a grand scale in space and time."[60] Improvement and expansion were intertwined; "increase" had material as well as moral and political meanings. Franklin was a well-known land speculator—one of his generation's "most audacious"—but profit was not his (only) motive in encouraging plans of settlement. Though he never crossed the Allegheny Mountains, he was confident that land to the west was among the "finest" in North America. Rich and fertile, blessed with a mild climate and an extensive network of lakes and rivers, it would be an extraordinary "accession of power" to Great Britain. Or to France, he worried, if Britain dithered. Franklin's *Observations concerning the Increase of Mankind* identified the demographic foundation of a continental empire; the Albany Plan was its political correlate.[61]

The government imagined by the Albany Plan had two branches: a "President General" appointed by the crown and a "Grand Council" whose members were elected by the colonial assemblies. The president had the right to veto acts of the council, giving him "one half of the legislative power" as well as "the whole executive power." The council represented the people and was comparable in "nature and intention" to the British House of Commons.[62] Taken together, the president and council constituted a "General Government" with the power to regulate Indian affairs (from purchasing land and managing trade to declaring war and peace), settle new colonies (from defining boundaries to making laws), and provide for defense (from raising troops to building forts and equipping warships).

Each colony retained its constitution, laws, and privileges, subject only to the limits imposed by the union. Strictly speaking, however, the Albany Plan would not have established a federal system, "since the devolution of powers to the colonies was enacted [by Parliament], and so could be modified or withdrawn" by it. But within the union, authority was "divided between the general government and the several colonial governments by a man-made law superior to both."[63]

One of the primary purposes of union was to ease territorial expansion. "A single old colony does not seem strong enough to extend itself otherwise than inch by inch." This was especially true of charter colonies, whose original land grants extended in "long narrow slips of land" from the Atlantic to the South Sea. Though only one or two hundred miles in length, they were over three thousand miles wide. These dimensions were inhospitable to good government. How could colonists in the east effectively communicate with, much less supply, those living in the west? Growth required the creation of new colonies, not the extension of old ones. Only a colonial union would have the strength and energy needed to accomplish this task.[64]

Imperial expansion was not simply a matter of strength, however. Franklin insisted that successful growth was dependent on the maintenance of civil and political liberty. "Thousands of families" were "ready to swarm" into the Ohio valley. But they could not do so unassisted. Territorial government was a prerequisite to large-scale settlement; political integration was a precondition to economic development. The union would purchase Indian lands, make grants to settlers, and establish codes of law. This would provide a stable foundation for growth. Once the new colonies were established, however, they would be admitted to the union as equal members. Each would have its own constitution and possess the same governing rights as the original thirteen members.[65]

The Rights of Britons

In December 1754 William Shirley, governor of Massachusetts, wrote Thomas Robinson, secretary of state, about the prospects for colonial union. Copies of the Albany Plan had been presented to eleven colonies. Five ignored it, four rejected it, and two sought to devise alternatives.[66] Franklin was distressed by this result, but Shirley was coolly pleased. The conduct of the colonies confirmed his belief that they were incapable of cooperation. Besides, he did not favor the Albany Plan. The powers it gave the General Council—powers to tax, to declare war and make peace with the Indians, to appoint military officers, and make laws for new territories—were "a great strain upon the prerogative of the Crown and contrary to the English Constitution." Shirley sketched an alternative, which he offered to send to the Board of Trade. Shirley's plan has been lost, but it apparently transformed the council into an appointed, not elected, body. It also placed the power to tax squarely in the hands of Parliament. When Franklin saw the sketch he was incensed. "It is supposed an undoubted Right of Englishmen not to be taxed but by their own Consent given through their Representatives."[67] Franklin's words, private in 1754, were made public during the Stamp Act crisis and repeatedly invoked in the decade prior to the Revolution. What did he mean by them?

Political theorists sometimes distinguish between two kinds of consent, "constitutional" and "legislative." Roughly, constitutional consent occurs when the members of civil society agree to a basic frame of government, while legislative consent occurs when citizens authorize, directly or through their representatives, specific acts of government. The former concerns the choice of institutions, the latter concerns decisions and actions taken by individuals within those institutions. To some, particularly within the social contract tradition, constitutional consent takes priority. Specific policies are justified only if the government itself is legitimate, and governments are legitimate only if they have received the consent of the governed. Thomas Jefferson thought this way, arguing that the Constitution ought to expire every nineteen years so that each new generation had the opportunity to accept, revise, or reject it.[68]

Franklin initially thought "a voluntary Union . . . preferable to one imposed by Parliament." A voluntary union would have embodied the ideal of constitutional consent—though, characteristically, Franklin's reasons for favoring it were practical, not ethical. A voluntary union would be easier to "alter and improve, as Circumstances should require, and Experience direct." By 1754 he had changed his mind. If there was to be a union, it had to be imposed by Parliament. This was a controversial position at Albany and was hotly debated by the commissioners. Historians have suggested that Franklin (temporarily) lost his faith in the political capacity of the colonies.[69] This is true, but it is only part of the story. Franklin was disgusted by the "weak Noodles" that dominated colonial assemblies, and some of his friends disparaged assemblies almost as a matter of principle.[70] But the pettiness and jealousy of the colonies was not Franklin's only concern. No less threatening was the possibility of secession. Even if the colonies unanimously approved the plan of union, "any colony, on the least dissatisfaction, might repeal its own act" and withdraw from the union. Other colonies, in turn, "might think it unjust and unequal that they, by continuing in the union, should be at the expense of defending a colony which refused to bear its proportional part, and would therefore one after another, withdraw, till the whole crumbled into its original parts." Paradoxically, the fruits of cooperation—collective security, economic integration, territorial expansion—were contingent on the colonies' willingness to accept the union as work of a higher authority. In 1787 the authors of the Constitution appealed to the American people, mobilized through special ratification committees. In 1754 that option simply did not exist, either practically or imaginatively. To Franklin, a devoted subject of the British Empire, the higher authority that ensured the integrity of the union "could be only the sovereign parliament."[71]

The rights of Britons did not include the right to select the basic institutions of government. What, then, were they? Don Herzog has argued that constitutional consent is "a special case . . . properly relegated to the sidelines" of consent theory. The "root idea" of consent, the one that best captures both moral ideal and lived practice, is that government ought to be "responsive to the expressed wishes of the people." This is akin to the concept of legislative consent. Responsive governments track the wishes of the people. If the people favor a specific policy, then it will be enacted; if the people do not want it, then it won't.[72]

Elections help make governments accountable to the people and are an important means of generating responsiveness. They are not the only way: protests and riots, as well as polls and study groups, are capable of linking the wishes of the people and the conduct of the government.[73] But elections have their advantages. As Franklin argued in his letters to Shirley, "It is very possible, that this general Government might be as well and faithfully administered without the people, as with them; but where heavy burdens are to be laid on them, it has been found useful to make it, as much as possible, their own act; for they bear better when they have, or think they have some share in the direction; and when any public measures are generally grievous or even distasteful to the people, the wheels of Government must move more heavily." Taxation by elected representatives was tolerable; taxation by a distant government, in which the colonists had no elected representatives, was disquieting. Self-imposed obligations are less obnoxious than ones inflicted by others. Elections enlist the will of the people, linking the passions and intentions of citizens to acts of state. That is one reason why Franklin thought it crucial to listen to what colonists actually said, not simply govern on the basis of what they "ought to think."[74]

During the Stamp Act crisis, defenders of the British constitution argued that elections were unnecessary to representation. A Member of Parliament (MP) represented the entire nation, not just his constituents. The distribution of votes in the House of Commons bore no consistent relationship to the distribution of the population; many inhabitants were drastically underrepresented, while others were dramatically overrepresented. But that did not matter; all were "virtually represented" in "that august Assembly," the House of Commons. When MPs deliberated, they represented "one interest, that of the whole."[75] Colonists were quick to point out that this argument assumed the very thing being contested: the existence of a single common good. Worse yet, the institutional guarantee of virtual representation—the impossibility of treating one region different from another—was absent in the colonies. In Great Britain Parliament could not pass laws that treated Birmingham any differently from Old Sarum. (At least, that is what the theory required. Parliamentary practice was a different matter.) But Parliament could and did pass laws that treated colonists differently from subjects living in England. For those living in North America, there could be no substitute for elections.

Franklin also thought that elections conveyed vital ideas and information. Consider the problem of colonial defense. "The People in the Colonies, who are to feel the immediate Mischief of Invasion and Conquest by an Enemy, in the Loss of their Estates, Lives and Liberties, are like to be better Judges of the Quantity of Forces necessary to be raised and maintained, Forts to be built and supported, and of their own Abilities to bear the Expense, than the Parliament of England at so great a Distance." Parliamentarians had no direct experience of the problems confronting colonists. They had to rely on reports from governors, men who often had neither a permanent interest in the colonies nor "natural Connections" with the colonists. Experience and interest gave the colonists insight and information that was essential to effective public policies. To ignore the colonists was irresponsible.[76]

Every Briton was entitled to legislative representation, whether he lived in London or Boston, Edinburgh or Philadelphia. In a commercial empire, bound together by the division of labor and a wide market, it did not matter where an individual lived. "I look on the Colonies as so many Counties gained to Great Britain, and more advantageous to it than if they had been gained out of the sea around its coasts, and joined to its land: For being in different climates, they afford greater variety of produce, and materials for more manufactures; and being separated by the ocean, they increase . . . its shipping and seamen. . . . What imports it to the general state, whether a merchant, a smith, or a hatter, grow rich in *Old* or *New* England?" Commerce dissolved the territorial priorities that governed older empires. In the mid-eighteenth century there could be no justification for depriving the settlers of the New World in order to satisfy the needs and interests of the Old. And how much greater a hardship, Franklin added, "if the people of the new country should be allowed no Representatives in the Parliament"?[77]

Franklin's criticisms of Shirley's proposed changes to the Albany Plan of Union suggested an obvious solution: elect MPs from the colonies. Scotland, as a consequence of the Act of Union of 1707, was entitled to forty-five seats in the Commons and sixteen in the Lords. Why not the colonies? Shirley floated this idea in conversation. Franklin's response was subtle and satiric, demolishing the idea by appearing to embrace it: "I . . . am of opinion, that such an Union would be very acceptable to the Colonies, provided they had a reasonable number of Representatives allowed them; and that all the old Acts of Parliament restraining the trade or cramping the manufactures of the Colonies, be at the same time repealed, and the British Subjects on this side the water put, in those respects, on the same footing with those in Great Britain, 'til the new Parliament, representing the whole, shall think it for the interest of the whole to re-enact some or all of them." No numbers were discussed. At the time England returned 489 MPs, to which were added 45 from Scotland and 24 from Wales. A decade later Franklin thought 100 colonial MPs sufficient to gain "the Attention of any Ministry." But numbers were not the point. The conditions Franklin imposed on colonial representation—dismantling virtually the entire imperial apparatus and making a fresh start with a new and enlarged Parliament—were comical. No metropolitan authority would have given them a second thought. Franklin knew this, and he used their implausibility to highlight the subordinate position of the colonies. Slyly mirroring language he had used to advocate the Albany Plan, he suggested that "by such an union, the people of Great Britain and the people of the Colonies would learn to consider themselves, not as belonging to different Communities with different Interests, but to one Community with one Interest." Given his prediction of a demographic explosion in North America, of course, it would not be long before Great Britain felt itself the junior partner and began clamoring for equality. Shirley, who was bringing *Observations concerning the Increase of Mankind* to print at precisely this moment, cannot have missed Franklin's ironic intentions.[78]

The Albany Plan of Union, with its elected General Council, was the best hope for preserving the rights of Britons living in North America. Before leaving this topic, one final aspect of Franklin's argument needs attention. Unlike in the British House of Commons, representation in the council was intended to be roughly proportional to population. Before the great reforms of the nineteenth century, representation in the Commons bore no necessary relationship to British population. Electoral districts were not adjusted regularly or systematically to reflect changes in population. As a consequence, once-vibrant towns that had shrunk to nothingness, like Old Sarum, continued to elect MPs, while bustling new cities, like Manchester, were not entitled to any representatives. By contrast, the council established by the Albany Plan guaranteed each colony a minimum of two, and a maximum of seven, representatives. Two, it was felt, was the minimum needed to ensure representation. Given the difficulty of intercolonial transportation, travelers could not plan arrivals and departures with precision. If a colony sent two representatives, then the likelihood that at least one would be present in congress was increased.

The maximum of seven representatives, on the other hand, is puzzling. Neither Franklin's "Short Hints" nor the report of the draft committee set an upper limit to the number of representatives a colony might claim, and the record is silent on the reasons for this change. But from start to finish Franklin insisted that the number of representatives bear a positive relationship to the proportion of money contributed to the common treasury. At first glance this looks like an attempt to represent property, not persons. On closer examination, however, it appears to be an ingenious solution to a difficult problem. As Franklin knew from personal experience, the exact population of each colony was unknown. Instruments needed for an accurate count simply did not exist. But taxes were a different matter. The council had the authority to "lay and levy such general duties, imports, or taxes, as to them shall appear most equal and just, (considering the ability and other circumstances of the inhabitants in the several colonies,) and such as may be collected with the least inconvenience to the people." Franklin favored an excise on "strong liquors" because they were "pretty equally drank in the Colonies." Others favored "Stamps on all Legal Writings." The precise form of the tax, to be levied directly on the colonists, is less important than the principle that governed it: the funds should "arise" from a source that was proportionate to the population of each colony. Lacking an accurate census, select articles of trade provided a suitable substitute.[79]

"Magna Britannia"

The Albany Plan fared no better in London than it did in the colonies. In June, just as the congress was convened, the king asked the Board of Trade to prepare a "Plan of General Concert." The draft, returned in August, conceived of union in military and administrative terms: the colonial council was appointed, not elected, and its primary purpose was to determine how much each colony should contribute to the common defense. No provision was made for broad political and legislative responsibilities, as in the Albany Plan. Even this was politically problematic, however; the speaker of the House of Commons warned that many MPs feared that union would lead to independence.[80] Compounding matters was news of Washington's defeat at Fort Necessity on the Ohio, which reached London in early September. Faced with a military crisis, delay was unacceptable. The prime minister ordered an imperial expedition under the command of Edward Braddock. As he explained to the attorney general, "You will have heard all that is passed, about the General Concert for establishing some provision for the joint defense of our Northern Colonies, but as no scheme of that kind can be of service in the present exigency, that may be a matter for future consideration." When copies of the Albany Plan finally arrived, in early October, they were judged "curious" and promptly set aside. Events on both sides of the Atlantic had rendered the plan moot.[81]

Thirty-five years later Franklin suggested that if the Albany Plan had been adopted and executed, the Revolution might not have happened for "another Century." If the colonies had been "united," and thus able to defend themselves, Britain would not have had to send an army to North America. And without an army in North America, "the Pretences for framing the Stamp-Act would then not have existed, nor the other Projects for drawing a Revenue from America to Britain by Acts of Parliament, which were the Cause of the Breach, and attended with such terrible Expense of Blood and Treasure."[82] (Franklin's initial qualification—"another Century"—is crucial. A separation would have occurred, just not as soon.)

The Albany Plan (1754) and the Stamp Act (1765) were colonial bookends to the Seven Years' War, "the greatest of Europe's eighteenth-century wars." Franklin, so prescient in 1754, was slow to appreciate the consequences of war for public opinion in the colonies. The public cost of the Seven Years' War was unprecedented. When George Grenville floated the idea of raising money in the colonies by imposing a tax on papers used to transact business, Franklin's first reaction was pragmatic. He proposed what he believed would be a less troubling alternative and, when it was dismissed, bowed to Grenville's plan as distasteful yet unavoidable. "We might as well have hindered the Sun's setting," he concluded. He was shocked by the

Virginia Resolves, which declared parliamentary taxation "illegal, unconstitutional, and unjust." As his letters to Shirley in 1754 indicated, he accepted the basic principle of the Resolves, linking taxation and representation. But in 1765 he did not think announcing that principle, especially in such a provocative way, to be productive. Far better to remain flexible and able to negotiate; who knows what might emerge? Sometimes, in politics, it was useful to be hypocritical.[83]

Franklin was no less dismayed by attempts to intimidate stamp distributors, and he was horrified by mobs who suspected his loyalty and threatened his home. (Living in London, Franklin was removed from immediate threat. Deborah, who remained in Philadelphia, was protected by the White Oaks, a fraternal club of Philadelphia laborers.)[84] Only gradually did Franklin come to understand the intensity and determination of colonial opposition to the Stamp Act. He was quicker to appreciate the intransigence of Parliament, and by the end of 1765 he had come to fear that metropolitan authorities would attempt to compel colonial obedience through force of arms. He worked to ease tensions and lessen hostilities. One facet of his campaign was an extraordinary political cartoon, "Magna Britannia."

Like "Join, or Die," "Magna Britannia" uses a severed body to explore the themes of union and disunion. Unlike the snake cartoon, which suggested that the colonies constituted a distinct and coherent community, "Magna Britannia" called attention to the interdependence of Great Britain and her colonies. In the foreground is a woman, fallen from her seat on top of the globe, dismembered and despondent. Each of her limbs bears the name of a colony; lying across her is a sash with the motto *Date Obolum Bellisario.* On one border is a denuded oak tree; in the background, three empty ships.

Franklin printed this image on cards, which he then used as writing paper during the time Parliament was debating whether to use the army to enforce the Stamp Act. As he explained to his sister, "The Moral is, that the Colonies might be ruined, but that Britain would thereby be maimed." This explanation is compact and accurate, but it does not do justice to the rich and multilayered iconography of the print. Franklin knew this; he also printed the cartoon on half sheets of paper with an "Explanation" and "Moral":

EXPLANATION.
  GREAT BRITAIN is supposed to have been placed upon the globe; but the COLONIES, (that is, her limbs,) being severed from

"Magna Britannia," designed by Benjamin Franklin, c. 1766. (Courtesy the Library Company of Philadelphia.)

her, she is seen lifting her eyes and mangled stumps to heaven; her shield, which she is unable to wield, lies useless by her side; her lance has pierced New England: the laurel branch has fallen from the hand of Pennsylvania: the English oak has lost its head, and stands a bare trunk, with a few withered branches; briars and thorns are on the ground beneath it; the British ships have brooms at their top-mast heads, denoting their being on sale; and BRITANNIA herself is seen sliding off the world, (no longer able to hold its balance) her fragments overspread with the label, DATE OBOLUM BELLISARIO.

THE MORAL.

History affords us many instances of the ruin of states, by the prosecution of measures ill suited to the temper and genius of their people. The ordaining of laws in favor of *one* part of the nation, to the prejudice and oppression of *another*, is certainly the most erroneous and mistaken policy. An *equal* dispensation of protection, rights, privileges, and advantages, is what every part is entitled to, and ought to enjoy; it being a matter of no moment to the state, whether a subject grows rich and flourishing on the Thames or the Ohio, in Edinburgh or Dublin. These measures never fail to create great and violent jealousies and animosities between the people

favored and the people oppressed: whence a total separation of affections, interests, political obligations, and all manner of connections, necessarily ensue, by which the whole state is weakened, and
perhaps ruined forever![85]

As Franklin had argued in 1754, Great Britain and her colonies were interdependent and ought to be considered as a single community. The Stamp Act,
like every other measure that treated the colonies differently from the
mother country, was shortsighted and self-destructive.

This exegesis is incomplete, however; it leaves unexplained the inscription *Date Obolum Bellisario*. Franklin may have thought this unnecessary; the
print was intended for a sophisticated metropolitan audience, for whom the
reference would have been familiar. (By contrast, when reprinted in Philadelphia, "Magna Britannia" included a lengthy explanation of the inscription.)
Belisarius (c. 505–565 CE) was one of the greatest military heroes of the ancient world. Under the emperor Justinian he led campaigns in Mesopotamia,
North Africa, and Italy. Though Belisarius added vast territories to the
Byzantine Empire, his victories aroused envy and suspicion. Late in life he
was accused of plotting against Justinian's life. According to legend, the emperor had him blinded and forced him to live on the streets, begging
passersby to "give a penny to Belisarius" (*Date Obolum Bellisario*). For eighteenth-century Europeans, Belisarius's fate was a powerful reminder of the
consequences of ingratitude. Poems were written, plays were performed,
and pictures were painted on Justinian's "savage Ingratitude." Alexander
Pope spoke for many when he wondered, "Was there a generous, a reflecting
mind, / But pitied Belisarius old and blind?"[86]

Gratitude is a feeling, a warm sense of appreciation for a kindness done,
as well as a desire to do something in return. It can also be a moral obligation,
a duty to acknowledge and reciprocate benefits received.[87] Gratitude has little
to do with contracts or explicit agreements; it thrives in relationships defined
by trust. Its natural habitat is the family. Children owe a debt of gratitude to
parents for the care and support they receive. When children fail to acknowledge that debt, they are considered ungrateful. And to many Britons, nothing
was more odious than ingratitude. According to Jonathan Swift, "He that
calls a man ungrateful, sums up all the Evil that a Man can be guilty of."
David Hume concurred: "Of all crimes that human creatures are capable of
committing, the most horrid and unnatural is ingratitude."[88]

The family was a potent model and metaphor for political relationships—many still referred to the king as the nation's "father" and to England as the "mother country"—and gratitude and ingratitude played important roles in public life. Accusations of ingratitude expressed scorn, disdain, and contempt. They suggested that a person was base and unworthy. And in the social world of eighteenth-century Britain, still largely defined by relations of hierarchy and inequality, these emotions had palpable consequences.[89] When the charge of ingratitude stuck, it altered a person's position in society. As ungrateful children ought to be reprimanded and brought low, so ought ungrateful adults. And ungrateful communities. Franklin noted with foreboding the frequency with which colonists were charged with ingratitude during the Stamp Act crisis. A London writer was "surprised" at the colonists' "want of gratitude": "they knew very well that a great part of our national debt was contracted in establishing them on a firm foundation, and protecting them from the arbitrary attempts of their implacable enemies." Robert Nugent, MP for Bristol, "expatiated on the extreme ingratitude of the colonies" on the floor of the House of Commons. The esteemed political economist Josiah Tucker remonstrated that "you Americans do not choose to remember anything, which we have done for you." Even in the colonies charges of ingratitude were flying. The loyalist lawyer Martin Howard Jr., engaged in a "Paper War" in Rhode Island, wrote Franklin that he had "taken the Side of [the] Mother Country against her Ungrateful Sons."[90]

Franklin was alarmed by these sentiments. "Ingratitude is so odious, I cannot be unconcerned, when my countrymen are unjustly charged with it." When he appeared before the Commons in February 1766 to testify on American sentiment regarding the Stamp Act, he made a special point of addressing this accusation. "America has been greatly misrepresented and abused here, in papers, and pamphlets, and speeches, as ungrateful, and unreasonable, and unjust, in having put this nation to immense expense for their defense, and refusing to bear any part of that expense." The government's own records, Franklin countered, proved otherwise; during the Seven Years' War the colonies contributed "beyond their abilities" and at a proportionately higher rate than the people of Great Britain.[91] It was at this time that Franklin first decried the "common but mistaken Notion here, that the Colonies were planted at the Expense of Parliament." In truth, he claimed, they were planted at private expense. "Parliament had no hand in their

Settlement."[92] This story of origins was the basis for an important constitutional claim: Parliament's sovereign powers were limited to the territory of Great Britain. But it was also an attempt to undercut the charge of ingratitude. If no benefit had been conferred by Parliament, then no debt of gratitude could have been incurred by the colonies.

Franklin was too savvy a controversialist—and too sophisticated a moral psychologist—to think that British scorn could be countered effectively by reciting the facts and figures of colonization. Political passions, like the human character, were complex and multilayered. Indirect strategies were often more effective than straightforward appeals to reason. We have seen how, in his attempts to mobilize Pennsylvanians for self-defense in 1747, Franklin invoked shame to counter the pride and envy of the Proprietary Party. In 1766 he used the same strategy to influence opinion in Great Britain. Sneers and contempt could be upended and turned against themselves. When one writer predicted that the colonists would prove unable to maintain their resolution to stop drinking tea because of the wretched quality of American produce, Franklin responded with an impassioned defense of Indian corn, "one of the most agreeable and wholesome grains in the world." When military talk filled the air, Franklin sought to defuse it with satire. As the fateful vote on the Stamp Act neared, Franklin suggested that the cheapest way to bring the colonies to heel would be to send a coalition of Highlanders, Canadians, and Indians to level the largest cities, scalping every inhabitant within them. "No Man in his Wits, after such terrible Military Execution, will refuse to purchase stamped Paper." (Eight years later Franklin upped the ante, suggesting that the "most feasible Method of humbling our rebellious Vassals of North America" was to castrate all male colonists. "This will be laying the Axe to the Root of the Tree.") And finally, resentment and indignation could be met with a blend of countervailing passions and interests. Great Britain was poised on a knife-edge. Should it persist in treating the colonies as unequal and inferior, it would fall from "the Zenith of Glory and Honor" to "the most Abject State of Disgrace Misery and Ruin." Sympathy for blind Belisarius and horror at his fall from greatness merged with national pride and economic self-interest. Ingratitude was a dangerous and destructive political passion. For union to endure and for the empire to prosper each part must enjoy "an *equal* dispensation of protection, rights, privileges, and advantages."[93]

"We Are One"

Franklin's short-term objective in distributing "Magna Britannia"—repeal of the Stamp Act—was achieved. But in the longer term relations between Great Britain and the colonies worsened. Like many others, Franklin spent the late 1760s and early 1770s searching for a way to "preserve from breaking, that fine and noble China Vase the British Empire." Were the colonies "virtually" represented in Parliament, as many parts of Great Britain were? Would it be possible to elect American MPs to Parliament, as Scotland did? Could a new imperial configuration, in which Great Britain and the colonies were politically distinct, linked only by a common king, succeed? Each of these options was explored and rejected. In mid-1775 Franklin publicly committed himself to independence. Conciliation was no longer possible, and half measures would not do. "He does not hesitate at our boldest Measures," John Adams wrote his wife Abigail, "but rather seems to think us, too irresolute, and backward."[94]

By the time the Second Continental Congress convened in Philadelphia, on 10 May 1775, the battles of Lexington and Concord had already been fought. Within a month Congress voted to create the Continental Army, under the command of George Washington. To fund the war effort, new federally issued money—Continental Currency—was authorized: $3,000,000 in June, $3,000,000 in November, and another $4,000,000 in February 1776. Franklin, as one of Pennsylvania's representatives to Congress, was appointed to the committee responsible for these issues.[95]

Franklin had been designing and printing paper money for decades and was keenly interested in the expressive power of its emblems and mottos. Money was a medium with a message, and every time it was handled, it made "an Impression upon the Mind." Instead of repeating tired stories and dull facts, the faces of coins and bills could be stamped with new and constructive messages. Money could be used, quite literally, to improve people's minds. Thus the new $8 bill contained the figure of a harp with the motto *Majora minoribus consonant* (The greater and smaller ones sound together). As the harp was made of different strings, so "the several colonies of different weight and force, or the various ranks of people" were "united" by the Continental Congress in "the most perfect *harmony*." The $20 bill portrayed "a *tempestuous sea;* a face, with swollen cheeks, wrapped up in a black cloud, appearing to blow violently on the waters, *the waves high,* and *all rolling one way:* The motto VI CONCITATE; which may be rendered, *raised by force.*"

Unlike the harp, this design originated with Franklin; a rough draft still exists. Astute consumers would have recalled that Franklin had twice before used the phrase "The waves never rise but when the winds blow" to blame Great Britain for colonial unrest.[96]

Franklin's most sophisticated designs appeared on "fractional" bills, ranging in value from one-sixth to two-thirds of a dollar. On one side of each bill is a rebus, consisting of a shining sun, a sundial, and the Latin word *Fugio* (I fly). Underneath this rebus is the phrase "Mind your business." Taken together, the elements of the rebus suggest that time flies, and colonists should get to work. On the other side of the bills was a chain with thirteen links, each bearing the name of a colony. Within the chain was a sunburst and within the sunburst the words "American Congress." At the very center was the phrase "We Are One." With slight modifications, these designs were used on the first coin minted by the United States, the so-called Fugio cent of 1787. Franklin may not have designed the rebus, but his original sketches of the chain device have survived. This image was extremely popular, and during the coming decade it appeared on everything from plates and pitchers to buttons, flags, and carpets.[97] What did it mean?

At the center of Franklin's design are the words "We Are One." The phrase is an oxymoron, a conflation of plural and singular. How can "we" be "one"? As written expression, the phrase is confusing. But when drawn as a

Franklin's sketch for Continental currency, 1775.
(Courtesy American Philosophical Society.)

One-third dollar note, Continental currency. (Reproduced from the original held by the Department of Special Collections of the University Libraries of Notre Dame.)

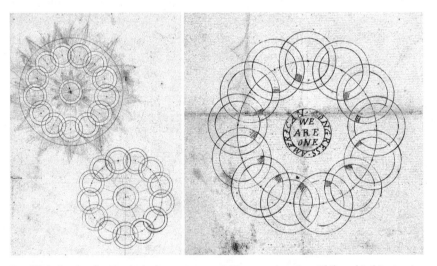

Franklin's sketches for Continental currency, 1776. (Courtesy American Philosophical Society.)

chain ring, it makes perfect sense. Each of the links is distinct, yet when joined together they form an unbroken circle. In just the same way, each of the states was distinct, yet when joined together they formed a single nation. The design does not resolve the underlying tension between the independence of the states and the unity of the nation, but it does imply that those conflicts can—and should—be negotiated. To understand the terms of that negotiation, we need to ask two further questions. Who are the "we" referred to in the phrase "We Are One," states or individual citizens? And what kind of unity was achieved when they came together? Clues to the answers to these questions can be found in the "Articles of Confederation and perpetual Union" Franklin submitted to Congress in July 1775.

Franklin's "Articles" proposed a "firm League of Friendship" between the colonies of North America. From the perspective of the twenty-first century this language sounds quaint. But in the summer of 1775 it was explosive—it signaled an end to attempts at reconciliation—and Franklin was not permitted to read his plan into the journals of Congress. Instead, on 21 July Congress resolved itself into a committee of the whole, and Franklin was permitted to present his plan without leaving a trace on the official record.[98]

Franklin proposed that each colony remain distinct, like the links in a chain, retaining "as much as it may think fit of its own present Laws, Customs, Rights, Privileges, and peculiar Jurisdictions." In tandem with the provision that the "Articles" be returned to the provincial assemblies and conventions for ratification, this gives the impression that the union was to be a confederation of independent states, akin to an international treaty. Many members of the Continental Congress thought this way. Roger Sherman, a merchant from Massachusetts, argued that "we are representatives of States, not Individuals"; John Witherspoon, president of the College of New Jersey, declared that "every Colony is a distinct Person." Men like Sherman and Witherspoon viewed the national government as "a compact between individual states, each considered as a self-sufficient community." The basic units out of which the union was composed were territorial and legal corporations, not individual citizens. This abstract idea had two immediate practical consequences. It meant that the national government should act on states, not directly upon individuals living within states. It also meant that in Congress, each state should be represented as a state, equal to every other state, regardless of its size or wealth. In compact federalism, one state is entitled to one vote.[99]

Franklin vigorously resisted this idea. "Let the smaller Colonies give equal money and men," he retorted, "and then have an equal vote. But if they have an equal vote without bearing equal burdens, a confederation upon such iniquitous principles will never last long." Votes in Congress "should be in proportion to numbers. . . . The Number of Delegates to be elected and sent to the Congress by each Colony, shall be regulated from time to time by the Number of such Polls returned, so as that one Delegate be allowed for every 5000 Polls. And the Delegates are to bring with them to every Congress an authenticated Return of the number of Polls in their respective Provinces, which is to be annually taken, for the Purposes abovementioned." Franklin averred that if he lived in a state where representation "had become unequal by time and accident," he might accept it as an unavoidable compromise. But "we should be very wrong" to start out this way, "when it is in our power to establish what is right." Each citizen was entitled to equal representation in Congress.[100]

Witherspoon, Sherman, and others were anxious that proportional representation would allow larger states to dominate smaller ones. Tiny states like Rhode Island and New Jersey would not stand a chance against behemoths like Virginia or Pennsylvania. These worries persisted into the 1780s and played a key role in the drafting of the Constitution in 1787. Franklin was a participant in those debates as well, and the width of the chasm separating him from men like Witherspoon—men dedicated to preserving the corporate and territorial integrity of the states—was graphically illustrated by a playful injection into a very serious exchange. To eliminate conflicts between small and large states, "an honorable Gentleman"—Franklin delighted in ventriloquism—had "hinted" at a method for "equalizing the States. It appears to me an equitable one and I should for my own Part, not be against such a Measure, if it might be found practicable. . . . The Interest of a State is made up of the Interests of its individual Members. If they are not injured, the State is not injured. Small States are more easily well and happily governed than large ones. If therefore in such an equal Division, it should be found necessary to diminish Pennsylvania, I should not be averse to the giving a Part of it to New Jersey, and another to Delaware." Sadly, Franklin added with a sly wink, this scheme was not practical: every change in population distribution would require redrawing state boundaries. This was a fabulous proposal, never intended to be taken seriously. But as a flight of political imagination it is revealing. From the point of view of the nation, state boundaries were arbitrary and ought to be politically irrelevant. The basic unit of the union was the individual citizen. As Franklin's friend and fellow Pennsylvanian James Wilson put it in 1776, in "those matters which are referred to Congress, we are not so many states; we are one large state."[101]

John Adams also favored proportional representation, but this apparent harmony of views masked a sharp disagreement. "The question," Adams asserted, was not "what we are now," but what we will become. Correctly understood, union was like a blast furnace, fusing "separate parcels of metal, into one common mass." With this Franklin would have agreed: "We Are One." But the "common mass" Adams referred to was composed of interests, not persons. "Reason, justice and equity" did not "govern the councils of men." Interest did. "Therefore the interests within doors should be the mathematical representatives of the interests without doors. . . . A. has 50£, B. 500£ C. 1,000£ in partnership. Is it just they should equally dispose of the monies of the partnership?" Franklin found this analogy disturbing, since it implied that the rights of representation were tied to the ownership of property. "The Combinations of Civil Society are not like those of a Set of Merchants who club their Property in different Proportions for Building and Freighting a Ship, and may therefore have some Right to vote in the Disposition of the Voyage in a greater or less Degree according to their respective Contributions; but the important Ends of Civil Society are the personal Securities of Life and Liberty; these remain the same in every Member of the Society; and the poorest continues to have an equal Claim to them with the most opulent, whatever Difference Time, Chance or Industry may occasion in their Circumstances."[102]

The distance between Adams and Franklin is extraordinary, and at first glance more than a little puzzling. Franklin argued that commerce was the foundation of the modern republic, yet he insisted that representation and citizenship be blind to wealth and property. Adams worried that commerce, and the luxury that came in its train, threatened to destroy the Republic, yet he insisted that property be represented in politics. Shouldn't their positions be reversed?

Disagreements between Adams and Franklin are sometimes treated as personality conflicts, a clash of colonial titans: the stern and haughty Bostonian versus the familiar and indulgent Philadelphian. There is some truth to this. In the Continental Congress, Adams was thin skinned and argumentative, while Franklin was complaisant. As ambassadors to the court of Louis

XVI, Adams disapproved of lax French morals and manners, while Franklin relished in them. But the differences between these two men were not simply personal; they had deep intellectual roots as well. Adams was a keen student of the seventeenth-century English republican James Harrington. Like Harrington, he believed that the institutions of government should reflect the distribution of power in society. In all nations there are inequalities of virtue, talent, wealth, knowledge, and wit. No "human legislator" could eradicate these differences, for they were "planted" by God and nature. But every individual *could* and *did* aspire to distinction. All life was a "scramble" for the top. Inevitably, societies divided into two broad groups: "the rich and the poor, the laborious and the idle, the learned and the ignorant." Between these groups there could be no permanent peace. Harrington had taught that the key to a stable republic was "dividing and equalizing" the forces in society. Conflicts between the few and the many, destructive when left unchecked, could be contained and channeled by political institutions. Adams concurred. On this basis, he argued that legislatures ought to be bicameral, with an upper house representing the few and a lower house representing the many.[103]

Franklin railed at this idea. It stoked the pride of the rich and degraded everyone else. A single legislative branch was "much the safest and best." Franklin had read Harrington, but he did not accept Harrington's claim that the balance of property determined the optimal structure of government.[104] Nor did he share Adams's belief that all societies fracture into two basic groups, the few and the many. When thinking about the relationship between politics and economics, Franklin participated in a different circle of conversation. From the 1750s onward his principal interlocutors were men committed to free trade: Hume and Smith in Scotland; Lord Shelburne, Richard Price, and Joseph Priestley in England; Turgot, Condorcet, and Mirabeau in France. The key insight shared by these men was captured by Hume in "Of the Jealousy of Trade": "The increase of riches and commerce in any one nation, instead of hurting, commonly promotes the riches and commerce of all its neighbors." Economic growth was not a zero-sum contest, in which one nation was pitted against the others. The monopolistic practices of the British Empire were unnecessary and counterproductive. Free trade, in this view, was an engine of growth and development. Franklin invoked this argument in 1760 in an attempt to ease British anxieties about America's explosive economic growth. After 1776 it provided a touchstone for thinking about terms of union in the new nation.[105]

The liberalization of trade was not simply an economic doctrine; it was also viewed as "a means to knit the world together in a single community of cosmopolitan fellowship." Recall that in Franklin's day, commerce involved much more than buying and selling; it included a wide range of relationships in which needs and interests were met through the circulation of objects and ideas, people and passions. Recall also that utility and usefulness were not narrow economic categories; they referred to the ability of something to be advantageous or beneficial. Commerce, in this complex sense, was useful; it softened manners, strengthened morals, and fostered communication. To succeed, a merchant must understand the needs and interests of others. The empire of trade was an engine of reciprocity.[106]

(Franklin embraced free trade but, true to form, he was not doctrinaire. In 1787 and 1788 friends from England and France wrote to chide him. The United States had turned to import and excise taxes to fund its debt. Had the Americans forgotten "the Principles of Public Economy"? Direct taxes—taxes levied on individuals—preserved freedom of trade; taxes imposed through customs houses were inefficient and unrewarding. Franklin protested that he had not abandoned his commitment to "Freedom of Commerce." But, he punned, "To get the bad Customs of a Country changed, and new ones . . . introduced . . . is not the Work of a Day." Besides, direct taxes were not practical in a country that was "sparsely settled." The distance between homes was often five or six miles, and the cost of administering a direct tax would exceed the amount it could bring in. Once the country was filled with people, and its debts were paid, "we may leave our trade free." But until then, it was not practical. Improvement was not a rigid ideology or a program but a set of priorities expressed in decisions and actions.)[107]

To many Europeans, unicameralism was the constitutional correlate of free trade. This was especially evident in France, where *américanistes* argued that it was necessary to set aside "antiquated English notions" in politics as well as economics. All persons were equal in principle; all ought to be equal in practice as well. Bicameral legislatures echoed the division of Parliament into a House of Lords for the privileged few and a House of Commons for the unprivileged many. Anne-Robert Turgot, friend of Franklin and leader of the américanistes, had hoped that the new states of North America would embrace unicameralism. Instead, he lamented, most states had slavishly imitated the English: "They have established different bodies . . . [and] endeavor to balance [them] . . . as if this equilibrium . . . could be of any use in

Republics founded upon the equality of all the Citizens; and as if establishing different orders of men, was not a source of divisions and disputes. In attempting to prevent imaginary dangers they create real ones."[108] Only Pennsylvania had managed to avoid this trap: due, no doubt, to Franklin's influence. (Years later Adams grumbled, "Mr. Turgot, the Duke de la Rochefoucauld, and Mr. Condorcet and others, admired Mr. Franklin's Constitution and reprobated mine.")[109]

In the ideology of free trade, political integration and economic development were linked. At times Franklin expressed this idea in terms that suggest a middle-class idyll of peace and prosperity. To Europeans he proclaimed that "a general happy Mediocrity" prevailed in America.[110] This claim had more than a hint of salesmanship to it and neglected to mention the brutal inequalities of slavery. But it does capture an important dimension of Franklin's thought. Franklin was conscious of economic inequalities and the clashes they gave rise to. But they were not the only, or even the primary, cause of enduring social conflict. Religious practice, ethnic identity, and national origin were no less potent, and they did not all neatly line up into two groups. To a man coming from Pennsylvania, this would have been almost intuitive. Quakers' beliefs and practices were at the center of social and political conflicts from the colony's founding. Immigrants, from Scotland and Ireland as well as Germany, challenged preexisting community practices.

When Franklin reflected on the optimal design of a legislature, he focused on qualities like transparency, responsiveness, and resoluteness. In 1776 he supported Pennsylvania's controversial unicameral constitution with a parable. Two houses, each having the ability to check the other, were like a wagon with horses hitched to both ends, pulling in opposite directions. Thirteen years later he opposed a campaign to introduce a bicameral legislature with another allegory. "Has not the famous political Fable of the Snake with two Heads and one Body some useful Instruction contained in it? She was going to a Brook to drink, and in her Way was to pass through a Hedge, a Twig of which opposed her direct Course; one Head chose to go on the right side of the Twig, the other on the left; so that Time was spent in the Contest, and before the Decision was completed, the poor Snake died with Thirst."[111] As he wrote this, Franklin had in mind the logjams that clogged Pennsylvania's colonial government during the 1750s. With the governor and Assembly pitted against each other, the flow of legislation ground to a halt, with disastrous consequences. A government divided against itself threatened the public interest. A representative government, Franklin argued, must be able to act with resolution.

Adams feared the resoluteness of unicameral legislatures. "A single Assembly is liable to all the vices, follies and frailties of an individual": "fits of humor, starts of passion, flights of enthusiasm, partialities of prejudice, and consequently productive of hasty results and absurd judgments." Simplicity was a vice; the "complexity" of a bicameral legislation permitted one branch to check the passions of the other. This was a common complaint against unicameral legislatures: they were less rational than bicameral legislatures. Franklin did not agree; he saw no reason to believe that wisdom divided was more intelligent than wisdom united.[112] But what drew his ire especially was the association of wisdom and virtue with rank and class. In the *Essex Result* of 1778, the Massachusetts lawyer Theophilus Parsons argued that in designing a constitution "we are to look further than to the bulk of the people, for the greatest wisdom, firmness, consistency, and perseverance." Parsons argued that the best index of these qualities was property. The Massachusetts constitution of 1780—whose principal author was John Adams—incorporated this idea and based representation in the upper house on the proportion of taxes paid in each district. Franklin dismissed these arguments for bicameralism and the representation of property. "Some of the greatest rogues he was ever acquainted with, were the richest rogues." But among his American contemporaries he was in the minority. With the exception of Pennsylvania, no state fully embraced unicameralism, and Pennsylvania abandoned its experiment in 1790. At the Constitutional Convention of 1787, bicameralism was adopted "without debate or dissent." The Pennsylvania delegates withheld their vote, to be sure; but James Madison was not worried. This was nothing more than a polite gesture of respect for the well-known views of the convention's most senior member.[113]

The Morals of Politics

Franklin's French friends were fascinated by American politics. Approaching reforms of their own, they looked to America for insight and example. Many were deeply disappointed when they learned that the Constitution established a bicameral legislature. The marquis de Condorcet was pained to learn that "the aristocratic spirit seeks to introduce itself among you in spite of so many wise precautions."[114] Pierre-Samuel du Pont de Nemours, the

duc de La Rochefoucauld, and Louis-Guillaume Le Veillard expressed similar sentiments. To Le Veillard—a devoted friend and neighbor from Passy—
Franklin responded, "As to the two Chambers, I am of your Opinion, that
one alone would be better; but my dear Friend, nothing in human Affairs and
Schemes is perfect, and perhaps that is the Case of our Opinions.—" This
was vintage Franklin: moderate, self-effacing, pragmatic. To the political
economist du Pont Franklin suggested a different metaphor, with a different
lesson. "We must not expect that a new government may be formed, as a
game of chess may be played, by a skilful hand, without a fault. The players
of our game are so many, their ideas so different, their prejudices so strong
and so various, and their particular interests independent of the general
seeming so opposite, that not a move can be made that is not contested; the
numerous objections confound the understanding; the wisest must agree to
some unreasonable things, that reasonable ones of more consequence may
be obtained, and thus chance has its share in many of the determinations, so
that the play is more like tric-trac with a box of dice."[115] This, too, was vintage Franklin. Union was the fruit of negotiation, persuasion, and compromise. And, of course, luck. Accident and chance could not be escaped;
politics was not like chess.

Franklin's letter to du Pont is a reminder of the importance of chess to
his life. We do not know when he first learned the game, but by the age of
twenty-seven he was an avid player. Competition in Philadelphia was intense, and Franklin collected books on chess to improve his game. When he
traveled to London in 1757, he carried his books with him.[116] In England, and
later in France, he delighted in matches, sometimes playing late into the
night. His correspondence is littered with invitations to play; intriguingly,
the majority of these letters are from women.[117] Late in life he gave a traveling chess set to a dear friend, Polly Hewson, née Stevenson. The board of
this set is made of leather; the ivory pieces are held in a silver egg. The scale
is Lilliputian: the king is less than three-quarters of an inch tall.

Franklin memorialized his love of the game in a famous bagatelle,
"The Morals of Chess." "The game of Chess is not merely an idle Amusement," he reminded his readers. ("Not merely." Which is to say, of course it
is amusing—why else would we play?—but it is much more than that.)
"Several very valuable qualities of the mind, useful in the course of human
Life, are to be acquired or strengthened by it, so as to become habits, ready
on all occasions. For Life is a kind of Chess, in which we have often points to

Traveling chess set, c. 1786. (Courtesy American Philosophical Society.)

gain, and Competitors or Adversaries to contend with; and in which there is a vast variety of good or ill Events, that are in some degree the Effects of Prudence or the want of it." By playing chess a person learned *foresight,* or the knack of anticipating the future consequences of present actions; *circumspection,* or the ability to comprehend complex situations at a single glance; *caution,* or the habit of moving slowly and self-consciously; and *perseverance,* or the ability to see beyond the temporary vicissitudes of the game. To learn these virtues, it was necessary that players agree to play "according to the strict rules." Bending the rules undermined play; so, too, did distracting, amusing, or deceiving an opponent. Gloating was absolutely forbidden; victors ought to endeavor to console their adversaries.[118]

"The Morals of Chess" suggests an Apollonian perspective on life: serene, balanced, and rational. This was the spirit in which Franklin wrote his friend Horatio Gates in the summer of 1779, anticipating the day "when we shall meet again in cheerful Converse, talk of our Adventures, and finish with a quiet Game of Chess." At the time Gates was a commander in the Continental army. In three short years his fortunes had ranged from a triumphant victory over Burgoyne at Saratoga to nasty accusations that he was plotting to replace Washington as commander in chief. Politics was a brutal game, marked by chance and accident, passion and conflict, confusion and mistakes. It was a collective activity—the work of coalitions and groups, not individuals. Often, as Gates painfully learned, it was difficult to distinguish friends and enemies, colleagues and competitors. Chess offered a welcome respite from the tribulations of political life. (Chess was not always played at Apollonian heights, of course. According to the family lore of Franklin's Passy landlord, Franklin was not a particularly courteous or fair player. "He grew impatient at the slowness of his partners, was prone to rearranging the board if his opponent left the room, and often drummed his fingers on the table." When reprimanded for the latter, he replied, "Mon cher, c'est une bagatelle, et ce n'est pas la peine d'en parler" [My friend, it is a trifle and not worth talking about]. In other words, "he played to win.")[119]

Politics was not like chess. Neither was it a free-for-all. It had its own rules and patterns, structure and logic. And just as success at chess required the cultivation of specific habits and virtues, so, too, did politics. Personal character, no less than formal institutions, was essential to a successful union.

What were the virtues of a politician? Franklin did not give a general or abstract answer to this question (or any other question, for that matter). But he delighted in using his own life for instructive purposes, and we may turn to it for clues. As a conversationalist, Franklin's most distinctive trait was his complaisance. He was courteous, obliging, and politely agreeable. As much as possible, he avoided direct conflict with others. Thomas Jefferson thought this made him "the most amiable of men in society." Franklin made it a rule "never to contradict anybody. If he was urged to announce an opinion, he did it rather by asking questions, as for information, or by suggesting doubts." John Adams observed the same behavior but came to a different conclusion. Franklin's "whole life" was "one continued Insult to good Manners and Decency": he "hates to offend, and seldom gives any opinion till obliged to do it. . . . Although he has as determined a soul as any man, yet it is his constant policy never to say yes or no decidedly but when he cannot avoid it." Jefferson and Adams each recognized that Franklin's complaisance was a conscious choice—a "rule" or "policy"—and not simply a habit or an affectation. Adams, who was sent with Franklin as ambassador to France in 1776, thought Franklin's complaisance self-serving and nationally humiliating. Adams boiled with indignation at Franklin's willingness to blandly tolerate the precise and complex rituals dictated by the court of Louis XVI. Had Franklin comported himself with greater candor, Adams implied, he would have been a more effective ambassador. Jefferson, by contrast, thought Franklin's mode of conduct expressed a valuable political ideal. "I never yet saw an instance of one or two disputants convincing the other by argument," he warned his grandson. "I have," on the other hand, "seen many on their getting warm, becoming rude, and shooting one another."[120]

Jefferson and Adams knew Franklin as a man in his seventies, coping with the challenges of war making and state building. The personal style they observed had been honed during five decades of public life. As was so often the case, Franklin's defense of complaisance linked method and purpose with personal narrative. In a letter to Samuel Mather, he recalled a hard lesson learned at the hands of Samuel's father, Cotton:

> The last Time I saw your Father was in the Beginning of 1724 when I visited him after my first Trip to Pennsylvania. He received me in his Library, and on my taking Leave showed me a shorter way out of the House thro a narrow Passage which was crossed by a Beam overhead. We were still talking as I withdrew, he accompanying me behind, and I turning partly towards him, when he said hastily Stoop, Stoop! I did not understand him till I felt my Head hit against the Beam. He was a Man that never missed any Occasion of giving Instruction, and upon this he said to me, *You are young and have the World before you; Stoop as you go through it, and you will miss many hard Thumps.* This Advice, thus beat into my head has frequently been of use to me, and I often think of it when I see Pride mortified, and Misfortunes brought upon People by their carrying their Heads too high.

Franklin was too proud to be humble, but he relished the slapstick humor of the scene and cherished Mather's advice. (Cotton was a notoriously short-tempered and impatient man. Samuel may have found the anecdote especially witty, as he undoubtedly would have recalled a sign posted above Cotton's study door, admonishing all who entered to "Be Short.")[121]

Franklin took Mather's advice to heart. As a young man he delighted in vigorous arguments and allowed himself to be brash and aggressive. But this gained him more enemies than friends, and he had to teach himself to be less "positive" and dogmatic. "The great Secret of succeeding in Conversation," he noted in his commonplace book of the early 1730s, "is, to admire little, to hear much; always to distrust our own Reason, and sometimes that of our

Friends; never to pretend to Wit, but to make that of others appear as much as possibly we can: to hearken to what is said, and to answer to the purpose. *Ut iam nunc dicat iam nunc debentia dici* [To say just now what ought to be said just now]."[122] To those who believe that there is a true or authentic self that ought to be revealed in conversation—to people like D. H. Lawrence—this advice sounds crass and boorish. These are the stratagems of a salesman, aren't they? A good conversation ought to be bracing, vibrant, and revealing, not pleasant, comfortable, and ingratiating. Shouldn't it?

According to Franklin, "Man is a sociable being," "born for Society and mutual Solace." Recall Franklin's observations and reflections on board ship during his journey home in 1726. A fellow passenger, caught cheating at cards, was "excommunicated"; a prisoner, locked deep in the Bastille, was denied all human contact. Each found isolation grievous. Death itself seemed preferable. But life among others is often little better. Some talk too much, "robbing others of their Share of the Discourse." Others prattle on and on about themselves—a vice matched only by "the impertinent Inquisitiveness" of those who ask "ten thousand Questions about the Business of others." Many make themselves disagreeable by "wrangling and disputing" about the slightest matters. What they lack in knowledge they make up for "by Obstinacy, Noise and Fury," and when pressed hard, they resort to "personal Reproaches and Invectives." Then there are those "ill-natured People" who are drawn like flies to an open wound, delighting in their ability to make others wince at painful truths.[123] These untutored habits are painful and corrosive. To thrive in the company of others, individuals need to be improved. Character is achieved through the cultivation of good habits, and the measure of those habits is their usefulness, their ability to sustain and deepen the ties of society.

Franklin's contemporaries sometimes lamented a decline in public virtue after the Revolution. "Self-sacrifice and patriotism" seemed to give way to "greed and profiteering at the expense of the public good." The ills of the new nation were frequently catalogued using a binary framework organized around the concepts of virtue and corruption. A virtuous citizen ought to be disciplined, not licentious; frugal, not luxurious; courageous, not cowardly; firm and unyielding, not flexible and adaptive; plainspoken and honest, not strategic or diplomatic. Even the white lies and gentle deceptions of everyday life were suspect. A man of principle ought to speak his mind, even—perhaps especially—when among others who did not share his beliefs. The masculine ideal of republican citizenship was captured by the motto of the revered seventeenth-century Whig martyr, Algernon Sidney: *Manus haec inimica tyrannis/Ense petit placidam sub libertate quietem* (This hand, hostile to tyrants/Seeks by the sword the tranquil peace of freedom). Compromise with corruption, whether it was found on the throne or in the tavern, was deplorable. John Adams expressed this ideal when, in the lap of Parisian luxury, he prided himself on remaining "a stern and haughty Republican."[124]

Franklin was not immune to the charms of Roman virtue, but he did not think it appropriate to modern life. Modesty and flexibility were the hallmarks of good character. Unyielding candor and self-righteous certainty were obstacles to cooperation. Improvement was a collective achievement; even the best projects were futile unless embraced by others. But as Franklin's experiences mobilizing Pennsylvanians in 1747 had demonstrated, even well-intentioned persons can disagree over the meaning of that seemingly innocuous phrase "the public good" as well as over the means needed to attain it. Modern politics was inseparable from negotiation, persuasion, and compromise. Even hypocrisy had its place, especially the kind that accompanied the complex roles of public life. In Paris Adams congratulated himself on maintaining his integrity—and in the process managed to alienate everyone. The French minister for foreign affairs, the comte de Vergennes, feared that the American from Massachusetts would "only incite difficulties and vexations, because he has an inflexibility, a pedantry, an arrogance, and a conceit that renders him incapable of dealing with political subjects, and especially of handling them with the representatives of great powers, who assuredly will not yield either to the tone or to the logic of Mr. Adams."[125] Franklin, meanwhile, donned a beaver cap, wore a plain wool coat, and charmed the French with his easy confidence, bad grammar, and affable manners.

All these qualities were on display at the Constitutional Convention. We have already taken note of Franklin's brilliant concluding speech. Franklin began with a skeptical confession ("I do not entirely approve of this Constitution at present, but Sir, I am not sure I shall never approve it") and ended with an endorsement ("I consent, Sir, to this Constitution because I expect no better, and because I am not sure it is not the best"). This speech is a perfect illustration of Franklin's habit of expressing himself "in Terms of modest Diffidence." Avoiding words that gave his opinions "the Air of

Positiveness," like *certainly* and *undoubtedly,* had been "of great Advantage" when he "proposed new Institutions, or Alterations in the old."[126]

No less revealing was Franklin's call for prayers on 28 June. The convention appeared to have reached an impasse over representation. The smaller states feared that unless they had an equal voice with the larger states they would be overwhelmed; the larger states were convinced that it would be unjust for Delaware to have the same representation as Virginia. On the 27th Luther Martin, the attorney general of Maryland, had railed against the proposed constitution for three hours; on the 28th he picked up where he had left off the day before. Tempers were hot, feelings "acrimonious," and "a rupture appeared almost inevitable." It appeared as if the smaller states were on the verge of issuing an ultimatum: return to the system of equal representation found under the Articles of Confederation or dissolve the convention. In this explosive context, Franklin spoke. "The small Progress we have made after 4 or 5 Weeks close Attendance and continual Reasonings with each other, our different Sentiments on almost every Question, several of the last producing as many *Noes* as *Ayes,* is methinks a melancholy Proof of the Imperfection of the Human Understanding." The members of the convention had looked everywhere and applied to everyone for guidance. Why then had they not thought of "humbly applying to the Father of Lights to illuminate our Understandings?" Without God's aid, "we shall be divided by our little partial local Interests, our Projects will be confounded and we ourselves shall become a Reproach and a Byword down to future Ages. And what is worse, Mankind may hereafter, from this unfortunate Instance, despair of establishing Government by human Wisdom, and leave it to Chance, War and Conquest."[127]

To escape this fate, Franklin moved that the convention begin every morning with prayers. This was an extraordinary gesture—really, an act of desperation—from a well-known freethinker who attended worship services only rarely. Some have stumbled over Franklin's words: "The longer I live, the more convincing proofs I see of this Truth, *That GOD governs in the Affairs of Men!*—And if a Sparrow cannot fall to the Ground without his Notice, is it probable that an Empire can rise without his Aid?" Did he truly believe this? Had he, late in life, regained the providential faith of his Puritan forebears? These are interesting and potentially important biographical questions. But if we focus too closely on what Franklin *said,* then we will miss what he *did:* he stopped the convention dead in its tracks. Destructive debates ground to a halt, and men were given a chance to go home, cool down, and return with clearer heads. It did not matter whether Franklin sincerely believed in the power of prayer. Nor did it matter that his motion was tabled without a vote. (At the bottom of his manuscript for the speech, Franklin wryly penciled, "The Convention, except three or four Persons, thought Prayers unnecessary!") What *did* matter was that it was "received and treated with the respect due to it"—and that an adjournment promptly followed.[128] Fatal deadlock had been avoided.

When the convention resumed on the 29th, temperatures had dropped a degree or two. Not much, perhaps, but just enough to permit a new round of deliberation. On the 30th Franklin called for compromise: "When a broad table is to be made, and the edges of planks do not fit, the artist takes a little from both, and makes a good joint. In the like manner here both sides must part with some of their demands, in order that they may join in some accommodating proposition." His own plan was cast aside, but he was elected to a committee charged with finding a scheme of representation acceptable to both large and small states. In mid-July a solution—the "Grand Compromise," representing population in the House and states in the Senate—squeaked through the convention.[129] Franklin did not devise this final solution, but he had helped hold the convention together long enough for compromise to be possible.

Franklin's final speech to the convention was less immediately successful. Despite concerted efforts to achieve unanimity, it was clear that three members—Edmund Randolph, George Mason, and Elbridge Gerry—did not want to sign. Each was in the minority in his state. This created an interesting dilemma: though individual delegates dissented, the states, voting as states, were unanimous in their support. Franklin delivered his speech, then proposed an ambiguous oath: "Done in Convention by the unanimous consent of the States." Randolph, Mason, and Gerry saw through Franklin's gambit, and the Constitution went forward without their signatures. Complaisance was no guarantee of success. How could it be? Politics was not like chess.

5. Slavery

There are now eight hundred and fifty thousand Negroes in the English Islands and Colonies; and . . . the yearly importation is about one hundred thousand, of which number about one third perish by the gaol distemper on the passage, and in the sickness called the *seasoning* before they are set to labor. . . . Can sweetening our tea, etc. with sugar, be a circumstance of such absolute necessity? Can the petty pleasure thence arising to the taste, compensate for so much misery produced among our fellow creatures, and such a constant butchery of the human species by this pestilential detestable traffic in the bodies and souls of men?
—Benjamin Franklin, "The Somersett Case and the Slave Trade" (1772)

An American Paradox

Benjamin Franklin enacted the paradox of American slavery in his own life. In June 1776 the Continental Congress took up a resolution stating that the "United Colonies are, and of right ought to be, free and independent States." Final vote was scheduled for early July; in the meantime, a committee was appointed to write a declaration justifying this momentous step. Thomas Jefferson composed the first draft. On 21 June he asked Franklin if he would "be so good as to peruse it and suggest such alterations as his more enlarged view of the subject will dictate." Franklin's most memorable change came at the beginning of the crucial second paragraph. Where Jefferson had written, "We hold these truths to be sacred and undeniable," Franklin suggested, "We hold these truths to be self-evident." Left standing was the subordinate clause, "that all men are created equal."[1] Franklin undoubtedly made these changes while sitting at his desk in Market Street, in the home he shared with his daughter, Sally, her husband, Richard Bache, and their two children, Benjamin ("Benny") and Will. And George, a domestic slave Franklin had acquired in the 1760s. None has improved upon the British author Samuel Johnson's caustic question, "How is it that we hear the loudest yelps for liberty among the drivers of Negroes?"[2]

Jefferson's tortured relationship to slavery—his moral revulsion at the slave trade was matched only by his complete immersion in and dependence on America's "peculiar institution"—is well known. Less familiar is Franklin's involvement with slavery.[3] This is partly a matter of scale and context. The earliest reference to a "Negro" in Franklin's household is in 1735, the last in 1781.[4] At any given point in between, it appears that Franklin owned between one and three domestic slaves. Pennsylvania's slave population, never large, peaked before the Revolution; at the first census, in 1790, there were approximately 3,760 slaves in a population of 435,000 (0.9 percent). Jefferson, by contrast, employed as many as two hundred slaves at Monticello, in occupations ranging from cooking and cleaning to farming and nail making. To be sure, Jefferson belonged to a small elite; most slaveholders, even in the South, owned only a few slaves. But there were many, many slaveholders. In 1790 there were approximately 293,000 slaves in Virginia, out of a population of 748,000 (39 percent). In a numeric sense, Franklin lived on the margins of American slaveholding, while Jefferson inhabited its center.[5]

Franklin's engagement with slavery is masked, moreover, by the apparent clarity of his final public acts. In contrast to Jefferson—who could not bring himself to free his slaves, even in his will—Franklin ended his life a vocal abolitionist. In 1787 he was elected president of the newly constituted Pennsylvania Society for Promoting the Abolition of Slavery, and the Relief of Free Negroes Unlawfully Held in Bondage (commonly referred to as the Pennsylvania Abolition Society). The society litigated on behalf of blacks who had been illegally enslaved and worked to improve the living conditions of those who were already free. It also sought to mobilize support, locally, nationally, and internationally, for the abolition of slavery. As part of this campaign, in early 1790 the society called on Congress to "step to the very verge of the Powers vested in you, for discouraging every Species of Traffic in the Persons of our fellow Men." The society's petition arrived over Franklin's signature. When it met with cries of outrage by James Jackson of Georgia, Franklin responded with a hoax, a bitter parody "defending" the custom of enslaving Christians by Barbary pirates.[6] What is sauce for the goose, Franklin suggested, is sauce for the gander. It was his last public act.

Finally, the vividness of the contrast between the lofty ideals of the Declaration and the brutal practices of American slaveholders has obscured the distinctiveness of Franklin's ideas. The Declaration was framed in the language of natural rights: "We hold these truths to be self-evident, that all men are created equal, that they are endowed by their Creator with certain unalienable Rights, that among these are Life, Liberty, and the pursuit of Happiness." These rights could be seized or thwarted, lost or regained, but they could not be permanently renounced. This claim, classically articulated by John Locke in his *Two Treatises of Government*, provided an account of legitimacy as well as a justification for rebellion. Governments are instituted to secure the rights of men. When they fail to do so, they lose their moral authority. Legal command is replaced by naked power. And when such governments demonstrate a settled design—when "a long train of abuses and usurpations" becomes visible—then resistance is both necessary and just. The alternative was slavery.

To be a slave was to be subject to the arbitrary and absolute will of another. In the 1760s and 1770s increasing numbers of colonists came to believe that they already were, or would soon become, slaves. This was not "mere exclamation and hyperbole." Slavery "referred to a specific political condition . . . characteristic of the lives of contemporary Frenchmen, Danes, and Swedes as well as of Turks, Russians, and Poles." As early as the 1750s, we have seen, British authorities were contemplating the advantages of the French Empire, with a central state exercising control over far-flung colonies. It was an unrealistic plan, but the simple fact that it could be whispered in the corridors of power gave colonists in North America cause for concern. The fiscal and political strains of the Seven Years' War only added to their anxieties.[7]

The political significance of the concept of slavery was magnified by the fact that there were slaves, real slaves, living and working in the colonies. The condition of black plantation laborers "was only a more dramatic, more bizarre variation of the condition of all who had lost the power of self-determination."[8] North Americans did not have to look abroad to see what a life of slavery was like. The charge of hypocrisy, as Samuel Johnson instinctively knew, was difficult to evade and—short of embracing the potentially explosive ideal of abolitionism—almost impossible to answer. To revolutionaries who hated slavery, but valued the creation and preservation of the Union even more, this was an intractable dilemma.

Franklin has been accused of hypocrisy on numerous occasions and for many reasons, from his day to ours. But on the topic of slavery, the charge does not stick easily, at least not in the way that it does to someone like Jefferson. As a youth, Franklin read Locke carefully and thoroughly. But he did not think in Lockean terms; government was not founded on a social contract, nor was the ownership of property a natural right. As I have suggested throughout this book, Franklin framed his arguments using a quite different vocabulary. He spoke the language of improvement: of profit and gain, progress and perfection, increase and expansion, benefit and amelioration. Utility was the goal, sociability the means. This was the language of commercial society. And it was argued, by Franklin and others, that the spread of commerce was a civilizing, humanitarian force. Trade would replace war, peace and prosperity would supplant conflict and domination. The puzzle we face with Franklin concerns the intersection of commercial society and chattel slavery. How did someone steeped in the language of commerce, and committed to improvement, think about slavery? What were the strengths and weaknesses, the insights and blind spots, of the approach Franklin took?

Masters and Slaves

Franklin lived with slavery most of his life. As a boy in Boston, he would have seen slaves shown and sold by boarders living in his house on Union Street.[9] As a printer in Philadelphia, he routinely ran ads for the sale of slaves as well as for the recovery of runaways. And though he was not a slave trader, on numerous occasions he acted as intermediary between buyers and sellers, owners and captors.[10] There was nothing unusual about this; printers and their shops were centers of communication and exchange in colonial America, and slaves had been part of Pennsylvania's economy from the beginning.

Franklin also ran ads for apprentices and bound laborers. In southern colonies, staple crop production shifted from white to black bondsmen and women in the late seventeenth and early eighteenth centuries. Slavery, tied to tobacco, rice, and sugar, was a distinct sector of the labor market. Pennsylvania's mixed economy did not permit that kind of bifurcation; slaves were part of a general labor pool. "Farmers, rural and urban artisans, merchants, and professionals turned to white indentured servants, black slaves, free laborers, and family members as the supply and price of different kinds of labor varied and their labor needs changed. . . . Most producers viewed black and white labor as interchangeable and . . . no occupation became associated solely with slaves."[11]

Franklin's own experience with apprenticeship was mixed. He learned vital skills, gained access to many more books, and got his start as a writer. He also had to endure his master's "harsh and tyrannical Treatment." That his master was also his brother only added salt to his wounds; family ties ought to have softened the blows, he thought. (Family ties did give the brothers a unique board of arbitration, however: their father. "Our Disputes were often brought before our Father, and I fancy I was either generally in the right, or else a better Pleader, because the Judgment was generally in my favor." Fifty years later, Franklin's rancor still burned hot; the alternative to justice—"or else a better Pleader"—did not deserve further consideration.)[12]

These experiences instilled in Franklin a lifelong "Aversion to arbitrary Power." They did not, however, lead him to express qualms about apprenticeship itself. To the contrary, he considered apprenticeship a vital institution, providing inexpensive labor for masters and teaching important skills to apprentices. Behind this public position lay intense personal feelings. Franklin was proud of his identity as an artisan; it distinguished him from aristocratic gentlemen like Washington and Jefferson and college-educated professionals like Adams. He had been "bred to a manual art, printing." He had not inherited a single shilling, and was able to set up shop in Philadelphia only with "kind loans of money from two friends." In a sense, everything he had accomplished in life could be traced to those loans. In an extraordinary codicil to his will, Franklin expressed the desire "to be useful even after my death, if possible, in forming and advancing other young men, that may be serviceable to their country." He designated that £2,000 of his estate be used to create trusts in Boston and Philadelphia, out of which loans to set up businesses would be provided to "young married artificers, under the age of twenty-five years" who had successfully completed their apprenticeship.[13]

Among all the forms of bound labor in eighteenth-century North America, only slavery received Franklin's sustained reflection. Unlike apprenticeship and indentured servitude, slavery could not be integrated into a narrative of social mobility and individual improvement. There was no route for slaves that led from poverty to prosperity. To be sure, small numbers of slaves were able to purchase (or have purchased for them) their freedom. But they were the exception; for the vast majority there was no escape.

By 1751 Franklin had begun to experience qualms about slavery. As we have seen, large chunks of his demographic treatise, *Observations concerning the Increase of Mankind*, were given over to proving that slavery was economically inefficient and morally corrupting. British manufacturers feared that cheap slave labor would enable the colonies to compete economically with the mother country. Franklin thought this impossible. "Anyone may compute it. Interest of Money is in the Colonies from 6 to 10 per Cent. Slaves one with another cost £30 Sterling per Head. Reckon then the Interest of the first Purchase of a Slave, the Insurance or Risk on his Life, his Clothing and Diet, Expenses in his Sickness and Loss of Time, Loss by his Neglect of Business (Neglect is natural to the Man who is not to be benefited by his own Care or Diligence), Expense of a Driver to keep him at Work, and his Pilfering from Time to Time, almost every Slave being *by Nature* a Thief, and compare the whole Amount with the Wages of a Manufacturer of Iron or Wool in *England*, you will see that Labor is much cheaper there than it ever can be by Negroes here."[14]

Franklin's language is cool, calculating, and slightly disturbing. It verges on Jonathan Swift's savage satire "A Modest Proposal for Preventing the Children of Poor People from Being a Burthen to Their Parents or the Country, and for Making Them Beneficial to the Public" (1729). Swift, born in Dublin, railed against the conditions of life in British-dominated Ireland. Poverty was endemic, famine routine. But, he slyly told his readers, he had a solution. "I have been assured by a very knowing American of my acquaintance in London, that a young healthy child, well nursed, is at a year old a most delicious, nourishing, and wholesome food, whether *stewed, roasted, baked,* or *broiled,* and I make no doubt that it will equally serve in a *fricassee,* or a *ragout.*"[15] Let the children of the poor be rendered useful in the kitchen. Here was utility with a vengeance.

Franklin was a brilliant and witty writer, and on other occasions he used cost-benefit calculations to mock things he abhorred. In the fall of 1775 he asked his English friend the demographer and political radical Richard Price to run a few numbers. "Britain, at the expense of three million [pounds], has killed 150 Yankees this campaign, which is £20,000 a head; and at Bunker's Hill she gained a mile of ground, half of which she lost again. . . . During the same time 60,000 children have been born in America. From these *data* [your] mathematical head will easily calculate the time and expense necessary to kill us all, and conquer our whole territory." But the discussion of slavery in the *Observations* lacked this letter's mordant humor. Slavery was extremely costly. Only the extraordinarily high profits yielded by tobacco and sugar production made it feasible. What made it economically advantageous? It gave colonists virtually complete control over their labor supply. "Slaves may be kept as long as a Man pleases, or has Occasion for their Labor; while hired Men are continually leaving their Master (often in the midst of his Business) and setting up for themselves."[16] Franklin had done so himself, when at the tender age of seventeen he fled Boston for Philadelphia. Migration was the domestic face of population growth and territorial expansion in North America.

Some may think an economic evaluation of slavery in poor taste or morally obtuse; what matters is the cruel injustice of the institution, not its inefficiency. Franklin might respond that there was no point pounding on the table, declaiming the rights of man and warning of God's vengeance. These things did not motivate the owners of slaves; money did. To strike a critical blow, it was necessary to prove that slavery was less efficient than free labor. Calculating the costs of slavery was a prudent moral and political strategy.

As a skilled politician, Franklin surely would have accepted this line of thought. But like many of his contemporaries, he would have resisted the suggestion that political economy and moral judgment were distinct. Consider Adam Smith's treatment of slavery in the *Wealth of Nations:* "The experience of all ages and nations, I believe, demonstrates that the work done by slaves, though it appears to cost only their maintenance, is in the end the dearest of any." Why? Because "a person who can acquire no property, can have no other interest but to eat as much, and labor as little as possible. Whatever work he does beyond what is sufficient to purchase his own maintenance, can be squeezed out of him by violence only, and not by any interest of his own." Smith's French contemporary—and Franklin's close friend—Anne-Robert Turgot agreed. Slavery relied on coercion and belonged to an earlier stage of economic development. Hunters did not keep slaves; when they captured a prisoner, they killed him. Agricultural societies, reliant on backbreaking labor, discovered the value of slaves. The wealthiest ceased working altogether, and "slavery became harsher and more degrading." The rise of commerce introduced a "spirit of equality," however, and ate at the foundations of slavery.[17]

Slavery was an economic atavism, a holdover from an earlier time. The consequences for slaves were devastating. Overworked and underfed, they died faster than they reproduced. Only "a continual Supply . . . from *Africa*" prevented demographic collapse. The consequences for masters were less physically destructive than morally corrupting. Slaves "pejorate [make worse] the Families that use them." Children learn to be proud, and sneer at those who work with sweat on their brows. "Educated in Idleness," they are "rendered unfit to get a Living by Industry."[18]

Idleness was not the same as inactivity. A person could be fluent in Greek or Latin, or skilled at riding horses, yet still feel contempt for those who work with their hands or have sweat on their brows. A slaveholding society was like society with a hereditary aristocracy: each inverted the proper relationship between industry and reputation. When officers of the Continental army and navy formed a hereditary honor society, the Order of the Cincinnati, in 1784, Franklin lampooned them in terms that resonated with his earlier assessment of slaveholders:

> Honor worthily obtained . . . is in its Nature a personal Thing, and incommunicable to any but those who had some Share in obtaining it. Thus among the Chinese . . . Honor does not *descend* but *ascends*. If a man from his Learning, his Wisdom or his Valor, is promoted by the Emperor to the Rank of Mandarin, his Parents are immediately entitled to all the same Ceremonies of Respect . . . on this Supposition, that it must have been owing to the Education, Instruction, and good Example afforded him by his Parents that he was rendered capable of serving the Public. This *ascending Honor* is therefore useful to the State. . . . But the *descending Honor*, to Posterity who could have no Share in obtaining it, is not only groundless and absurd, but often hurtful to that Posterity, since it is apt to make them proud, disdaining to be employed in useful Arts, and thence falling into Poverty and all the Meanness, Servility and Wretchedness attending it; which is the present case with much of what is called the *Noblesse* in Europe.

After mathematically demonstrating the foolishness of hereditary honor— once nine generations had passed, a descendant's share in the blood of the founder would be "but a 512th part"—Franklin turned to an equally troubling development: the decision to make the bald eagle the national bird. "He is a Bird of bad moral Character. He does not get his living honestly. You may have seen him perched on some dead Tree near the River, where, too lazy to fish for himself, he watches the Labor of the Fishing Hawk; and, when that diligent Bird has at length taken a Fish, and is bearing it to his Nest for the support of his Mate and young Ones, the Bald Eagle pursues him and takes it from him." A far better choice would have been the turkey, "a true original Native of America." Though "a little vain and silly," the turkey was also "a Bird of Courage." Franklin's juxtaposition of the Cincinnati and the bald eagle was rhetorically brilliant, cagy and inflammatory at the same time. Would the descendents of George Washington really be birds of bad moral character, living off the labors of others? Were the Cincinnati pointing the nation in the direction of Spain, with its "odious Mixture of Pride and Beggary and Idleness"?[19]

Some nations attempted to "keep up the Dignity of the Family" by passing the entire estate on to the eldest male heir. But primogeniture was just "another Pest to Industry and Improvement," bringing pride to the eldest and penury to the rest. In 1785 the English abolitionist Granville Sharp urged Americans to embrace "the old salutary Law of Gavelkind," which granted every son an equal inheritance in cases of intestacy. Franklin concurred. In six states, if parents died without leaving a will, their lands were "divided equally among the Children if all Girls; but there is a double Share given to the eldest Son, for which I see no more Reason than in giving such Share to the eldest Daughters; and think there should be no Distinction." This was a matter not of rights but of consequences. The sons of southern planters, dissipating their wealth in European travel, graphically demonstrated the ills of primogeniture. Distribution, not concentration, encouraged industry and improvement. In this, sex was irrelevant.[20]

Franklin's anxieties about the political economy of slavery did not immunize him from the racialized prejudices of his age. The original draft of the *Observations* ended with potentially explosive comments about German immigrants and African slaves. As we have seen, Franklin's language and logic are baffling and controversial. He may have recognized this; when he reprinted the *Observations* in 1760, he removed the offending paragraphs. Tellingly, he also revised his utterly unambiguous declaration that "almost every Slave" was "*by Nature* a Thief." By 1760 he had come to argue that "almost every Slave" was "from the nature of slavery a thief."[21] The institution of slavery explained the character of the slave, not vice versa.[22]

What can explain these changes? Did they express a moral awakening? Were they the fruit of personal experience? A consequence of lobbying by abolitionists and other advocates for Africans? Or simply strategic adaptations to a new environment, yet another example of Franklin's extraordinary flexibility? These explanations are not exhaustive. Nor are they mutually exclusive, as Franklin would have been the first to admit. The self is a congeries of passions and interests, customs and beliefs. Purity of heart and simplicity of character were not possible. But that was no obstacle to improvement. The habits of virtue could not make a man pure, but they did make him more useful. Franklin never mastered his vanity or his pride, but nonetheless he led a productive life.

At the time Franklin revised the text of the *Observations*, he was living in London with his son William and his "Negro Man Peter." Peter was a domestic servant, and though he had his "Faults . . . I see with only one Eye, and hear with only one Ear; so we rub on pretty comfortably." Not so King, the slave brought from Philadelphia to serve William. "He was of little Use, and often in Mischief," and so when he ran away and found shelter in a Suffolk household, Franklin consented to let him stay. Whether King would eventually return to America or be sold to his new masters was unclear; but "in the meantime he is no Expense to us."[23]

Weighing against these gruff and irascible sentiments were Franklin's experiences with the education of blacks in Philadelphia. In 1757 John Waring, London secretary of the Associates of Dr. Bray, approached Franklin for advice. A spin-off of Thomas Bray's Society for the Propagation of the Gospel in Foreign Parts, the Associates' mission was conveyed by its full title: Dr. Bray's Associates for Founding Clerical Libraries and Supporting Negro Schools. What scheme for schooling blacks would work best in Philadelphia? Waring wondered. Franklin recognized the importance of the task; in method and purpose it resembled the German charity schools he had supported a few years earlier. He also acknowledged the obstacles. "At present few or none give their Negro Children any Schooling, partly from a Prejudice that Reading and Knowledge in a Slave are both useless and dangerous; and partly from an Unwillingness in the Masters and Mistresses of common Schools to take black Scholars, lest the Parents of the white Children should be disgusted and take them away, not choosing to have their Children mixed with Slaves in Education, Play, etc." In light of these impediments, Franklin recommended "a separate School for Blacks," under the care of "a good Master." Accordingly, a school for thirty boys and girls was opened in 1758. It was the first successful school of its kind in North

America. Deborah was so impressed that she immediately enrolled Othello, a young slave in her household.[24]

Franklin's involvement with the Associates deepened. In 1760 he was elected a member and provided help and advice on the foundation of sister schools in New York, Williamsburg, and Newport. When he returned to North America in 1763, he made a point of visiting the schools. In Philadelphia he "thoroughly examined" the children. "I was on the whole much pleased, and from what I then saw, have conceived a higher Opinion of the natural Capacities of the black Race, than I had ever before entertained. Their Apprehension seems as quick, their Memory as strong, and their Docility [readiness to receive instruction] in every respect equal to that of white Children." As to his old attitudes, Franklin was characteristically unapologetic: " You will wonder perhaps that I should ever doubt it, and I will not undertake to justify all my Prejudices, nor to account for them."[25] It is possible that he himself found his old views inexplicable.

Franklin's realization that the intellectual capacities of black and white children were equal was an extraordinary imaginative accomplishment. It looks like a perfect demonstration of the civilizing power of commercial societies. Here were many of the basic elements: a voluntary association, dedicated to education, organizing men and women on both sides of the Atlantic in a philanthropic venture that transformed and humanized a range of beliefs and practices. And indeed it is difficult to imagine the Associates of Dr. Bray fulfilling its mission without the social, political, and economic opportunities made available by the spread of commercial society. But this is a cumbrous explanation of Franklin's reaction to the children in the Philadelphia academy. Why did Franklin come to this realization and not others? Why did Franklin come to it at this particular point in time and not another? We simply do not have the kind of fine-grained biographical evidence that would be needed to adequately answer those questions. True to his word, Franklin refused to publicly reflect on his change of heart.

Franklin was not the first to conclude that the intellectual capacities of blacks and whites were equal. The Philadelphia educator and abolitionist Anthony Benezet, who began informally instructing slave children in 1750, insisted that only "pride" and "ignorance" prevented masters from recognizing the capacities of their slaves.[26] Benezet began life as a merchant and was embedded in one of the most sophisticated economies in North America. But his beliefs were grounded in religious faith, not commercial ideals. There were many routes to humanitarian practices in the eighteenth century.

In this context, Franklin's first forays into intellectual life are worth recalling. As a young man he taught himself to write by rewriting Addison and Steele's *Spectator*, a brilliant series of essays on the cultivation of manners and the refinement of taste. From Shaftesbury Franklin learned the virtue of politeness; from Hutcheson, the power of moral sentiments, especially sympathy. One of Franklin's first publications, "Silence Dogood, No. 11," begins with the confession that "from a natural Compassion to my Fellow-Creatures, I have sometimes been betrayed into Tears at the Sight of an Object of Charity, who by a bare Relation of his Circumstances, seemed to demand the Assistance of those about him." At precisely the same moment, Franklin was reading the books of the humane English vegetarian Thomas Tryon. According to Tryon, "Greater Evil and Misery attends Mankind, by killing . . . and oppressing his Fellow-Creatures, and eating their Flesh . . . than is generally apprehended or imagined." When animals are killed, gross and violent passions infuse their bodies; when their flesh is eaten, those passions are passed on to humans. To bring home the suffering of animals taken to slaughter, Tryon perfected the rhetorical art of ventriloquism. In his pamphlets, fish and fowl speak directly to the reader, exhibiting "all the sensible Powers and Faculties" of men. Animals are "equally sensible of Hunger, Thirst, Cold, Heat, Pain, Weariness, and an infinite train of Distempers." They experience the abattoir as a human would: with fear and trembling.[27]

To Franklin, Tryon's vegetarianism was not a philosophical doctrine to reflect on but an ideal to be put into practice. When Franklin first mentions Tryon in the *Autobiography*, he emphasizes the utilitarian virtues of "a Vegetable Diet": it cost less, and it left him feeling lighter and more clearheaded. But these were not his only motives. A few pages later he elaborates, noting that for two years he had "stuck by my Resolution of not eating animal Food. . . . I considered with my Master Tryon, the taking every Fish as a kind of unprovoked Murder, since none of them had or ever could do us any Injury that might justify the Slaughter.——All this seemed very reasonable." Then, on a fateful trip from Boston his fellow passengers caught and fried some cod. "Hot out of the Frying Pan, it smelt admirably well. I balanced sometime between Principle and Inclination: till I recollected, that when the Fish were opened, I saw smaller Fish taken out of their Stomachs.

Then thought I, if you eat one another, I don't see why we may not eat you. So I dined upon Cod very heartily and . . . return[ed] only now and then occasionally to a vegetable Diet. So convenient a thing it is to be a *reasonable Creature*, since it enables one to find or make a Reason for everything one has a mind to do.———" This was Franklin at his best, using raillery, ridicule, and good humor—at his own expense—as "antidotes to the morose single-mindedness of the spiritual zealot."[28]

Tryon was also an early and vocal critic of the slave trade. He used many of the same arguments and strategies to oppose human bondage that he had mobilized against eating animals. In his books, slaves spoke with devastating effect, testifying to the cruelty and hypocrisy of their masters. Compassion, attachment, and brotherhood were bonds of identification in the human world as well as the natural.[29]

By the time Franklin visited the Associates' school in Philadelphia, he had practiced and abandoned the humane vegetarianism of Thomas Tryon. He had printed two editions of Ralph Sandiford's *A Brief Examination of the Times* (1729), an early antislavery tract. And he had edited and printed Benjamin Lay's explosive reflections on slavery, *All Slave-Keepers That keep the Innocent in Bondage, Apostates* (1738).[30] Lay was notorious for his theatrical and confrontational interruptions of Quaker meetings. In 1738 he dramatized the sin of slavery by thrusting a knife into a hollowed-out Bible that contained a bladder of red pokeberry juice; as the juice poured out, he told the gathering, "Thus shall God shed the blood of those who have enslaved their fellow creatures." Both men were condemned by Philadelphia Quakers; Sandiford left for England, while Lay lived in a cave as an ascetic to demonstrate his independence from slave labor.[31]

Tryon, Sandiford, and Lay were, at various points in their lives, merchants, but their arguments had little to do with the new discipline of political economy. Tryon was a disciple of the German mystic Jakob Böhme; Lay, in Franklin's characterization, was a "Pythagorean-cynical-christian Philosopher." And yet their commitment to compassion and brotherhood resonated with the moral psychology of Addison and Steele, Hutcheson and Hume. Adam Smith's first book was *The Theory of Moral Sentiments;* his opening words were "How selfish so ever man may be supposed, there are evidently some principles in his nature, which interest him in the fortune of others, and render their happiness necessary to him. . . . Of this kind is pity or compassion, the emotion which we feel for the misery of others, when we

either see it, or are made to conceive it in a very lively manner." Tryon, Sandiford, Lay, and others may have planted the "seed" of abolitionism, but the
soil was rich with many and various nutrients.[32]

Abolition

Franklin's change of heart in 1763 did not make him a single-minded or thor-
oughgoing abolitionist, any more than his reading of Tryon made him a lifelong vegetarian. That was his nature; he was not single-minded about
anything. He continued to own slaves. And as London agent for the state of
Georgia, he struggled to have that colony's slave code accepted by the British
government.

Another small turn came in 1770. When forced to confront charges
that the colonists were hypocrites—clamoring for liberty while keeping
slaves—Franklin penned "A Conversation on Slavery," proclaiming the
British responsible for the greatest "Enormities" and "Wickedness" of the
slave trade. This complaint, focusing on the slave trade and not slaveholding,
was increasingly common. Thomas Jefferson's *Summary View of the Rights
of British America* (1774) blasted George III for vetoing every colonial attempt to slow or stop the importation of slaves. He repeated the charge in his
draft of the Declaration of Independence: the king was "determined to keep
open a market where MEN should be bought and sold."[33] (Southern delegates
to the Continental Congress had this passage removed.) But this argument
was rhetorically compromised and thus difficult to sustain: it required that
colonial opposition to the slave trade, as well as colonial slaveholding practices, be captured in an extremely favorable light.

Franklin was on firmer ground in June 1772, when James Somersett, an
American slave who had escaped when brought to England, sued for his
freedom. In a landmark decision, Chief Justice Mansfield declared slavery
"so odious" that it was inconsistent with English law. Somersett was set free,
and—absent an act of Parliament—slavery was forbidden in England. But
British participation in the slave trade, and slavery in other parts of the empire, was unaffected. Franklin used the Somersett decision to launch his first
public call for abolition:

> There are now eight hundred and fifty thousand Negroes in the En-
> glish Islands and Colonies; and . . . the yearly importation is about

one hundred thousand, of which number about one third perish by the gaol distemper on the passage, and in the sickness called the *seasoning* before they are set to labor. The remnant makes up the deficiencies continually occurring among the main body of those unhappy people, through the distempers occasioned by excessive labor, bad nourishment, uncomfortable accommodation, and broken spirits. Can sweetening our tea, etc. with sugar, be a circumstance of such absolute necessity? Can the petty pleasure thence arising to the taste, compensate for so much misery produced among our fellow creatures, and such a constant butchery of the human species by this pestilential detestable traffic in the bodies and souls of men? ——— *Pharisaical Britain!* to pride thyself in setting free *a single Slave* that happens to land on thy coasts, while thy Merchants in all thy ports are encouraged by thy laws to continue a commerce whereby so many *hundreds of thousands* are dragged into a slavery that can scarce be said to end with their lives, since it is entailed on their posterity!

Franklin rarely wrote with such passion. His outrage may reflect the influence of the Quaker abolitionist Anthony Benezet, or possibly the English abolitionist (and key figure in the Somersett case) Granville Sharp. In the early 1770s, Franklin, who had remained active in the Associates of Dr. Bray, began cooperating with Benezet, Sharp, and others to bring about an end to slavery and the slave trade.[34]

Ambiguities remained. As previously noted, the home Franklin inhabited while editing the Declaration of Independence included a domestic slave. And like every other leader of the Revolution, Franklin was preoccupied with the struggle for independence and appears to have given little thought to abolition during the war. Many of his closest friends—Richard Price and Joseph Priestley in England, Condorcet and Turgot in France—expressed grief at the new nation's failure to take a clear stand against slavery. They were thus relieved at Franklin's election as first president of the Pennsylvania Abolition Society in 1787. At eighty and suffering from the gout, Franklin was incapable of providing active leadership. But his international reputation ensured that the antislavery cause could not be ignored and would not be forgotten. The British pottery manufacturer Josiah Wedgwood—Franklin's friend since the days of the Lunar Society—demonstrated his support for abolition with a small jasperware cameo. In

Josiah Wedgwood, "Am I Not a Man and a Brother?" c.
1788. Deep blue ceramic (jasperware) with white overlay,
1¼ in. high. This example is believed to have been among
those given by Josiah Wedgwood to Franklin. (Courtesy
American Philosophical Society.)

1788 Wedgwood shipped a packet of cameos to Franklin, who had a keen understanding of the power of images and symbols in political campaigns.[35]
Among abolitionists and antislavery sympathizers, the cameos quickly became an important fashion statement, and were worn as pins, bracelets, and
hair ornaments. They were even used to decorate snuffboxes.

Not all Franklin's friends were pleased with his actions. The English political economist (and free trader) George Whatley thought it an imprudent
and ultimately irrelevant concession to the Quakers.[36] But with Franklin's support and over his signature, Pennsylvania abolitionists churned out a vast number of letters, petitions, and pamphlets. The "blessings of liberty" ought to be
administered "without distinction of Color, to all descriptions of People." Increasingly, calls for abolition were framed using the language of natural rights:
liberty was "the Birthright of all Men." But older claims retained their power.
"Were lands to be cultivated by freemen, they would be much more productive
than those cultivated by slaves. In this as in every other case the obligations of
Justice and Interest both inculcate the same line of Conduct."[37]

In February 1790 Congress was presented with petitions calling for the abolition of the slave trade. Southern representatives bristled. Thomas Tucker of South Carolina threatened "civil war." James Jackson of Georgia promised that if a federal judge attempted to emancipate slaves in his state, the judge's very "existence . . . might be in danger." James Madison sought to calm the House by reassuring these men that the Constitution guaranteed their right to import slaves for eighteen more years.[38]

Franklin was not a member of the House and had no standing on its floor. He did, however, have over six decades' experience as a writer, and he knew how to use satire to isolate and unmask his enemies. Franklin's final contribution to abolitionism was a hoax, purported to be a speech by Sidi Mehemet Ibrahim to the Divan of Algiers, defending the custom of enslaving Christians captured by Barbary pirates. Every shibboleth of slaveholding was held up for mockery. "If we forebear to make slaves" of the Christians, wrote Sidi Mehemet Ibrahim, "who are to perform the common labors of our city, and in our families? Must we not then be our own slaves? And is there not more compassion and more favor due to us as Muslims, than to these Christian dogs?" Ah, but enslaving the Christians *was* compassionate, for their condition has been made better. "While serving us, we take care to provide them with everything, and they are treated with humanity. The laborers in their own countries, are, as I am well informed, worse fed, lodged and clothed. The condition of most of them is therefore already mended, and requires no further improvement." And "how grossly are they mistaken in imagining slavery to be disallowed by the Koran!" All knew that "God has given the World all that it contains to his faithful Muslims, who are to enjoy it of right as fast as they can conquer it." The very idea of manumission was "detestable."[39]

This extraordinary performance was published the *Federal Gazette* on 25 March 1790. Three weeks later Franklin died.

Epilogue

Words may show a man's Wit, but *Actions* his Meaning.
—Benjamin Franklin, *Poor Richard Improved* (1749)

In February 1787 Franklin presided over the creation of the Society for Political Enquiries. He was eighty-one years old; it was to be his final act of association. War with England had been won, and new governments had been formed. But the nation had achieved only "partial independence." The "fetters of foreign power" had been broken, but "the influence of foreign prejudices" remained, embedded in laws, opinions, and manners that originated in the "ancient and corrupted monarchies" of Europe. New "maxims of policy" were needed for a "situation" itself quite new. To date, however, the "associated labors of learned and ingenious men" had ignored this need. "The arduous and complicated science of government, has been generally left to the care of practical politicians, or the speculations of individual theorists." To supply this deficiency, Franklin and his fellows proposed "a society for mutual improvement in the knowledge of government, and for the advancement of political science."[1]

   Twenty-two of the society's thirty-four founders were also members of the American Philosophical Society. The fathers of six members had helped found the Library Company and the Union Fire Company. These were Franklin's kind of men. They would have been familiar with the society's rules defining offices, providing for new members, scheduling meetings, establishing dues, and authorizing medals for prize essays. They also would have been prepared for the society's fifteenth and final rule: "There shall be a penalty of one shilling paid by every member not attending . . . any meeting . . .

provided he be not out of town or confined by sickness."[2] The Junto and the American Philosophical Society had imposed small fines on members who were argumentative or abusive during meetings, while the Union Fire Company had fined men who failed to keep their buckets and bags ready for use. Only the Association, Franklin's militia of 1747, did not use formal sanctions to ensure good conduct. But as we have seen, even the Association did not rely upon unalloyed virtue to motivate its members; commercial interests and masculine pride were no less important than the call of duty. Reading, reflection, and life experience had taught Franklin that the self was a bundle of contradictions, loosely bound by customs, habits, and conventions. Any attempt to reduce the motives for action to a single source, whether moral virtue or material self-interest, was doomed to failure. Successful associations, like the individuals who composed them, were impure amalgams.

The first meeting of the society was in the City Tavern, but members subsequently assembled at Franklin's house on Market Street. The first paper, delivered by Benjamin Rush, concerned the "effects of public punishments upon criminals and upon others"; the second, by Tench Coxe, addressed "the principles on which a commercial system for the United States should be founded." No meetings were held from June to September. This was according to the rules, a concession to Philadelphia's summer heat. Had it not been so, a break still would have been unavoidable: nine of the society's founders were also delegates to the Constitutional Convention. (Six had also signed the Declaration of Independence.) When the society reconvened in October, it confronted problems familiar from the early years of the American Philosophical Society: low attendance and a lack of business. Fourteen members came to one meeting, seven to the next, eleven to another. These stalwarts met briefly and then adjourned so that they could set aside their official topics—"government and political economy"—and discuss whatever interested them. Franklin's declining health forced several meetings to be cancelled. The last recorded meeting of the society was on 9 May 1789; after that, it simply fades from the historical record.[3]

The Society for Political Enquiries had a short and uneventful life. It receives scant mention in Franklin biographies, and none at all in most histories of the early Republic. Franklin's extraordinary insights into clubs and associations have been largely forgotten. Small wonder that when Alexis de Tocqueville visited the United States in the 1830s, he imagined that he was the first to fully appreciate the importance of voluntary associations to

American life. "At the head of any new undertaking" in France, "you would find the government." In England, you would find "some territorial magnate." But "in the United States you are sure to find an association." Tocqueville believed that the patterns of life he observed in Jacksonian America were unprecedented, proclaiming that "a new political science is needed for a world itself quite new."[4] His own *Democracy in America* was intended to fill that void. It is a magnificent book, beautifully written and brimming with ideas. But the analytic gap Tocqueville perceived was of his own making. Many of the phenomena he observed, ideas he discussed, and arguments he advanced had already been canvassed by Franklin and his contemporaries.

Tocqueville's failure to appreciate Franklin's contributions to the theory and practice of American politics is all too common. For a century and more, scholars and activists have argued that the United States is based on liberal ideals and institutions. Americans are unconsciously wedded to the philosophy of John Locke and obsessively committed to the right to private property. American politics, in turn, is bland and uniform, especially when compared with the ideological and class struggles of Europe. Liberalism is "a drab and cheerless heritage, a poor thing, but our own." More recently, the classical republicanism of Machiavelli and Harrington has been trumpeted as a vibrant alternative to liberalism. The Revolution was fought and argued on republican principles. Civic virtue was crushed by the liberal Constitution of 1787. But if it can be revived, then the seemingly anemic quality of public life in modern America can be overcome.[5]

Neither liberal nor republican narratives of American identity fit perfectly. Each seeks to capture complex webs of beliefs and practices using the abstract language of political theory, and in the process each overlooks or excludes important aspects of lived experience. Some have suggested that liberalism and republicanism must be supplemented with the moral and religious ideals of Puritanism. Others, following Tocqueville, have focused on the importance of associational life. And a few have challenged the very idea that American identity is tied to distinct and coherent intellectual traditions. Americans do not have and do not need theories. They are practical and pragmatic, embodying the common sense of men and women who have learned to shift for themselves.[6]

Benjamin Franklin is virtually invisible in these frameworks. To be sure, he embraced many liberal ideas, like religious toleration and free trade. And like a classical republican, he called on his fellow citizens to bear arms in defense of their country. But unlike a Lockean liberal, he did not think property rights natural; and unlike a classical republican, he did not think that a good citizen had to be morally pure or selflessly devoted to the commonwealth. He spoke of virtue, but he did not share the moral psychology of American Puritanism. He praised associations, but with the insight of an organizer and participant, not a distant observer. And by no stretch of the imagination was he a simple frontiersman, improvising solutions to the problems he encountered using nothing more than his native wit and the strength of his body. Franklin was one of the most intellectually sophisticated and politically creative men of the eighteenth century. Though he considered Philadelphia his home, and focused his attention on the dilemmas of civic life in North America, the resources he drew on were not parochial. He was a cosmopolitan, participating in every facet of life in the eighteenth-century Atlantic world.

Because Franklin does not fit easily into accepted narratives, his contributions to American politics have been obscured. We have inherited a series of caricatures: Franklin the wacky scientist, who flew a kite in a rainstorm; Franklin the womanizer, who as an octogenarian chased the skirts of Paris; Franklin the apostle of industry, who subordinated all his life to the making of money. And, of course, Franklin the practical improver, the founder of libraries and fire companies. A spate of recent biographies and specialized studies has helped restore balance to our understanding of Franklin's life.[7] We know more about him than we ever have. Yet the richness and depth of Franklin's engagement with the civic challenges of North America have remained elusive. We have looked for an integrating theory, an abstract statement of method and purpose, parallel to Locke's *Second Treatise of Government* or Harrington's *Commonwealth of Oceana*. Not finding that, we have assumed that there was little to be said about Franklin's political thought.

Franklin had a "projecting public Spirit" and conceived of his activities using the concept of improvement and the language of commercial society. To improve something is to increase its value or excellence, to bring it to a more desirable state. Land is improved by cultivation; minds are improved by education; inventions are improved by use and experience. Improvement is best understood as a set of priorities, not as a philosophical doctrine or a well-defined political program. It cannot be captured in general formulas, nor can it be separated from the contingent social, political, and intellectual contexts within which it is pursued. Recall Richard Saunders's 1749 declaration, "*Words* may show a man's Wit, but *Actions* his Meaning." A man's wit was his mental capacity, his intellect or understanding. "True wit," said Alexander Pope, was "a justness of thought, and a facility of expression." Words showed a man's wit by exhibiting his talent with ideas and phrases. The "meaning" of something, by contrast, was its importance or purpose. Clever words were necessary but not sufficient; consequences mattered. Actions measured a man's meaning with the yardstick of his experiences and accomplishments.[8]

This book has traced Franklin's wit and meaning in five areas: political economy, associational life, population growth, political union, and slavery. European debates over trade and commerce provided vital tools for thinking about economic development and social order. Cooperation was based on utility, on reciprocal relationships of need and interest, and not on moral virtue or mortal fear. Franklin did not think of utility in narrowly economic terms, nor did he think usefulness could be straightforwardly measured in terms of profits and losses. Knowledge was useful; so, too, were friendship and freedom. Moreover, usefulness was not a natural property of groups or individuals. It had to be cultivated personally, through the formation of habits of virtue, and collectively, through the cooperation of men and women who held different beliefs and had conflicting interests. The pursuit of prosperity did not signal the release of uninhibited greed; instead, it provided the material base for the development of sociability and civility.

Associational life created vital resources for individual and collective improvement. Franklin is best known for founding the Library Company and the American Philosophical Society. But he faced his greatest challenges, and gained some of his deepest insights, in his efforts to mobilize Pennsylvania for defense in 1747. Every soldier should be a citizen, but not every citizen could be, or should be, a soldier. Improvement through association required carefully negotiating conflicts between personal beliefs and interests, and civic roles and responsibilities.

The growth of population and movement of people posed a complex set of scientific and political challenges. What are the determinants of expansion and contraction? What are the consequences, political and economic, of international migration? If improvement is predicated on cooperation, then on what terms can groups divided by language, culture, and nationality coexist within a single territory? Answers to these questions had profound consequences for men and women living in British North America. Franklin never doubted the value of population growth, and he saw no conflict between international migration and national wealth. But as he learned in Pennsylvania, a thriving, migrating population gives rise to a host of challenges that do not admit of easy solution.

Political union was an adjunct to economic growth and associational activity. Without union, improvement was not possible. Political institutions defined the conditions under which groups and regions interacted; individual character contributed to the proper functioning of those institutions. From the Albany Plan of Union forward, Franklin held that men and women living in North America were best served by a federal system that distributed power and authority between the national center and colonial or state peripheries. The fundamental unit of the polity, however, was the individual; for both moral and prudential reasons, a broad and equal franchise was essential to responsive government. Ironically, these ideas were first formulated not to foment revolution but to shore up the British Empire.

Slavery was the last major challenge Franklin confronted. His thoughts, steeped in the beliefs and practices of commercial society, developed slowly. Initially Franklin complained of slavery's economic inefficiency. Subsequently he came to object on moral grounds, out of sympathy for the suffering of those held in bondage. Improvement was inconsistent with relationships founded on domination.

These themes and topics overlap and intersect in complex and interesting ways. The Association, a private army funded by a lottery, linked individual economic interests, voluntary associations, and the logic of security. Miss Polly Baker, the fecund creation of Franklin's imagination, addressed the interplay of population growth, moral virtue, and masculine power. Promoting colonial economic development required a potent combination of personal habits, monetary policies, and political alliances.

The problems Franklin identified, and the strategies he pursued, look astonishingly familiar. Consider three examples. In 1790 Representative Thomas Tucker of South Carolina promised that the attempt to end slavery would bring civil war. But already Franklin and the Pennsylvania Abolition Society were looking beyond emancipation. Slavery was "such an atrocious debasement of human nature" that simply ending it was insufficient. Without education for the young and suitable employment for the able-bodied, freedom itself might prove a "misfortune." The members of the Pennsylvania Abolition Society could not have imagined the extraordinary, tumultuous, and ultimately failed attempts to secure the freedom of emancipated slaves during Reconstruction (1865–77). They would have been amazed by the vigor and valor of freedmen, shocked by the violence and intransigence of southern states, and dismayed by the persistence of inequality in American society. But they would have intuitively understood the challenges facing Americans who hoped to forge bonds of cooperation based on needs and interests, not threats and violence.[9]

Population studies have changed dramatically since Franklin's day. Though Franklin handled "Figures" with ease, he was innocent of higher mathematics and could not have understood the work of present-day demographers. But population and migration remain crucial determinants of human well-being. They affect virtually every aspect of life, from an individual's decision to have children to a state's ability to provide adequate schools and hospitals. In many parts of the world, rapid population growth threatens to overwhelm available resources. Governmental and nongovernmental agencies struggle to limit population growth in an attempt to diminish human misery. In Franklin's own Atlantic world, by contrast, population decline is particularly worrisome. Fertility rates have fallen, cities have shrunk, jobs have been lost, lives have been devastated. Between 1960 and 2000, for example, Glasgow lost over 400,000 inhabitants, leading Scottish authorities to seek changes in United Kingdom immigration policies. The Czech Republic, faced with a dramatic decline in fertility rates and a substantial increase in life expectancy, has embraced immigration as its preferred solution to a "demographic slump." Even Philadelphia has suffered a precipitous decline, falling from 2.1 million inhabitants in 1950 to 1.6 million in 1990. Over this same period, suburban counties grew at an even faster rate. Urban redevelopment, tax breaks for homeowners, diversification of the local economy: all have been attempted to help staunch the flow.[10]

And what of credit? It is no secret that the United States is a debtor nation. The development of sophisticated instruments of credit has been crucial to the growth of both public finance and private wealth. It has also exposed Americans to new risks. As this book goes to press the United States teeters on the brink of recession, faced with a deep economic chasm created by the collapse of the home mortgage market. Aggressive lending and unwise borrowing have wreaked havoc on individual lives and on the economy as a whole. But the United States is not the only debtor nation, nor was it the first. In modern economies, credit and commerce are coextensive. During the eighteenth century Great Britain met the challenges of costly international wars through the creation of a "fiscal-military state," combining a massive increase in public debt with a huge administrative apparatus to collect taxes. In prerevolutionary France powerful private credit markets played a crucial role in mobilizing capital at all levels of the economy. But the importance of credit is not restricted to the eighteenth century, or to nations bordering the Atlantic. In 2006 the Nobel Peace Prize was given to Muhammad Yunus, a Bangladeshi banker and economist who has been a pioneer in the use of microcredit, in which small loans are extended to entrepreneurs too poor to qualify for traditional bank loans. According to the Nobel Prize announcement, Yunus and the funding institution he founded, Grameen Bank, "have shown that even the poorest of the poor can work to bring about their own development."[11]

What gives Franklin's thought such resonance? Is it his power of imagination, his ability to think and act in new ways? Is it his gift for language, his ability to write vigorously and provocatively about matters of public concern? Is it his confident optimism, his steady pursuit of improvements small and large? Or is it the simple fact that he and we live in commercial societies, in which cooperative relationships are (or ought to be) based on the ability of men and women to respond to each other's needs and interests? Franklin focused his attention on the possibilities and pitfalls of that world. As long as we share it with him, we will find meaning in his ideas and actions.

If we were to ask Franklin to address some of the problems that continue to bedevil the world, how might he respond? He would surely begin by modestly insisting that he had no special expertise—while inwardly glowing, the mere question having stoked his pride. He would have ideas; he was always thinking, probing, and imagining, his mind seemingly never at rest. After a few well-placed and diplomatic utterances of "it appears to me" or "it is so if I am not mistaken," he might launch into the description of a clever and well-designed plan of action. But in all likelihood, he would also call for the creation of a group—a "society for mutual improvement"—to pursue the matter. The world was constantly changing. New discoveries might lead to improvements in the quality of human life. There could be no substitute for individual industry and cooperative effort. In a scatological moment, Richard Saunders exclaimed, "He that lives upon Hope, dies farting." Perhaps that is too coarse an expression with which to end a book. Franklin delighted in mimicking the authors he read. Here is the same thought, in the voice not of Rabelais but of Shakespeare: "Dost thou love Life? then do not squander Time; for that's the Stuff Life is made of."[12]

Appendix: Franklin and Weber

In *The Protestant Ethic and the Spirit of Capitalism* (1905), Max Weber argued that Franklin illustrated the spirit of rational acquisition with "almost classical purity."[1] Every aspect of Franklin's life was subordinated to the task of making more and more money. As Franklin once urged, "Remember that Time is Money. He that can earn Ten Shillings a Day by his Labor, and goes abroad, or sits idle one half of that Day, though he spends but Sixpence during his Diversion or Idleness, ought not to reckon That the only Expense; he has really spent or rather thrown away Five Shillings besides."[2]

The broad features of Weber's sketch are well known and widely accepted, even as its finer details are often ignored. As indicated in chapter 1, I believe it fundamentally mistaken. For analytic and expository reasons, however, I did not there pursue Weber's argument in detail. I do so here, devoting more attention to explicating Weber than to my articulating my own qualms. For the latter, condensed claims made in this appendix may be supplemented with arguments and evidence found throughout this book, especially in chapter 1.

Weber used the concept of "the 'spirit' of capitalism" to help answer a single thorny question: Why did modern capitalism emerge in the West and not elsewhere? The grasp of traditional institutions, practices, and ideas was strong. What enabled innovation and change? Weber rejected historical materialism; economic processes alone could not explain the uniqueness of the Occident. He was no less skeptical of arguments that appealed to putatively modern personality traits like greed or the pursuit of profit; these were found everywhere and always. According to Weber, the defining feature of modern capitalism is "the striving for profit" and "for *more and more* profit" through "continuous" and "rational" activity. This is not natural; "a person does not 'by nature' want to make more and more money, but simply to live—to live in the manner in which he is accustomed to live, and to earn as much as is necessary for this."[3] Faced with inertia and sometimes hostile opposition, entrepreneurs needed "unusual strength of character" to succeed. At its origin, capitalism required a "spiritual ally to help it become a system, or a ruling economic order." This was provided by the "calling" of Puritanism, an ascetic discipline that demanded "systematic self-control" in a life of labor lived in service to God.[4]

As incipient capitalism displaced traditional forms of enterprise and older economic attitudes, its religious roots withered and were replaced by utilitarian ideals. Benjamin Franklin, a "nonsectarian [*konfessionell farbloser*] Deist," exemplified this secularized spirit: "sober," "rigorous," and "completely devoted" to business, with "strictly bourgeois opinions and principles." These traits were useful to Franklin. But they were not mere business techniques, laudable for their efficacy; they expressed an "ethos," an ethically charged set of maxims governing "the conduct of life" (*Lebensführung*). From the point of view of the individual, Franklin's ethic had nothing to do with happiness or utility. It appeared "wholly transcendent," and the only thing the capitalist entrepreneur got out of his wealth was "the irrational sense of 'fulfilling his vocation.'"[5]

Weber's use of Franklin prompts a string of interpretive and evidentiary questions. According to Weber, a sense of calling distinguished capitalist entrepreneurs, enabling them to innovate in the face of traditional habits and institutions. Did Franklin possess the requisite sense of personal identity? What of his audience? How would it have understood his references to time and money, either as goals or as standards of measurement? Weber presents the calling as a catalyst that energized people to transform themselves and the world around them. What kinds of changes, either personal or collective, did Franklin propose? Was he successful in bringing them to pass? Did anyone challenge him? If, so, how did they do so, and with what consequences? Weber sought to explain capitalism's origins; he resolutely focused on what he took to be the first instances of a constellation of ideas and practices that, once firmly established, were self-sustaining. But eighteenth-century North Americans were neither attempting to create capitalism from scratch nor were they already within its steely grasp. Instead, they struggled for survival on the margins of the British Empire, itself already highly commercialized. What is the relationship between the spirit of capitalism and the political economy of development?

According to Weber, greed and avarice are found among every class of people, in every kind of society, and in every epoch of human history. The distinctive mark of capitalism is "striving for profit" through "continuous, rational . . . exploitation of opportunities for exchange." The "'ideal type' of the capitalist entrepreneur . . . shuns ostentation and unnecessary show, spurns the conscious enjoyment of his power, and is embarrassed by the outward signs of the social esteem in which he is held." His manner of life is characterized by "a form of *asceticism*. . . . He 'gets nothing out of' his wealth for his own person—other than the irrational sense of 'fulfilling his vocation.'" Where does the "irrational element" of this ethos originate? In the Protestantism of Martin Luther, John Knox, and above all John Calvin. The religious valuation of continuous and systematic work was a "powerful lever" in human history. "Rational conduct of life on the foundation of the *idea of the calling*, was born . . . out of the spirit of *Christian asceticism*."[6]

The calling was not a set of techniques or prudential maxims but a disciplinary regimen in which human passions, desires, and feelings were subordinated through rational, methodical action. Puritan fears of damnation were purged through work: not occasional work, or incidental good works, but work that expressed "systematic self-control." Puritan theology held that the fate of each individual was predetermined by God, but there was no way of knowing whether you were one of the elect or damned. Such profound uncertainty is humanly unbearable, and in time Puritans came to view worldly success as a sign of God's favor. Labor in a calling was, in the final analysis, "the *sole* means of making sure of one's state of grace."[7]

The "worldly asceticism" of Puritanism called on men to make profit without succumbing to the temptations of profit.[8] "Puritanism placed a tremendous premium" on "the transformation of the self into a unified personality." The godly person is "an *agent* of godly purposes" whose "self had been transformed into a transparent medium of godly action." The calling or vocation is "the office or station in which God places us for his employment, not for our enjoyment; it is a special burden taken on as our only spiritual hope and purpose, not for personal fulfillment." This "strength of character," this "sober self-control," was crucial to the success of capitalist entrepreneurs. At its inception, capitalism met with suspicion, hostility, and "moral indignation." The calling provided men with strength, energy, and clarity of purpose. It imbued them with the qualities needed to "wrestle" with these obstacles.[9]

By Franklin's day the religious basis of "Puritan asceticism" had withered; what remained was its "spirit," embodied in the ascetic discipline of the capitalist entrepreneur. Franklin expressed this spirit with "almost classical purity." Or did he? Franklin's conceptions of the self and of the habits of virtue cannot be fit within a Puritan mold. They captured the possibilities of self-fashioning, not the logic of being called. (Franklin's "bold and arduous Project" was of his own design.) They treated the self as an impure but workable constellation of habits, not an organized and disciplined unity. (As Franklin quipped, vanity and pride made him a better man.) And they were predicated on the possibility of harmony between the man of action and the world around him, not an ineluctable conflict between them. (On board a ship in 1726, Franklin realized that "Man is a sociable being" who thrives in the company of others.)

What of making money? Wasn't that one of Franklin's primary goals? In a striking addition to the 1920 edition of *The Protestant Ethic*, Weber observed that the "ethical tone" of Franklin's "Advice to a Young Tradesman" was "unmistakable": "Carelessness with money is equivalent to the *murder* of embryonic capital." In Franklin's words, "He that kills a breeding Sow, destroys all her Offspring to the thousandth Generation. He that murders a Crown, destroys all it might have produced, even Scores of Pounds." This certainly *sounds* like the spirit of capitalism. But, as noted previously, Franklin's writings cannot always be taken at face value. According to Weber, men infused with the spirit of capitalism considered money a living thing, possessed of soul and spirit. It was a trust to be cherished and nurtured, as life itself was to be cherished and nurtured. To squander money, whether rashly, recklessly, or through simple inattention, was a sin. The man of calling was obligated to cherish and preserve it; he was not its master but its "servant or steward."[10] Franklin's language belies this perspective. An ambitious young tradesman who views money through the eyes of a pig wrangler is unlikely to think of himself as a "servant" or "steward." (Shepherd, perhaps; but unlike servants and stewards, shepherds sometimes lead their flock to slaughter.)

Weber also quoted from Franklin's 1737 "Hints for those that would be Rich": "He that wastes idly a Groat's worth of his Time per Day, one Day with another, wastes the Privilege of using 100£ each day," and "He that idly loses 5s. worth of time, loses 5s. and might as prudently throw 5s. in the River."[11] Franklin's praise of industry and frugality certainly *seems* ascetic. Are the virtues of Poor Richard directed at the restless and methodical pursuit of profit? Perhaps. But the weight of Franklin's words falls on the behavior appropriate to a tradesman living on credit, not on the rational and systematic pursuit of profit. In the economy of colonial North America, success rested on a reputation for industry and frugality. Short-term passions and interests had to be subordinated to the long-term demands of credit and debt.

How could Weber have so mistaken the meaning of Franklin's ideas and actions? We know precious little about the personal and intellectual background to *The Protestant Ethic,* and hence cannot fully answer this question.[12] The textual evidence, however, is stunning. Weber was given a German translation of the *Autobiography* for his twelfth birthday.[13] Given his voracious reading habits, we may assume that he read it at that time. The only other texts by Franklin that show up in *any* of Weber's writings—and the two on which his interpretation in *Protestant Ethic* is built—are "Advice to a Young Tradesman" and "Hints for those that would be Rich." Weber first read excerpts from these essays in Ferdinand Kürnberger's roman à clef, *Der Amerikamüde: Amerikanisches Kulturbild* (The Man Tired of America: Portrait of American Culture). According to Kürnberger, Americans are selfish, grasping, and vulgar, and Franklin is their avatar. Franklin's philosophy was reduced to the savage thought "They turn cattle into tallow, and people into money." Weber thought Kürnberger's prose "indigestible," but he did not doubt that the quotations from "Advice" and "Hints" expressed "the characteristic voice of the 'spirit of capitalism.' "[14] A colleague of Weber, the economist Lujo Brentano, charged that Weber had allowed Kürnberger's acid portrait of American culture to mislead him. The charge is badly put; whether or not Weber was unduly influenced by Kürnberger, Weber's own analysis of Franklin was defined by the texts he encountered in *Der Amerikamüde.* Precisely the same selections appear in each.[15] Put simply: Weber derived Franklin's economic ethos from a literal interpretation of fewer than seven hundred words. For reference, the *Autobiography* is approximately sixty-five-thousand words long, while Franklin's *Papers* is now in its thirty-ninth volume, with seven eventful years of Franklin's life still to be covered.

Chronology

1706   Born 17 January (6 January 1705, Old Style) in Boston

1714   Studies at South Grammar School

1715   Studies at George Brownell's school

1718   Apprenticed to brother James, a printer

1722   "Silence Dogood" essays published in *New-England Courant;* adopts Thomas Tryon's vegetable diet

1723   Runs away to Philadelphia, arriving 6 October; finds work in Samuel Keimer's print shop

1724   Befriended by William Keith, governor of Pennsylvania; sails for London to buy type and other printing supplies, arriving 24 December, accompanied by James Ralph

1725   Works in London printing shops of Samuel Palmer and John Watts; meets Bernard Mandeville, Sir Hans Sloane

1726   Returns to Philadelphia, arriving 11 October; works for Thomas Denham as shopkeeper

1727   Nearly dies of pleurisy; rejoins Keimer's print shop; forms Junto in the fall

1728   Opens print shop with Hugh Meredith

1729   Buys *Pennsylvania Gazette* from Samuel Keimer

1730   Birth of son, William; common-law marriage to Deborah Read, 1 September

1731   Joins Freemasons; founds Library Company of Philadelphia

1732	First volume of *Poor Richard's Almanac* published (continued annually until 1758)
1733	Conceives "bold and arduous Project of arriving at moral Perfection"
1735	Defends sermons of Rev. Mr. Samuel Hemphill
1736	Appointed clerk of Pennsylvania Assembly; establishes Union Fire Company; prints New Jersey currency, using nature-printing technique
1737	Appointed postmaster of Philadelphia
1739	George Whitefield visits Philadelphia for first time
1741	Pennsylvania Fireplace ("Franklin stove") advertised for sale
1743	Founds American Philosophical Society; birth of daughter, Sarah (Sally)
1745	Begins electrical experiments
1747	Sends letters on electrical experiments to Peter Collinson; writes *Plain Truth;* organizes the Association; conducts Philadelphia lottery
1748	Forms partnership with David Hall; retires as printer
1749	Proposes Philadelphia Academy (future University of Pennsylvania)
1751	*Experiments and Observations on Electricity,* part 1, published in London; elected to Pennsylvania Assembly (reelected annually until 1764); writes *Observations concerning the Increase of Mankind*
1752	Performs kite experiment; Pennsylvania Hospital opens
1753	Appointed joint deputy postmaster general of North America; awarded Copley Medal of Royal Society
1754	Prints "Join, or Die" cartoon; attends Albany Congress, proposes intercolonial union
1755	Supplies General Braddock with wagons; struggles with Proprietors
1756	Commands defense of Northampton County; elected Fellow of the Royal Society

1757   Appointed agent of Pennsylvania Assembly to negotiate dispute with Proprietors; sails for London, arriving 30 July; writes preface to *Poor Richard* later known as "The Way to Wealth"

1758   Joins Club of Honest Whigs at St. Paul's Coffeehouse; meets David Hume

1759   Tours northern England and Scotland; meets Adam Smith, William Robertson, and Lord Kames

1760   Elected chairman of Associates of Dr. Bray; writes *The Interest of Great Britain Considered* (the "Canada" pamphlet)

1761   Coronation of George III

1762   Returns to Philadelphia, arriving 1 November

1763   Visits Philadelphia school for blacks sponsored by Associates of Dr. Bray; Seven Years' War ends with Peace of Paris; Paxton Boys' massacre of Indians in Lancaster County

1764   Paxton Boys' march on Philadelphia; Franklin defeated in Assembly election but sent to London as its agent, arriving 10 December

1765   Stamp Act passed

1766   Designs "Magna Britannia" cartoon; testifies against Stamp Act in Parliament; Stamp Act repealed

1768   Appointed agent of Georgia Assembly; prints maps showing course of the Gulf Stream

1769   Joins Ohio Company; appointed agent by New Jersey House of Representatives; elected president of American Philosophical Society (reelected annually until death)

1770   Appointed agent by Massachusetts House of Representatives

1771   Writes part 1 of *Autobiography*; tours Ireland and Scotland

1772   Writes "The Somersett Case and the Slave Trade"; sends Hutchinson-Oliver letters to Massachusetts

1773   Writes "Rules by Which a Great Empire May Be Reduced to a Small One" and "An Edict by the King of Prussia"; Boston Tea Party

1774   Denounced in Parliament; dismissed from post office; Deborah Franklin dies in Philadelphia, 19 December

1775   Returns to Philadelphia, arriving 5 May; battles of Lexington and Concord; elected to Second Continental Congress; designs devices and mottoes for Continental currency; George III declares colonies in open rebellion

1776   William Franklin, royal governor of New Jersey, imprisoned; Benjamin Franklin designs Continental currency; helps draft Declaration of Independence; elected commissioner to France, leaving Philadelphia on 27 October

1777   Settles in Paris suburb of Passy

1778   Treaties of amity and commerce with France; John Adams arrives in Paris as commissioner; Congress appoints Franklin minister plenipotentiary

1779   First edition of Franklin's *Political, Miscellaneous, and Philosophical Pieces*

1781   Cornwallis surrenders at Yorktown

1782   Negotiates, with John Adams and John Jay, peace treaty with Great Britain

1783   Treaty of Paris, marking end of American Revolution; prints French translations of American state constitutions and Articles of Confederation

1784   Mocks Society of the Cincinnati; writes part 2 of *Autobiography*

1785   Replaced by Jefferson as minister to France; returns to Philadelphia, arriving 14 September; elected president of Pennsylvania's Supreme Executive Council

1787   Delegate to Constitutional Convention; helps found Society for Political Enquiries; elected president of the Pennsylvania Society for Promoting the Abolition of Slavery

1788   Begins writing part 3 of *Autobiography*

1790   Petitions Congress against slavery; dies of pleurisy, 17 April

Notes

ABBREVIATIONS

APS	American Philosophical Society, Philadelphia
Autobiography	*Franklin: The Autobiography and Other Writings on Politics, Economics and Virtue,* ed. Alan Houston (Cambridge: CUP, 2004)
Beinecke	Beinecke Rare Book and Manuscript Library, Yale University, New Haven
BF	Benjamin Franklin
BL	British Library, London
CUP	Cambridge University Press
Farrand	Max Farrand, ed., *The Records of the Federal Convention of 1787,* 4 vols. (New Haven: YUP, 1966)
Gazette	*Pennsylvania Gazette*
Houghton	Houghton Library, Harvard University, Cambridge
HSP	Historical Society of Pennsylvania, Philadelphia
HUP	Harvard University Press
JCC	*Journals of the Continental Congress,* 34 vols. (Washington, DC: U.S. Government Printing Office, 1904–37)
LC	Library of Congress, Manuscripts Division, Washington, DC
LCP	Library Company of Philadelphia

Miller	C. William Miller, *Benjamin Franklin's Philadelphia Printing, 1728–1766: A Descriptive Bibliography* (Philadelphia: American Philosophical Society, 1974)
NYCD	E. B. O'Callaghan, ed., *Documents Relative to the Colonial History of the State of New York*, 15 vols. (Albany: Weed, Parsons, 1853–87)
OED	*Oxford English Dictionary Online*
OUP	Oxford University Press
PA	Samuel Hazard et al., eds., *Pennsylvania Archives*, 9 series (Philadelphia: Joseph Severns, 1852–1935)
Papers	*The Papers of Benjamin Franklin*, 39 vols., ed. Leonard W. Labaree et al. (New Haven: YUP, 1959–)
PMHB	*Pennsylvania Magazine of History and Biography*
PR	*Poor Richard* (1733–47) and *Poor Richard Improved* (1748–58)
PRO	Public Record Office, the National Archives of the UK, Kew
PUP	Princeton University Press
Temple	William Temple Franklin, ed., *Memoirs of the Life and Writings of Benjamin Franklin*, 3 vols. (London: Henry Colburn, 1817–18)
UCP	University of Chicago Press
UNCP	University of North Carolina Press
WMQ	*William and Mary Quarterly*, 3rd series
Yale	Papers of Benjamin Franklin, Yale University Library, New Haven
YUP	Yale University Press

INTRODUCTION

1. The history of Turgot's famous epigram "Eripuit coelo fulmen sceptrumque tyrannis" is traced in A. O. Aldridge, *Benjamin Franklin and His French Contemporaries* (New York: New York University Press, 1957), 124–36; John Penn to Thomas Penn, 19 October 1764, HSP Penn Papers,

Official Correspondence, 9:274–76; William Allen to D. Barclay and Sons, 15 February 1762, in *The Burd Papers*, ed. Lewis Burd Walker (Pottsville, PA: 1897), 49; John Adams, *Diary and Autobiography*, ed. Lyman H. Butterfield (Cambridge: HUP, 1961), 4:118.

2. *PR* 1737, 1749; BF to Benjamin Vaughan, 9 November 1779, in *Papers* 31:158; Clinton Rossiter, "The Political Thought of Benjamin Franklin," *PMHB* 76 (1952):261.

3. Puritan, Deist, and atheist: David Levin, "The *Autobiography* of Benjamin Franklin: Puritan Experimenter in Life and Art," *Yale Review* 53 (1963): 258–75; Alfred Owen Aldridge, *Benjamin Franklin and Nature's God* (Chapel Hill: UNCP, 1967); Norman Fiering, "Benjamin Franklin and the Way to Virtue," *American Quarterly* 30 (1978): 199–223; Kerry Walters, *Benjamin Franklin and His Gods* (Urbana: University of Illinois Press, 1999); Douglas Anderson, *The Radical Enlightenments of Benjamin Franklin* (Baltimore: Johns Hopkins University Press, 1997). Empiricist and rationalist: I. Bernard Cohen, *Franklin and Newton* (Philadelphia: American Philosophical Society, 1956); Paul Conner, *Poor Richard's Politics: Benjamin Franklin and the New American Order* (Oxford: OUP, 1965); Cohen, *Benjamin Franklin's Science* (Cambridge: HUP, 1990); Joyce Chaplin, *The First Scientific American: Benjamin Franklin and the Pursuit of Genius* (New York: Basic, 2006). Populist and individualist: Louis Hartz, *The Liberal Tradition in America* (New York: Harcourt, Brace and World, 1955); Gerald Stourzh, *Benjamin Franklin and American Foreign Policy*, 2nd ed. (Chicago: UCP, 1969); Michael Warner, *The Letters of the Republic: Publication and the Public Sphere in Eighteenth-Century America* (Cambridge: HUP, 1990). Bourgeois and capitalist: Max Weber, *The Protestant Ethic and the Spirit of Capitalism*, 1905, ed. and trans. Peter Baehr and Gordon C. Wells (Harmondsworth: Penguin, 2002). Pragmatist and scoundrel: Robert Mitchell Breitweiser, *Cotton Mather and Benjamin Franklin* (Cambridge: CUP, 1984); James Campbell, *Recovering Benjamin Franklin: An Exploration of a Life of Science and Service* (Chicago: Open Court, 1999).

4. "Celia Single," *Gazette*, 24 July 1732; "Advice to a Young Tradesman," 21 July 1748, in *Papers* 3:304; *PR* 1745, 1735.

5. Robert Lawson, *Ben and Me* (Boston: Little Brown, 1988); Candace Fleming and Robert Andrew Parker, *The Hatmaker's Sign* (New York: Orchard, 1999); Carl Japikse, *Fart Proudly* (Columbus, OH: Enthea, 1990).

6. H. W. Brands, *The First American: The Life and Times of Benjamin Franklin* (New York: Doubleday, 2000); Walter Isaacson, *Benjamin*

Franklin: An American Life (New York: Simon and Schuster, 2003); David Waldstreicher, *Runaway America: Benjamin Franklin, Slavery, and the American Revolution* (New York: Hill and Wang, 2004); Philip Dray, *Stealing God's Thunder: Benjamin Franklin's Lightning Rod and the Invention of America* (New York: Random House, 2005); Joyce Chaplin, *The First Scientific American: Benjamin Franklin and the Pursuit of Genius* (New York: Basic, 2006). The most sophisticated treatment—Gordon S. Wood's *The Americanization of Benjamin Franklin* (New York: Penguin, 2004)—depicts a Franklin who was not born American but had to become so. Wood is generally uninterested in Franklin's intellectual life; key moments are explained in terms of feelings and passions, not ideas and arguments. For example, Franklin's relationship to the British Empire is described in terms of "emotional commitment" and "emotional separation." The crucial turning point in Franklin's becoming an "American" was his humiliating interview with Lord Hillsborough in January 1771 (91, 151, 135–38).

7. *Autobiography*, 68–72; D. H. Lawrence, "Benjamin Franklin," in *Studies in Classic American Literature* (New York: T. Seltzer, 1923), 20, 25–26. "When I was a little boy, my father used to buy a scrubby yearly almanac. . . . crammed in corners it had little anecdotes and humorisms, with a moral tag. . . . The author of these bits was Poor Richard, and Poor Richard was Benjamin Franklin, writing in Philadelphia well over a hundred years before" (ibid., 20).

8. In Franklin's last surviving letter to Richard Price, he was still worrying over the fate of a set of English books he had ordered years before (31 May 1789, LC Franklin Papers, box 25). Books borrowed: Samuel Vaughan Jr. to BF, 18 July 1789, APS B F85, 56:165. Books lent: "Domestic accounts," APS B F85, f6(7), fol. 29. The definitive study of Franklin's library is Edwin Wolf II and Kevin J. Hayes, *The Library of Benjamin Franklin* (Philadelphia: American Philosophical Society, 2006).

9. Louis Hartz, *The Liberal Tradition in America* (New York: Harcourt Brace and World, 1955). The literature on republicanism is voluminous. Key first-generation works are Bernard Bailyn, *The Ideological Origins of the American Revolution* (Cambridge: HUP, 1967); Gordon S. Wood, *The Creation of the American Republic, 1776–1787* (New York: W. W. Norton, 1969); J .G. A. Pocock, *The Machiavellian Moment* (Princeton: PUP, 1975). My own contribution to these debates is *Algernon Sidney and the Republican Heritage in England and America* (Princeton: PUP, 1991).

10. Crèvecoeur, *Letters from an American Farmer*, ed. Albert E. Stone (Harmondsworth: Penguin, 1986), 69. The Puritan heritage is emphasized in Sacvan Bercovitch, *The American Jeremiad* (Madison: University of Wisconsin Press, 1978), and John Patrick Diggins, *The Lost Soul of American Politics* (Chicago: UCP, 1984). Rogers Smith pursues a "multiple traditions" approach to American citizenship in *Civic Ideals: Conflicting Visions of Citizenship in U.S. History* (New Haven: YUP, 1997).

11. These themes are elegantly discussed in Joyce Appleby, *Liberalism and Republicanism in the Historical Imagination* (Cambridge: HUP, 1992).

12. The qualifier "fully" deserves emphasis. I do not mean to imply that Franklin embodies or represents American identity or that his actions uniquely determined the course of American history. Franklin is neither metonym nor prime mover. He is, nonetheless, a vital part of American history.

13. *PR* 1733.

14. *Autobiography*, 6, 10; "The Whistle," 10 November 1779, in *Papers* 31:73–75.

15. *Autobiography*, 10–13, 17; *OED*, s.v. "essay."

16. *Autobiography*, 13–15.

17. Ibid., 14, 76–77. "I cannot boast of much Success in acquiring the *Reality* of this Virtue [humility]; but I had a good deal with regard to the *Appearance* of it" (76).

18. Ibid., 7; Mark Twain, *The Adventures of Tom Sawyer*, in *Mark Twain: Mississippi Writings*, ed. Guy Cardwell (New York: Library of America, 1982), 10.

19. Mark Twain, "The Late Benjamin Franklin," in *Mark Twain: Collected Tales, Sketches, Speeches, and Essays, 1852–1890*, ed. Louis J. Budd (New York: Library of America, 1992), 425; *OED*, s.v. "projector."

20. We often assume that a person's true beliefs are revealed in private, free from the harsh glare of publicity. But that intuition relies on a fairly clear and relatively stable distinction between "public" and "private" life. In Franklin's world, that boundary was still being negotiated. Conversations rarely lacked an audience, whether fellow tavern-goers or household servants. Letters were routinely shared and frequently intercepted by persons other than the intended recipient. There is no obvious reason to give "private" communication interpretive priority.

21. Joan Thirsk, *Economic Policy and Projects: The Development of a Consumer Society in Early Modern England* (Oxford: Clarendon, 1978); David

Hancock, *Citizens of the World: London Merchants and the Integration of the British Atlantic Community, 1735–1785* (Cambridge: CUP, 1995); Paul Slack, *From Reformation to Improvement: Public Welfare in Early Modern England* (Oxford: Clarendon, 1999); Richard Drayton, *Nature's Government: Science, Imperial Britain, and the 'Improvement' of the World* (New Haven: YUP, 2000).

22. Contrast the quite different conception in Norbert Elias's *The Civilizing Process* [*Über den Prozess der Zivilisation*], trans. Edmund Jephcott (Oxford: Blackwell, 2000). Elias's argument is based on the norms of civility developed at the royal court by the French nobility; the civilizing process he describes concerns the refinement of aristocratic manners, not the "useful" improvements entailed in the founding, building, extending, and developing of colonial society.

23. This threefold typology was first laid out by Adam Smith in *The Theory of Moral Sentiments,* ed. D. D. Raphael and A. L. Macfie (Oxford: OUP 1976), 2.2.3. The secondary literature is voluminous; I have learned a great deal from Istvan Hont and Michael Ignatieff, eds., *Wealth and Virtue* (Cambridge: CUP, 1983), and Hont, *Jealousy of Trade* (Cambridge: HUP, 2005).

24. *Autobiography,* 35. Hutcheson's *Inquiry* carried the subtitle "In which the Principles of the late Early of Shaftesbury are Explained and Defended, against the Author of the *Fable of the Bees*" (London: J Darby, 1725), title page.

25. "Humble Address," 15 May 1733, LCP, *A Book of Minutes. Containing an Account of the Proceedings of the Directors of the Library Company of Philadelphia* (MS Yi2 5960F), fols. 27–28; "A Proposal for Promoting Useful Knowledge," 1743, in *Papers* 2:380–81; Jack P. Greene, *Pursuits of Happiness* (Chapel Hill: UNCP, 1988), 193–205, esp. 197.

26. BF to Sir Joseph Banks, 27 July 1783, LC Franklin Papers, box 21; BF to John Lathrop, 31 May 1788, LC Franklin Papers, box 24.

27. BF to John Lathrop, 31 May 1788, LC Franklin Papers, box 24; BF to Joseph Priestley, 8 February 1780, in *Papers* 31:455–56. "When will human Reason be sufficiently improved to see the Advantage" of settling disputes without recourse to war? (BF to Richard Price, 6 February 1780, in *Papers* 31:453).

28. Three influential examples: Theodor Adorno and Max Horkheimer's *Dialectic of Enlightenment* (1944), Martin Heidegger's *The Question of Technology* (1954), and Michel Foucault's *Discipline and Punish* (1975). More recently, scholars have questioned the assumption that the Enlightenment was a single, coherent, international movement of people and ideas; see,

for example, the first volume of J. G. A. Pocock's *Barbarism and Religion* (Cambridge: CUP, 1999). Without entering into the details, I note my general agreement with this line of criticism.

29. My formulation of Franklin's ethos of improvement is indebted to Peter Lake's extraordinary studies of Puritanism; see, for example, "Feminine Piety and Personal Potency: The 'Emancipation' of Mrs. Jane Ratcliffe," *Seventeenth Century* 2 (1987): 143–65.

30. *Autobiography*, 105–7. Cf. Lord Kames to BF, 12 February 1768, and BF's response, 28 February 1768, in *Papers* 15:50–51, 60–61.

31. "Speech at the Convention," 17 September 1787, in *Autobiography*, 362–63.

32. Franklin's complex and shifting relationship to Brillon is captured by the titles of two chapters in Claude-Anne Lopez's sophisticated treatment of the topic, "Madame Brillon's Suitor" and "Madame Brillon's Papa," in *Mon Cher Papa: Franklin and the Ladies of Paris* (New Haven: YUP, 1966).

33. Carl Van Doren, *Benjamin Franklin* (New York: Viking, 1938), 782.

34. John Dunn, "The Identity of the History of Ideas," *Philosophy* 43 (1968): 99. For Dunn's application of these ideas, see *The Political Thought of John Locke: An Historical Account of the Argument of the Two Treatises of Government* (Cambridge: CUP, 1969). For Skinner on methods, see *Meaning and Context: Quentin Skinner and His Critics*, ed. James Tully (Princeton: PUP, 1978); for application, see *The Foundations of Modern Political Thought*, 2 vols. (Cambridge: CUP, 1978). For Pocock, see *Politics, Language, and Time: Essays on Political Thought and History* (Chicago: UCP, 1971).

35. I have framed these arguments in terms of the task of making sense of Franklin's political thought, but I take them to be generally true. I have been especially influenced by the arguments and examples provided by John Dunn—whose work is importantly different from that of Skinner and Pocock—and Don Herzog; see especially Dunn, *Western Political Theory in the Face of the Future*, 2nd ed. (Cambridge: CUP, 1993); Dunn, *The Cunning of Unreason: Making Sense of Politics* (London: Harper Collins, 2000); Dunn, *Democracy: A History* (Harmondsworth: Penguin, 2005); Herzog, *Without Foundations: Justification in Political Theory* (Ithaca: Cornell University Press, 1985); Herzog, *Happy Slaves: A Critique of Consent Theory* (Chicago: UCP, 1989); Herzog, *Poisoning the Minds of the Lower Order* (Princeton: PUP, 1998).

36. "Atlantic history is the history of a world in motion" (Bernard Bailyn, *Atlantic History: Concept and Contours* [Cambridge: HUP, 2005], 61). To date,

however, Atlantic historians have shown little interest in the circulation of political ideas and practices, and they have largely ignored Franklin.

CHAPTER I. COMMERCE

1. *Autobiography*, 40.
2. *Gazette*, 24 July 1732; *Autobiography*, 23, 33. See also *PR* 1737; BF to Edward Bridge, 2 October 1779, in *Papers* 30:429–30. Repetition does not make truth; we have no record of Franklin's using the familiar formulation "A penny saved is a penny earned."
3. *Autobiography*, 33–36.
4. J. A. Leo Lemay, *The Life of Benjamin Franklin* (Philadelphia: University of Pennsylvania Press, 2006), 1:269; Thomas Denham, "Account Book," HSP Am.9055, fol. 18; *PR* 1739. Lemay suggests that Denham's loans were in the fall of 1726, after Franklin's return to Philadelphia (*Benjamin Franklin: A Documentary History*, entry for 1 September 1728, http://www .english.udel.edu/lemay/franklin/printer.html). To be sure, the loans are recorded on a page dated 1726. But the order of entry—20, 21, 27 October; then 7 and 25 December; finally 1 April—suggests that the October and December loans occurred first, in the fall of 1725. Of the £10 Denham lent for Franklin's passage home, however, there is no doubt; nor is there any lack of clarity concerning the fact that this debt was not repaid by Franklin but forgiven by Denham in an oral addition to his will made sometime between 15 March 1728 and his death on 4 July 1728.
5. Dennie, quoted in Gordon S. Wood, *The Americanization of Benjamin Franklin* (New York: Penguin, 2004), 5; Nathaniel Hawthorne, *Biographical Stories for Children*, in *The Works of Nathaniel Hawthorne*, ed. William Charvat (Columbus: Ohio State University Press, 1963), 6:274; Mark Twain, "The Late Benjamin Franklin," in *Mark Twain: Collected Tales, Sketches, Speeches, and Essays, 1852–1890*, ed. Louis J. Budd (New York: Library of America, 1992), 425–26; Max Weber, *The Protestant Ethic and the Spirit of Capitalism*, ed. and trans. Peter Baehr and Gordon C. Wells (Harmondsworth: Penguin, 2002), 9, 11, 120.
6. "Advice to a Young Tradesman," 21 July 1748, in *Papers* 3:306. Retirement: *Autobiography*, 100; BF to Cadwallader Colden, 29 September 1748, in *Papers* 3:318. Proverbs: *PR* 1758; *Autobiography*, 80. "A penny saved," "No gains," "Haste," and "Early to go to bed" can be found in John Ray, *A Collection of English Proverbs*, 2nd ed. (Cambridge: John Hayes, 1678), 349,

131, 151, 39. The root form of "Rather go to bed" can be found in George Herbert, *Outlandish Proverbs* (London: T.P., 1640), no. 93. " 'Tis hard for an empty bag" can be found in N.R., *Proverbs English, French, Dutch, Italian, and Spanish* (London: Simon Miller, 1659), 15. The provenance of Poor Richard's proverbs is traced in Robert H. Newcomb, "The Sources of Benjamin Franklin's Sayings of Poor Richard" (Ph.D. diss., University of Maryland, 1957); for a recent discussion, see Lemay, *Life of Franklin*, 192–213.

7. *Modest Enquiry*, 1729, in *Papers* 1:148; *OED*, s.v. "commerce"; BF to Cadwallader Colden, 12 April 1753, in *Papers* 4:464.

8. BF to Joshua Babcock, 26 February 1770, in *Papers* 17:78.

9. Daniel Defoe, *An Essay upon Projects* (London: R. R. for Tho. Cockerill, 1697), 10, 132–42; "Silence Dogood," 13 August 1722 and 16 April 1722, in *Papers* 1:32–36, 13.

10. *OED*, s.vv. "economy, " "economist."

11. *PR* 1755.

12. "Journal of a Voyage, 1726," in *Papers* 1:74; Niccolò Machiavelli, *The Prince*, in *Selected Political Writings*, ed. and trans. David Wootton (Indianapolis: Hackett, 1994), 52–53, 59. As Poor Richard put it in 1744, "Those who are feared, are hated."

13. "Journal," in *Papers* 1:87, 86.

14. Ibid., 1:83–85.

15. Ibid., 1:85–86; Blaise Pascal, *Pensées*, trans. A. J. Krailsheimer (London: Penguin, 1995), #8, p. 37. Franklin read Pascal's *Lettres provinciales* as a boy and considered it one of the finest books in the French language (Pierre Cabanis, *Œuvres posthumes de Cabanis* [Paris: Bossange Frères, 1823–25], 5:228).

16. Thomas Hobbes, *Leviathan*, ed. Richard Tuck (Cambridge: CUP, 1996), 88–89.

17. "It may be perceived what manner of life there would be, where there were no common Power to fear; by the manner of life, which men that have formerly lived under a peaceful government, use to degenerate into, in a civil War" (ibid., 89–90).

18. Francis Hutcheson, *On the Social Nature of Man*, 1730, in *Two Texts on Human Nature*, ed. Thomas Mautner (Cambridge: CUP, 1993), §24, p. 137; Hutcheson, *An Inquiry into the Original of Our Ideas of Beauty and Virtue*, 1725, ed. Wolfgang Leidhold (Indianapolis: Liberty Fund, 2004), 118.

19. BF to James Logan, 1737? in *Papers* 2:184.

20. Pufendorf, *The Whole Duty of Man,* ed. Ian Hunter and David Saunders (Indianapolis: Liberty Fund, 2003), I.iii, pp. 52–60; Smith, *Wealth of Nations* 1.2.2, quoted in Istvan Hont, *Jealousy of Trade* (Cambridge: HUP, 2005), 40. I am indebted to Hont for my formulation of this general context for Franklin's ideas.

21. John Locke, *An Essay concerning Human Understanding,* ed. Peter Nidditch (Oxford: OUP, 1975), 2.21.29–39; Proverbs 13:12.

22. "Old Mistresses Apologue," 25 June 1745, in *Papers* 3:30–31.

23. *Autobiography,* 41; "Plan of Conduct," in *Papers* 1:99–100.

24. *Autobiography,* 68, 1–2; BF to Benjamin Vaughan, 24 October 1788, in Temple, 2:113.

25. *Autobiography,* 68; Douglas Anderson, *The Radical Enlightenments of Benjamin Franklin* (Baltimore: Johns Hopkins University Press, 1997), 105.

26. Locke, *Essay,* 2.21.47–48, 2:13.27, 2:21.70. John Dunn, *The Political Thought of John Locke: An Historical Account of the Argument of the Two Treatises of Government* (Cambridge: CUP, 1969); Dunn, *Locke* (Oxford: OUP, 1984); Don Herzog, *Without Foundations: Justification in Political Theory* (Ithaca: Cornell University Press, 1985).

27. *Autobiography,* 68–69, 76.

28. Ibid., 73–75. Wood argues that this section of the *Autobiography* is "morally ambiguous" and implies that this is a weakness (*Americanization,* 206). We might say instead that it is ironic and uses multiple points of view to add depth and sophistication.

29. Cotton Mather, *Bonifacius: An Essay upon the Good,* 1710, ed. David Levin (Cambridge: HUP, 1966), 29.

30. *PR* 1747; *Autobiography,* 76; Cotton Mather, *Manuductio ad Ministerium* (1726), quoted in Norman Fiering, *Moral Philosophy at Seventeenth-Century Harvard* (Chapel Hill: UNCP, 1981), 40. Thus Poor Richard wrote in 1739, "Sin is not hurtful because it is forbidden but it's forbidden because it is hurtful. Nor is duty beneficial because it is commanded, but it is commanded, because it's beneficial."

31. Lemay, *Life of Franklin,* 2:28–29; *Autobiography,* 67, 82–83. Only a few months before, Franklin's name had surfaced in the trial of men charged with the death of a young Philadelphian during a mock initiation ceremony (Julius Sachse, "Franklin as a Freemason," in *Proceedings of the Right Worshipful Grand Lodge . . . of Pennsylvania* [Philadelphia: Grand Lodge of Pennsylvania, 1906], 49–71).

32. BF, "Commonplace Book," HSP Ferdinand J. Dreer Collection. The final version, with some but not all variations, is printed in *Papers* 2:202–4.

33. BF to Josiah Franklin, May? 1738, in *Papers* 2:206; *PR* 1749; *A Defence of the Rev. Mr. Hemphill's Observations*, 1735, in *Papers* 2:53.

34. Jonathan Edwards, miscellany 73, quoted in Norman S. Fiering, "Benjamin Franklin and the Way to Virtue," *American Quarterly* 30 (1978): 221; Fiering, *Jonathan Edwards' Moral Thought and Its British Context* (Chapel Hill: UNCP, 1981), 346–53.

35. Richard Lester, "Currency Issues to Overcome Depressions in Pennsylvania, 1723 and 1729," *Journal of Economic History* 46 (1938): 324–75; John McCusker, *Money and Exchange in Europe and America, 1600–1775* (Chapel Hill: UNCP, 1978); Margaret Ellen Newell, *From Dependency to Independence: Economic Revolution in Colonial New England* (Ithaca: Cornell University Press, 1998); Keith Arbour, *Benjamin Franklin's First Government Printing* (Philadelphia: American Philosophical Society, 1999); Claire Priest, "Currency Policies and Legal Development in Colonial New England," *Yale Law Journal* 110 (June 2001): 1303–405. In 1717 the "want of running Cash" in Pennsylvania was so severe that 183 citizens petitioned the Assembly that "wheat Flour Bread" be made "lawful pay in the general way as not to be refused or rejected" (quoted in Harrold Gillingham, *Counterfeiting in Colonial Pennsylvania* [New York: American Numismatic Society, 1939], 9).

36. *A Modest Enquiry*, 1729, in *Papers* 1:141–57.

37. William Petty, *A Treatise of Taxes and Contributions*, 1662, in *The Economic Writings of Sir William Petty*, ed. Charles Henry Hull (Cambridge: CUP, 1899), 1:1–97; [John Wise], *A Word of Comfort to a Melancholy Country* [Boston, 1721]. Franklin would also have known the labor theory of value from his reading of John Locke (*Two Treatises of Government*, ed. Peter Laslett [Cambridge: CUP, 1960], 2:25–51).

38. [Wise], *Word of Comfort*, 52–54. On the context for Wise's comments, see Elizabeth Dunn, " 'Grasping at the Shadow': The Massachusetts Currency Debate, 1690–1751," *New England Quarterly* 71 (1993): 54–76.

39. "All Property, indeed except the Savage's temporary Cabin, his Bow, his Matchcoat, and other little Acquisitions absolutely necessary for his Subsistence, seems to me to be the Creature of public Convention" (BF to Robert Morris, 25 December 1783, in *Autobiography*, 329).

40. *Modest Enquiry*, in *Papers* 1:146.

41. Stephen Holmes, "The Secret History of Self-Interest," in *Beyond Self-Interest*, ed. Jane Mansbridge (Chicago: UCP, 1990), 267–86; Alan Houston, "Republicanism, the Politics of Necessity, and the Rule of Law," in *A Nation Transformed: England After the Restoration*, ed. Houston and Steve Pincus (Cambridge: CUP, 2001), 241–71.

42. Miller, 4; Arbour, *First Government Printing*, 15, 22–23; *Autobiography*, 53–54.

43. "Advice to a Young Tradesman," 3:306; *PR* 1737. The clearest statement of this interpretation is Max Weber, *Die protestantische Ethik und der Geist des Kapitalismus*, in *Gesammelte Aufsätze zur Religionssoziologie* (Tübingen: Mohr, 1920), 1:40n1. Thanks to Doug Anderson for sharpening my appreciation of Franklin's language in this passage.

44. T. H. Breen, *The Marketplace of Revolution: How Consumer Politics Shaped American Independence* (Oxford: OUP, 2004), 137; Adam Smith, *An Inquiry into the Nature and Causes of the Wealth of Nations*, ed. R. H. Campbell and A. S. Skinner (Oxford: OUP, 1976), 4.7.c, §38, p. 2:601.; Bernard Bailyn, *The New England Merchants in the Seventeenth Century* (Cambridge: HUP, 1955); John McCusker and Russell Menard, *The Economy of British America, 1607–1789* (Chapel Hill: UNCP, 1985); Kenneth Morgan, "Business Networks in the British Export Trade to North America, 1750–1800," in *The Early Modern Atlantic Economy*, ed. McCusker and Morgan (Cambridge: CUP, 2000), 36–62.

45. Ledgers A, B, and D, APS B F85, f6(5), f6(6); Wilbur Plummer, "Consumer Credit in Colonial Philadelphia," *PMHB* 66 (1942): 399. For detailed discussions of the use of credit as a medium of exchange in colonial North America, see Bruce Mann, *Neighbors and Strangers: Law and Community in Early Connecticut* (Chapel Hill: UNCP), ch. 1; Mann, *Republic of Debtors: Bankruptcy in the Age of American Independence* (Cambridge: HUP, 2002). For seventeenth-century English use of book credit, see Craig Muldrew, *The Economy of Obligation: The Culture of Credit and Social Relations in Early Modern England* (New York: Palgrave, 1998).

46. "During the number of years I was in business as a stationer, printer, and postmaster, a great many small sums became due for books, advertisements, postage of letters, and other matters, which were not collected when, in 1757, I was sent by the Assembly to England as their agent. . . . These, as they are stated in my great folio ledger E, I bequeath to the contributors to the Pennsylvania Hospital. . . . I am sensible that much must inevitably be lost, but I hope something considerable may be recovered. It

is possible, too, that some of the parties charged may have existing old, un-settled accounts against me; in which case the managers of the said hospi-tal will allow and deduct the amount, or pay the balance if they find it against me" ("Will, July 17, 1788; [and] Codicil," APS B F85, 212).

47. *Autobiography*, 54, 49.

48. A. A. Sykes, *A Letter to a Friend* (London, 1717), quoted in Peter Mathias, "Risk, Credit and Kinship in Early Modern Enterprise," in McCusker and Morgan, *Early Modern Atlantic Economy*, 29; Mann, *Republic of Debtors*, 7; *The Tradesman's Director, or the London and Country Shopkeeper's Useful Companion* (London: W. Owen, S. Crowder and H. Woodgate, 1756), 10.

49. Quoted in John Smail, "Credit, Risk, and Honor in Eighteenth-Century Commerce," *Journal of British Studies* 44 (2005): 450; Benjamin Vaughan to John Vaughan, 23 September 1784, APS Benjamin Vaughan Papers, B V46p, series I.

50. Breen, *Marketplace of Revolution*, 137–18; Defoe, *An Essay upon Projects*, 194; Joseph Addison and Richard Steele, *The Spectator*, ed. Donald Bond (Oxford: Clarendon, 1965), #428 (11 July 1712). Imprisonment for debt: Mann, *Republic of Debtors*, 79, 87; for English parallels, see Julian Hoppit, *Risk and Failure in English Business, 1700–1800* (Cambridge: CUP, 1987).

51. "Advice to a Young Tradesman," 3:307.

52. Muldrew, *Economy of Obligation*, 148–52.

53. Finding fault with Franklin: editorial note to letter from BF to Deborah, 1 May 1771, in *Papers* 18:90–91; Claude-Anne Lopez and Eugenia W. Her-bert, *The Private Franklin* (New York: W. W. Norton, 1975), 218–35; Wal-ter Isaacson, *Benjamin Franklin: An American Life* (New York: Simon and Schuster, 2003), 375–77; Wood, *Americanization*, 132. Exchange with Sarah: BF to Sarah Franklin Bache, 3 June 1779, in *Papers* 29:612–15; Sarah to BF, 14 September 1779, in *Papers* 30:333.

54. *Autobiography*, 66.

55. Breen, *Marketplace of Revolution*, 175–76. "From all that I had read of History and Government, of human Life and manners," John Adams con-fided, "I had drawn this Conclusion, that the manners of Women were the most infallible Barometer, to ascertain the degree of Morality and Virtue in a Nation." In particular, the "Modesty and Domestic Virtues" of women "are the surest Criterion by which to determine whether a Republican Government is practicable, in a Nation or not" (*Diary and Autobiography*, ed. Lyman H. Butterfield [Cambridge: HUP, 1961], 4:123).

56. *Autobiography*, 48–49, 164–66.

57. John Locke, "Rules of a Society," in *A Collection of Several Pieces of Mr. John Locke* (London, 1720), 358–62; Cotton Mather, *Proposals for the Revival of Dying Religion, By Well Ordered Societies* (Boston, 1724); Daniel Defoe, *The Complete English Tradesman* (London, 1726), 235; William Maitland, *The History and Survey of London*, 1739, quoted in John Brewer, "Commercialization and Politics," in *The Birth of a Consumer Society*, ed. Neil McKendrick, John Brewer, and J. H. Plumb (Bloomington: Indiana University Press, 1982), 203.

58. McCusker and Menard, *Economy of British America*, 28–87. See also Morgan, "Business Networks," in McCusker and Morgan, *Early Modern Atlantic Economy*, 36; Breen, *Marketplace of Revolution*, 33–101.

59. Archibald Kennedy, *Observations on the Importance of the Northern Colonies Under Proper Regulation* (New York, 1750), 9; *PR* 1758. At midcentury, Europeans grumbled that everyone talked about luxury, but no one dared say precisely what it was (Istvan Hont, "The Early Enlightenment Debate on Commerce and Luxury," in *The Cambridge History of Eighteenth-Century Political Thought*, ed. Mark Goldie and Robert Wokler [Cambridge: CUP, 2006], 379).

60. "Publius Agricola," *Maryland Gazette*, 23 December 1746, and "X," *Connecticut Journal, and New-Haven Post-Boy*, 16 February 1770, quoted in Breen, *Marketplace of Revolution*, 185–86.

61. BF to Benjamin Vaughan, 26 July 1784, LC Franklin Papers, box 22 ; Hont, *Jealousy of Trade*, 115–22.

62. Bernard Mandeville, *The Fable of the Bees: Or, Private Vices, Publick Benefits*, ed. F. B. Kaye (Oxford: Clarendon, 1924), 1:67. Mandeville's taunt: Shelley Burtt, *Virtue Transformed: Political Argument in England, 1688–1740* (Cambridge: CUP, 1992), 39–63, 128–49.

63. BF to Benjamin Vaughan, 26 July 1784, LC Franklin Papers, box 22.

64. Anderson, *Radical Enlightenments*, 11; E. J. Hundert, *The Enlightenment's Fable: Bernard Mandeville and the Discovery of Society* (Cambridge: CUP, 1994), 34.

65. Mann, *Republic of Debtors*, 3.

66. "Examination by the House of Commons," 13 February 1766, in *Papers* 13:143; Breen, *Marketplace of Revolution*, 263–64. See also Thomas Horne, "Bourgeois Virtue: Property and Moral Philosophy in America, 1750–1800," *History of Political Thought* 4 (Summer 1983): 317–40. For contrasting views, see Edmund S. Morgan, "The Puritan Ethic and the American Revolution," *WMQ* 24 (January 1967): 3–43; J. E. Crowley,

This Sheba, Self: The Conceptualization of Economic Life in Eighteenth-Century America (Baltimore: Johns Hopkins University Press, 1974), 125–46.

67. BF to Lord Kames, 3 January 1760, in *Papers* 9:6–7; BF, *The Interest of Great Britain Considered, With Regard to Her Colonies*, 1760, in *Papers* 9:74–75.

68. *Reasons for Keeping Guadaloupe at a Peace, Preferable to Canada, Explained in Five Letters, from a Gentleman in Guadaloupe, to his Friend in London* (London: M. Cooper, 1761), 20, 6.

69. Such thoughts were not limited to continental colonists. Colonel Samuel Martin, the doyen of Antigua sugar planters, wrote to his son on 22 September 1767 that "as it is highly probable that N[orth] America will be the seat of [the] British Empire in half a century, so I think it would be prudent in your eldest brother, yourself and me to make our [home?] there" (BL Add. MS 41350, fol. 56, quoted in McCusker and Menard, *Economy of British America*, 353n4).

70. BF, *Interest of Great Britain*, 9:90.

71. BL Lansdowne MS 85:27–35, quoted in Clarence Walworth Alvord, *The Mississippi Valley in British Politics* (Cleveland: Arthur H. Clark, 1917), 1:50–51.

72. David Hume, "Of the Jealousy of Trade," 1758) in *Essays: Moral, Political, and Literary*, ed. E. F. Miller (Indianapolis: Liberty, 1985), 327–31.

73. Franklin to Hume, 27 September 1760, in *Papers* 9:229. Most attempts to regulate trade were either "political Blunders" or "Jobs obtained by artful Men, for private Advantage under Pretence of Public Good." When the seventeenth-century French finance minister Colbert "assembled some wise old Merchants of France, and desired their Advice and Opinion, how he could best serve and promote Commerce, their Answer, after Consultation, was, in three Words only, *Laissez nous faire*. Let us alone. It is said, by a very solid Writer of the same Nation, that he is well advanced in the Science of Politics, who knows the full Force of that Maxim, *Pas trop gouvernor:* Not to govern too strictly. Which, perhaps, would be of more Use when applied to Trade, than in any other public Concern" ("Contributions to a Pamphlet by George Whatley," 1774, in *Papers* 21:175).

CHAPTER 2. ASSOCIATION

1. *Minutes of the Provincial Council of Pennsylvania* (Harrisburg: Theo. Fenn, 1851), 5:89, 92, 93, 99. Privateering was the North American rump of the

War of the Austrian Succession, which had begun in 1740 with Prussia's invasion of Silesia. Britain, initially pitted against Spain, declared war on France in 1744. After the brilliant and unexpected capture of Fort Louisbourg on Cape Breton Island in 1745, the colonial phase of the conflict disintegrated into a series of indiscriminate and inconclusive raids. The war—known in America as King George's War—ended with the treaty of Aix-la-Chapelle in 1748.

2. *Plain Truth,* in *Papers* 3:199; *Minutes of the Provincial Council,* 5:231.

3. Alexis de Tocqueville, *Democracy in America,* ed. J. P. Mayer, trans. George Lawrence (New York: Doubleday Anchor, 1969), 513.

4. Peter Clark, *British Clubs and Societies, 1580–1800: The Origins of an Associational World* (Oxford: Clarendon, 2000), 4. Tocqueville claimed that the English did not use associations "nearly so constantly or so adroitly" as the Americans (*Democracy in America,* 514). But, as Hugh Brogan suggests, this conclusion was based on very limited and highly selective experience (*Alexis de Tocqueville* [New Haven: YUP, 2006]).

5. Edmund S. Morgan, *Inventing the People: The Rise of Popular Sovereignty in England and America* (New York: W. W. Norton, 1988), 170. Colonial militias also served as a reservoir of men and matériel for expeditionary forces and for the British army, especially during the 1740s and 1750s (Lawrence Delbert Cress, *Citizens in Arms: The Army and the Militia in American Society to the War of 1812* [Chapel Hill: UNCP, 1982], 4–7; Fred Anderson, *A People's Army: Massachusetts Soldiers and Society in the Seven Years' War* [Chapel Hill: UNCP, 1984], 26, 41).

6. Josiah Quincy Jr., *Observations on the Act of Parliament Commonly Called the Boston Port-Bill* (Boston: Edes and Gill, 1774), 32, 34, 41; "Resolution of Committee of Safety, 17 January 1775," in George Mason, "Fairfax County Militia Plan," 6 February 1775, *The Papers of George Mason,* ed. Robert Rutland (Chapel Hill: UNCP, 1970), 1:215.

7. General Nathaniel Greene, 28 September 1776, quoted in Don Higginbotham, *War and Society in Revolutionary America* (Columbia: University of South Carolina Press, 1988), 107–8; George Washington, "Sentiments on a Peace Establishment," 2 May 1783, in *The Writings of George Washington from the Original Manuscript Sources, 1745–1799,* ed. John C. Fitzpatrick (Washington, DC: Government Printing Office, 1931–44), 26:388.

8. The republican militia ideal is charted in Caroline Robbins, *The Eighteenth-Century Commonwealthman* (Cambridge: HUP, 1961); Bernard Bailyn, *The Ideological Origins of the American Revolution* (Cambridge: HUP,

1967); Gordon S. Wood, *The Creation of the American Republic, 1776–1787* (New York: W. W. Norton, 1969); Lois Schwoerer, *"No Standing Armies!" The Antiarmy Ideology in Seventeenth-Century England* (Baltimore: Johns Hopkins University Press, 1974); J. G. A. Pocock, *The Machiavellian Moment* (Princeton: PUP, 1975); Cress, *Citizens in Arms.*

9. Quentin Skinner, *Liberty Before Liberalism* (Cambridge: CUP, 1998), 95. According to J. G. A. Pocock, "the ideals of virtue and commerce could not . . . be reconciled" (*Virtue, Commerce and History* [Cambridge: CUP, 1985], 386). The backward-looking nature of republican political economy is brilliantly captured by Steve Pincus in "Neither Machiavellian Moment nor Possessive Individualism: Commercial Society and the Defenders of the English Commonwealth," *American Historical Review* 103 (1998): 705–36.

10. In the language of economics, free riding caused Pennsylvania to suffer a market failure in the provision of a key public good, defense.

11. *Autobiography,* 7, 56–57, 64–65.

12. *Plain Truth,* in *Papers* 3:202. In addition to ordering books, directors were forced to devise policies for the return of late and damaged books as well as means to increase the rate of return on subscriptions (LCP, *A Book of Minutes. Containing an Account of the Proceedings of the Directors of the Library Company of Philadelphia* [MS Yi2 5960F], 1:5, 14–15, 19).

13. George Fox et al., *A Declaration from the Harmles & Innocent People of God, Called Quakers . . . Against all Plotters and Fighters in the World* (London: Robert Wilson, 1660), 1–2. Quakers were by no means the only pacifists in Pennsylvania, but they were politically the most salient. Many German sects shared their opposition to war; see, for example, "Petition of Mennonites," 15 May 1755, APS Penn Letters and Ancient Documents (974.8 P365), 3:27. The relationship between religious unity and social order in seventeenth-century England is deftly explored in Conrad Russell, "Arguments for Religious Unity in England, 1530–1650," *Journal of Ecclesiastical History* 18 (1967): 201–26, and Don Herzog, *Happy Slaves: A Critique of Consent Theory* (Chicago: UCP, 1989), 39–71.

14. The complex history of Quaker pacifism is traced in Meredith Baldwin Weddle, *Walking in the Way of Peace: Quaker Pacifism in the Seventeenth Century* (Oxford: OUP, 2001).

15. William Livingston, "A History of the American Revolution," John Jay Papers, reel 1, New York Historical Society, as quoted in Alan Tully, *Forming American Politics: Ideals, Interests, and Institutions in Colonial New York and Pennsylvania* (Baltimore: Johns Hopkins University Press, 1994), 292.

Native Americans shared this judgment. In 1756 the Oneida chief
Scarouady attributed the rise of violence along the frontier to the (mis-
taken) belief that William Penn's "children" had all died: "this
Misfortune . . . came upon us as if an evil Spirit had arisen from under the
Ground" ("Minutes of Several Meetings with Indians," APS B F85, 58:3).

16. Franklin recounts this practice in *Autobiography*, 95–96. On the background, see Hermann Wellenreuther, "The Political Dilemma of the
Quakers in Pennsylvania, 1681–1748," *PMHB* 94 (1970): 135–72.

17. Expressing gratitude: "Neither Soldier, nor mercenary Bonds of any other
Denomination, burden or injure us" (*A Dialogue Shewing, What's therein to
be found* [Philadelphia: Samuel Keimer, 1725], 39). Antimilitarism was especially strong among German immigrants: some felt a spiritual kinship to the
Quakers, while others had suffered from militarization in their homeland.
Showing opposition: Governor Andrew Hamilton remonstrated in 1702,
"The Golden Rule in this Case ought to be the Standard, for if those who
profess themselves under a scruple to bear arms would think it a hardship to
be forced to it, so (I hope) they'll also think it one to Invade the principles of
others by Disabling them to Effect what they in Conscience ought to do,
which is to Provide, under God, for the Defense of the Inhabitants against
the insults of an Enemy" (*Minutes of the Provincial Council*, 2:78). This tension is explored by Tully in *Forming American Politics*, 108–10, 289–94;
"King George's War and the Quakers: The Defense Crisis of 1732–1742 in
Pennsylvania Politics," *Journal of the Lancaster County Historical Society* 82
(1978): 174–98; "Politics and Peace Testimony in Mid-Eighteenth-Century
Pennsylvania," *Canadian Review of American Studies* 13 (1982): 159–77.

18. Franklin was sufficiently anxious that he argued that the Association ought
to be disbanded if the mutiny act were not adopted (*Papers* 6:266–73,
433–37; *Votes and Proceedings of the House of Representatives of the
Province of Pennsylvania* [Philadelphia: B. Franklin, 1756], 74–75).

19. *Votes and Proceedings*, 103–4; BF to Peter Collinson, 15 June 1756, in *Papers*
6:456–57. The resignations protected the local Meeting; as Ralph Ketcham
has argued, nothing would have been more destructive to the community
of the faithful than "to have Quakers in government responsible for punishing other Quakers who felt obliged to 'suffer' for conscience sake"
("Conscience, War and Politics in Pennsylvania, 1755–1757," *WMQ* 20
[1963]: 436–37). But the departures exacerbated conflicts between Pennsylvania and London Friends (Jack D. Marietta, "Conscience, the Quaker
Community, and the French and Indian War," *PMHB* 95 [1971]: 3–27).

20. James Logan to BF, 3 December 1747, in *Papers* 3:219. As early as 1741 Logan was urging Quakers unwilling to embrace defensive war to not seek election to the Assembly (J[ames] L[ogan], *To Robert Jordan, and others the Friends of the Yearly Meeting for Business, now conven'd in Philadelphia* [Philadelphia: Benjamin Franklin, 1741]).

21. Tully, "Politics and Peace Testimony," 162, 165–66. In 1756 James Pemberton, one of the six who resigned rather than embrace military measures, admitted that "there is indeed a majority amongst us who show little regard to the Principles of their profession" (Pemberton to Jonah Thompson, 25 April 1756, quoted in Tully, *Forming American Politics*, 478n159).

22. The logic of differentiation is brilliantly explored in Michael Walzer, "Liberalism and the Art of Separation," *Political Theory* 12 (1984): 315–30, and Herzog, *Happy Slaves*, 148–81.

23. *Autobiography*, 94–95; Tom Paine, *Common Sense; Addressed to the Inhabitants of America* (Philadelphia: R. Bell, 1776), 29; Judith N. Shklar, *Ordinary Vices* (Cambridge: HUP, 1984), 48, 72.

24. *Autobiography*, 96. On the emergence of print culture, see Elizabeth Eisenstein, *The Printing Press as an Agent of Change: Communications and Culture in Early-Modern Europe*, 2 vols. (Cambridge: CUP, 1979). For a vigorous challenge, see Adrian Johns, *The Nature of the Book: Print and Culture in the Making* (Chicago: UCP, 1998). Many of Johns's criticisms of Eisenstein are telling, but he overstates the case against uniformity and fixity.

25. *Autobiography*, 96–97; *Papers* 1:109–11. This theme is elegantly discussed in Douglas Anderson, "Franklin [and/among] the Revisionists," paper presented at the annual meeting of the North American Conference on British Studies, Boston, 17 November 2006.

26. *Gazette*, 22 October and 5 November 1747. "Among other Prejudices which it has removed with me . . . is this: I had always imagined" that Quakers "were absolutely against all *Defensive War*, and looked upon it as their Duty, not only to decline it themselves, but to discourage it as much as possible in others." But Barclay was "very moderate on this Head," allowing that "WAR, undertaken upon a JUST OCCASION (and no Occasion can be more just than that of *defending* one's Country) is unlawful only *to such Christians as have attained Perfection*" (*Gazette*, 5 November 1747).

27. *Gazette*, 19 November 1747. Franklin quoted Proverbs 22:3 ("A prudent Man foreseeth the Evil, and hideth himself; but the simple pass on, and are punished") and 24:5–6 ("A wise Man is strong, yea, a Man of Knowledge increaseth Strength. For by wise Counsel thou shalt make thy War; and in

Multitude of Counselors there is Safety"). The reference is to William Edmundson, *A Journal of the Life, Travels, Sufferings and Labour of . . .
William Edmundson* (Dublin: Samuel Fairbrother, 1715), 119–26.

28. Whitefield, quoted in *Papers* 2:313n9; Gilbert Tennent, *The late Association
for Defence, encourag'd, Or, The lawfulness of a Defensive War*, 2nd ed.
(Philadelphia: William Bradford, 1748), 5, 35, 41. Franklin called attention
to Tennent's "excellent Sermon" in the *Gazette*, 29 December 1747. Tennent was seconded by William Currie, *A Treatise on the Lawfulness of Defensive War* (Philadelphia: Franklin and Hall, 1748). The relationship
between Franklin and Tennent was widely known; cf. Benjamin Gilbert,
Truth Vindicated, And The Doctrine of Darkness Manifested (Philadelphia:
1748), 10.

29. Quoted in *Papers* 3:240n1. John Smith, *The Doctrine of Christianity, As held
by the People called Quakers, Vindicated* (Philadelphia: Franklin and Hall,
1748). Like Tennent's *Late Association*, it quickly went through two editions. See also Samuel Smith, *Necessary Truth: Or, Seasonable Considerations for the Inhabitants of the City of Philadelphia, and Province of
Pennsylvania* (Philadelphia, 1748); *A Treatise Shewing the Need We Have to
Rely upon God as Sole Protector of This Province* (Philadelphia: Godhard
Armbrister, 1748); Gilbert, *Truth Vindicated*. German-language responses
to the Association will be discussed below.

30. Tennent, *Late Association*, 10; Gilbert Tennent, *Sermon Preach'd At
Philadelphia, January 7. 1747–8* (Philadelphia: William Bradford, 1748),
19; Smith, *Doctrine of Christianity*, 3, 17, 33.

31. Tennent, *Sermon*, 19; Tennent, *Late Association*, 9. According to Smith, by
contrast, "the Design of the Gospel Dispensation, was to redeem Man
from the deplorable Corruption which was the Consequence of his Fall,
and to restore him into the State of Purity and Peace, wherein he was created; by informing his Judgment, rectifying his Will, governing his Passions, and making him a *New Creature*" (*Doctrine of Christianity*, 1).

32. Tennent, *Sermon*, 16. "Who can, without the utmost Horror, conceive the
Miseries" of an attack by "*licentious Privateers*": "when your Persons, Fortunes, Wives and Daughters, shall be subject to the wanton and unbridled
Rage, Rapine and Lust, of *Negroes, Mulattos*, and others, the vilest and
most abandoned of Mankind" (*Plain Truth*, in *Autobiography*, 187–88).
"We have an Enemy in Head of us, the most barbarous and cruel of any of
the human Race; if we have any Regard, therefore, either for our selves, or
for our Families, for our Country, or our fellow Subjects, let us fall upon

some Means or other, to keep off those Enemies of human Nature; I mean a lawless Crew of *French* and *Spanish* Privateers; and which is a worse Enemy than even those, the barbarous, cruel, and inhuman *Indians;* who, wherever they come, will turn the richest Soil to a barren Wilderness, ravish our Women in the Sight of the Sun, and afterwards slay them before our Eyes; imbrue their Hands in the Blood of our innocent Children; and after all, put ourselves to Death, by the most painful Tortures the savage Cruelty can invent" (William Currie, *A Sermon, Preached in Radnor Church* [Philadelphia: Franklin and Hall, 1748], 17).

33. "It is justly esteemed Wisdom in a Nation to think of War and prepare for it in a Time of Peace" (Tennent, *Late Association*, 9). Franklin's phrasing was more mellifluous: " 'Tis a wise and true Saying, that *One Sword often keeps another in the Scabbard. The Way to secure Peace is to be prepared for War*" (*Plain Truth*, in *Autobiography*, 192). The motto originated with Flavius Vegetius Renatus, a fourth-century Roman military writer (*De re militari* III).

34. Smith, *Doctrine of Christianity*, 11–12. The quotation is from Matthew 16:25–26.

35. Thomas Hobbes, *Leviathan*, 1651, ed. Richard Tuck (Cambridge: CUP, 1996), 89, 491, 153. *Plain Truth*, in *Papers* 3:199. Franklin had read Hobbes a decade or more before writing *Plain Truth* (BF to James Logan, 1737? in *Papers* 2:185).

36. "Should not the *Magistrate* protect his Subjects from unjust violence? . . . Nor is it reasonable he should expect Support, Honor and Obedience from his Subjects, if they . . . do not obtain Protection from him" (Tennent, *Late Association*, 18, 77). The Quaker Anthony Benezet retorted that this suggestion was "a device of the enemy. There is no distinction in Christianity between civil and religious matters" (quoted in Marietta, "Conscience, Quaker Community," 14).

37. This judgment is shared by some modern historians. Both Tully ("Politics and Peace Testimony") and Marietta ("Conscience, Quaker Community") assume that violence is necessary to governance and dismiss out of hand the Quaker belief that nonviolence was itself a source of power.

38. Or rather, so much for the standard account of Hobbes. For a spirited alternative, which takes seriously Hobbes's appreciation for the limited appeal of self-preservation in the midst of a religious civil war, see Herzog, *Happy Slaves*, 72–109.

39. Plautus, *Asinaria* 2.495; Thomas Hobbes, *On the Citizen (De Cive)*, ed. and trans. Richard Tuck and Michael Silverthorne (Cambridge: CUP, 1998),

3–4; Anthony Ashley Cooper, third Earl of Shaftesbury, *Characteristics of Men, Manners, Opinions, Times*, ed. Lawrence E. Klein (Cambridge: CUP, 1999), 288, 51–52; Francis Hutcheson, *An Inquiry into the Original of Our Ideas of Beauty and Virtue*, 1725, ed. Wolfgang Leidhold (Indianapolis: Liberty Fund, 2004), 225.

40. Franklin read Shaftesbury as a young man in Boston (*Autobiography*, 14). Hutcheson's *Inquiry* was published to great acclaim during Franklin's first trip to London. In Philadelphia, Franklin sold both Shaftesbury and Hutcheson (*Gazette*, 25 May 1738 and 14 December 1742), and copies could be found in the private libraries of leading members of the community (Frederick Tolles, *Meeting House and Counting House: The Quaker Merchants of Colonial Philadelphia 1682–1763* [Chapel Hill: UNCP, 1948], 177). And when it came time to design a curriculum for the Philadelphia Academy, Franklin relied heavily on Hutcheson's disciple George Turnbull ("Proposals Relating to the Education of Youth," in *Papers* 3:397–421).

41. Shaftesbury, *Characteristics* 31. On politeness: Lawrence Klein, *Shaftesbury and the Culture of Politeness* (Cambridge: CUP, 1994); Nicholas Phillipson, "Adam Smith as Civic Moralist," in *Wealth and Virtue: The Shaping of Political Economy in the Scottish Enlightenment*, ed. Istvan Hont and Michael Ignatieff (Cambridge: CUP, 1983), 179–202; Phillipson, "Politeness and Politics in the Reigns of Anne and the Early Hanoverians," in *The Varieties of British Political Thought*, ed. J. G. A. Pocock (Cambridge: CUP, 1993), 211–45.

42. *Fog's Weekly Journal*, 2 May 1730, quoted in Clark, *British Clubs and Societies*, 1; Francis Drake, *A Speech Deliver'd to the Worshipful and Antient Society of Free and Accepted Masons* (London, 1729), 19, 24; Steven Bullock, "The Revolutionary Transformation of American Freemasonry, 1752–1792," *WMQ* 47 (1990): 352; John Brewer, "Commercialization and Politics," in Neil McKendrick, John Brewer, and J. H. Plumb, *The Birth of a Consumer Society: The Commercialization of Eighteenth-Century England* (Bloomington: Indiana University Press, 1982), 217–22.

43. Clark, *British Clubs and Societies*, 491; "Journal of William Black, 1744," *PMHB* 1 (1877): 405. Another visitor in the same year spoke of the "very mixed company" at a tavern he visited: "There were Scots, English, Dutch, Germans, and Irish; there were Roman Catholics, Church men, Presbyterians, Quakers, Newlightmen, Methodists, Seventh day men, Moravians, Anabaptists, and one Jew" (Alexander Hamilton, *Gentleman's Progress: The Itinerarium of Dr. Alexander Hamilton, 1744*, ed. Carl Bridenbaugh [Chapel Hill: UNCP, 1948], 20). In the words of a Philadelphia

clubman of the period, "We meet, converse, laugh, talk, smoke, drink, differ, agree, argue, Philosophize, harangue, pun, sing, dance and fiddle together" (quoted in Carl Bridenbaugh and Jessica Bridenbaugh, *Rebels and Gentlemen: Philadelphia in the Age of Franklin* [New York: OUP, 1962], 22).

44. *Plain Truth*, in *Papers* 3:200–201.

45. Douglas Anderson, *The Radical Enlightenments of Benjamin Franklin* (Baltimore: Johns Hopkins University Press, 1997), 10–11; Shaftesbury, *Characteristics*, 54. This insight is brilliantly explored in Stephen Holmes, "The Secret History of Self-Interest," in *Beyond Self-Interest*, ed. Jane Mansbridge (Chicago: UCP, 1990), 267–86.

46. Hutcheson, *Inquiry*, 115; Francis Hutcheson, *An Essay on the Nature and Conduct of the Passions and Affections, with Illustrations on the Moral Sense*, ed. Aaron Garrett (Indianapolis: Liberty Fund, 2002), 46–47. On the powers of reason, see Hutcheson, *Inquiry*, 133. Shaftesbury pointed to "envy, malice, forwardness or other such hateful passions" as the cause of "an ill creature" (*Characteristics*, 172).

47. *Plain Truth*, in *Papers* 3:201; *Gazette*, 19 November 1747. Apparently this was deemed insufficient; in late November the Proprietary Party was still considering a "vindication" of its conduct (Richard Peters to the Proprietaries, 29 November 1747, in *Papers*, 3:216).

48. *Plain Truth*, in *Papers* 3:201.

49. Ibid., 3:195.

50. Richard Morison, *A Remedy for Sedition* (London: Thomae Bertheleti, 1536), fol. B.ii^v; Elizabeth I, speech of 5 November 1566, in J. E. Neale, *Elizabeth I and Her Parliaments* (London: Cape, 1953), 1:148. E. M. W. Tillyard, *The Elizabethan World Picture* (London: Chatto and Windus, 1943) contains a wealth of examples.

51. *Plain Truth*, in *Papers* 3:195–96.

52. Istvan Hont, "Commercial Society and Political Theory in the Eighteenth Century: The Problem of Authority in David Hume and Adam Smith," in *Main Trends in Cultural History*, ed. Willem Melding and Wyger Velma (Amsterdam: Ridopi, 1994), 60–61.

53. "Proposals and Queries" and "Standing Queries for the Junto," in *Papers* 1:255–64.

54. Bernard Bailyn, *Education in the Forming of American Society* (New York: W. W. Norton, 1960), 36; *Autobiography*, 137.

55. Kenneth Lockridge, "Literacy in Early America, 1650–1800," in *Literacy and Social Development in the West*, ed. H. J. Graff (Cambridge: CUP,

1981), 183–200; F. W. Grubb, "Growth of Literacy in Colonial America: Longitudinal Patterns, Economic Models, and the Direction of Future Research," *Social Science History* 14 (1990): 452–82; David Galenson, "Settlement and Growth of the Colonies: Population, Labor and Economic Development," in *The Cambridge Economic History of the United States,* ed. Stanley Engerman and Robert Gallman (Cambridge: CUP, 1996), 1:135–207 . On signature literacy, see Kenneth Lockridge, *Literacy in Colonial New England* (New York: W. W. Norton, 1974); David Cressy, *Literacy and the Social Order* (Cambridge: CUP, 1980). On literacy rates among servants in England prior to immigration, see David Galenson, *White Servitude in Colonial America* (Cambridge: CUP, 1981).

56. BF to William Franklin, 6 October 1773, in *Papers* 20:436–39; BF to Noah Webster Jr., 26 December 1789, LC Franklin Papers, box 24.

57. Alexander Pope, *An Essay on Man. In Four Epistles to a Friend. Corrected by the Author,* 7th ed. (London: J. Wilford, 1736), 1:152, p. 10; *Gazette,* 19 November 1747. Franklin reprinted this translation—with one small change and slightly different formatting—in the second edition of *Plain Truth.*

58. Lawrence Cremin, *American Education: The Colonial Experience, 1607–1783* (New York: Harper and Row, 1970), 501; Ian Michael, *The Teaching of English from the Sixteenth Century to 1870* (Cambridge: CUP, 1987), 437; *Gazette,* 28 January 1746, 3 February 1747.

59. Thomas Dilworth, *A New Guide to the English Tongue* (Philadelphia: B. Franklin, 1747), 139. Alternate versions: Samuel Croxall, *Fables of Aesop and Others* (London: J. Tonson and J. Watts, 1722), 102–3; *Aesop's Fables, with Their Morals,* 16th ed. (London: J. Phillips, H. Rhodes, J. Taylor, 1706), 161–62.

60. *Plain Truth,* in *Papers* 3:188–91; *Gazette,* 5 February 1735. Harrington wrote that "the people cannot see, but they can feel" ("Valerius and Publicola," in *The Political Works of James Harrington,* ed. J. G. A. Pocock [Cambridge: CUP, 1977], 798). Thanks to Leo Lemay for helping me track down this reference. Machiavelli's original inverts the terms but carries the same meaning: "Most men judge more by their eyes than by their hands. For everyone is capable of seeing you, but few can touch you. Everyone can see what you appear to be, whereas few have direct experience of what you really are" (*The Prince,* ed. Quentin Skinner and Russell Price [Cambridge: CUP, 1988], 63).

61. *Plain Truth,* in *Papers* 3:191.

62. Richard Peters to the Proprietors, 29 November 1747, in *Papers*, 3:216; Ledger D (APS B F85, f6[6], 155). This figure probably includes a second edition, printed three weeks later (Miller, 220).

63. Richard Peters to the Proprietors, 29 November 1747, in *Papers*, 3:216–17; *Gazette*, 26 November 1747 and 3 December 1747; *Autobiography*, 92; BF to Cadwallader Colden, 27 November 1747, in *Papers*, 3:213. In the *Autobiography* Franklin claimed that twelve hundred men subscribed on the first day; I have followed the more conservative figure he gave in the *Gazette*.

64. "An Act to Regulate the Militia of this Colony," in *Acts Passed in October and November 1739* (New York: William Bradford, 1739), 1–10; "An Act for the settling and better regulation of the Militia," 9 May 1723, in *The Statutes at Large . . . of Virginia*, ed. William Waller Hening (Richmond: Samuel Pleasants, 1809–23), 4:118–19; Higginbotham, *War and Society*, 23; George Webb, *The Office and Authority of a Justice of Peace* (Williamsburg: William Parks, 1736), 221–22; Linda Kerber, *No Constitutional Right to Be Ladies: Women and the Obligations of Citizenship* (New York: Hill and Wang, 1998), 236–42.

65. *Autobiography*, 92; "Articles of Association," 1 July 1731, LCP; "Articles of the Union Fire Company," 7 December 1736, in *Papers* 2:150.

66. *Autobiography*, 48; Edward Shippen to Thomas Stretch, 26 January 1754, Edward Shippen Letterbook, APS B Sh62.

67. Anderson, *People's Army*, 120. For example, in 1758 five soldiers on the western frontier were court-martialed for refusing to work until they received "more Pay and Victuals." Their punishments ranged from one hundred to six hundred lashes with a cat-o'-nine-tails (HSP Shippen Papers, 3:195). See also Anderson, *People's Army*, 137–40.

68. Shklar, *Ordinary Vices*; Judith N. Shklar, "The Liberalism of Fear," in *Liberalism and the Moral Life*, ed. Nancy Rosenblum (Cambridge: HUP, 1989), 21–38; William Ian Miller, *Humiliation and Other Essays on Honor, Social Discomfort, and Violence* (Ithaca: Cornell University Press), 1993.

69. For Massachusetts, "An Act for Regulating of the Militia," in *Acts and Laws, Of His Majesty's Province of the Massachusetts-Bay* (Boston: B. Green, 1726), 42–43; for Connecticut, "An Act for forming and regulating the Militia," in *Acts and Laws of His Majesty's English Colony of Connecticut* (New-London: Timothy Green, 1750), 162; for Virginia, Webb, *Office and Authority*, 222.

70. Anderson, *People's Army*, 125, 189; David Underdown, *Revel, Riot, and Rebellion: Popular Politics and Culture in England, 1603–1660* (Oxford:

Clarendon, 1985), 21. In Maryland, Virginia, and South Carolina, the relationship between freedom, slavery, and military service was further inflected by the fact that one of the primary responsibilities of the militia was
to provide slave patrols (Saul Cornell, *A Well-Regulated Militia: The
Founding Fathers and the Origins of Gun Control in America* [Oxford: OUP,
2006], 18–19).

71. *Papers*, 3:225–26, 239; *Minutes of the Provincial Council*, 5:174–75; *Gazette*,
5 January 1748; William Blakeney and Humphrey Bland, *The New Manual
Exercise*, 2nd ed. (Philadelphia: B. Franklin, 1747); Miller, 217–18.

72. *Gazette*, 19 January, 9 June, and 26 May 1748. Richard Peters reported to
the Proprietors that the Association's "Conduct hitherto has been remarkably regular and moderate, without any angry Expressions or blustering
behavior" (Peters to Proprietaries, 1 February 1748, HSP Penn Papers,
Official Correspondence, 4:89). Thomas Penn thought the Association illegal and unconstitutional but still found reason to report that he was "well
pleased to hear . . . that the Effects of the Association have been carried so
regularly on" (Penn to Peters, 9 June 1748, HSP Peters Papers, 2:108).

73. *Plain Truth*, in *Papers* 3:199; 195; Niccolò Machiavelli, *The Discourses*, ed.
Bernard Crick, trans. Leslie Walker (Harmondsworth: Penguin, 1970),
218; Pocock, *Machiavellian Moment*, 452, 464; J. G. A. Pocock, "Machiavelli, Harrington and English Political Ideologies in the Eighteenth Century," *WMQ* 22 (1965): 567. Alternately, and ominously, "a republic of
free warriors" (J. G. A. Pocock, "*The Machiavellian Moment* Revisited: A
Study in History and Ideology," *Journal of Modern History* 53 [1981]: 61).

74. Cornell, *Well-Regulated Militia;* Cress, *Citizens in Arms;* Robert Shalhope,
"The Armed Citizen in the Early Republic," *Law and Contemporary Problems* 49 (1986): 125–41; David Williams, "Civic Republicanism and the
Citizen Militia: The Terrifying Second Amendment," *Yale Law Journal*
101 (1991): 551–613.

75. Classical republicanism was an explicitly masculine ideology. The worst
that could be said of a man, or of a class of men, was that he (or it) was
"too effeminate for Arms" ([William Thornton], *The Counterpoise. Being
Thoughts on a Militia and a Standing Army* [London: M. Cooper, 1752], 35).

76. Harrington, *The Commonwealth of Oceana*, in *The Political Works of James
Harrington*, ed. J. G. A. Pocock (Cambridge: CUP, 1977), 212–13. On militias and social hierarchy: J. R. Western, *The English Militia in the Eighteenth Century* (London: Routledge and Kegan Paul, 1965), 94; John
Robertson, *The Scottish Enlightenment and the Militia Issue* (Edinburgh: J.

Donald, 1985), 91; Eliga Gould, "To Strengthen the King's Hands: Dynastic Legitimacy, Militia Reform and Ideas of National Unity in England, 1745–1760," *Historical Journal* 34 (1991): 345–46.

77. Morgan, *Inventing the People*, 169; "Form of Association," in *Papers* 3:205–12.

78. Massachusetts: T. H. Breen, "English Origins and New World Developments: The Case of the Covenanted Militia in Seventeenth-Century Massachusetts," *Past and Present* 57 (1972): 74–96; John Shy, "A New Look at Colonial Militia," *WMQ* 20 (1963): 176–77. Officer lists: *Gazette*, 5 January 1748.

79. "Form of Association," 3:209. Whether consciously or not, Franklin's words echo those of Colonel Thomas Rainborough in the Putney debates of 1747: "The poorest he that is in England hath a life to live, as the greatest he." Rainborough and the junior officers who joined him—supporters of the Levellers's "Agreement of the People"—also insisted that decision making within the army be more democratic. "We are not a mere mercenary Army, hired to serve any Arbitrary power of a State." Some of the most radical developments in the theory and practice of civic equality occurred within the military in the seventeenth and eighteenth centuries. Ironically, these innovations were invisible to writers like James Harrington, who were imbued with the spirit of classical republicanism ("The Putney Debates," 29 October 1747, in *Puritanism and Liberty*, ed. A. S. P. Woodhouse [Chicago: UCP, 1951], 53–54; *A Declaration, or Representation from His Excellency, Sir Thomas Fairfax, And the Army under his command* [London, 1747], 4).

80. *Plain Truth*, in *Papers* 3:198–99.

81. *Papers* 22:208–9.

82. BF, "Commonplace Book," HSP Ferdinand J. Dreer Collection, fol. 17; "Standing Queries," in *Papers* 1:259. According to the rules of the Freemasons, to enable "*easy* and *free* Conversation . . . no private Piques or Quarrels must be brought within the Door of the *Lodge*, far less any Quarrels about *Religion*, or *Nations*, or *State-Policy*" (*The Constitutions of the Free-Masons* [Philadelphia: B. Franklin, 1734], 54). One Masonic sermon proclaimed that this "excellent institution has been a means of conciliating persons, who otherwise must have lived . . . in perpetual discord and contention" (Arthur Browne, *Universal Love recommended in a Sermon* [Boston: J. and T. Leverett, 1755], 20). Tension within and between modern and ancient Masons are traced in Steven Bullock, *Revolutionary Brotherhood:*

Freemasonry and the Transformation of the American Social Order, 1730–1840 (Chapel Hill: UNCP, 1996).

83. "Rules of a Society meeting weekly in the City of Philadelphia for their mutual improvement in useful knowledge," American Philosophical Society Notes and Extracts, 1726–1841, HSP DuPonceau Papers; "Articles of Association," 1 July 1731, LCP.

84. In the "Form of Association" Franklin suggested that "most People" already had a firelock of some kind. He appears to have been overly optimistic. In January he advertised a "ready Market" for "any Quantities of Small Arms to spare," and in March he began selling military kits (muskets equipped with bayonets, belts, cartridge boxes and leather slings) that were geared to the needs of Associators (*Gazette*, 19 January and 8 March 1748; *Papers* 3:310–11).

85. Peters to Penn, 29 November 1747, in *Papers* 3:217. They had the support of the mayor and Corporation of Philadelphia as well as the president and Council of the Province (*Minutes of the Common Council of the City of Philadelphia, 1704–1776* [Philadelphia: Crissy and Markley, 1847], 488–89; *Minutes of the Provincial Council*, 5:158, 161).

86. Thomas Penn to Council, 30 March 1748, in *Minutes of the Provincial Council*, 5:240–41.

87. Shirley to Council, 1 February 1748, in *Minutes of the Provincial Council*, 5:198–99, 206; Clinton to Council, 5 January 1748, in *Minutes of the Provincial Council*, 5:187; *Autobiography*, 93. Franklin's memory was faulty; Clinton actually sent twelve 12-pounders and two 18-pounders (*Papers*, 222n5).

88. Thomas Jefferson, "Thoughts on Lotteries," February 1826, in *The Writings of Thomas Jefferson*, ed. Andrew A. Lipscomb and Albert Ellery Bergh (Washington, DC: Thomas Jefferson Memorial Association, 1905), 11:437; *The Diaries of George Washington*, ed. Donald Jackson (Charlottesville: University Press of Virginia, 1976), 2:106, 148; Washington to Edmund Randolph, 10 July 1784, in *The Papers of George Washington: Confederation Series*, ed. W. W. Abbot (Charlottesville: University Press of Virginia, 1992), 1:494–95. The indispensable source on this topic is John Samuel Ezell, *Fortune's Merry Wheel: The Lottery in America* (Cambridge: HUP, 1960).

89. John Adams to Abigail Adams, 17 February 1777, in *Adams Family Correspondence*, ed. L. H. Butterfield (Cambridge: HUP, 1963), 2:162–63.

90. On Providence: "He that makes use of a Lot wholly commits his affair to a superior Cause than either nature or art, therefore unto God. But this

ought not to be done in a Sportful Lusory way" (Increase Mather, *Testimony against Several Prophane and Superstitious Customs*, 1687, quoted in Ezell, *Fortune's Merry Wheel*, 17). See also Benjamin Coleman, *A Humble Discourse of the Incomprehensibleness of God*, 2nd ed. (Boston: J. Draper, 1714), 75–76. Poem on cullies: *Prologue, Design'd for the last new Farce, Call'd, The Fool's Expectation: Or, The Wheel of Fortune* (London: 1698).

91. Joseph Addison and Richard Steele, *The Spectator*, ed. Donald Bond (Oxford: Clarendon, 1965), #191 (9 October 1711), 2:248. Modern social science confirms this basic insight (Jonathan Guryan and Melissa Kearney, "Lucky Stores, Gambling, and Addiction: Empirical Evidence from State Lotteries" [working paper 11287, National Bureau of Economic Research, Cambridge, April 2005]). Consequences of lotteries: Parliamentary debate of 15 January 1755, in William Cobbett, ed., *The Parliamentary History of England* (London: T. C. Hansard, 1813), 15:515.

92. *Charter to William Penn, and Laws of the Province of Pennsylvania*, quoted in Asa Earl Martin, "Lotteries in Pennsylvania Prior to 1833," *PMHB* 47 (1923): 310; *Anno Regni Georgii II . . . At a General Assembly of the Province of Pennsylvania . . . 1729* (Philadelphia: Franklin and Meredith, 1730), 40–41; Ezell, *Fortune's Merry Wheel*, 22.

93. *The Secretary's Guide, Or, Young Man's Companion*, 5th ed. (Philadelphia: Andrew Bradford, 1737), 92; George Fisher, *The American Instructor: Or, Young Man's Best Companion*, 9th ed. (Philadelphia: Franklin and Hall, 1748), 58. These books were originally printed in England; the latter was edited by Franklin to make it especially appropriate for colonists.

94. *Gazette*, 22 December 1747, 2 February and 1 March 1748.

95. *Gazette*, 2 June 1748.

96. *Autobiography*, 107; Nathaniel Hazard to Alexander Hamilton, 5 October 1790, in *The Papers of Alexander Hamilton*, ed. Harold C. Syrett (New York: Columbia University Press, 1963), 7:93; Alexander Hamilton, "Idea Concerning a Lottery," January 1793, in *Papers of Hamilton*, 13:518.

97. "The industrious habits of the people of the present day, absorbed in the pursuits of gain, and devoted to the improvements of agriculture and commerce are incompatible with the condition of a nation of soldiers" (Alexander Hamilton, James Madison, and John Jay, *The Federalist*, ed. Terence Ball [Cambridge: CUP, 2003], #8, p. 33; Hamilton, *Federalist*, #29, pp. 132–36; Don Higginbotham, "The Federalized Militia Debate: A Neglected Aspect of Second Amendment Scholarship," *WMQ* 55 [1998]: 39–58).

98. *Gazette*, 19 January and 28 April 1748; *Philadelphia Lottery Accounts* (Philadelphia: Franklin and Hall, 1752); "Philadelphia Lottery Papers," Beinecke Uncat Ms. Vault Franklin, Bound Oversize.

99. *Gazette*, 12 January, 16 April, 28 April, 2 June, 18 August, 1 September 1748; *PA*, 1st ser., 12:440.

100. BF to Sir Joseph Banks, 27 July 1783, LC Franklin Papers, box 25. See also "Journal of Negotiations," September 1775, in *Papers* 21:555; BF to David Hartley, 2 February 1780, in *Papers* 31:437; BF to Jonathan Shipley, 10 June 1782, in *Papers* 37:323; BF to Josiah Quincy Sr., 11 September 1783, APS B F85.228.

101. *Autobiography*, 123–24; John Locke, *An Essay concerning Human Understanding*, ed. Peter Nidditch (Oxford: OUP, 1975), 2.21.29–39. See also a letter from the camp at Gnadenhütten dated 20 January, in *Gazette*, 29 January 1756, and William Hunter, *Forts on the Pennsylvania Frontier, 1753–1758* (Harrisburg: Pennsylvania Historical and Museum Commission, 1960), 233–37.

102. Penn to Peters, 30 March 1748, quoted in *Papers* 3:186; Penn to Peters, 9 June 1748, HSP Peters Papers, 2:108. On Franklin's leadership of the Association, see James Logan to Peter Collinson, 28 February 1750, in *Papers* 3:470–72.

103. Robert Middlekauff, *Benjamin Franklin and His Enemies* (Berkeley and Los Angeles: University of California Press, 1996), 35; Penn to Peters, 9 June 1748, HSP Peters Papers, 2:108.

104. Franklin "there broaches a Doctrine, though very true in itself, that Obedience to Governors is no more due than protection to the people, Yet it is not fit to be always in the heads of the Wild unthinking Multitude" (Penn to Peters, 9 June 1748, HSP Peters Papers, 2:108).

105. Alden T. Vaughan, "Frontier Banditti and the Indians: The Paxton Boys' Legacy, 1763–1775," *Pennsylvania History* 51 (1984): 1; [Joseph Galloway], *A True and Impartial State of the Province of Pennsylvania* (Philadelphia: W. Dunlap, 1759), 15.

106. William Parsons to Timothy Horsfield, 9 March 1756, APS Horsfield Papers (974.8 H78), fol. 109; Timothy Horsfield to Governor Hamilton, 3 September 1761, APS Horsfield Papers (974.8 H78), fol. 441.

107. "John Potts, James Reed, Conrad Weiser, William Maugridge, Jonas Seeley, et al to Robert Hunter Morris, Reading, 31 October 1755," APS Horsfield Papers (974.8 H78), fol. 33; Dan Clark to Samuel Burd, 21 May 1755, HSP Shippen Papers, 2:183; John R. Dunbar, ed., *The Paxton Papers* (The Hague: Martinus Nijhoff, 1957), 9–10.

108. Governor Hamilton to Timothy Horsfield, 13 October 1763, APS Horsfield Papers (974.8 H78), fol. 499; Brooke Hindle, "The March of the Paxton Boys," *WMQ* 3 (1946): 466–67; William Henry, in *Colonial Records of Pennsylvania* (Harrisburg, 1851–53), 9:103–4, quoted in Dunbar, *Paxton Papers*, 29.

109. Hindle, "March of the Paxton Boys," 470; BF to Lord Kames, 2 June 1765, in *Papers*, 12:158; *Gazette*, 9 February 1764. Even Franklin was overwhelmed by the pace of events: "You may judge what Hurry and Confusion we have been in for this Week past. I was up two Nights running, all Night, with our Governor; and my Rest so broken by Alarms on the other Nights, that the whole Weeks seems one confused Space of Time, without any such Distinction of Days, as that I can readily and certainly say, on such a Day such a thing happened" (BF to Richard Jackson, 11 February 1764, in *Papers* 11:77).

110. Hindle, "March of the Paxton Boys," 463n5; *A Declaration and Remonstrance Of the distressed and bleeding Frontier Inhabitants* ([Philadelphia], 1764), 11. "For God's sake," one supporter cried out, "are we always to be slaves, must we groan for ever beneath the yoke of three Quaker counties?" ([Hugh Williamson], *The Plain Dealer: Or, Remarks on Quaker Politicks in Pennsylvania. Numb. III* [Philadelphia, 1764], 22).

111. *The Journals of Henry Melchior Muhlenberg*, trans. Theodore Tapper and John Doberstein (Philadelphia: Muhlenberg, 1942), 6 February 1764, 2:21; *An Apology of the Paxton Volunteers addressed to the candid & impartial World*, 1764, HSP Am.283.

112. For a fascinating example of an attempt to shore up this distinction through education and specially adopted forms of dress and behavior, see "Description of the Nain and Wechquetane Indians, and distinction from wild Indians," c. 1756, APS Horsfield Papers (974.8 H78), fol. 525.

113. *An Historical Account, of the late Disturbance, between the Inhabitants of the Back Settlements . . . and the Philadelphians* (Philadelphia: Anthony Armbruster, 1764), 7; *A Narrative of the Late Massacres, in Lancaster County*, 1764, in *Papers* 11:55; Vaughan, "Frontier Banditti," 2.

114. South Carolina Regulators, for example, complained that "the bands of society and government hang loose and ungirt about us" and called for the creation of a regular police force to subdue "cunning, rapine, fraud, and violence" (quoted in Eric Hinderaker and Peter Mancall, *At the Edge of Empire: The Backcountry in British North America* [Baltimore: Johns Hopkins University Press, 2003], 137–38).

115. Joseph Shippen to Edward Shippen, 19 January 1764, HSP Shippen Papers, 6:81; Thomas Penn to James Hamilton, 13 June 1764, HSP Penn Letter Books, 8:93.

CHAPTER 3. POPULATION

1. "The Speech of Miss Polly Baker," 15 April 1747, in *Papers* 3:123–25.

2. Max Hall, *Benjamin Franklin and Polly Baker: The History of a Literary Deception* (Chapel Hill: UNCP, 1960); "Editorial Introduction," in *Papers* 3:120–23.

3. David Hume, "Of Civil Liberty," in *Essays: Moral, Political, and Literary*, ed. E. F. Miller (Indianapolis: Liberty, 1985), 88; Istvan Hont, "The Political Economy of the 'Unnatural and Retrograde' Order: Adam Smith and Natural Liberty," in *Französische Revolution und Politische Ökonomie* (Trier: Friedrich-Ebert-Stiftung, 1989), 132. The emergence of sovereign states is skillfully analyzed by Hendrik Spruyt in *The Sovereign State and Its Competitors* (Princeton: PUP, 1994).

4. Charles Davenant, *Discourses on the Public Revenues, and on Trade*, 1698, in *The Political and Commercial Works of . . . Charles D'Avenant,,* ed. Charles Whitworth (London: R. Horsfield, 1771), 1:128.

5. Temple, 1:447.

6. "Silence Dogood, No. 10," 13 August 1722, in *Papers* 1:32–33; *PR* 1750; *Observations*, in *Papers* 4:225–34. The first U.S. census was in 1790, the year of Franklin's death. Using census data, Conway Zirkle calculates that the doubling period between 1790 and 1860 was twenty-three years and four months. Franklin fares better with a hundred-year interval. Comparison of a figure based on Franklin's twenty-five year doubling and the actual population of 1890 shows a difference of just 0.13 percent. Zirkle also calculates that in 1850 the white population of the United States exceeded the population of England and Wales ("Benjamin Franklin, Thomas Malthus, and the United States Census," *Isis* 48 [1757]: 58–62).

7. I have learned a great deal on this topic from the writings of John Dunn; see, for example, his introduction to *The Economic Limits to Modern Politics* (Cambridge: CUP, 1990). On the ethics of false necessities, see Judith Shklar, *The Face of Injustice* (New Haven: YUP, 1990).

8. *Observations*, 4:234.

9. As demographic study: James H. Cassedy, *Demography in Early America: Beginnings of the Statistical Mind, 1600–1800* (Cambridge: HUP, 1969);

Michael R. Haines and Richard H. Steckel, *A Population History of North America* (Cambridge: CUP, 2000); Joseph J. Spengler, "Malthusianism in Late Eighteenth Century America," *American Economic Review* 25 (December 1935): 691–707; Zirkle, "Benjamin Franklin, Thomas Malthus." As expression of nativism: Roger Daniels, *Coming to America: A History of Immigration and Ethnicity in American Life* (New York: HarperCollins, 1990); Matthew Frye Jacobson, *Whiteness of a Different Color: European Immigrants and the Alchemy of Race* (Cambridge: HUP, 1998); Ronald Takaki, *Iron Cages: Race and Culture in Nineteenth-Century America* (New York: Knopf, 1979).

10. *OED*, s.vv. "electrician," "plus," "positive," "minus," "negative," electrify," "non-conducting," "battery"; I. Bernard Cohen, *Benjamin Franklin's Science* (Cambridge: CUP, 1990), 4; Carl Van Doren, *Benjamin Franklin* (New York: Viking, 1938), 173–74. The details of the kite experiment—when and how it was performed, by whom, and what it demonstrated—are hotly contested. For recent assessments, see Joyce Chaplin, *The First Scientific American: Benjamin Franklin and the Pursuit of Genius* (New York: Basic, 2006), 127–29; James Delbourgo, *A Most Amazing Scene of Wonders: Electricity and Enlightenment in Early America* (Cambridge: HUP, 2006); Philip Dray, *Stealing God's Thunder: Benjamin Franklin's Lightning Rod and the Invention of America* (New York: Random House, 2005), 83–87.

11. Isaac Watts, *Logick: Or, The Right Use of Reason in the Enquiry after Truth*, 2nd ed. (London: John Clark and Richard Hett, 1726), 180; *A Proposal for Promoting Useful Knowledge*, in *Papers* 2:381–82; *OED*, s.v. "academician." For early members of the APS, see Whitfield Bell Jr., *Patriot-Improvers: Biographical Sketches of Members of the American Philosophical Society*, vol. 1, *1743–1768* (Philadelphia: American Philosophical Society, 1997).

12. *Autobiography*, 35; BF to Sloane, 2 June 1725, in *Papers* 1:54; Peter Collinson to Joseph Breintall, 20 February 1736, APS B F85, 69:48; Collinson to John Bartram, 20 or 22 September 1751 and 10 December 1762, and Bartram to Collinson, 22 November 1764, in *The Correspondence of John Bartram, 1734–1777*, ed. Edmund Berkeley and Dorothy Smith Berkeley (Gainesville: University Press of Florida, 1992), 332, 581; Cadwallader Colden to BF, October 1743, in *Papers* 2:305. On this circle, see Nicholas Wrightson, "Franklin's Networks: Aspects of British Atlantic Print Culture, Science, and Communication, c. 1730–1760" (D.Phil. thesis, Oxford University, 2007).

13. Chaplin, *First Scientific American*, 84; Jan Ingenhousz to BF, 28 January 1783, APS B F85, 27:54; BF to Ingenhousz, 28 August 1785, Yale 43:u409;

A Proposal, in *Papers* 2:382. See also Ellen Cohn, "Benjamin Franklin, Georges-Louis Le Rouge and the Franklin/Folger Chart of the Gulf Stream," *Imago Mundi* 52 (2000): 124–42.

14. John Adams, *Diary and Autobiography,* ed. Lyman H. Butterfield (Cambridge: HUP, 1961), entry for 9 September 1776. Samuel Cooper was minister of the Brattle Street Church; see BF to Samuel Cooper, 7 July 1773, in *Papers* 20:268–71.

15. Willem Jakob 's-Gravesande, *Mathematical Elements of Natural Philosophy Confirmed by Experiments,* 2nd ed., trans. J. T. Desaguliers (London: J. Senex and W. Taylor, 1721), xv; William Derham, *Physico-Theology: Or, A Demonstration of the Being and Attributes of God, From His Works of Creation,* 3rd ed. (London: W. Innys, 1714), 36.

16. Douglas Anderson, *The Radical Enlightenments of Benjamin Franklin* (Baltimore: Johns Hopkins University Press, 1997), 128; Ray, *Wisdom of God,* 153–56. The lengthy title is from the second edition of Ray's treatise (London: Samuel Smith, 1692); the first edition, with a more compact title, was issued in 1691.

17. *Proposals Relating to the Education of Youth in Pennsylvania,* 1749, in *Papers* 3:416–17; "Articles of Belief and Acts of Religion," 20 November 1728, in *Papers* 1:105; *Autobiography,* 66–68; Anderson, *Radical Enlightenments,* 129.

18. *Papers* 4:17; Van Doren, *Benjamin Franklin,* 706; BF to Sir Joseph Banks, 21 November 1783, LC Franklin Papers, box 21.

19. *Autobiography,* 13; Wilbur Samuel Howell, *Logic and Rhetoric in England, 1500–1700* (Princeton: PUP, 1956), 351; Antoine Arnauld and Pierre Nicole, *Logic; or, The Art of Thinking,* 1662, trans. Jill Vance Buroker (Cambridge: CUP, 1996), 263; Ian Hacking, *The Emergence of Probability* (Cambridge: CUP, 1975), 73.

20. Arnauld and Nicole, *Logic,* 274–75; *PR* 1736. For a good example of this logic, see Franklin's introduction to a pamphlet on smallpox inoculation, 16 February 1759, in *Papers* 8:286. Franklin's debt to Port Royal probabilism: Jessica Riskin, "Poor Richard's Leyden Jar: Electricity and Economy in Franklinist France," *Historical Studies in the Physical and Biological Sciences* 28 (1998): 309–10.

21. I. Bernard Cohen, *Science and the Founding Fathers* (New York: W. W. Norton, 1995), 142. On Franklin's conceptual language: I. Bernard Cohen, *Franklin and Newton* (Philadelphia: American Philosophical Society, 1956), 299; Chaplin, *First Scientific American,* 77; Dray, *Stealing God's Thunder,* 139; Riskin, "Poor Richard's Leyden Jar," 329.

22. BF to Peter Collinson, 9 May 1753, in *Papers* 4:480. See also "Peter Kalm: Conversations with Franklin," in *Papers* 4:60. As Clarence Glacken has argued, "Once the design argument is eliminated as a fundamental explanation of the distribution of various kinds of life, what often remains is some form of environmental theory" (*Traces on the Rhodian Shore* [Berkeley and Los Angeles: University of California Press, 1967], 520).

23. Ezra Stiles, "Journals and Memoirs, 1760–1762," Beinecke MS Vault Stiles—Itineraries, I:302, 298.

24. In the sixteenth and early seventeenth centuries, by contrast, populousness was associated with unemployment, idleness, and beggary. This worry returned at the end of the eighteenth century.

25. Sir William Petty, *A Treatise of Taxes & Contributions,* 1662, in *The Economic Writings of Sir William Petty,* ed. Charles Henry Hull (Cambridge: CUP, 1899), 1:34; Johann Peter Süssmilch, *Die göttliche Ordnung,* (Berlin, 1775–76), 1:1 ("Ein Staat, welcher nur de Hälfte der Einwohner hat, die er vermöge seines Umfangs und seiner Nahrungsmittel haben könnte, wird auch nur half so glücklich, mächtic und reich seyn, als er seyn konnte und solte").

26. Steve Pincus, "From Holy Cause to Economic Interest: The Study of Population and the Invention of the State," in *A Nation Transformed: England After the Restoration,* ed. Alan Houston and Steve Pincus (Cambridge: CUP, 2001), 272–98; Anthony Pagden, *Lords of All the World: Ideologies of Empire in Spain, Britain and France, c. 1500–c. 1800* (New Haven: YUP, 1995). Richard Drayton's extraordinary study of natural science and imperial expansion is weakened by his focus on agricultural improvement to the exclusion of trade and commerce (*Nature's Government* [New Haven: YUP, 2000]).

27. Classic statements of this argument can be found in the writings of Otto Hintze and Max Weber; for a sophisticated reformulation, see Brian Downing, *The Military Revolution and Political Change* (Princeton: PUP, 1992).

28. Istvan Hont, "Free Trade and the Economic Limits to National Politics: Neo-Machiavellian Political Economy Reconsidered," in Dunn, *Economic Limits,* 43–44.

29. Charles Davenant, *An Essay upon the Probable Methods of making a People Gainers in the Balance of Trade,* 1699, in *Works,* 2:192.

30. Sir William Petty, *Political Arithmetick, or, A Discourse,* 1690, in *Economic Writings,* 1:307–9; Gregory King, *Natural and Political Observations and conclusions upon the State and Condition of England,* 1696?, in *Two Tracts by*

Gregory King, ed. George E. Barnett (Baltimore: Johns Hopkins University Press, 1936), 11–56. "The bodies of men are without doubt the most valuable treasure of a country. . . . But a country may be populous and yet poor. . . . He who does not some way serve the commonwealth, either by being employed, or by employing others, is not only a useless, but hurtful member of it" (Davenant, *Balance of Trade,* 2:202–3).

31. "When *England* shall be thicker peopled . . . the very same People shall then spend more, than when they lived more sordidly and inurbanely, and further asunder, and more out of sight, observation, and emulation of each other; every Man desiring to put on better Apparel when he appears in Company, than when he has no occasion to be seen" (Petty, *Political Arithmetick,* 1:290). In Bernard Mandeville's *Fable of the Bees,* the triumph of virtue over vice—of honesty and simplicity over vanity and pride—leads directly to depopulation.

32. Thus John Locke: "In all manufactures the greatest part of the value lies in the labor. Where therefore labor is cheapest there 'tis plain commodities may be afforded [at] the cheapest rates and here I demand whether plenty of hands do not everywhere make work cheaper. And what so ever at market can be afforded cheapest shall of course be first sold and beat out others of the same sort" ("For a General Naturalisation," 1693, in *Political Essays,* ed. Mark Goldie (Cambridge: CUP, 1997), 323. See also Daniel Statt, *Foreigners and Englishmen: The Controversy over Immigration and Population, 1660–1760* (Newark: University of Delaware Press, 1995), 44–47; Hont, "Free Trade," 44. The preference for low wages was widespread but not universal; for contrasting evidence, see Richard C. Wiles, "The Theory of Wages in Later English Mercantilism," *Economic History Review,* n.s., 21 (1968): 113–26. On the labor-leisure trade-off, see John Hatcher, "Labor, Leisure and Economic Thought Before the Nineteenth Century," *Past and Present* 160 (August 1998): 64–115.

33. Davenant, *Public Revenues,* 1:128; John Graunt, *Natural and Political Observations made upon the Bills of Mortality* (London, 1662), 78. For Süssmilch's Manichaean contrast between "natural, uncorrupted, rapidly growing but sparsely populated" regions and "manmade, corrupt, stagnating or declining, and evil societies," see James C. Riley, *Population Thought in the Age of the Demographic Revolution* (Durham: Carolina Academic Press, 1985), 27–28.

34. Sir William Petty, *Another Essay in Political Arithmetic, Concerning the City of London,* 1683, in *Economic Writings,* 462. According to R. R. Kuczynski, there was a "consensus of opinion among British demographers in the

century preceding the Industrial Revolution that fertility, i.e. the actual production of children, lagged considerably behind fecundity, i.e. the child-bearing capacity" ("British Demographers' Opinions on Fertility, 1660 to 1760," in *Political Arithmetic: A Symposium of Population Studies*, ed. Lancelot Hogben [London: George Allen and Unwin, 1938], 283).

35. Graunt, *Natural and Political Observations*, 52–53; E. A. Wrigley, "Urban Growth and Agricultural Change: England and the Continent in the Early Modern Period," in *The Eighteenth-Century Town*, ed. Peter Borsay (London: Longman, 1990), 42; C. G. A. Clay, *Economic Expansion and Social Change: England, 1500–1700* (Cambridge: CUP, 1984), 1:20; R. A. Houston, *The Population History of Britain and Ireland, 1500–1750* (London: Macmillan, 1992), 28–32; Statt, *Foreigners and Englishmen*, 74–76. Similar calculations were being made in the colonies in the eighteenth century; see, for example, Ezra Stiles's analysis of Indians (Beinecke MS Vault Stiles—Miscellaneous, MP 200:240–41).

36. Thus Graunt: "As to the causes of Barrenness in *London*, I say, that . . . the intemperance in feeding and especially the Adulteries and Fornications, supposed more frequent in *London* then elsewhere, do certainly hinder breeding. For a Woman, admitting 10 Men, is so far from having ten times as many Children, that she hath none at all. Add to this, that the minds of men in *London* are more thoughtful and full of business then in the Country, where their work is *corporal* Labor, and Exercises. All which promote Breeding, whereas *Anxieties* of the mind hinder it" (*Natural and Political Observations*, 56). See also Thomas Short, *New Observations on the City, Town and Country Bills of Mortality* (London, 1750), 1.

37. Edmund Halley, *Degrees of Mortality of Mankind*, 1693, ed. Lowel J. Reed (Baltimore: Johns Hopkins University Press, 1934), 20. "The law for marriages is that which will cause the most increase of people" (Sir William Petty, "Concerning Marriages," in *The Petty Papers*, ed. Marquis of Lansdowne [London: Constable, 1927], 2:49); population is dependent upon "the number and fruitfulness of marriages, and on the encouragement given to marry" (Robert Wallace, *A Dissertation on the Numbers of Mankind*, 1753, 2nd ed. [Edinburgh, 1809], 19).

38. Graunt, *Natural and Political Observations*, 61; Halley, *Degrees of Mortality*, 20; Davenant, *Balance of Trade*, 190–92; Short, *New Observations*, 159; Petty, "Of Marriages" and "Californian Marriages with the Reasons Thereof," in *Petty Papers*, 2:50–52; Rachel Weil, "The Family in the Exclusion Crisis," in Houston and Pincus, *A Nation Transformed*, 100–124.

39. Charles-Louis de Secondat, baron de Montesquieu, *The Persian Letters*, 1721, trans. C. J. Betts (Harmondsworth: Penguin, 1973), letters 112, 122; Montesquieu, *The Spirit of the Laws*, trans. Anne Cohler, Basia Miller, and Harold Stone (Cambridge: CUP, 1989), book 23.

40. Wallace, *Numbers of Mankind*, 14n, 81. The most famous version of this argument was Rousseau's; see especially the comments on population and political health in *On the Social Contract*, II:9.

41. Hume, "Populousness," in *Essays*, 421, 420.

42. Allan I. Macinnes, "Highland Society in the Era of 'Improvement,'" in *Modern Scottish History*, ed. Anthony Cook et al. (East Lothian: Tuckwell, 1998), 2:186; Wallace, *Numbers of Mankind*, 157–61. "Through want of Improvement, Trade, and Converse with Mankind, are not the Vulgar of the Inhabitants, rude, uncivilized, cruel, barbarous, given to Robbery, Sedition, Rebellion, and Murder, mere two-legged Savages?" (Short, *New Observations*, 130). As Macinnes demonstrates, however, commercialization of the Highlands predated the '45 by many decades. The purported backwardness of the clans served to legitimate "the commercial promotion of agriculture, fisheries and manufactures" as part of the "civilizing" process (Allan I. Macinnes, *Clanship, Commerce and the House of Stuart, 1603–1788* [East Lothian: Tuckwell, 1996]).

43. Bernard Bailyn, *The Peopling of British North America: An Introduction* (New York: Knopf, 1986); Bailyn, *Voyagers to the West: Emigration from Britain to America on the Eve of the Revolution* (New York: Knopf, 1986); Marilyn C. Baseler, *Asylum for Mankind: America, 1607–1800* (Ithaca: Cornell University Press, 1998); Marianne Wokeck, *Trade in Strangers: The Beginnings of Mass Migration to North America* (University Park: Pennsylvania State University Press, 1999); Eric Hinderaker and Peter Mancall, *At the Edge of Empire: The Backcountry in British North America* (Baltimore: Johns Hopkins University Press, 2003).

44. *Journals of the House of Commons*, 21 March 1738, 23:113.

45. "So in Paisley, Scotland, in 1773, when weavers struck for higher wages and blocked employers' efforts to use scab labor, the authorities undertook a resolute, all-out prosecution of the ringleaders for creating 'an unlawful combination'—until they discovered that several thousand of the workers 'threatened to go off in a body to America.' At that point the trial became, in the words of one of the judges, 'very delicate.' The court drew back and imposed lenient sentences, and not on all but only on some of the leaders, freeing the rest; the judges contented themselves with lecturing all

concerned on 'the criminality of their conduct.' Privately, the chief judge breathed a sigh of relief that 'all thoughts of going over to America are for the present laid aside'" (Bailyn, *Peopling* 38); 23 George II, c. 29; PRO CO 30/8/97, 2:73–74.

46. *Observations,* §22, 4:233. In France at roughly the same time, and without apparent knowledge of Franklin's work, Cantillon said that "Men multiply like Mice in a barn if they have unlimited Means of subsistence" (R. Cantillon, *Essai sur la Nature du Commerce Général,* 1755, ed. and trans. H. Higgs [London, 1931], 83). The phrase was repeated by Mirabeau in an early brief for Physiocratic ideas: "Les hommes multiplient comme les rats dans une grange, s'ils ont les moyens de subsister. C'est un axiome que je n'ai pas inventé, & qu'il est temps qu'on prenne pour base de tout calcul en ce genre" (Victor de Riquetii, marquis de Mirabeau, *L'Ami des homes, ou, Traité de la population,* rev. ed. [La Haye: B. Gilbert, 1758–60], 1:19). Neither Cantillon nor Mirabeau, however, expressed the relationship between population and means of subsistence in terms of a fixed relationship amenable to quantitative measure.

47. *Observations,* §§15, 21, 4:232–32. "Who can now find the Vacancy made in Sweden, France or other Warlike Nations, by the Plague of Heroism 40 Years ago; in France, by the Expulsion of the Protestants; in England, by the Settlement of her Colonies; or in Guinea, by 100 Years Exportation of Slaves, that has blackened half America?"

48. Ibid., §§2–7, 4:227–28.

49. Ronald Meek, *Social Science and the Ignoble Savage* (Cambridge: CUP, 1976), 2. Turgot's *On Universal History* was drafted in 1751 but not published until 1808. Helvétius's *De L'Esprit* was published in 1758; Kames's *Essays on the Principles of Morality and Natural Religion* appeared the same year. Smith probably began working with four stages theory in his lectures on jurisprudence during the 1750s (Meek, *Social Science,* 68, 75, 93, 107). For Franklin in 1749, see James Logan to BF, 19 May 1749, in *Papers* 3:379; *Education of Youth,* October 1749, in *Papers* 3:413–14. For early examples of four stages theory in America, see J. A. Leo Lemay, "The Frontiersman from Lout to Hero: Notes on the Significance of the Comparative Method and the Stage Theory in Early American Literature and Culture," *Proceedings of the American Antiquarian Society* 88 (1978): 187–223.

50. *Autobiography,* 15–16; John Perkins to BF, 3 August 1752, and BF to Perkins, 13 August 1752, in *Papers* 4:336, 340; William Douglass, *A Summary, Historical and Political* (Boston: Rogers and Fowle, 1747), 1:153–54.

In July 1766 Franklin visited Göttingen, Germany. In conversation with Gottfried Achenwall, an esteemed statistician, Franklin said, "The most significant work on the British Colonies in North America is the *Summary historical and political* by William Douglass. . . . This physician collected material for many years in America itself, and gives valuable intelligence . . . but his book is not a systematic work. He wanted to make one out of it, but he began to drink too much brandy in his old age, so lost the power to do it" (*Papers* 13:348).

51. Ramsay was "ignorant that all the Indians of North America not under the Dominion of the Spaniards, are in that *Natural State*, being restrained by no Laws, having no Courts or Ministers of Justice, no Suits, no Prisons, no Governors vested with any legal Authority" (*Papers* 16:305–6).

52. BF to Peter Collinson, 9 May 1753, in *Papers* 4:481–82; James Axtell, "The White Indians of Colonial America," *WMQ* 32 (1975): 55–88; Adam Smith, *The Theory of Moral Sentiments*, ed. D. D. Raphael and A. L. Macfie (Oxford: OUP, 1976), 4.1.8–10, pp. 182–84.

53. *Observations*, §8, 4:228. As Franklin put it ten years later, "Manufactures are founded in poverty. It is the multitude of the poor without land in a country, and who must work for others at low wages or starve, that enables undertakers to carry on a manufacture" (*The Interest of Great Britain Considered, With Regard to Her Colonies*, 1760, in *Papers* 9:73).

54. Adam Smith, *An Inquiry in the Nature and Causes of the Wealth of Nations*, 1776, ed. R. H. Campbell and A. S. Skinner (Oxford: OUP, 1976), 3.4.19, p. 1:423; *Observations*, §9, 4:229.

55. *Observations*, §23, 4:233–34.

56. *PR* 1751. Franklin's description follows closely that of George Adams in *Micrographia Illustrata, or, The Knowledge of the Microscope Explained*, 2nd ed. (London: George Adams and Samuel Birt, 1747), 137–65.

57. In March 1741 Abraham Trembley presented his discovery to the Paris Academy of Sciences. The first full discussion in English was his "Observations and Experiments upon the Freshwater Polypus," *Philosophical Transactions* 42 (1742–43): iii–xi.

58. *Histoire de l'Académie Royale des Sciences, année 1741*, quoted in Virginia Dawson, *Nature's Enigma: The Problem of the Polyp in the Letters of Bonnet, Trembley and Réaumur* (Philadelphia: American Philosophical Society, 1987), 7.

59. Aram Vartanian, "Trembley's Polyp, La Mettrie, and Eighteenth-Century French Materialism," *Journal of the History of Ideas* 11 (1950): 259–86.

60. Jean-Jacques Rousseau, "Discourse on the Arts and Sciences," 1750, in *The First and Second Discourses*, ed. Roger Masters and Judith Masters (New York: St. Martin's, 1964); on Voltaire, see Vartanian, "Trembley's Polyp," 284; James Parsons, *Philosophical Observations On the Analogy between the Propagation of Animals and That of Vegetables* (London: C. Davis, 1752), title page. Spanning the debate in England: "Remarks on the Essay on Spirit," *London Magazine. Or, Gentleman's Monthly Intelligencer* 21 (July 1752): 312; "A Criticism on a Passage in Genesis," *London Magazine* 22 (March 1753): 117; John Wesley, *A Survey of the Wisdom of God in the Creation: Or, A Compendium of Natural Philosophy*, 1763, 3rd ed. (London, 1777), 1:187; 2:123–32, 205–6, 329; 4:178–237; 5:25–26; G.W., "Mr. Howlett's Treatise on Population Examined," *Gentleman's Magazine* (August 1782): 369–75; John Howlett, "Mr. Howlett's Defence of his Pamphlet on Population," *Gentleman's Magazine* 51 (October–November 1782): 473–75, 525–26.

61. Contemporaries saw other possibilities. As one beleaguered husband complained in mock despair, "Alas! I find it to my cost, that a wife, like a polypus, has the power of dividing and multiplying herself into as many bodies as she pleases" ("Humorous Matrimonial Complaint," *London Magazine. Or, Gentleman's Monthly Intelligencer* 24 [August 1755]: 379).

62. *Observations*, §22, 4:233. Nine years later Franklin changed metaphors to strengthen this point: "The human body and the political differ in this, that the first is limited by nature to a certain stature, which, when attained, it cannot, ordinarily, exceed; the other by better government and more prudent police, as well as by change of manners and other circumstances, often takes fresh starts of growth, after being long at a stand; and may add tenfold to the dimensions it had for ages been confined to. The mother being of full stature, is in a few years equaled by a growing daughter: but in the case of a mother country and her colonies, it is quite different. The growth of the children tends to increase the growth of the mother, and so the difference and superiority is longer preserved" (*Interest of Great Britain*, 9:78–79).

63. "Rattle-Snakes for Felons," *Gazette*, 11 May 1751; Bailyn, *Peopling*, 121. On transportation, see A. Roger Ekirch, *Bound for America: The Transportation of British Convicts to the Colonies, 1718–1775* (Oxford: Clarendon, 1987); Abbott Emerson Smith, *Colonists in Bondage: White Servitude and Convict Labor in America, 1607–1776* (Chapel Hill: UNCP, 1947).

64. Aaron S. Fogleman, "From Slaves, Convicts, and Servants to Free Passengers: The Transformation of Immigration in the Era of the American

Revolution," *Journal of American History* 85 (1998): 43. The figures given in this paragraph are from Fogleman. See also the chapters by Henry Gemery and Lorena Walsh in Haines and Steckel, *Population History of North America*.

65. *Observations*, §§12–13, 4:229–30.

66. Ibid., §§23–24, 4:233–34. As Franklin complained to James Parker, "Already the English begin to quit particular Neighborhoods surrounded by Dutch, being made uneasy by the Disagreeableness of dissonant Manners; and in Time, Numbers will probably quit the Province for the same Reason" (20 March 1751, in *Papers* 4:120).

67. Van Doren, *Benjamin Franklin*, 218; Edmund S. Morgan, *Benjamin Franklin* (New Haven: YUP, 2002), 77–78; Walter Isaacson, *Benjamin Franklin: An American Life* (New York: Simon and Schuster, 2003), 152.

68. Anderson, *Radical Enlightenments*, 160–62.

69. Paul W. Conner, *Richard's Politicks: Benjamin Franklin and His New American Order* (Oxford: OUP, 1965); Roger Daniels, *Coming to America: A History of Immigration and Ethnicity in American Life* (New York: Harper-Collins, 1990); John Higham, *Send These to Me: Patterns of American Nativism, 1860–1925* (New Brunswick: Rutgers University Press, 1988); Ronald Takaki, *A Different Mirror: A History of Multicultural America* (Boston: Little, Brown, 1993); Jacobson, *Whiteness of a Different Color;* A. Leon Higginbotham, *In the Matter of Color: Race and the American Legal Process; the Colonial Period* (New York: OUP, 1978); David Waldstreicher, *Runaway America: Benjamin Franklin, Slavery, and the American Revolution* (New York: Hill and Wang, 2004).

70. Philip Gleason, "Trouble in the Colonial Melting Pot," *Journal of American Ethnic History* 20 (2000): 11. See also Gleason, "A Scurrilous Colonial Election and Franklin's Reputation," *WMQ* 18 (1961): 68–84.

71. Roxann Wheeler, *The Complexion of Race: Categories of Difference in Eighteenth-Century British Culture* (Philadelphia: University of Pennsylvania Press, 2000), 7. See also Dror Wahrman, *The Making of the Modern Self* (New Haven: YUP, 2004), 101–3. On black and white in North America: Winthrop D. Jordan, *White over Black: American Attitudes toward the Negro, 1550–1812* (Chapel Hill: UNCP, 1968); Edmund S. Morgan, *American Slavery, American Freedom: The Ordeal of Colonial Virginia* (New York: W. W. Norton, 1975).

72. "Census of New Jersey," APS B F85, 58:18; *PR* 1750; APS Burd-Shippen Papers, Printed Forms 1747–1787, volume 3, B B892p. The story of how

the Irish became "white" in the late nineteenth century is well told by Jacobson in *Whiteness of a Different Color.*

73. Daniel Richter, *Facing East from Indian Country: A Native History of Early America* (Cambridge: HUP, 2001), 207. "Not until the middle of the eighteenth century did most Anglo-Americans view Indians as significantly different in color from themselves" (Alden T. Vaughan, "From White Man to Redskin: Changing Anglo-American Perceptions of the American Indian," *American Historical Review* 87 (October 1982): 918. On the ideas of Neolin, Pontiac, and other Indian leaders, see Gregory Evans Dowd, *A Spirited Resistance: The North American Indian Struggle for Unity, 1745–1815* (Baltimore: Johns Hopkins University Press, 1992).

74. George M. Fredrickson, *The Black Image in the White Mind* (Middletown: Wesleyan University Press, 1971); Fredrickson, *Racism: A Short History* (Princeton: PUP, 2002); Bruce Dain, *A Hideous Monster of the Mind: American Race Theory in the Early Republic* (Cambridge: HUP, 2002); Wheeler, *Complexion of Race,* esp. 248–66.

75. BF to Peter Collinson, 9 May 1753, in *Papers* 4:479–80; *A Narrative of the Late Massacres in Lancaster County,* 1764, in *Papers* 11:55.

76. Wahrman, *Making of the Modern Self,* 103; BF to John Lining, 17 June 1758, in *Papers* 8:108–9.

77. Colden to BF, 13 February 1754, in *Papers* 5:197. See also Peter Collinson to BF, 27 September 1752, and John Perkins to BF, 15 October 1752, in *Papers* 4:358; Richard Jackson to BF, 17 June 1755, in *Papers* 6:75–82.

78. BF to William Shirley, 30 December 1754, in *Papers* 5:455–56. "I delivered the night before I left Boston to Dr. Clark his manuscript *Essay upon the Importance of the Northern Colonies* etc. which he is now publishing. I wish I could have found time to correct it; but I had not a moment to do it in. Your treatise, which is to be annexed, hath been already printed off some time" (Shirley to BF, 10 July 1755, BL Add MSS 4478B, fol. 125).

79. "The Proprietary Party . . . carried (would you think it!) above 1000 Dutch from me, by printing part of my Paper sent to you 12 Years since on Peopling new Countries where I speak of the Palatine *Boors herding* together, which they explained that I called them a *Herd* of *Hogs.* This is quite a laughing matter" (Franklin to Richard Jackson, 11 October 1764, in *Papers* 11:397). Several pamphlets from the electoral campaign of 1764 have been reprinted in *Papers* 11:380–88.

80. Marianne Wokeck, "Harnessing the Lure," in *To Make America: European Emigration in the Early Modern Period*, ed. Ida Altman and James Horn (Berkeley: University of California Press, 1991), 216–28. In the late 1720s an average of 600 German immigrants landed at Philadelphia each autumn. In the late 1740s this grew to 1,800, and in 1749—at the end of the War of Austrian Succession—a peak of 9,500 newcomers arrived. The permanent population of Philadelphia in 1749 was roughly 10,000. For each of the next five years, an average of 5,600 per year arrived (224). See also A. G. Roeber, "'The Origin of Whatever Is Not English among Us': The Dutch-Speaking and the German-Speaking Peoples of Colonial British America," in *Strangers within the Realm: Cultural Margins of the First British Empire*, ed. Bernard Bailyn and Philip Morgan (Chapel Hill: UNCP, 1991), 244.

81. Roeber, "'Whatever Is Not English among Us,'" 252. Roeber suggests that Franklin's paper was fated to fail because it was obviously the work of an "outsider" (259).

82. Benjamin Franklin, *Die Lautere Wahrheit* (Philadelphia: Armbruester, 1747); *Ein Gründliches Zeugnüss Gegen das kurtzlich herausgegebene Büchlein Genande: Plain Truth* (Germantown: Christoph Saur, 1748); BF to Peter Collinson, 9 May 1753, in *Papers* 4:485; BF to James Parker, 20 March 1751, in *Papers* 4:117.

83. Loyalty oaths: Don Herzog, *Happy Slaves: A Critique of Consent Theory* (Chicago: UCP, 1989), 186–93. Mennonites: Petition of Mennonites, 15 May 1755, APS Penn Letters and Ancient Documents [974.8 P365], 3:27.

84. BF to Jared Eliot, 19 December 1752, in *Papers* 4:387; Peter Collinson to BF, 12 August 1753, in *Papers* 5:19; "Observations on the Present State of the Germans in Pennsylvania," 1753, BL Add MSS 32,420, fol. 147; Richard Jackson to BF, 17 June 1755, in *Papers* 6:75–86.

85. BF to Peter Collinson, 1753?, in *Papers* 5:158. Franklin was responding to proposals enclosed in Collinson's letter of 12 August 1753, in *Papers* 5:21.

86. The scheme is described in William Smith to Richard Peters and Benjamin Franklin, February 1754, in *Papers* 5:203–18. See also [Samuel Chandler], *Memorial of the Case of the German Emigrants* (London, 1754), 12–20; William Smith, *A Brief History of the Rise and Progress of the Charitable Scheme . . . For the Relief and Instruction of poor Germans, and their Descendants* (Philadelphia: B. Franklin and D. Hall, 1755). German sentiment is visible in extracts from Sauer's newspaper collected for the Proprietors (HSP Penn Papers, 4:84).

87. Roeber, "Whatever Is Not English among Us,'" 263–68, 274–78; Hermann Wellenreuther, "Image and Counterimage, Trade and Expectation: The German Immigrants in English Colonial Society in Pennsylvania, 1700–1765," in *America and the Germans*, vol. 1, *Immigration, Language, Ethnicity*, ed. Frank Trommler and Joseph McVeigh (Philadelphia: University of Pennsylvania Press, 1985), 85–105.

88. Anthony Pagden, *Empires and Peoples: A Short History of European Migration, Exploration, and Conquest, from Greece to the Present* (New York: Modern Library, 2001); Albert O. Hirschman, *The Passions and the Interests: Political Arguments for Capitalism before Its Triumph* (Princeton: PUP, 1977).

89. Richard Price, *Observations on the Expectations of Lives, The Increase of Mankind . . . In a Letter . . . to Benjamin Franklin* (London: Bowyer and Nichols, 1769); Price to BF, 3 April 1769, *Philosophical Transactions* 59 (1769): 89–125; Price, *Observations on Reversionary Payments* (London, 1771); Waldstreicher, *Runaway America*, 286n5.

90. Smith, *Wealth of Nations*, 1.8.23, pp. 1:87–88; Ezra Stiles, *A Discourse on the Christian Union* (Boston: Edes and Gill, 1761), 108–110; Price, *Observations on Reversionary Payments*, 159–60. On Stiles's knowledge of Franklin's population ideas: Beinecke MS Vault Stiles—Miscellaneous, MP 200:26, MP 445.

91. William Cobbett, ed., *The Parliamentary History of England* (London: T. C. Hansard, 1813), 14:1317–63; William Wales, *An Inquiry into the Present State of Population in England and Wales* (London: G. Bigg, 1781), 7–9. Wales identified two sorts of resistance to numbering the people. Some worried that the government might use the information to increase taxes. Others, citing 1 Chronicles 21:1 ("And Satan stood up against Israel, and provoked David to number Israel"), feared that a census would stir the wrath of God (ibid.). For background, see D. V. Glass, *Numbering the People: The Eighteenth-Century Population Controversy and the Development of Census and Vital Statistics in Britain* (London: Gordon and Cremonesi, 1973).

92. William Godwin, *Enquiry concerning political justice, and its influence on morals and happiness*, 2nd ed. (London, 1796), 1:8, 2:494. Godwin noted that "I have no authority to quote for this expression but the conversation of Doctor Price. I am happy to report that Mr. William Morgan, the nephew of Dr. Price, and editor of his works, distinctly recollects to have heard it from his uncle" (2:494n). Unfortunately, nothing in the historical record supports this thirdhand attribution.

93. Thomas Robert Malthus, *An Essay on the Principle of Population* (London: J. Johnson, 1798), iii–iv, 13–14; Frederick Rosen, "The Principle of Population

as Political Theory: Godwin's *Of Population* and the Malthusian Controversy," *Journal of the History of Ideas* 31 (1970): 33–48; Donald Winch, *Malthus* (Oxford: OUP, 1987), 17–18.

94. In a letter to his father of 4 February 1799, Malthus indicated that he would like a copy of *The Interest of Great Britain Considered*. We have no record of his receiving it. Malthus's Jesus College library, however, includes a marked copy of Franklin's *Political, Miscellaneous and Philosophical Pieces* (Thomas Robert Malthus, *The Malthus Library Catalogue* [Oxford: Pergamon, 1983], xviii, xxiii, 62). On Malthus's ambitions in the second edition: A. M. C. Waterman, *Revolution, Economics and Religion: Christian Political Economy, 1793–1833* (Cambridge: CUP, 1991), 56; Patricia James, *Population Malthus: His Life and Times* (London: Routledge and Kegan Paul, 1979), 70, 104. "Necessity": Malthus, *Essay,* 15.

95. Thomas Robert Malthus, *An Essay on the Principle of Population,* 1803, ed. Donald Winch (Cambridge: CUP, 1992), 13–14.

96. William Godwin, *Of Population* (London: Longman, 1820), 124–25. "Perhaps the saddest story about the quarto is that told by Dr. Currie in a long letter . . . dated 19 February 1804" concerning "a mental patient whose reason gave way after his indulgence in speculations on the perfectibility of man. Dr. Currie . . . explained to his patient the principle of population; his reaction was to produce 'a scheme for enlarging the surface of the globe, and a project for an act of parliament for this purpose, in a letter addressed to Mr. Pitt.' To show that even this measure could not solve the problem, Dr. Currie gave the young man Malthus's quarto. This he read twice, aloud the second time, not omitting a single word, and then, after a few distressing days, he quietly lay down and died. Dr. Currie added, 'At the moment that I write this, his copy of Malthus is in my sight; and I cannot look at it but with extreme emotion'" (James, *Population Malthus,* 112).

97. E. A. Wrigley, "Malthus's Model of Pre-industrial Economy," in *Malthus Past and Present,* ed. J. A. Dupâquier, A. Fauv-Chamoux, and E. Grebenik (London: Academic, 1983), 111–24; D. P. O'Brien, *Classical Economists Revisited* (Princeton: PUP, 2004), 66–77.

98. Charles Darwin, *Autobiography,* in *The Works of Charles Darwin,* ed. Paul Barrett and R. B. Freeman (London: William Pickering, 1989), 29:144. We ought not take Darwin's casual "happened to read for amusement" at face value. Malthus and his ideas were regular topics in the *Edinburgh Review* and *Quarterly Review,* journals that Darwin assiduously read. At the time

Darwin picked up Malthus, the Chartists were lambasting Malthusian ideas in speeches regularly reported in the *Times*. Darwin had family ties as well: Darwin's brother, Erasmus, was involved with the well-known Whig political economist Harriet Martineau; and Malthus was on close terms with the Wedgwood family (Silvan Schweber, "Darwin and the Political Economists: Divergence of Character," *Journal of the History of Biology* 13 [1980]: 195–96; Adrian Desmond and James Moore, *Darwin: The Life of a Tormented Evolutionist* [New York: Warner, 1991], 201, 218, 264).

99. David Kohn, "Theories to Work By," *Studies in the History of Biology* 4 (1980): 67–170; Dov Ospovat, *The Development of Darwin's Theory: Natural History, Natural Theology and Natural Selection, 1838–1859* (Cambridge: CUP, 1981), 60; Peter Bowler, *Charles Darwin: The Man and His Influence* (Oxford: Basil Blackwell, 1990), 82.

100. Robert Schofield, *The Lunar Society of Birmingham* (Oxford: Clarendon, 1963); Jenny Uglow, *The Lunar Men: Five Friends Whose Curiosity Changed the World* (New York: Farrar, Straus and Giroux, 2002); Darwin, *Autobiography*, 29:94; James Harrison, "Erasmus Darwin's View of Evolution," *Journal of the History of Ideas* 32 (1971): 247–64; Desmond King-Hele, *Erasmus Darwin: A Life of Unequalled Achievement* (London: Giles de la Mare, 1999).

101. Erasmus Darwin, *The Botanic Garden*, part 1, *The Economy of Vegetation*, 4th ed. (London, 1799), canto 2, line 365, p. 105; canto 1, lines 381–88, pp. 43–44; Charles Darwin to Charles Elliot Norton, 30 April 1881, Houghton bMS Am 1088 1598. See also Darwin to Norton, 1 June 1881, Houghton bMS Am 1088 1599.

102. Peter Vorzimmer, "The Darwin Reading Notebooks (1838–1860)," *Journal of the History of Biology* 10 (1977): 143 [entry for 12 September 1851]. The closest Darwin came to mentioning Franklin in his scientific writings was an exchange on the extinction of the North American shrub *Franklinia alatamaha* (Charles Darwin to Charles Lyell, 14–28 June 1849, in *The Correspondence of Charles Darwin*, ed. Frederick Burkhardt and Sydney Smith [Cambridge: CUP, 1988], 4:239–40).

103. Charles Darwin, *Charles Darwin's Notebooks, 1836–1844*, ed. Paul Barrett, Peter Gautrey, Sandra Herbert, David Kohn, and Sydney Smith (Ithaca: Cornell University Press, 1987), D 135e. According to the editors, this is "Darwin's first formulation of natural selection. . . . It is unambiguously crystallized by his reading of Malthus" (376n3).

104. This appears to be Joyce Chaplin's view (*First Scientific American*, 351–52).

105. M. Lémontey, ed., *Mémoires de l'abbé Morellet* (Paris, 1821), 1:294–97. Franklin once mock chastised the Quaker physician John Fothergill by asking, "Does your Conscience never hint to you the Impiety of being in constant Warfare against the Plans of Providence? Disease was intended as the Punishment of Intemperance, Sloth, and other Vices; and the Example of that Punishment was intended to promote and strengthen the opposite Virtues. But here you step in officiously with your Art, disappoint those wise Intentions of Nature, and make Men safe in their Excesses" (BF to Fothergill, 14 March 1764, in *Papers* 11:101). Further examples of Franklin's ridicule of the argument from design—including his poignant 1734 essay, "The Death of Infants"—can be found in J. A. Leo Lemay, *The Life of Benjamin Franklin* (Philadelphia: University of Pennsylvania Press, 2006), 1:275–76, 365; 2:75–79.

CHAPTER 4. UNION

1. Farrand, 2:582, 606–7, 615–16. Albert Gallatin later charged that the Committee of Style had attempted, in changing the punctuation of the "general welfare" clause, to change a "limitation" on Congress into a "distinct power" (Farrand, 3:379).
2. BF to John Mitchell, 29 April 1749, in *Papers* 3:372–73, reprinted in *Experiments and Observations;* BF to John Pringle, 10 May 1768, in *Papers* 15:115–18. See also BF to Alexander Small, 12 May 1760, in *Papers* 9:112.
3. Canal construction in England reached its height between 1768 and 1776 (Paul Langford, *A Polite and Commercial People: England, 1727–1783* [Oxford: Clarendon, 1989], 391–92). In late 1769 Franklin began following a vigorous debate over the construction of a canal between the Chesapeake and Delaware bays (Thomas Gilpin to BF, 10 October 1769, in *Papers* 16:216–19; BF to Gilpin, 18 March 1770, in *Papers* 17:103–9). Interest was sufficiently strong that Philadelphia merchants subscribed £200 to fund a survey of the proposed route ("An Abstract of sundry Papers and Proposals for improving the Inland Navigation," *Transactions of the American Philosophical Society* 1 [1 January 1769–1 January 1771]: 293–300). The poles of the debate are visible in "Patrius," *Pennsylvania Chronicle* 156 (8 January 1770): 1–2; *To the Merchants and other Inhabitants of Pennsylvania* (Philadelphia, 1771); *To the Public* (Philadelphia, 1772).
4. BF to Samuel Rhoads, 22 August 1772, in *Papers* 19:279; BF to John Pringle, 10 May 1768, in *Papers* 15:118. The famed Bridgewater Canal,

completed in 1761, cut the cost of coal by 75 percent in Manchester (Charles Hadfield, *The Canal Age* [Newton Abbot: David and Charles, 1968]). Franklin toured the Bridgewater Canal in 1771 ("Journal of Jonathan Williams," May 1771, in *Papers* 18:113–17). Franklin was still studying canals in the final years of his life (BF to Rodolphe-Ferdinand Grant, 20 March 1786 and 8 October 1786, LC Franklin Papers, box 23).

5. Adam Smith, *An Inquiry into the Nature and Causes of the Wealth of Nations,* 1776, ed. R. H. Campbell and A. S. Skinner (Oxford: OUP, 1976), 1.11.b.5, p. 1:163; Alexander Hamilton, "Report on Manufactures," 5 December 1791, in *The Papers of Alexander Hamilton,* ed. Harold C. Syrett (New York: Columbia University Press, 1966), 10:310–11. See also George Washington to Jacob Read, 3 November 1784, in *The Writings of George Washington,* ed. John C. Fitzpatrick (Washington, DC: Government Printing Office, 1938), 27:489. Washington was an investor in and first president of the Potomac Company, founded in 1785.

6. Alexander Hamilton, James Madison, and John Jay, *The Federalist,* ed. Terence Ball (Cambridge: CUP, 2003), #10, p. 45. The republican "problem of scale" is explored in Samuel H. Beer, *To Make a Nation: The Rediscovery of American Federalism* (Cambridge: HUP, 1993).

7. Hamilton, Madison, and Jay, *Federalist,* #14, pp. 60, 62; James Madison, "Seventh Annual Message," 5 December 1815, in *The Writings of James Madison,* ed. Gaillard Hunt (New York: G. P. Putnam's Sons, 1900–1910), 8:342–43; Thomas Jefferson, "Sixth Annual Message," 2 December 1806, in *The Works of Thomas Jefferson,* ed. Paul Leicester Ford (New York: G. P. Putnam's Sons, 1905), 8:482–96.

8. Thus Richard John concludes that postal policy in the early Republic created "an imagined community in which the government encouraged its far-flung citizenry to participate directly in the political process through an ongoing discussion of the leading events of the day" (*Spreading the News: The American Postal System from Franklin to Morse* [Cambridge: HUP, 1995], 112).

9. As Albert Gallatin later put it, "The national legislature alone, embracing every local interest, and superior to every local consideration, is competent to the selection of such national objects" (*The Report of the Secretary of Treasury on the Subject of Public Roads and Canals* [Washington, DC: R. C. Weightman, 1808], 73–75).

10. Farrand, 2:615–16.

11. Most famously in Madison's veto of John Calhoun's "Bonus Bill of 1817," a bill that sought to "bind the republic together with a perfect system of

roads and canals" (*Annals of Congress*, 14th Cong., 2nd sess. [4 February 1817], 854). Finding no express or implied constitutional warrant and fearing the loss of all "landmarks" limiting the powers of Congress, Madison vetoed legislation he had actively encouraged ("Veto Message," 3 March 1817, in *Writings*, 8:386–88). See also Madison to Spencer Roane, 6 May 1821, in *Writings*, 9:55–63; Thomas Jefferson, "Draft Declaration and Protest of the Commonwealth of Virginia, on the Principles of the Constitution of the United States of America, and on the Violations of Them," December 1825, in *The Writings of Thomas Jefferson*, ed. Andrew Lipscomb and Albert Ellery Bergh (Washington, DC: Thomas Jefferson Memorial Association, 1905), 17:442–48.

12. Stephen Minicucci, "Internal Improvements and the Union, 1790–1860," *Studies in American Political Development* 18 (2004): 161. Minicucci focuses on institutions. Constitutional issues are highlighted in Mark Killenbeck, "Pursuing the Great Experiment: Reserved Powers in a Post-ratification, Compound Republic," *Supreme Court Review* 1999 (1999): 81–140. Political and cultural themes dominate John Lauritz Larson, " 'Bind the Republic Together': The National Union and the Struggle for a System of Internal Improvements," *Journal of American History* 74 (1987): 363–87; and Paul Chen, "The Constitutional Politics of Roads and Canals: Interbranch Dialogue over Internal Improvements, 1800–1828," *Whittier Law Review* 28 (2006): 625–62.

13. John Dunn, *The Cunning of Reason: Making Sense of Politics* (London: HarperCollins, 2000); Don Herzog, *Cunning* (Princeton: PUP, 2006).

14. David Hume, *A Treatise of Human Nature*, ed. David Fate Norton and Mary Beth Norton (Oxford: OUP, 2000), 3.2.7.

15. BF to Francis Maseres, 26 June 1785, in Temple, 2:80–81; BF to Sir Joseph Banks, 27 July 1783, LC Franklin Papers, box 21. Franklin expressed similar sentiments in letters to David Hartley (16 October 1783, Yale 40:u477) and Jane Mecom (20 September 1787, LC Franklin Papers, box 24).

16. BF to James Parker, 20 March 1751, in *Papers* 4:117–21.

17. [Archibald Kennedy], *The Importance of Gaining and Preserving the Friendship of the Indians to the British Interest, Considered* (New York: James Parker, 1751), 5–7.

18. Ibid., 7–9, 13, 17. Kennedy was adamant that these changes would come at little or no expense to Great Britain: "It is high Time we should look to our own Security, and most unnatural to expect, that we should hang forever upon the Breasts of our Mother-Country" (7).

19. Ibid., 6–7, 19, 26. "From Assemblies, by Experience," he lamented, "we have little to hope for" (*Observations on the Importance of the Northern Colonies under Proper Regulations* [New York: James Parker, 1750], 7). See also *An Essay on the Government of the Colonies* [New York: James Parker, 1752], 39: "If this Affair, of so much Importance to the *British* Interest, be left much longer to the Caprice of Assemblies, we may easily guess what will be the Consequence."

20. BF to James Parker, 20 March 1751, in *Papers* 4:118. Gordon S. Wood mocks Franklin's suggestion: the Albany Plan was "totally out of touch with the political realities of the day, which was often the case when one relied on a few reasonable men for solutions to complicated political problems" (*The Americanization of Benjamin Franklin* [New York: Penguin, 2004], 76). This overlooks the context of Franklin's proposal. The alternative to a New York lobbying campaign was parliamentary imposition.

21. BF to James Parker, 20 March 1751, in *Papers* 4:118–19. Kennedy wrote six pamphlets between 1750 and 1755. All call attention to the importance of trade to Indian relations; most express disdain for colonial assemblies; many invoke the ideas of placing blacksmiths among the Indians, holding annual fairs, building new forts, or using Highlanders to settle and pacify the frontier. Only in *Importance*, however, does Kennedy discuss the structure of intercolonial institutions.

22. *Autobiography*, 225, 220–21.

23. BF to Collinson, 28 May 1754, in *Papers* 5:332. In a superb study of the Albany Congress, Timothy Shannon argued that Franklin fits Benedict Anderson's model of "Creole pioneers." It is true that Franklin was a Creole (born in America, but of European descent), that he chafed at what he considered to be misguided metropolitan decisions, and he was a pivotal figure in colonial print culture. But the "imagined community" he claimed membership in was not national (American) but imperial (British) (Timothy Shannon, *Indians and Colonists at the Crossroads of Empire* [Ithaca: Cornell University Press, 2000], 100n44; Benedict Anderson, *Imagined Communities*, rev. ed. [New York: Verso, 1991], esp. 6–8, 50, 56–58.).

24. Richard Koebner, *Empire* (Cambridge: CUP, 1961), 4–11; Samuel Johnson, *A Dictionary of the English Language* (London: W. Strahan, 1755), s.v. "empire"; Anthony Pagden, *Lords of All the World: Ideologies of Empire in Spain, Britain and France, c. 1500–c. 1800* (New Haven: YUP, 1995), 18–19. In these passages Pagden is describing the Roman Empire, for, he argues,

Rome provided "the language and political models" for "modern European overseas empires" (11).

25. David Armitage, "The British Conception of Empire in the Eighteenth Century," in *Imperium/Empire/Reich: Ein Konzept Politischer Herrschaft Im Deutsch-Britischen Vergleich,* ed. Franz Bosbach and Hermann Hiery (Munich: K. G. Saur, 1999), 94. See also Armitage, "Making the Empire British: Scotland in the Atlantic World, 1542–1707," *Past and Present* 155 (1997): 63; Armitage, *The Ideological Origins of the British Empire* (Cambridge: CUP, 2000), 8.

26. Linda Colley, *Britons: Forging the Nation, 1707–1837* (New Haven: YUP, 1992), 17–18, 33. After the conquest of Nova Scotia, Lord Halifax wondered why the children of the Acadians—who were French-speaking Catholics—had not been taken from their parents and brought up "in the Protestant religion, by which means they at least, however stubborn their parents might prove, would have become good and useful subjects" (Halifax to W. Lyttelton, 13 August 1756, quoted in P. J. Marshall, "A Nation Defined by Empire," in *Uniting the Kingdom? The Making of British History,* ed. Alexander Grant and Keith Stringer (London: Routledge, 1995), 213. Peter Lake crisply captures the logic of anti-Catholic sentiment in "Anti-Popery: The Structure of a Prejudice," in *Conflict in Early Stuart England: Studies in Religion and Politics, 1603–1642,* ed. Richard Cust and Ann Hughes (London: Longman, 1989), 72–106.

27. Charles Davenant, *An Essay upon the Probable Methods of making a People Gainers in the Balance of Trade,* 1699, in *The Political and Commercial Works of . . . Charles D'Avenant,* ed. Charles Whitworth (London: R. Horsfield, 1771), 2:192; Richard Price, "Who Cared about the Colonies? The Impact of the Thirteen Colonies on British Society and Politics, circa 1714–1775," in *Strangers within the Realm: Cultural Margins of the First British Empire,* ed. Bernard Bailyn and Philip Morgan (Chapel Hill: UNCP, 1991), 417–19.

28. Price, "Who Cared about the Colonies?" 410. Contemporary interest: Henry McCulloh to the Duke of Bedford, 28 July 1748, PRO CO 5/5/294–95; Thomas Robinson to Lord Holdernesse, 29 August 1755, BL Egerton MS. 3432, fols. 297–98.

29. "Rule, Britannia, rule the waves: / Britons never will be slaves" (James Thomson, *Alfred: A Masque* [London: A. Millar, 1740], 43); Daniel Baugh, "Great Britain's 'Blue-Water' Policy, 1689–1815," *International History Review* 10 (1988): 33–58; Baugh, "Maritime Strength and Atlantic

Commerce," in *An Imperial State at War*, ed. Lawrence Stone (London: Routledge, 1994), 185–223.

30. Eliga Gould, *The Persistence of Empire: British Political Culture in the Age of the American Revolution* (Chapel Hill: UNCP, 2000), ch. 1.

31. Kathleen Wilson, "Empire of Virtue: The Imperial Project and Hanoverian Culture, c. 1720–1785," in Lawrence, *Imperial State at War*, 132. On popular support for empire: Gould, *Persistence of Empire;* Wilson, "Empire of Virtue"; Wilson, "Empire, Trade and Popular Politics in Mid-Hanoverian Britain: The Case of Admiral Vernon," *Past and Present* 121 (1988): 74–109; Wilson, *The Sense of the People: Politics, Culture and Imperialism in England, 1715–1785* (Cambridge: CUP, 1995).

32. "No Nation in the World is more commodiously situated for Trade or War, than the *British* Empire, taking all together as ONE BODY, *viz.* Great Britain, Ireland, and the *Plantations* and *Fishery* in *America*, besides its Possessions in the *East-Indies* and *Africa*" (John Ashley, *The Second Part of Memoirs and Considerations Concerning the Trade and Revenues of the British Colonies in America* [London: H. Kent, 1743], 94).

33. Henry McCulloh to the Earl of Halifax, 10 December 1751, BL Add MSS 11514, fol. 11; [Earl of Halifax?], "Some Considerations relating to the present Condition of the plantations; with Proposals for a better Regulation of them," PRO CO 5/5/313; James Abercromby, *An Examination of the Acts of Parliament Relative to the Trade and the Government of our American Colonies*, 1752, in *Magna Charta for America*, ed. Jack Greene, Charles Mullett, and Edward Papenfuse (Philadelphia: American Philosophical Society, 1986), 45; Malachy Postlethwayt, *Britain's Commercial Interest Explained and Improved* (London: D. Browne, 1757), 153.

34. Jack P. Greene, "A Posture of Hostility: A Reconsideration of Some Aspects of the Origins of the American Revolution," *Proceedings of the American Antiquarian Society* 87 (1977): 33; Peter Collinson to BF, 11 July 1750, in *Papers* 4:5; Thomas Penn to Governor Hamilton, 12 February 1750, in *Papers* 4:5n2.

35. [Halifax?], "Some Considerations," PRO CO 5/5/313–14; P. J. Marshall, "The Eighteenth-Century Empire," in *British Politics and Society from Walpole to Pitt, 1742–1789*, ed. Jeremy Black (Basingstoke: Macmillan, 1990), 177–80.

36. "Proceedings of the French in America, delivered to Sir Tho. Robinson by the Earl of Halifax," April 1754, PRO CO 5/5/96–100; McCulloh to Halifax, 10 December 1751, BL Add MSS 11514, fols. 35–36; [Archibald

Kennedy], *Serious Advice to the Inhabitants of the Northern-Colonies, on the Present Situation of Affairs* (New York: 1755), 13.

37. Linda Colley has argued that British national identity was forged in opposition to France. But as Peter Miller astutely argues, Colley's emphasis on Francophobia misses "the ambivalence of this relationship" (Peter Miller, *Defining the Common Good: Empire, Religion, and Philosophy in Eighteenth-Century Britain* [Cambridge: CUP, 1994], 167n72).

38. David Hume, "Of Civil Liberty," in *Essays: Moral, Political, and Literary,* ed. E. F. Miller (Indianapolis: Liberty, 1985), 92–98; Malachy Postlethwayt, *Great-Britain's True System* (London: A. Millar, 1757), 272. This opinion was held by some living in North America as well: William Clarke, *Observations on the Late and Present Conduct of the French* (Boston: S. Kneeland, 1755), 33–34.

39. Abercromby, *An Examination,* 45, 72, 162; [Halifax?], "Some Considerations," PRO CO 5/5/313–17; McCulloh to the Earl of Halifax, 10 December 1751, BL Add MSS 11514, fols. 6, 26. Ironically, McCulloh observed, the French Council of Commerce was modeled on the original constitution of Britain's Board of Trade. But while the British deviated from that foundation, the French steadfastly adhered to it ([Henry McCulloh], *The Wisdom and Policy of the French in the Construction of their Great Offices* [London: R. Baldwin, 1755], 53).

40. Lords of Trade to Sir Danvers Osborne, 18 September 1753, in *NYCD* 6:800–801. The Six Nations of the Iroquois were the Mohawk, the Oneida, the Onondaga, the Cayuga, the Seneca, and the Tuscarora. Osborne committed suicide on 20 October and was replaced by Delancey.

41. Fred Anderson, *Crucible of War: The Seven Years' War and the Fate of Empire in British North America, 1754–1766* (New York: Knopf, 2000), 7. According to one witness to Washington's surrender at Fort Necessity, "what is most severe upon us" was the discovery that the Indians who had contributed to their defeat "were all *our own Indians,* Shawnesses [*sic*], Delawares and Mingoes" (quoted in Anderson, *Crucible of War,* 65).

42. Lester C. Olson, *Benjamin Franklin's Vision of American Community* (Columbia: University of South Carolina Press, 2004), 27–76; Olson, *Emblems of American Community in the Revolutionary Era* (Washington, DC: Smithsonian Institution, 1991), 21–74; Karen Severud Cook, "Benjamin Franklin and the Snake That Would Not Die," *British Library Journal* 22 (1996): 88–111.

43. J. A. Leo Lemay, "The American Aesthetic of Franklin's Visual Cre-
ations," *PMHB* 111 (1987): 479; Genesis 2:17, 3:13–14; *OED*, s.v. "snake."

44. Reading Milton: BF to Peter Collinson, 9 May 1753, in *Papers* 4:486. Milton
and James Thomson were "the two best English Poets that ever were"
(*Gazette*, 4 March 1735). Satan's mouthpiece: John Milton, *Paradise Lost*,
9:613. Franklin's debt was not all cautionary; he included part of Milton's
"Hymn to the Creator" in his private liturgy of 1728, "Articles of Belief
and Acts of Religion" (*Papers* 1:106–7). Douglas Anderson provides a spirited account of Franklin's debt to Milton in *The Radical Enlightenments of
Benjamin Franklin* (Baltimore: Johns Hopkins University Press, 1997), esp.
65–67, 164–67. Lurking in the shadows is a potentially quite radical implication. As Blair Worden has demonstrated, Milton's Satan—embodied as a
snake—was a republican ("Milton's Republicanism and the Tyranny of
Heaven," in *Machiavelli and Republicanism*, ed. Gisela Bock, Quentin Skinner and Maurizio Viroli [Cambridge: CUP, 1990], 225–46).

45. "An American Guésser," *Pennsylvania Journal*, 27 December 1775. For the
attribution of this letter, see J. A. Leo Lemay, *The Canon of Benjamin
Franklin, 1722–1776* (Newark: University of Delaware Press, 1986),
124–26. This was the first public appearance of the image found on the so-
called Gadsden flag.

46. Although "sporadic" reference to separation can be found "almost from
the first settlement in America," before 1763 "only a few individuals on either side of the Atlantic were openly predicting American independence in
the foreseeable future" (J. M. Bumsted, " 'Things in the Womb of Time':
Ideas of American Independence, 1633 to 1763," *WMQ* 31 [1974]: 536).

47. *Gazette*, 9 May 1751. To be sure, the rhetorical force of "Felons" also relied
on the association of snakes with base, corrupt, and vicious behavior. This
remained a liability up to the Revolution. As an anonymous bit of doggerel
put it in 1774: "Ye Sons of Sedition, how comes it to pass, / That America's typed by a SNAKE—in the grass? / Don't you think 'tis a scandalous,
saucy reflection, / That merits the soundest, severest Correction, / NEW
ENGLAND's the HEAD too;————NEW ENGLAND's abused; / For the *Head
of the Serpent* we know *should be* BRUISED." (*New-York Gazeteer*, 25 August
1774; *The Boston News-Letter*, 8 September 1774). For contemporary responses, see Olson, *Emblems*, 34–37.

48. Andrew Burnaby, *Travels Through the Middle Settlements in North-
America*, 2nd ed. (London: 1775), 159; Shannon, *Indians and Colonists*, 86;

Gazette, 9 May 1754. See also BF to Collinson, 28 May 1754, in *Papers* 5:332. This was a common complaint; as Governor Dinwiddie of Virginia reported to Sir Thomas Robinson, "The French too justly observe the want of Connection in the Colonies and from thence conclude (as they declare without Reserve) that although we are vastly superior to them in Numbers, yet they can take and secure the Country before we can agree to hinder them" (18 June 1754, PRO CO 5/14/198).

49. Theodore Atkinson's "Memo Book," printed in Beverly McAnear, "Personal Accounts of the Albany Congress of 1754," *Mississippi Valley Historical Review* 39 (1953): 729–39; *NYCD* 6:859. Representatives were sent by New Hampshire, Massachusetts Bay, Rhode Island, Connecticut, New York, Pennsylvania, and Maryland. Virginia and New Jersey were invited but chose not to attend.

50. *NYCD* 6:859–60; Atkinson, "Memo Book," 734; *Autobiography*, 108–9. "Though I projected the Plan and drew it, I was obliged to alter some Things contrary to my Judgment, or should never have been able to carry it through" (BF to Peter Collinson, 29 December 1754, in *Papers* 5:454). No other plan—with the possible exception of Richard Peters's "Rough Draft of a Plan for a General Union" (*PA*, 1st ser., 2:197–99)—has been found.

51. The two strongest challenges are the "Hutchinson Thesis" and the "Iroquois Influence Thesis." The former holds that Thomas Hutchinson is the plan's primary author; the latter holds that the basic ideas of the Albany Plan were drawn from Iroquois models of government. For sources and arguments concerning the Hutchinson thesis, see *Papers* 5:374–87; for the Iroquois influence thesis, see Shannon, *Indians and Colonists*, 6–7, 103–4.

52. *Papers* 5:399. On the problems of trust: Diego Gambetta, "Can We Trust Trust?" in *Trust: Making and Breaking Cooperative Relations*, ed. Gambetta (Oxford: Basil Blackwell, 1988), 216; Bernard Williams, "Formal Structures and Social Reality," in Gambetta, *Trust*, 7–8.

53. Thomas Hobbes, *Leviathan*, 1651, ed. Richard Tuck (Cambridge: CUP, 1996), 96. The alternative, Hobbes contended, was a war "of every man, against every man." Hobbes's depiction of the state of nature was intended to shift the relative cost of trust and distrust. Franklin attempted something similar in his "Join, or Die" cartoon. By raising the cost of independence (death), Franklin hoped to make cooperation (joining) more acceptable.

54. Clarke, *Observations*, 33–34. Cf. William Shirley to Secretary Robinson, 24 December 1754, in *NYCD* 6:930–33.

55. *Papers* 5:399. As Franklin lamented six years later, "Their jealousy of each other is so great that however necessary an union of the colonies has long been, for their common defense and security against their enemies, and how sensible soever each colony has been of that necessity, yet they have never been able to effect such an union among themselves, nor even to agree in requesting the mother country to establish it for them" (*Papers* 9:90).

56. *Papers* 5:401–2. On the constraining power of ongoing relationships, see Russell Hardin, "Trusting Persons, Trusting Institutions," in *The Strategy of Choice*, ed. Richard Zeckhauser (Cambridge: MIT Press, 1991), 185–209, and "The Street-Level Epistemology of Trust," *Politics and Society* 21 (1993): 505–29.

57. *Papers* 5:401; Shannon, *Indians and Colonists*, 183. The only surviving example of a plan of partial union is Richard Peters's "Rough Draft."

58. *Papers* 5:401.

59. Madison, *Federalist*, #10.

60. Beer, *To Make a Nation*, 153. Others have described Franklin's commitment to growth in less charitable terms. Gerald Stourzh argues that Franklin was "America's first great expansionist"; Paul Conner paints Franklin with the brush of National Socialism, suggesting that his "true motive" was the pursuit of *"Lebensraum"* (Stourzh, *Benjamin Franklin and American Foreign Policy*, 2nd ed. [Chicago: UCP, 1969], 250; Conner, *Poor Richard's Politicks: Benjamin Franklin and His New American Order* [Oxford: OUP, 1965], 164).

61. James Hutson, "Benjamin Franklin and the West," *Western Historical Quarterly* 4 (1973): 425; BF, "A Plan for Settling Two Western Colonies," 1754, in *Papers* 5:457. Compare Madison: "It is now no longer a point of speculation and hope that the Western territory is a mine of vast wealth to the United States. . . . We may calculate . . . that a rich and fertile country, of an area equal to the inhabited extent of the United States, will soon become a national stock" (*Federalist*, #39, pp. 180–81).

62. "Reasons and Motives," in *Papers* 5:409, 404.

63. Beer, *To Make a Nation*, 156–57. This may explain why no mention was made of a judicial power. All laws were subject to metropolitan approval, with Parliament retaining the power to judge disputes.

64. "Two Western Colonies," 5:439; "Reasons and Motives," 5:411.

65. Thirty-three years later this idea was embodied in the Northwest Ordinance, key to the expansion of the new republic. The link between political

integration and economic development is perceptively analyzed by Peter S. Onuf in "Settlers, Settlements, and New States," in *The American Revolution: Its Character and Limits*, ed. Jack P. Greene (New York: New York University Press, 1987), 171–96.

66. *Ignored:* New Hampshire, New York, North Carolina, South Carolina, and Virginia. *Rejected:* Maryland, New Jersey, Pennsylvania, and Rhode Island. *Revised:* Connecticut and Massachusetts.

67. Shirley to Robinson, 24 December 1754, in *NYCD* 6:930–33; BF to Shirley, 4 December 1754, in *Papers* 5:444.

68. Thomas Jefferson to James Madison, 6 September 1789, in *Works*, 5:115–24.

69. BF to James Parker, 20 March 1751, in *Papers* 4:118. Debates at Albany: Atkinson, "Memo Book," 737; Richard Peters, "Rough Notes on a Debate at Albany," 1 July 1754, in *Papers* 5:364–66. Historians: Edmund S. Morgan, *Benjamin Franklin* (New Haven: YUP, 2001), 85–86; Wood, *Americanization*, 75–76.

70. BF to Peter Collinson, 20 December 1754, in *Papers* 5:454; Archibald Kennedy, *Observations on the Importance of the Northern Colonies Under Proper Regulation* (New York, 1750); 7; Cadwallader Colden, "The Present State of the Indian Affairs," 8 August 1751, in *NYCD* 6:745–46.

71. "Reasons and Motives," 5:400; Beer, *To Make a Nation*, 156.

72. Don Herzog, *Happy Slaves: A Critique of Consent Theory* (Chicago: UCP, 1989), 182, 203.

73. Adam Przeworski, Susan Stokes, and Bernard Manin, introduction to and "Elections and Representation," in *Democracy, Accountability and Representation* (Cambridge: CUP, 1999), 1–54.

74. BF to William Shirley, 3 December 1754 and 4 December 1754, in *Papers* 5:443.

75. Thomas Whately, *The Regulations Lately Made* (London, 1765), 109; Edmund Burke, "Speech to the Electors of Bristol, 3 November 1774," in *The Works of the Right Honourable Edmund Burke* (London: J. Dodsley, 1792), 2:15.

76. BF to William Shirley, 3 December 1754, in *Papers* 5:443; BF to Shirley, 4 December 1754, in *Papers* 5:444. Interest and information were linked: Parliament was dependent on governors and councils for its information; the interests of the latter skewed their reports and gave rise to misinformation (*Papers* 5:444).

77. BF to William Shirley, 22 December 1754, in *Papers* 5:450–51.

78. Ibid., 5:449–50; "Marginalia," 1766, in *Papers* 16:280–81; BF to Shirley, 30 December 1754, in *Papers* 5:456; Shirley to BF, 10 July 1755, BL Add MSS 4478B, fol. 125.

79. "Reasons and Motives," 5:405–6, 413; "Short Hints," in *Papers* 5:338; Committee "Short Hints," 28 June 1754, in *Papers* 5:362.

80. Secretary Robinson to the Board of Trade, 14 June 1754, in *NYCD* 6:844; "The Draught of a Plan or Project for a General Council," 9 August 1754, PRO CO 5/6/112–19; Newcastle Memorandum, 9 September 1754, BL Add MSS 32,995, fol. 309, quoted in Alison Olson, "The British Government and Colonial Union, 1754," *WMQ* 17 (1960): 31.

81. Hardwicke to Newcastle, 7 September 1754, BL Add MSS 32,736, fols. 436–38; Newcastle to Murray, 28 September 1754, BL Add MSS 32,736, fol. 591; Robinson to Newcastle, 12 October 1754, BL Add MSS 32,737, fols. 135–36; Board of Trade to the King, 29 October 1754, PRO CO 5/6/138–45.

82. "Remark," 9 February 1789, in *Papers* 5:417. Franklin claimed that "the Crown disapproved it, as having placed too much Weight in the democratic part of the Constitution." This was William Shirley's view, and it resonated with fears expressed by the plan's drafting committee (Shirley to Secretary Robinson, 24 December 1754, in *NYCD* 6:930–33; Committee "Short Hints," 5:361). But as an explanation for what actually happened in London, it is woefully inadequate. See also Olson, "Colonial Union."

83. Anderson, *Crucible of War*, 11; BF to Charles Thomson, 11 July 1765, in *Papers* 12:207; "Virginia Resolves," 29 May 1765, reprinted in *Prologue to Revolution*, ed. Edmund S. Morgan (New York: W. W. Norton, 1959), 48.

84. BF to Charles Thomson, 11 July 1765, in *Papers* 12:207; "Virginia Resolves,"48; BF to John Hughes, 9 August 1765, in *Papers* 12:234; Deborah Franklin to BF, 22 September 1765, in *Papers* 270; Joseph Galloway to William Franklin, 14 November 1765, APS B F85, I:170; James Hutson, "An Investigation of the Inarticulate: Philadelphia's White Oaks," *WMQ* 28 (1971): 3–25.

85. BF to Jane Mecom, 1 March 1766, in *Papers* 13:189; "Magna Britannia," January 1766?, in *Papers* 13:70–71. Franklin may also have had copies handed to MPs as they entered Parliament (APS B F85, 76:43).

86. *Papers* 13:71–72 (note that Franklin did not compose this explanation); *A Pocket Companion and History of Free-Masons* (London: J. Scott, 1754), 60; Alexander Pope, "A Prologue to a Play for Mr. Dennis' Benefit," 1733, in

The Works of Alexander Pope (London: J. and P. Knapton, 1751), 6:55. Jean François Marmontel's *Bélisaire,* printed one year after "Magna Britannia," was an international best seller. Belisarius was painted by David, Vincent, and West; at midcentury, a Van Dyck reportedly fetched £1,000 (Horace Walpole, *Anecdotes of Painting in England,* 2nd ed. [1765], 2:101).

87. *OED,* s.v. "gratitude." The two senses of "gratitude," as feeling and as moral obligation, are perfectly captured in Samuel Johnson's *Dictionary* "1. Duty to benefactors" and "2. Desire to return benefits" (*Dictionary of the English Language,* 2nd ed. [London: W. Strahan, 1755–56]).

88. Jonathan Swift, "A Tritical Essay upon the Faculties of the Mind," in *Miscellanies. The First Volume* (London: Benjamin Motte, 1731), 190; David Hume, *A Treatise of Human Nature,* ed. David Fate Norton and Mary Beth Norton (Oxford: OUP, 2000), 3.1.1.

89. I have learned a great deal about the historical sociology of emotions from William Ian Miller, *Humiliation and Other Essays on Honor, Social Discomfort and Violence* (Ithaca: Cornell University Press, 1993); Miller, *The Anatomy of Disgust* (Cambridge: HUP, 1997); Don Herzog, *Poisoning the Minds of the Lower Orders* (Princeton: PUP, 1998).

90. "William Pym," *London General Evening Post,* 20 August 1765, reprinted in Morgan, *Prologue to Revolution,* 97–99; William Pitt, *Political Debates* (Paris [i.e., London]: Chez J.W., 1766), 2; Josiah Tucker, *A Letter from a Merchant in London to his Nephew in North America* (London: J. Walter, 1766); Martin Howard Jr. to BF, 14 May 1765, in *Papers* 12:129. Howard is referring to *A Letter from a Gentleman at Halifax, To His Friend in Rhode Island,* which lamented the existence of "so much ingratitude in the colonies to the mother country" ([Newport: S. Hall, 1765], 20).

91. "A Virginian," 5 September 1765, in *Papers* 12:253; "Examination by the Commons," 13 February 1766, in *Papers* 13:149. See also: BF to ――― 6 January 1766, in *Papers* 13:24; "Benevolus," *London Chronicle,* 11 April 1767, in *Papers* 14:110.

92. BF to Lord Kames, 25 February 1767, in *Papers* 14:68–69. See also "On the Tenure of the Manor of East Greenwich," 11 January 1766, in *Papers* 13:22.

93. "Homespun," *Gazetteer and New Daily Advertiser,* 2 January 1766, in *Papers* 13:7; "Pacificus," *Public Advertiser,* 26 January 1766, in *Papers* 13:57. On castration: "A Freeholder of Old Sarum," *Public Advertiser,* 21 May 1774, in *Papers* 21:220–22. Conditions of union: "Magna Britannia," in *Papers* 13:71.

94. John Adams to Abigail Adams, 23 July 1775, in *Adams Family Correspondence*, ed. L. H. Butterfield (Cambridge: HUP, 1963), 1:253.

95. Olson, *Franklin's Vision*, 116–21; Eric P. Newman, *The Early Paper Money of America* (Racine, WI: Western, 1967), 34–37.

96. BF to Edward Bridgen, 2 October 1779, in *Papers* 30:429–30; "Account of the Devices on the Continental Bills of Credit," *Gazette*, 20 September 1775. On the attribution of this essay, see Lemay, *Canon*, 122–24. Previous use of wind and waves: *The Interest of Great Britain Considered, With Regard to Her Colonies*, 1760, and "Causes of the American Discontents before 1768," 1768, in *Papers* 9:91, 15:3. See also Eric P. Newman, "Continental Currency and the Fugio Cent: Sources of Emblems and Mottoes," *Numismatist* 79 (1966): 1587–98.

97. Fractional bills: Lemay, "American Aesthetic," 489; Newman, "Continental Currency," 1595. Chain device: Olson, *Franklin's Vision*, 133–40; David McBride, "Linked Rings: Early American Unity Illustrated," *Numismatist* 92 (1979): 2373–93.

98. Editorial note, in *Papers* 22:120–22; "Articles," in *Papers* 22:122–25.

99. "Notes of Debates," 30 July and 1 August 1776, in *JCC* 6:1079, 1081; Donald S. Lutz, "The Articles of Confederation as the Background to the Federal Republic," *Publius* 20 (1990): 62; Jack P. Greene, "The Background of the Articles of Confederation," *Publius* 12 (1982): 42. In the language of the day, it was to be a "federal" and not an "incorporating" union (Witherspoon, in *JCC* 6:1103).

100. *Papers* 22:123 (silently incorporating Franklin's interlineal additions); *JCC* 6:1102–3. Franklin maintained this position at the Constitutional Convention as well: "Decisions should be by the majority of members, not by the majority of States" (Farrand, 1.197).

101. BF, "Speech in A Committee of the Convention," 11 June 1787, in *Autobiography*, 358; Wilson, 1 August 1776, in *JCC* 6:1105.

102. Adams, 1 August 1776, in *JCC* 6:1104; "Queries and Remarks Respecting Alterations in the Constitution of Pennsylvania," November 1789, in *Autobiography*, 367–68.

103. John Adams, *A Defence of the Constitutions of Government of the United States of America* (Philadelphia: Hall and Sellers, 1787), 105–10; "Discourses on Davila," 1790, in *The Works of John Adams*, ed. Charles Francis Adams (Boston: Little, Brown, 1851), 6:249–50.

104. "Queries and Remarks," 368; *Gazette*, 31 March 1779; James Harrington, *The Commonwealth of Oceana*, in *The Political Works of James Harrington*,

ed. J. G. A. Pocock (Cambridge: CUP, 1977), 161–66. The Library Company acquired a copy of Harrington's works between 1737 and 1741 (*A Catalogue of Books belonging to the Library Company of Philadelphia* [Philadelphia: B. Franklin, 1741]); Franklin had a copy in his library in Paris in 1782 (*Papers* 36:339).

105. David Hume, "Of the Jealousy of Trade," 1758, in *Essays: Moral, Political, and Literary,* ed. E. F. Miller (Indianapolis: Liberty, 1985), 328. See also note 73 to ch. 1.

106. Laurence Dickey, "Doux-Commerce and Humanitarian Values," *Grotiana* 22–23 (2001–2): 283; Pagden, *Lords of All the World,* 179–81. Reciprocity need not be founded on altruism. As Smith briskly argued, "it is not from the benevolence of the butcher, the brewer, or the baker, that we expect our dinner, but from their regard to their own self-interest" (*Wealth of Nations,* 1.2.2, p. 1:27).

107. BF to Abbé Morellet, 22 April 1787, LC Franklin Papers, box 24; Alexander Small to BF, 3 July 1787, APS B F85, 35:89; BF to Small, 28 September 1787, LC Franklin Papers, box 24; BF to Louis-Guillaume Le Veillard, 17 February 1788, LC Franklin Papers, box 24.

108. "Condorcet's *The Influence of the American Revolution on Europe,*" trans. Durand Echeverria, *WMQ* 25 (1968): 91; Turgot, "Mémoire" of 6 April 1776, quoted in J. Paul Selsam and Joseph G. Rayback, "French Comment on the Pennsylvania Constitution of 1776," *PMHB* 76 (1952): 320; Turgot to Richard Price, 22 March 1778, printed in Price, *Observations on the Importance of the American Revolution* (London: T. Cadell, 1785), 113–14. Mirabeau warned, "What is well adapted to England, is ill calculated for America. Let there be no balance of powers—no complicated constitutions . . . think not of counteracting the interests of one body of men by those of another" (quoted in Selsam and Rayback, "French Comment," 322).

109. Adams to Samuel Perley, 19 June 1809, quoted in Joyce Appleby, "America as a Model for the Radical French Reformers of 1789," *WMQ* 28 (1971): 276. Franklin holds a French translation of the Pennsylvania constitution in the portrait on the dust jacket of this book.

110. *Information to Those Who Would Remove to America,* February 1784, in *Autobiography,* 341.

111. *Gazette,* 31 March 1779; "Queries and Remarks," 366.

112. John Adams, *Thoughts on Government* (Philadelphia: John Dunlap, 1776), 11–13. As Franklin retorted, "If the Wisdom brought by the Members to the Assembly is divided into two Branches may it not be too weak in each

to support a good Measure, or obstruct a bad one?" ("Queries and Remarks," 366).

113. Theophilus Parsons, *Essex Result*, 1778, reprinted in *Popular Sources of Authority: Documents on the Massachusetts Constitution of 1780*, ed. Oscar Handlin and Mary Handlin (Cambridge: HUP, 1966), 324–65; Gordon S. Wood, *The Creation of the American Republic, 1776–1787* (New York: W. W. Norton, 1969), 217–18; Farrand, 2:249, 1:48.

114. "Je vois avez peine l'esprit aristocratique chercher a s'introduire chez vou malgré tant de sages précautions" (Condorcet to BF, 8 June 1788, APS B F85, 36:68).

115. Bicameralism: BF to Le Veillard, 24 October 1788, Houghton bMS Am 1408 (147); BF to du Pont, 9 June 1788, in Temple, 2:231–33; La Rochefoucauld to BF, 6 February 1788 and 12 July 1788, APS B F85, 36:16, 36:70. Politics and chess: BF to du Pont de Nemours, 9 June 1788, in Temple, 2:232.

116. *Autobiography*, 83; BF to William Strahan, 22 September 1751 and 20 June 1752, in *Papers* 4:196, 322; BF to Deborah Franklin, 29 April 1757, in *Papers* 7:205.

117. Katherine French to BF, 19 May 1767, in *Papers* 14:163; John Foxcroft to BF, 14 January 1771, in *Papers* 18:7; Sir John Pringle to BF, December 1773, in *Papers* 20:528; Georgiana Shipley to BF, 22 December 1774, in *Papers* 21:397; Caroline Howe to BF, 3 January 1775, in *Papers* 21:436; BF to Anne-Louise Boivin d'Hardancourt Brillon de Jouy, 29 November 1777 and 27 July 1778, in *Papers* 25:204, 27:174–72; Jean-Baptiste Le Roy, October 1778, in *Papers* 27:672; BF to comtesse de Forbach, June 1779, in *Papers* 29:748.

118. BF, "The Morals of Chess," before 28 June 1779, in *Papers* 29:753–57.

119. BF to Horatio Gates, 2 June 1779, in *Papers* 29:604; editorial note, in *Papers* 29:753; Claude-Anne Lopez, *My Life with Benjamin Franklin* (New Haven: YUP, 2000), 112.

120. Thomas Jefferson to Samuel Smith, 22 August 1798, and Thomas Jefferson to Thomas Jefferson Randolph, 24 November 1808, in Lipscomb and Berg, *Writings*, 7:275–76, 9:232–33; John Adams to James Warren, 13 April 1783, in *Warren-Adams Letters* (Boston: Massachusetts Historical Society, 1925), 2:209; John Adams, *Diary and Autobiography*, ed. Lyman H. Butterfield (Cambridge: HUP, 1961), 4:118.

121. BF to Samuel Mather, 12 May 1784, LC Franklin Papers, box 22; also told in BF to Mather, 7 July 1773, in *Papers* 20:286. The sign over Cotton's door

was memorialized in Nathaniel Hawthorne's *Famous Old People* (1840): "Of the door of his library were painted these words, BE SHORT,—as a warning to visitors that they must not do the world so much harm as needlessly to interrupt this great man's wonderful labors" (*The Works of Nathaniel Hawthorne,* ed. William Charvat [Columbus: Ohio State University Press, 1963], 6:93).

122. "Commonplace book," HSP Ferdinand J. Dreer Collection, fol. 50. The Latin quotation is from Horace, *Ars poetica* 43.

123. "Journal," in *Papers* 1:85–86; *Gazette,* 12 July 1733, 15 October 1730.

124. Wood, *Creation,* 415; Alan Houston, *Algernon Sidney and the Republican Heritage in England and America* (Princeton: PUP, 1991), 34–35, 223–67; John Adams to Abigail Adams, 12 April 1778, in *Adams Family Correspondence,* 3:9.

125. Vergennes to Luzerne, 7 August 1780, quoted in Stacy Schiff, *A Great Improvisation* (New York: Henry Holt, 2005), 249n. "A stiff-necked refusal to compromise would ruin democratic civility in a political society in which people have many serious differences of belief and interest" (Judith Shklar, *Ordinary Vices* [Cambridge: HUP, 1984], 78).

126. *Autobiography,* 361, 14, 77.

127. Farrand, 1:436–59; William Steele to Jonathan Steele, September 1825, in Farrand, 3:469; "Motion for Prayers," 28 June 1787, in *Autobiography,* 360–61.

128. *Autobiography,* 360–61; Madison to Thomas Grimke, 6 January 1834, in Farrand, 3:531. Prayer as act of desperation: Judith Shklar, *Redeeming American Political Thought* (Chicago: UCP, 1998), 164.

129. Farrand, 1:488.

CHAPTER 5. SLAVERY

1. *JCC,* 10 June 1776, 5:428–29; Thomas Jefferson to BF, 21 June 1776, in *Papers* 22:485. Jefferson's "rough draft," with Franklin's emendations, may be viewed on the Library of Congress American Memory Web site (The Thomas Jefferson Papers, series 1, General Correspondence, 1651–1827, images 545–48): http://memory.loc.gov/master/mss/mtj/mtj1/001/0500/0545.jpg (accessed 14 February 2008).

2. Samuel Johnson, *Taxation no Tyranny; An Answer to the Resolutions and Address of the American Congress* (London: T. Cadell, 1775), 89. George was sold to Franklin as part of a debt settlement. Earliest references to him are

Deborah Franklin to BF, 10 February 1765, in *Papers* 12:43; BF to Deborah Franklin, 6 April 1766, in *Papers* 13:233. George remained a member of the Franklin household until his death in 1781 (Sarah Franklin Bache to BF, 23 June 1781, in *Papers* 35:193–94).

3. The basic narrative was established by Claude-Anne Lopez and Eugenia W. Herbert in *The Private Franklin* (New York: W. W. Norton 1975), 296–307. Gary B. Nash and Jean R. Soderlund skillfully set Franklin in his Pennsylvania context in *Freedom by Degrees: Emancipation in Pennsylvania and Its Aftermath* (Oxford: OUP, 1991), esp. ix–xiv. David Waldstreicher's *Runaway America: Benjamin Franklin, Slavery, and the American Revolution* (New York: Hill and Wang, 2004) is a provocative revisionist account.

4. Franklin's first direct reference to household slaves is in a letter to his mother of 12 April 1750 (*Papers* 3:474). On 16 December 1735 he bought a pair of shoes for a "Negro boy" (APS B F85, 66:46a); on 14 August 1745 Franklin ordered a "Raccoon hat" for his "Negro" (APS B F85, 66:71a).

5. Nash and Soderlund, *Freedom by Degrees*, 4–7; "Census Data for Year 1790," Historical Census Browser, Geospatial and Statistical Data Center, University of Virginia Library, http://fisher.lib.virginia.edu/collections/stats/histcensus/php/start.php?year=V1790#1 (accessed 28 May 2007).

6. *Annals of Congress*, 1st Cong., 2nd sess. (1791), 1223–32, 1239–46, 1465–66; *The Constitution of the Pennsylvania Society, for Promoting the Abolition of Slavery, and the Relief of Free Negroes, Unlawfully Held in Bondage* (Philadelphia, Joseph James, 1787); "The Pennsylvania Abolition Society to the United States Congress," 3 February 1790, HSP PAS; "On the Slave Trade," 25 March 1790, in *Autobiography*, 369–71. This entire episode is memorialized as "The Silence" by Joseph Ellis in *Founding Brothers* (New York: Knopf, 2001), 81–119.

7. Bernard Bailyn, *The Ideological Origins of the American Revolution* (Cambridge: HUP, 1967), 234.

8. Ibid. On the definition of slavery: John Locke, *Two Treatises of Government*, ed. Peter Laslett (Cambridge: CUP, 1960), 2.24, 2.172.

9. "Three able Negro Men and three Negro Women to be Sold by Messieurs *Henry Dewick* and *William Astin*, and to be seen at the House of Mr. *Josiah Franklin* at the Blue-Ball in Union Street near the Star Tavern, Buston" (*Boston News-Letter*, 15 June 1713).

10. Two early examples: in the *Gazette* of 9 April 1730 Franklin advertised "A Likely Negro Woman to be Sold. Enquire at the Widow Read's in Market-Street, Philadelphia." On 11 May 1732 he advertised "A likely young

Negro Fellow, about 19 or 20 Years of Age, to be disposed of: He is very fit for Labor, being used to Plantation Work, and has had the Small-Pox. Enquire of the Printer hereof" (*Papers* 1:186, 272).

11. Advertisements: In the *Gazette* of 21 October 1731 he advertised "A Likely Servant Lad's Time for near Seven Years, to be disposed of; He is fit for Town or Country Business. Enquire of the Printer hereof" (*Papers* 1:220). Labor pool: Edmund S. Morgan, *American Slavery, American Freedom: The Ordeal of Colonial Virginia* (New York: W. W. Norton, 1975); Nash and Soderlund, *Freedom by Degrees*, 8.

12. *Autobiography*, 16.

13. Ibid.; "Will, July 17, 1788, [and] Codicil," APS B F85, 212. The trusts lasted longer than the practice of apprenticeship; two centuries after Franklin's death, they were still being used to fund individuals and organizations in Boston and Philadelphia. For details, see Walter Isaacson, *Benjamin Franklin: An American Life* (New York: Simon and Schuster, 2003), 473–75.

14. *Papers* 4:229–30.

15. Jonathan Swift, *Major Works*, ed. Angus Ross and David Woolley (Oxford: OUP, 2003), 493–94.

16. BF to Joseph Priestley, 3 October 1775, in *Papers* 22:218; "Observations," in *Papers* 4:230.

17. Adam Smith, *An Inquiry into the Nature and Causes of the Wealth of Nations*, 1776, ed. R. H. Campbell and A. S. Skinner (Oxford: OUP, 1976), 3.2.9, pp. 1:387–88; Anne-Robert Turgot, "On Universal History," in *Turgot on Progress, Sociology and Economics*, ed. Ronald L. Meek (Cambridge: CUP, 1973), 81–83, 73–74. See also "The Formation and Distribution of Wealth," 129–31. The intellectual engagement between Turgot and Franklin dates to the 1760s. During Franklin's residence in France, they met often to share a meal and discuss economic policies and political ideas (A. R. J. Turgot, *Œuvres de Turgot*, ed. Gustave Schelle [Paris: Librarie Félix Alcan, 1913], 3:13, 5:510–19, 528, 532, 542–43, 578, 584, 587, 602, 629). See also *Papers* 23:550; 24:228; 25:302, 737; 26:259, 531; 27:475, 495; 30:549.

18. *Papers* 4:231. Smith added an intriguing twist: nothing mortifies the pride of man more than having to justify his decisions to others, especially those he considers inferior. In a system of free labor, this was an unavoidable necessity; slavery eliminated this indignity (Smith, *Wealth of Nations*, 3.2.10, p. 1:388).

19. BF to Sarah Franklin Bache, 26 January 1784, in *Autobiography*, 336–40.

20. Ibid., 337; Granville Sharp to BF, 17 June 1785, Yale 43:u215; BF to Sharp, 5 July 1785, Yale 43:u281 (corrected against copy of original, also at Yale). As a youngest son, of course, Franklin had a personal stake in dislodging the custom and law of primogeniture.

21. *The Interest of Great Britain Considered* (London: T. Becket, 1760), 56. The editors of the *Papers* erroneously identify the 1769 edition of *Experiments and Observations* as the first instance of this change in wording (*Papers* 4:229n9). The earlier date is critical because it suggests that Franklin began revising his views in the 1750s, long before most historians allow.

22. Even this did not satisfy everyone. Franklin's French editor and translator, Jacques Barbeu-Dubourg, balked at the word *thief:* it denoted a violation of the law, and between a slave and his master there could be no justice ("J'aurois dit simplement que tout esclave est pillard; car le mot *vol* suppose une atteinte portée aux loix d'une just propriéte: or il n'y a aucuns rapport d'équité entre le tyran et l'esclave" [Barbeu-Dubourg to BF, 19 December 1772, in *Papers* 19:434–35]).

23. "Last Will and Testament," 28 April 1757, in *Papers* 7:203; BF to Deborah Franklin, 21 March 1756, in *Papers* 6:425; BF to Deborah, 27 June 1760, in *Papers* 9:174–75. See also BF to Deborah, 19 February 1758, in *Papers* 7:380.

24. John Waring to BF, 24 January 1757, in *Papers* 7:100–101; BF to Waring, 3 January 1758, in *Papers* 7:356; BF to Waring, 17 February 1757, in *Papers* 7:377. See also William Sturgeon to BF, 22 August 1757, in *Papers* 7:252; E. L. Pennington, "The Work of the Bray Associates of Pennsylvania," *PMHB* 58 (1934): 7–9; Deborah to BF, 9 August 1759, in *Papers* 8:425.

25. BF to John Waring, 17 December 1763, in *Papers* 10:395–96; *OED*, s.v. "docility." In 1773 the marquis de Condorcet asked after the conditions of free blacks. Franklin responded that they are "generally improvident and poor. I think they are not deficient in natural Understanding, but they have not the Advantage of Education" (BF to Condorcet, 20 March 1774, in *Papers* 21:151; see also Condorcet to BF, 2 December 1773, in *Papers* 20:489–91).

26. Quoted in Lopez and Herbert, *Private Franklin*, 302.

27. "Silence Dogood, No. 11," 20 August 1722, in *Papers* 1:37; Thomas Tryon, *The Ways to Health, Long Life and Happiness*, 2nd ed. (London: H. C., 1691), 249–50; Tryon, *The Planter's Speech to his Neighbours & Country-Men of Pennsylvania, East & West Jersey* (London: Andrew Sowle, 1684), part 2; Tryon, *Tryon's Letters, Upon Several Occasions* (London: Geo.

Conyers, 1700), 82. I have learned much from Norman Fiering, "Irresistible Compassion: An Aspect of Eighteenth-Century Sympathy and Humanitarianism," *Journal of the History of Ideas* 37 (1976): 195–218; and Nigel Smith, "Enthusiasm and Enlightenment: Of Food, Filth and Slavery," in *The Country and the City Revisited,* ed. Gerald Maclean, Donna Landry, and Joseph P. Ward (Cambridge: CUP, 1999), 106–18.

28. *Autobiography,* 13, 28; Douglas Anderson, *The Radical Enlightenments of Benjamin Franklin* (Baltimore: Johns Hopkins University Press, 1997), 9.

29. [Thomas Tryon], *Friendly Advice to the Gentlemen-Planters of the East and West Indies* (London: Andrew Sowle, 1684).

30. Miller, 6–8, 64–65; BF to John Wright, 4 November 1789, in Temple, 2:119–21; "Excerpts from the Papers of Dr. Benjamin Rush," *PMHB* 29 (1905): 25.

31. Roberts Vaux, *Memoirs of the Lives of Benjamin Lay and Ralph Sandiford* (Philadelphia: Solomon W. Conrad, 1815); *Papers* 1:189n3; *American National Biography,* s.v. "Benjamin Lay."

32. *Gazette,* 25 March 1742; Smith, *The Theory of Moral Sentiments,* ed. D. D. Raphael and A. L. Macfie (Oxford: OUP, 1976), 1.1.1, p. 9; BF to John Wright, 4 November 1789, in Temple, 2:120.

33. "A Conversation on Slavery," 30 January 1770, in *Papers* 17:37; Thomas Jefferson, Draft Declaration of Independence, in *The Papers of Thomas Jefferson,* ed. Julian Boyd (Princeton: PUP, 1950), 1:318.

34. Somersett: Mansfield, quoted in Steven M. Wise, *Though the Heavens May Fall* (Cambridge: Da Capo, 2005), 182; "The Somersett Case and the Slave Trade," in *Papers* 19:187. Associates: BF to Francis Hopkinson, 16 December 1767, in *Papers* 14:339; BF to Hopkinson, 24 January 1768, in *Papers* 15:30; BF to Noble Wimberly Jones, 5 March 1771, in *Papers* 18:52–54. Cooperating: BF to Anthony Benezet, 22 August 1772, in *Papers* 19:269; BF to Benezet, 19 February 1773, in *Papers* 20:40; BF to Richard Woodward, 10 April 1773, in *Papers* 20:155; BF to Benezet, 14 July 1773, in *Papers* 20:296.

35. Josiah Wedgwood to BF, 29 February 1788, APS B F85, 36:28. Wedgwood was no innocent when it came to marketing (Neil McKendrick, "Commercialization and the Economy," in *The Birth of a Consumer Society,* ed. McKendrick, John Brewer, and J. H. Plumb [Bloomington: Indiana University Press, 1982], part 1).

36. Whatley suspected the English Quakers of wanting to be thought "enthusiastically humane" and anticipated the abolitionist outcry would end in

nothing more than a parliamentary inquiry into the condition of slaves— of which he professed no great concern (George Whatley to BF, 12 March 1788, APS B F85, 36:32).

37. Pennsylvania Abolition Society, "To the Senate and House of Representatives," 3 February 1790, Minutes of the Pennsylvania Abolition Society, 20 October 1787, HSP PAS Minutes, fols. 17–21.

38. *Annals of Congress*, 1st Cong., 2nd sess. (11 and 12 February 1790), 1224–26, 1239–47.

39. "On the Slave Trade," *Federal Gazette*, 25 March 1790, reprinted in *Autobiography*, 369–71.

EPILOGUE

1. *Rules and Regulations of the Society for Political Enquiries. Established at Philadelphia, 9th February, 1787* (Philadelphia: Robert Aitken, 1787), 1–2.

2. Ibid., 5.

3. [Benjamin Rush], *An Enquiry into the Effects of Publick Punishments upon Criminals, and Upon Others. Read . . . March 9th. 1787* (Philadelphia: Joseph James, 1787); [Tench Coxe], *An Enquiry Into The Principles On Which a Commercial System For the United States Should Be Founded . . . Read . . . May 11th 1787* (Philadelphia: Robert Aitken, 1787); "Minutes," HSP Am.311. The records of the society are sparse; see also Tench Coxe to BF, 18 May 1787, APS B F85, 35:62; Pelatiah Webster to BF, 18 December 1788, APS B F85, 36:109.

4. Alexis de Tocqueville, *Democracy in America*, ed. J. P. Mayer, trans. George Lawrence (New York: Doubleday Anchor, 1969), 513–15, 12. Franklin appears only once in *Democracy in America*, in a footnote to a paragraph asserting the power of the press (727).

5. Judith N. Shklar, "Redeeming American Political Theory," *American Political Science Review* 85 (1991): 3–4.

6. On Puritanism and American identity, see especially Sacvan Bercovitch, *The American Jeremiad* (Madison: University of Wisconsin Press, 1978); and John Patrick Diggins, *The Lost Soul of American Politics* (Chicago: UCP, 1984). Prominent neo-Tocquevillians include Robert Bellah et al., *Habits of the Heart* (Berkeley and Los Angeles: University of California Press, 1985); and Robert D. Putnam, *Bowling Alone* (New York: Simon and Schuster, 2000). Daniel Boorstin emphasized the nonphilosophical cast of American identity in *The Genius of American Politics* (Chicago: UCP,

1953). The most influential version of this argument, however, is that of Frederick Jackson Turner: "That coarseness and strength combined with acuteness and inquisitiveness; that practical, inventive turn of mind, quick to find expedients; that masterful grasp of material things, lacking in the artistic but powerful to effect great ends; that dominant individualism, working for good and for evil, and withal that buoyancy and exuberance that comes with freedom: these are traits of the frontier, or traits called out elsewhere because of the existence of the frontier" (*The Frontier in American History* [New York: Henry Holt, 1920]).

7. These books are listed in the notes to the introduction.

8. *OED,* s.vv. "wit," "meaning."

9. Pennsylvania Abolition Society, *An Address to the Public . . . 9 November 1789* (Philadelphia: Francis Bailey, 1789); Eric Foner, *Reconstruction: America's Unfinished Revolution* (New York: Harper and Row, 1988).

10. Lizette Alvarez, "Scotland Takes Action to Halt Drop in Population," *New York Times,* 30 November 2003; Milos Calda, "Demographic Slump vs. Immigration Policy: The Case of the Czech Republic" (working paper 127, Center for Comparative Immigration Studies, University of California, San Diego, November 2005); "Population of the 100 Largest Cities and Other Urban Places in the United States: 1790 to 1990," U.S. Census Bureau, http://www.census.gov/population/www/documentation/twps0027.html (accessed 30 July 2007); Lisa Chamberlain, "Tax Breaks Drive Philadelphia Boom," *New York Times,* 8 January 2006.

11. John Brewer, *The Sinews of Power: War, Money and the English State, 1688–1783* (New York: Knopf, 1989), 131; Philip Hoffman, Gilles Postel-Vinay, and Jean-Laurent Rosenthal, *Priceless Markets: The Political Economy of Credit in Paris, 1660–1870* (Chicago: UCP, 2000); "The Nobel Peace Prize 2006," http://nobelprize.org/nobel_prizes/peace/laureates/2006/press.html (accessed 30 July 2007).

12. *PR* 1736, 1746.

APPENDIX

1. The *Protestant Ethic* was first published as a two-part essay in 1904–5; Weber issued a revised edition in 1920. The best modern translation is of the 1905 essays: *The Protestant Ethic and the "Spirit" of Capitalism and Other Writings,* ed. and trans. Peter Baehr and Gordon Wells (Harmondsworth: Penguin, 2002). For the 1920 edition, I have relied on Weber's original:

Die protestantische Ethik und der Geist des Kapitalismus, in *Gesammelte Aufsätze zur Religionssoziologie* (Tübingen: J. C. B. Mohr [Paul Siebeck], 1920),
1:17–206.

2. "Advice to a Young Tradesman," in *Papers* 3:306. For methodological reasons Franklin is introduced as a "provisional illustration" (*eine provi-
   sorische Veranschaulichung*). Weber later states that Franklin speaks in the
   "characteristic voice of 'the spirit of capitalism'" (*aus ihm in charakter-
   ischer Weise redet*) and that he expresses its "essential elements" (*die
   wesentlichen Elemente*) (*Protestant Ethic,* 9, 11, 120; *Die protestantische
   Ethik,* 1:31, 33, 202).

3. Weber, *Protestant Ethic,* 359, 16, 22.

4. Harvey Goldman, *Max Weber and Thomas Mann: Calling and the Shaping
   of the Self* (Berkeley and Los Angeles: University of California Press,
   1988), 26; Weber, *Die protestantische Ethik,* 1:111.

5. Weber, *Die protestantische Ethik,* 1:53–54; Weber, *Protestant Ethic,* 11–12, 24.

6. Weber, *Protestant Ethic,* 359, 24, 120.

7. Ibid., 79, 119; Weber, *Die protestantische Ethik,* 1:111.

8. "Asceticism turns all its force . . . against one thing in particular: *the uninhibited enjoyment* of life and of the pleasures it has to offer" (Weber,
   Protestant Ethic, 112).

9. Goldman, *Weber and Mann,* 147, 42, 39; Weber, *Protestant Ethic,* 22, 15.
   "The capitalist spirit . . . had to prove itself in a hard struggle against a
   world of hostile forces" (14).

10. Weber, *Die protestantische Ethik,* 1:40n1; Weber, *Protestant Ethic,* 106, 115.

11. Weber, *Protestant Ethic,* 10.

12. What we do know can be found in Hartmut Lehmann, "Ascetic Protes-
    tantism and Economic Rationalism: Max Weber Revisited after Two Gen-
    erations," *Harvard Theological Review* 80 (1987): 307–20; Guenther Roth,
    Max Webers deutsch-englische Familiengeschichte 1800–1950 (Tübingen:
    Mohr Siebeck, 2001); Lawrence Scaff, "Young Man Weber," *International
    Journal of Politics, Culture and Society* 17 (2004): 639–50; Wolfgang J.
    Mommsen, "From Agrarian Capitalism to the 'Spirit' of Modern Capital-
    ism: Max Weber's Approaches to the Protestant Ethic," *Max Weber Studies*
    5 (2005): 185–203; Hartmut Lehmann, "Weber's Use of Scholarly Praise
    and Scholarly Criticism in *The Protestant Ethic and the 'Spirit' of Capital-
    ism,*" *Max Weber Studies* 5 (2005): 229–41.

13. Benjamin Franklin, *Sein Leben, von ihm selbst beschrieben,* mit einem Vor-
    wart von Berthold Auerbach und einer historisch-politischen Einleitung

von Friedrich Kapp (Stuttgart: A. B. Auerbach, 1876). For the gift, see Roth, *Webers Familiengeschichte*, 478.

14. "Aus dem Rinde macht man Talg, aus dem Menschen Geld" (Ferdinand Kürnberger, *Der Amerikamüde: Amerikanisches Kulturbild*, 1855 [Leipzig: P. Reclam, n.d.], 28); Weber, *Protestant Ethic*, 47n19, 11.

15. Franklin's "Advice to a Young Tradesman" is organized into nine paragraphs. *Der Amerikamüde* includes German translations of all of paragraphs 1–3, 5, 7, 8, and half of paragraph 6; *The Protestant Ethic* contains new translations of the same selections. "Hints for those that would be Rich" is organized into sixteen paragraphs. *Der Amerikamüde* translates paragraphs 2–4 and 7; *The Protestant Ethic* reprises this selection and adds paragraph 5.

Glossary of Names

Abercromby, James (1707–75). Scottish-born colonial agent and political writer.

Adams, John (1735–1826). Lawyer, leading statesman, and political philosopher from Massachusetts. Served in Continental Congress; helped negotiate with France and England during Revolution. Second president of the United States.

Allen, William (1704–80). Philadelphia merchant and chief justice of Pennsylvania. Early ally of Franklin's; broke during fight over proprietary privileges. Loyalist in the Revolution.

Bache, Sarah ("Sally") Franklin (1743–1808). Franklin's daughter.

Bartram, John (1699–1777). Philadelphia botanist and scientific friend of Franklin's. Helped form the American Philosophical Society.

Benezet, Anthony (1713–84). French-born Philadelphia educator and abolitionist.

Braddock, Edward (1695–1755). Commander of British forces in North America in 1755; fatally wounded in battle with French and Indians.

Brillon de Jouy, Anne-Louise Boivin d'Hardancourt (1744–1824). Neighbor and close friend of Franklin's at Passy.

Buffon, Georges-Louis LeClerc, comte de (1707–88). French naturalist and experimental scientist.

Colden, Cadwallader (1688–1776). Scottish-born American politician and naturalist. Loyalist; made lieutenant governor of New York in 1761.

Collinson, Peter (1694–1768). Quaker merchant in London. Patron and agent for Library Company. Naturalist and antiquary; corresponded with Franklin about science.

Condorcet, Marie Jean Antoine Nicolas Caritat, marquis de (1743–94). French philosopher and mathematician. Died in prison during the French Revolution.

Cooper, Anthony Ashley, third Earl of Shaftesbury (1671–1713). English moral theorist. Author of *Characteristics of Men, Manners, Opinions, Times.*

Coxe, Tench (1755–1824). Political economist and journalist. Alexander Hamilton's assistant secretary of the treasury.

Darwin, Charles (1809–82). English naturalist, geologist, and theorist of evolution.

Darwin, Erasmus (1731–1802). English physician and natural philosopher. Franklin's colleague in the Lunar Society; grandfather of Charles Darwin.

Davenant, Charles (1656–1714). English political economist.

Defoe, Daniel (1660?–1731). English writer and businessman. Author of novels (*Robinson Crusoe*) as well as political and economic tracts.

Denham, Thomas (d. 1728). Philadelphia merchant; employed Franklin in 1726–27.

Derham, William (1657–1735). Church of England clergyman and natural philosopher. Author of *Physico-Theology.*

Douglass, William (1681–1752). Scottish-born Boston physician and historian.

Fox, George (1624–91). English founder of the Religious Society of Friends (Quakers).

Franklin, Deborah Read (c. 1704–74). Franklin's wife; entered common-law union in 1730.

Franklin, James (1697–1735). Franklin's brother and first printing master.

Franklin, Josiah (1657–1745). Franklin's father.

Franklin, William (1730–1813). Franklin's son by an unknown mother. Raised in Franklin household. Last royal governor of New Jersey. Loyalist; imprisoned in 1776; released and fled to England in 1780.

Franklin, William Temple (c. 1760–1823). Illegitimate son of William, raised largely by Franklin. Printed collection of Franklin's writings.

Galloway, Joseph (1731–1803). Philadelphia lawyer and statesman. Franklin's ally in colonial Pennsylvania Assembly. Loyalist; fled to England in 1778.

Graunt, John (1620–74). English statistician and demographer.

Hall, David (1714–72). Scottish printer. Emigrated to Philadelphia at Franklin's invitation in 1744; became managing partner in 1748.

Harrington, James (1611–77). English political theorist. Author of *The Commonwealth of Oceana.*

Helvétius, Claude Adrien (1715–71). French philosopher and freethinker.

Hemphill, Samuel (dates unknown). Irish Presbyterian minister, installed in Philadelphia in 1734. Unorthodox views banned by synod in 1735; defended in print by Franklin.

Hillsborough, Wills Hill, Lord (1718–93). English president of Board of Trade, 1763–65, 1766–68; secretary of state for colonies, 1768–72. Opposed concessions to colonies.

Hobbes, Thomas (1588–1679). English philosopher and political theorist. Author of *Leviathan.*

Howe, Richard, Lord (1726–99). British admiral; commander in chief in North America, 1776–78. Attempted negotiation with Franklin in 1775.

Hume, David (1711–76). Scottish philosopher and historian.

Hutchinson, Thomas (1711–80). Boston-born royal governor of Massachusetts, 1771–74.

Ingenhousz, Jan (1730–99). Dutch physician and physicist; corresponded with Franklin about electricity.

Jackson, Richard (d. 1787). English lawyer and member of Parliament.

Jefferson, Thomas (1743–1826). Farmer, philosopher, inventor, and statesman from Virginia. Author of Declaration of Independence; third president of the United States.

Kames, Henry Home, Lord (1696–1782). Scottish judge and moral philosopher.

Keimer, Samuel (c. 1688–1742). London-born Philadelphia printer. Franklin's first employer and subsequent competitor.

Keith, Sir William (1680–1749). Scottish-born governor of Pennsylvania, 1716–26.

Kennedy, Archibald (1685–1763). Scottish-born New York colonial official and pamphleteer.

Le Veillard, Louis (1733–93). Franklin's next-door neighbor and close friend in Passy.

Locke, John (1632–1704). English philosopher and political theorist. Author of *An Essay concerning Human Understanding* and *Two Treatises of Government*.

Logan, James (1674–1751). Irish-born American scholar, scientist, and book collector. Member of Governor's Council; leader of Quaker party in Pennsylvania Assembly.

Machiavelli, Niccolò (1469–1527). Florentine diplomat and political theorist. Author of *The Prince* and *Discourses on Livy*.

Malthus, Thomas Robert (1766–1834). English clergyman and political economist. Author of *Principles of Population*.

Mandeville, Bernard (1670–1733). Dutch-born English political economist and satirist. Author of *Fable of the Bees*.

Mather, Cotton (1663–1728). Prominent Puritan clergyman in Boston.

McCulloh, Henry (dates unknown). London merchant, colonial agent, and colonial land speculator.

Mecom, Jane Franklin (1712–94). Franklin's sister and favored correspondent.

Montesquieu, Charles-Louis de Secondat, baron de La Brède et de (1689–1755). French writer, historian, political theorist. Author of *The Spirit of the Laws*.

Morellet, abbé André (1727–1819). French economist, philosopher, lover of wine.

Morris, Robert (1734–1806). English-born American banker. Signed Declaration of Independence. Superintendent of finance for Congress, 1781–84. Member of Constitutional Convention.

Penn, Thomas (1702–75). Son of William Penn. After 1746, became primary Proprietor of Pennsylvania; resided in London.

Penn, William (1644–1718). English Quaker; founder and Proprietor of Pennsylvania.

Petty, William (1623–87). English natural philosopher and political economist. Government administrator in Ireland.

Pitt, William, Earl of Chatham (1708–78). English statesman. Prime minister during Seven Years' War, 1756–63. Worked with Franklin in 1774–76 to avoid war.

Price, Richard (1723–91). English Unitarian minister, economist, and political philosopher. Publicly opposed war with America.

Priestley, Joseph (1733–1804). English scientist, educator, and Unitarian theologian.

Ralph, James (d. 1762). Historian and political writer. Accompanied Franklin to London in 1724.

Ray, John (1627–1705). English naturalist and natural theologian.

Rush, Benjamin (1746–1813). Physician and social reformer. Signed Declaration of Independence; represented Pennsylvania at Constitutional Convention.

Shelburne, William Petty, second Earl of (1737–1805). Whig member of Parliament; prime minister during negotiation of peace with America.

Shipley, Jonathan, bishop of St. Asaph (1714–88). Outspoken supporter of American cause. Part 1 of *Autobiography* written at his home in Twyford.

Shirley, William (1694–1771). London-born lawyer in Boston. Governor of Massachusetts, 1741–57.

Smith, Adam (1723–90). Scottish moral philosopher and political economist. Author of *The Theory of Moral Sentiments* and *An Inquiry into the Nature and Causes of the Wealth of Nations*.

Stiles, Ezra (1727–95). Congregational minister and president of Yale College.

Strahan, William (1714–85). London printer; published Hume, Smith, Gibbon, and others.

Tennent, Gilbert (1703–64). Irish-born Presbyterian preacher in New Brunswick and Philadelphia.

Tryon, Thomas (1634–1703). English writer; vegetarian, mystic, lay physician, and abolitionist.

Turgot, Anne-Robert-Jacques (1727–81). French economist and statesman. Finance minister to Louis XVI.

Vaughan, Benjamin (1751–35). English diplomat and political economist. Edited first edition of Franklin's writings, 1779. Helped negotiate Anglo-American peace in 1782.

Wallace, Robert (1697–1771). Church of Scotland minister; writer on population.

Washington, George (1732–99). Farmer, soldier, and statesman from Virginia. First president of the United States.

Whitefield, George (1714–70). English evangelist. Missions to America helped spark the Great Awakening.

Index

Page numbers in *italics* indicate illustrations.

democracy, 24, 60–61, 69, 172, 219

demography, 106–10, 116–22, 133–35,
    140–41, 266n6, 269–72nn30–38, 279n91;
    census table, *134*

Denham, Thomas, 22–24, 33, 242n4

Derham, William, 113–14, 129–30

design, argument from, 113–16, 129–30,
    143–46, *145*, 269n22, 282n105

Diderot, Denis, 130

differentiation, 67–68, 90–92

Dilworth, Thomas, 83–84

Dinwiddie, Robert, 290n48

division of labor, 118, 128, 173

dogmatism, 69

"Dogood, Silence" (Franklin), 2, 27, 108,
    125, 211

Douglass, William, 125–26, 274n50

Drayton, Richard, 269n26

Dunkers, 66, 69–70

Dunn, John, 19, 241n35, 266n7

Du Pont de Nemours, Pierre-Samuel, 191–92

economics. *See* political economy

education, 14, 79–81, 209–10. *See also*
    Philadelphia Academy, slavery

Edwards, Jonathan, 40

elections, 45, 136–37, 172–73

Elias, Norbert, 240n22

Elizabeth I, 79

emigration. *See* immigration and emigration

empire, 140, 152–53, 156–58; British, 52,
    56–59, 66, 130, 138, 147, 152, 156–61,
    169–70, 173, 177–82, *178;* French, 154,
    159–61, 166–67, 202, 288nn37,39

emulation, 24, 50, 53–54, 118, 270n31

England. *See* Great Britain

Enlightenment, 15–16, 240n28

envy, 13, 54–55, 76–77, 163, 179, 181, 257n46

equality, 90–91, 178–79, 187, 189, 200–201,
    210–11, 215

ethics. *See* morality

evolution, 130, 143–46

fear, 28, 73–74, 87–88

federalism, 169, 185–87, 222

Federalist, 148–49, 168

Fiering, Norman, 302n27

fireplaces, 112

flexibility, 69–70, 197, 209, 213

foresight, 84–85, 193

Fothergill, John, 282n105

four stages history, 124–28, 135, 206, 273n49

Fox, George, 65, 251n13

France and the French, 117, 154, 159–61, 224.
    See also empire

Franklin, Abiah Folger (mother), 38–39

Franklin, Benjamin

—Life: Boston, *1706–23,* 7–11, 26–27, 195,
    203–4, 211; London, *1724–25,* 13, 22–24,
    33, 110–11, 242n4; Philadelphia, *1726–57,*
    20, 23, 45, 51, 60, 81, 102–3, 136–37, 153,
    244n31; England, *1757–62, 1764–75,*
    177–81, 209; Philadelphia, *1762–64,* 103–5,
    136, *137,* 265n109; Philadelphia, *1775–76,*
    182–85, 200–201; Paris, *1776–85,* 18,
    187–88, 197, 300n17; Philadelphia,
    1785–90, 147, 197, 214–18

—As a person: appearance, *3;* character, 8,
    10, 18, 28–30, 36, *37,* 47–48, 108, 112–13,
    187–88, 192–94, *193,* 204, 209, 220, 223;
    cosmopolitanism, 5, 19–20, 25, 220,
    241n36, 267n12, 285n23; errata, 40, 70;
    experiments and inventions, 29, 80, 108,
    110–16, 124–28, 135, 148, 266n6, 267n10,
    282n4; family, xii, 50–51, 56–57, 177, 201,
    209; family slaves, xii, 200–201, 209–10,
    298n2, 299n4; finances, 18, 22–24, 45,
    50–51, 228–29, 242n4; flexibility, 70, 197,
    209, 213; projector, 10–11, 14–16, 26–27,
    51–52, 61, 64, 79–80, 166–70, 197, 217–18,
    220–21, 282n3; reading, 5, 7–8, 238n8,
    256n40; religion, 8, 38–40, 61, 71, 114, 198,
    228; skepticism, 17, 108, 192, 198, 211–12;
    women, 18, 22, 33, 50–51, 192, 241n32

—Reputation: "American," 2–7, 219–20,
    239n12; eighteenth-century, 1, 2, 36, 100,
    194–96, 236n1; nineteenth-century, 11, 24,
    141–46, 219, 279n92; twentieth-century,
    1–5, 24, 132–33, 219–20, 225–29, 237n3,
    237n6, 238n9, 285n23

—As a writer: method, xi, 2, 8, 20, 24–25, 30,
    33–34, 81, 84, 124–25, 162, 181; use of im-
    ages, 82, *83,* 84, 161–65, *162,* 177–85, *178,*
    183, 184, 215, 295n96; use of irony and
    satire: 2, 11, 20, 36–37, 106–7, 132–33, 136,
    144–46, 174, 181, 186, 201–2, 205–6,
    211–12, 216, 244n28; use of proverbs, 25,
    85, 162, 242n6